T0296764

Cognitive Big Data Intelligence with a Metaheuristic Approach

Cognitive Data Science in Sustainable Computing

Cognitive Big Data Intelligence with a Metaheuristic Approach

Series Editor

Arun Kumar Sangaiah

Volume Editors

Sushruta Mishra
School of Computer Engineering, Kalinga Institute of Industrial technology (KIIT) University, Bhubaneswar, Odisha, India

Hrudaya Kumar Tripathy
School of Computer Engineering, Kalinga Institute of Industrial technology (KIIT) University, Bhubaneswar, Odisha, India

Pradeep Kumar Mallick
School of Computer Engineering, Kalinga Institute of Industrial technology (KIIT) University, Bhubaneswar, Odisha, India

Arun Kumar Sangaiah
School of Computer Science, The University of Adelaide, Adelaide, SA, Australia

Gyoo-Soo Chae
Division of ICT, Baekseok University, Cheonan, South Korea

ACADEMIC PRESS

An imprint of Elsevier

Academic Press is an imprint of Elsevier
125 London Wall, London EC2Y 5AS, United Kingdom
525 B Street, Suite 1650, San Diego, CA 92101, United States
50 Hampshire Street, 5th Floor, Cambridge, MA 02139, United States
The Boulevard, Langford Lane, Kidlington, Oxford OX5 1GB, United Kingdom

Notices
Knowledge and best practice in this field are constantly changing. As new research and
experience broaden our understanding, changes in research methods, professional
practices, or medical treatment may become necessary.

Practitioners and researchers must always rely on their own experience and knowledge in
evaluating and using any information, methods, compounds, or experiments described
herein. In using such information or methods they should be mindful of their own safety
and the safety of others, including parties for whom they have a professional responsibility.

To the fullest extent of the law, neither the Publisher nor the authors, contributors, or
editors, assume any liability for any injury and/or damage to persons or property as a matter
of products liability, negligence or otherwise, or from any use or operation of any methods,
products, instructions, or ideas contained in the material herein.

Library of Congress Cataloging-in-Publication Data
A catalog record for this book is available from the Library of Congress

British Library Cataloguing-in-Publication Data
A catalogue record for this book is available from the British Library

ISBN: 978-0-323-85117-6

For information on all Academic Press publications visit our
website at https://www.elsevier.com/books-and-journals

Publisher: Mara Conner
Acquisitions Editor: Sonnini R. Yura
Editorial Project Manager: Michelle Fisher
Production Project Manager: Sreejith Viswanathan
Cover Designer: Christian J. Bilbow

Typeset by TNQ Technologies

Working together
to grow libraries in
developing countries

www.elsevier.com • www.bookaid.org

Contents

3. **Impacts of metaheuristic and swarm intelligence
approach in optimization** 71

*Abhishek Banerjee, Dharmpal Singh, Sudipta Sahana and
Ira Nath*

13. Optimization-based energy-efficient routing scheme for wireless body area network   279

Aradhana Behura and Manas Ranjan Kabat

14. Livestock health monitoring using a smart IoT-enabled neural network recognition system   305

Ricky Mohanty and Subhendu Kumar Pani

Contributors

Angelia Melani Adrian, Informatics Engineering Department, De La Salle Catholic University, Manado City, Indonesia

Abhishek Banerjee, Pailan College of Management and Technology, Pailan, Joka, Kolkata, West Bengal, India

Aradhana Behura, Department of Computer Science & Engineering, Veer Surendra Sai University of Technology, Burla, Odisha, India

Sukant Kishoro Bisoy, Department of Computer Science and Engineering, C.V. Raman Global University, Bhubaneswar, Odisha, India

Korhan Cengiz, Department of Telecommunication, Trakya University, Edirne, Turkey

Chandramouli Das, School of Computer Engineering, KIIT Deemed to be University, Bhubaneswar, Odisha, India

Ankit Desai, Embibe, Bengaluru, Karnataka, India

Pijush Dutta, Department of Electronics and Communication Engineering, Global Institute of Management and Technology, Krishnagar, West Bengal, India

Priyom Dutta, School of Computer Engineering, KIIT University, Bhubaneswar, Odisha, India

Manas Ranjan Kabat, Department of Computer Science & Engineering, Veer Surendra Sai University of Technology, Burla, Odisha, India

Nishant Kashyap, C.V. Raman Global University, Bhubaneswar, Odisha, India

Asok Kumar, Dean of Student Welfare Department, Vidyasagar University, Medinipur, West Bengal, India

B.S. Mahanand, Department of Information Science and Engineering, Sri Jayachamarajendra College of Engineering, JSS Science and Technology University, Mysuru, Karnataka, India

Anjana Mishra, C.V. Raman Global University, Bhubaneswar, Odisha, India

Sushruta Mishra, Kalinga Institute of Industrial Technology Deemed to be University, Bhubaneswar, Odisha, India

Ricky Mohanty, Department of Electronics & Telecommunication, Orissa Engineering College, Bhubaneswar, Odisha, India

Mihir Narayan Mohanty, ITER, Siksha 'O' Anusandhan (Deemed to be University), Bhubaneswar, Odisha, India

Saumendra Kumar Mohapatra, ITER, Siksha 'O' Anusandhan (Deemed to be University), Bhubaneswar, Odisha, India

Ira Nath, JIS College of Engineering, Kalyani, West Bengal, India

Subhendu Kumar Pani, Krupajal Computer Academy, Bhubaneswar, Odisha, India

Moushita Patnaik, School of Computer Engineering, KIIT University, Bhubaneswar, Odisha, India

Arabinda Pradhan, Department of Computer Science and Engineering, C.V. Raman Global University, Bhubaneswar, Odisha, India

Chittaranjan Pradhan, School of Computer Engineering, KIIT Deemed to be University, Bhubaneswar, Odisha, India

Rojanlina Priyadarshini, Department of Computer Science and Information Technology, C.V. Raman Global University, Bhubaneswar, Odisha, India

Deepak Rai, Department of Computer Science and Engineering, National Institute of Technology, Patna, Bihar, India

Priyanka Ray, Kalinga Institute of Industrial Technology Deemed to be University, Bhubaneswar, Odisha, India

Vaisnav Roy, School of Computer Engineering, KIIT University, Bhubaneswar, Odisha, India

Sudipta Sahana, JIS College of Engineering, Kalyani, West Bengal, India

Abhaya Kumar Sahoo, School of Computer Engineering, KIIT Deemed to be University, Bhubaneswar, Odisha, India

Prasan Kumar Sahoo, Department of Computer Science and Information Engineering, Chang Gung University, Taoyuan City, Taiwan

Qusay Sellat, Department of Computer Science and Engineering, C.V. Raman Global University, Bhubaneswar, Odisha, India

Hrushikesh Shukla, School of Computer Science and Engineering, Dr. Vishwanath Karad MIT World Peace University, Pune, Maharashtra, India

Dharmpal Singh, JIS College of Engineering, Kalyani, West Bengal, India

Hiren Kumar Thakkar, Department of Computer Science and Engineering, School of Engineering and Sciences, SRM University, Mangalagiri, Andhra Pradesh, India

Preface

In recent times, information industry has experienced rapid changes in both the platform scale and scope of applications. Computers, smartphones, clouds, social networks, and supercomputers demand not only high performance but also a high degree of machine intelligence. At present, Big data is playing a significant role in the field of information technology and, more specifically, in the Data Science domain. Many solutions are being offered in addressing big data analytics. Analysis of data by humans can be a time-consuming activity, and thus, the use of sophisticated cognitive systems can be utilized to crunch this enormous amount of data. Cognitive computing can be utilized to reduce the shortcomings of the concerns faced during big data analytics. Thus, we are entering an era of big data and cognitive computing. To meet these new computing and communication changes, we must upgrade the clouds and the computing ecosystem with new capabilities, such as machine learning, IoT sensing, data analytics, and cognitive machines mimicking human intelligence. Metaheuristic algorithms have proven to be effective, robust, and efficient in solving real-world optimization, clustering, forecasting, classification, and other engineering problems. The ability of metaheuristics algorithms includes managing a set of solutions, attending multiple objectives, as well as their ability to optimize various values, which allows them to fit in dealing with big data analytics. Metaheuristic algorithms have become powerful and famous in computational intelligence and many applications. This volume intends to project different frameworks and applications of cognitive big data analytics using the metaheuristics approach.

This book is designed as a self-contained edition so that readers can understand different aspects of recent innovations of metaheuristics to knowledge discovery problems in the context of Big Data and Cognitive computing. As many as 15 chapters are made as part of this book. Different application domains related to the scope of this book are discussed which include metaheuristics in clustering and classification, swarm intelligence, heuristics in virtual reality, deep learning, and big data with IoT and recommendation system among others.

Chapter 1

A discourse on metaheuristics techniques for solving clustering and semisupervised learning models

Nishant Kashyap, Anjana Mishra
C.V. Raman Global University, Bhubaneswar, Odisha, India

1. Introduction

A rapid surge of machine learning algorithms have been seen in the last decade which has also pointed out the need for state-of-the art optimization techniques to deal with the large amount of data involved. Metaheuristics involving data-driven methods have shown their effectiveness in better quality of solutions and better convergence rate.

Metaheuristics methods explore the solution space to find globally optimum solution and improve upon the general searching procedure provided by the heuristic methods. They guide a basic and simple heuristic method by inculcating various concepts to exploit the search space of the given problem [1]. Metaheuristics techniques are generally nondeterministic and approximate but give good enough solution in reasonable time. Besides, these methods are particularly well suited to solving nonconvex optimization problems including the likes of those encountered during clustering. A wide range of meta-heuristics have been discovered ranging from search-based methods like simulated annealing and tabu search to the popular nature inspired and the evolutionary algorithms. A brief discussion on the widely used metaheuristics is discussed in our study.

Clustering and semisupervised methods are a hot topic today, finding its uses in multiple important fields ranging from big data, wireless sensor networks to bioinformatics to name a few [2]. As such, it has become one of the most sought after areas in research to improve the performance of the existing methods involved. Most of the algorithms used for clustering and classification suffer from drawbacks related to being trapped in the local maxima or minima.

Cognitive Big Data Intelligence with a Metaheuristic Approach
https://doi.org/10.1016/B978-0-323-85117-6.00012-1
1

Due to this, we use various nature-inspired metaheuristic techniques to find globally optimal solutions in reasonable amount of computation time.

Before starting out with the metaheuristics, we start out with an overview of the standard methods for clustering.

2. Overview of clustering

2.1 K-means clustering

Clustering using k-means basically culminates to assigning the data vectors, Z_p accurately to k clusters. Basically, the aim is to minimize the sum of the squared errors, i.e., $\sum_{j=1}^{k} \left[\sum_{\text{for all } W_p \, \varepsilon \text{ cluster } k_i} \left|\left| W_p - k_i \right|\right|^2 \right]$ by repeating the following steps for some number of iteration (or till some termination condition is reached):

1. Randomly initialize the cluster centroids. Then, for each data vector Z_p, assign it the cluster with centroids $k_i(i = 1,2,3, ...,k)$ such that $\left|\left| Z_p - k_i \right|\right|$ is minimum (here, $\left|\left| x \right|\right|$ represents the Euclidean norm of x)
2. For each cluster, find a the new cluster centroid, K_i such that $K_i = \frac{1}{|k_i|} \sum_{\text{for all } W_p \, \varepsilon \text{ cluster } k_i} \left|\left| W_p \right|\right|$ (where $|k_i|$ is the number of data vectors in cluster k_i)

2.2 Hierarchical clustering

In hierarchical clustering, the required number of clusters is formed in a hierarchical manner. For some n number of data points, initially we assign each data point to n clusters, i.e., each point in a cluster in itself. Thereafter, we merge two points with the least distance between them into a single cluster. The distance of the other points from this cluster made of two points is the least distance from either of the two points from the other points. This process is continued until we get the required number of clusters (Fig. 1.1).

2.3 Fuzzy C-means

This is used when the data points are fuzzy, i.e., they can belong to two or more clusters at the same time. Each data point (there being n data points) belongs to some cluster with some weight (Fig. 1.2).

G_{ij} where G_{ij} denotes belongingness (weight) the ith data point to the jth cluster c_j (with centroids k_j). It is important to note that all weights of a data point add up to 1 as shown in Ref. [3]. In fuzzy c-means, the squared error function that we want to minimize is Eq. (1.1)

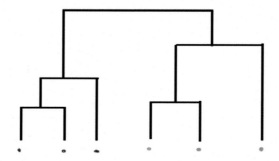

FIGURE 1.1   Hierarchical clustering, closest points clustered first.

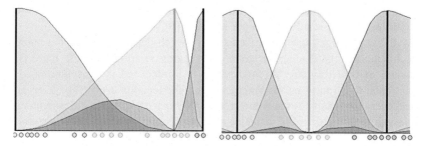

FIGURE 1.2   Clustering on fuzzy sets.

$$F = \sum_{j=1}^{k} \left[\sum_{p=1}^{n} G_{ij}^{d} \| Z_p - k_j \|^2 \right] \tag{1.1}$$

Here, d is some value from 1 to infinity which is used to control the weights.

At first all the values of the weights are initialized. Thereafter, the following steps are repeated till some termination condition:

I. Calculate the cluster centroids.
II. Update the weights.

The cluster centroids are updated as follows:

$$k_j = \left(\sum_{i=1}^{n} G_{ij}^{d} Z_i \right) \Big/ \left(\sum_{i=1}^{n} G_{ij}^{d} \right) \tag{1.2}$$

And the weights are updated as follows:

$$W_{ij} = \left(1 \Big/ \sum_{p=1}^{k} \left(\frac{\| Z_p - k_j \|}{\| Z_p - k_p \|} \right)^{2/(d-1)} \right) \tag{1.3}$$

2.4 Model-based clustering

This form of clustering is based on probabilistic distribution. Some models are used to cluster the data and then the relation between the data points and the model is optimized. Generally, Gaussian distribution is used for continuous points and Poisson for discreet points. In this regard, the EM algorithm is widely used to find the mixture of Gaussians [4]. For other models, refer to Ref. [5].

2.5 Particle swarm optimization

The particle swarm optimization (PSO) is a swarm-based optimization technique which draws inspiration from the foraging behavior of swarms of birds or that of fish schooling. This optimization technique is quite useful when continuous nonlinear functions are involved [6].

Let us indulge ourselves in a scenario which depicts the intuition behind technique in regard to the behavior of foraging swarms. Suppose there is a swarm of bird foraging for food which is limited and is concentrated in a particular location. A naïve strategy to reach the location is that (Fig. 1.3) each and every bird searches the entire area (search space); however, this might lead to some birds never reaching the location due to random nature of the search or some reaching so late that the resource is already depleted. Instead, what the birds do is that each of them considers the best position (position of the bird which is closest to the food source) among all the birds and keeps a memory of their previous best position (their closest individual position from the food source) to update their position and velocity. This connection amongst the birds and the fact that the best way to search is to follow the bird who is closest to the source form the basis of the technique [7].

FIGURE 1.3   Birds flocking together.

While dealing with a numeric optimization problem using PSO, initially there can be lot of solutions. Each solution is denoted as a particle and each is particle is associated with a position and velocity at each turn of updation [8]. Besides, each particle keeps track of its best position P_{best} (where it was closest to the global optimum) and that of the global best [9], G_{best} (position of the particle closest to the global optimum).The velocity and position equation are given as follows:

$$V(t + 1) = W * V(t) + [c_1 r_1 (P_{best} - X(t))] + [c_2 r_2 (G_{best} - X(t))] \qquad (1.4)$$

$$X(t + 1) = X(t) + V(t + 1) \qquad (1.5)$$

{position should be velocity*time, but since updation is done over a single turn time can be thought as 1}

Here, $V(t)$ is the velocity associated with the particle at time t.

$X(t)$ is the position of the particle at time t

r_1, r_2 are random values ranging from 0 to 1

c_1 is a constant called the cognitive (local or personal) weight

c_2 is a constant called the social (or global) weight.

W is a constant factor called the inertia weight.

Let us consider a function to understand the workings better. Suppose we have to find the global minima of

$$F(X) = X^2 + Y^2 + 2X$$

Now, although it is apparent that the plot will have a minima at $(x,y) = (0,0)$ with a value of 0, nonetheless, we can see the convergence of the PSO quite well here. Let us start at a point $(x,y) = (37.5, 18.75)$. Here, F(x) will be 1832.81. Let $V(t)$ be $(-1,-2)$, W be 0.6, c_1 and c_2 be 1.4, and r_1, r_2 be 0.4 and 0.5, respectively. Let the P_{best} be $(31.25, 12.5)$ yielding a value 1195.31 and the G_{best} be $(12.5, 18.75)$ yielding a value 532.81 (Fig. 1.4).

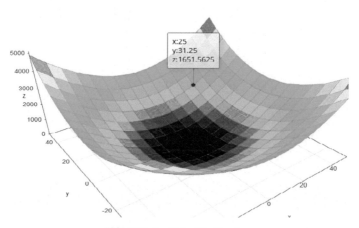

FIGURE 1.4 Plot of the function.

Now putting the above values, we get

$$
\begin{aligned}
V(t+1) &= \{0.6 * (-1, -2)\} + \{1.4 * 0.4 * (31.25, 12.5) - (37.5, 18.750)\} \\
&\quad + \{1.4 * 0.5 * (12.5, 18.75) - (37.5, 18.75)\} \\
&= (-0.6, -1.2) + (-3.5, -3.5) + (-17.5, 0) \\
&= (-21.6, -4.7)
\end{aligned}
$$

$$
\begin{aligned}
X(t+1) &= (37.5, 18.75) + (-21.6, -4.7) \\
&= (15.9, 14.05)
\end{aligned}
$$

which is closer to the optimal point (0,0).

2.6 Clustering using PSO

In a clustering problem, let W_p represent a data vector, k be the number of clusters, and k_i be the number of particles in cluster i.

Each particle can be thought of as a set of k cluster centroids, i.e., the ith particle is determined as follows:

$$
X_i = \{m_{i1}, m_{i2}, ..., m_{ik}\}
$$

where m_{ij} is the jth cluster centroid of the ith particle. Unless stated otherwise, we will be using the aforementioned symbols throughout the chapter.

The PSO equation for the ith particle can be then written as follows:

$$
V_{ik}(t+1) = w * V_{ik}(t) + [c_1 r_1 (P_{best} - X_i(t))] + [c_2 r_2 (G_{best} - X_i(t))] \quad (1.6)
$$

$$
X_i(t+1) = X_i(t) + V_{ik}(t+1) \quad (1.7)
$$

In general, lower the intracluster distance (the distance between all the data vectors and the centroid in a particular cluster), better the results are. Henceforth, we can define the quantization error for a particle i as the average intracluster error as

$$
E_c = \frac{1}{k} \sum_{j=1}^{k} \left[\sum_{\text{for all } W_p \, \epsilon \, \text{cluster } k_i} \|W_p - m_{ij}\| / K_i \right] \quad (1.8)
$$

Clustering using PSO runs on the following algorithm:

❖ Initially, each and every particle is randomly initialized, i.e., all the k cluster centroids of the particle are randomly initialized and some velocity associated with them.
❖ For some number of iteration t, we do the following:
  ▪ For each particle i:
    ➢ For data vector W_p, we first calculate $\|W_p - C_{ij}\|$ (Euclidean norm) to all the cluster centroids of particle i and then assign each data vector to the

cluster centroids with which it has the least Euclidean norm among all the cluster centroids.

➤ Then, the fitness for the particle is calculated using the fitness equation.

■ The G_{besst} and P_{best} are then changed accordingly after which the cluster centroids are updated using the aforementioned Eqs. (1.6) and (1.7).

While k-means for clustering suffers from the problem of being trapped in the local optimal positions (resulting in less accurate clusters) due to initial assumptions, clustering using PSO can give the global best resulting in more accurate clusters. However, it has the problem of very slow convergence rate toward the end. To do away with this problem, the hybrid PSO and k-means clustering algorithm can be used wherein the performance of PSO is improved by seeding the initial particle swarm with the results of k-mean. In this method, every particle is initialized randomly except one which is initialized with the result of k-mean. After that, the PSO clustering algorithm is run.

2.7 Ant colony optimization

The ant colony optimization (ACO) is another swarm algorithm which is inspired by the foraging behavior of ants. It is a stochastic metaheuristics technique for solving a bunch of nonlinear optimization problems. The main idea of the algorithm lies in its pheromone model which depends on probabilistic sampling.

Since most of the species of ants are devoid of eyesight or have blurry eyesight, they scatter along random routes from their nest to the food source when they initially start with each route having an equal probability. Each ant deposits a certain amount of pheromone on the path that it traverses. Eventually, they perceive the shortest path by following the path with the largest amount of pheromone entrails left over a period of time by all the ants.

The situation can be better understood by the following situation:

Initially, ants travel with equal probability along the paths a and b. Let us start from the situation when only two ants have started out (since both paths have equal probability). One moves along path a and the other along path b. Since path b is shorter, the ant on that path traverses to and fro from nest to food source back to nest quicker than the ant on the other path all while leaving pheromones. When another ant starts, it will move on the path with more pheromones that is b. Likewise, over time, the probability of choosing path b increases due to more pheromone concentration on that path compared to the other as path b has a shorter traverse time (Fig. 1.5).

The amount of pheromone on a path also depends on a lot of other factors like evaporation factor and other environmental factor. However, while considering ACO, only the factor is taken into consideration.

The ACO generally consist of two parts:

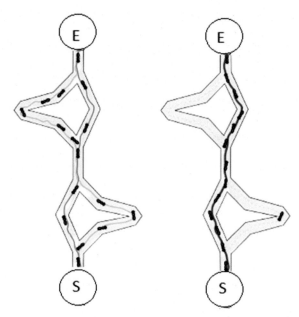

FIGURE 1.5   Ant movement initially and finally.

2.7.1 Constructing the ant probability solution

The ant probability solution refers to the probability, P_{ij}, that an ant moves from node i to j where i and j are some nodes along the path when the problem is represented as a graph problem. The probability P_{ij} is given by the following:

$$P_{ij} = \left(\left(\tau_{ij}^{\alpha} \right) \left(\eta_{ij}^{\beta} \right) \right) / \sum ((\tau ij\alpha)(\eta ij\beta)) \qquad (1.9)$$

Here, τ_{ij} indicates how much pheromone is deposited on the path from i to j.
α indicates the parameter that is used to control
η_{ij} indicates the ant's desirability to go through path from i to j
β indicates the control parameter of η_{ij}

2.7.2 Updating the pheromone amount

$$\tau_{ij} = (1 - \rho)\tau_{ij} + \Delta\tau_{ij} \qquad (1.10)$$

Here, ρ is the pheromone evaporation rate and the last term represents the amount of pheromone deposited which is given for some by 1/len, where len is the length of the path from i to j. If the ant does not travel via that route, the last term is taken as 0. This update when applied to all the ants includes a summation with the last term.

2.8 Clustering using ACO

Initially, all the data vectors are randomly projected on a 2d grid. The algorithm is based on the pickings and droppings of the data points on the 2d grid. The ants (agents) move around the 2d grid in a random manner picking and dropping the data points. The pickup and drop off probability of the data points, though random, are determined by neighborhood factors. The pickup probability increases in the case when the neighborhood data items have different labels, i.e., they are dissimilar [10]. On the other hand, if the neighborhood data items are similar, the drop off probability increases. The pickoff probability is given by

$$P_p = \left(\frac{I_1}{I_1 + f} \right)^2 \tag{1.11}$$

and the drop off probability is given by

$$P_p = \left(\frac{f}{I_2 + f} \right)^2 \tag{1.12}$$

Here, f is the fraction of items in the neighborhood of the agent.
I_1 and I_2 are threshold constants.

In the algorithm, we take the number of agents similar to the number of clusters that we want.

The algorithm consists of the following steps:

1. The following are run for some iteration, t:
   ❖ The k cluster centroids are initialized by the ACO. The P_{ij} of the ants as discussed determines the data points that are assimilated into clusters. The pickup and the drop off probabilities are considered alongside.
   ❖ While ensuring that every ant visits the corresponding occurrences, the data points are assigned to the neighboring cluster centroids and the value of the objective function is calculated for every agent.
   ❖ The best solution is found among all of the others by grading the agents by the norm and eliminating those agents with cluster less than given, i.e., k. The pheromone values are updated according to these best solutions.
2. The best agent globally is calculated using local best [11] while the agents are equal in number to the global best solutions. Thereafter, the mean is used to calculate the cluster centroids after evaluating initial and final f-measure and calculating entropy and moving data points to different cluster if the $F_{ij\text{-initial}} < F_{ij\text{-final}}$ where F_{ij} is the f-measure.
3. The above step is repeated till there is no case of reassigning the points.

Here, the f-measure for some data point p and cluster i is calculated as follows:

$$F(P, i) = \left(2* \frac{m_{ij}}{m_i} * \frac{m_{ij}}{m_j} \right) / \left(\frac{m_{ij}}{m_i} + \frac{m_{ij}}{m_j} \right) \tag{1.13}$$

Here, m_{ij} is the frequency of the class i in cluster j and m_i is the frequency of points in cluster I and the entropy E_p is defined as the probability sum of the fitting of some cluster into some class

$$E_P = -\sum_i p_{ij}\left(\log\left(p_{ij}\right)\right) \qquad (1.14)$$

and the total entropy for a cluster group is

$$E_{total} = \sum_{i=1}^{t}\left(n_i * E_p\right)/n \qquad (1.15)$$

2.9 Genetic algorithm

Genetic algorithms (GAs) are heuristic optimization techniques that take inspiration from the natural phenomena of evolution [12]. Despite being slow in nature, these techniques have the advantage of being easy to code and represent. An example of evolution is seen in giraffe that had a mix of long and short necks in the prehistoric times. However, with the passage of time, through the process of natural selection, only those having long necks were able to survive (Fig. 1.6).

As with natural selection, the GA is based on three steps:

❖ Selection
❖ Crossover
❖ Mutation

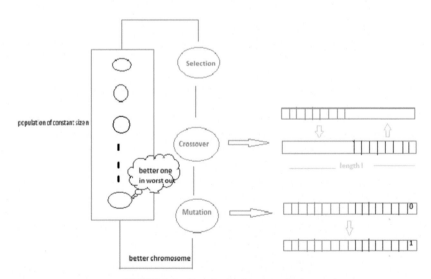

FIGURE 1.6   Genetic algorithms synthesis.

2.9.1 Selection

In a population of some size, any feature of the population is distinguished by a particular chromosome of the genome and each chromosome is made of genes (generally binary). Each chromosome in the population is associated with a certain fitness value (quantifies the optimality of the solution) which is inherent to the problem and the task that we wish to perform with our GA. The selection process determines which solutions are allowed to reproduce (crossover stage) and which are not according to fitness values while maintaining a constant population size for the solution space. This seems intuitively valid as we endeavor to weed unoptimal (low fitness value) solutions toward future generations (iterations) and perform crossover over solutions with high fitness values with the hope of getting a better solution to replace some other suboptimal solution in the population.

There are different techniques for selection like the following:

❖ Tournament selection
❖ Roulette-wheel selection
❖ Proportionate selection
❖ Rank selection, etc.

When the fitness values have sufficient difference, we may use tournament selection, and when the fitness values are close enough, generally, roulette-wheel selection is used.

2.9.2 Crossover

Suppose there are two chromosomes of size n for the purpose of crossover, we select a position k such that position [1,k] is covered by the genes of the first chromosome and the position [k+1,n] is covered by the genes of the other to create a new chromosome.

2.9.3 Mutation

Now any kind of mutation is used to create a new property out of our chromosomes which helps to improve to the rate of convergence. Mutation can be simply achieved by altering the bit of a specific position [13]. However, mutation is a risky process as too much can bring too much randomness which may completely disrupt our results. Likewise, applying mutation to the MSB of the chromosome can bring drastic changes which we want to avoid. However, mutation provided with low probability is useful.

2.9.4 Clustering using genetic algorithm

While considering to tackle the problem of clustering with the help of GA we must understand the restraints, i.e., what function we want to minimize or maximize [14]. This is crucial as the fitness function will depend on the task in hand. Subsequently, it is not difficult to see that what we seek is to actually minimize the sum of the Euclidean norm of the data vectors from their respective centroids, i.e., we need to minimize the function

$$\Delta = \sum_{j=1}^{k} \left[\sum_{\text{for all } W_p \ \varepsilon \ \text{cluster } k_i} \left\| W_p - m_j \right\| \right] \tag{1.16}$$

Here, m_j denotes the cluster centers.

For k clusters and data vector W_p with n features, we can represent this information using a chromosome of length n*k. The sequence of genes in the chromosome represents the k cluster centers. For e.g., for a data vector with two features and two clusters with their respective cluster centroids being (1,2) and (7,8), the chromosome can be represented [15] as shown below (Fig. 1.7).

For the purpose of our algorithm, we will consider a population of size N. Henceforth, with that population size, chromosomes will be created (with random cluster centroid initialization).

2.9.5 Computing the fitness function

For a chromosome, we assign the data vectors W_p in the clusters and then, the data vectors are assigned to those clusters with the Euclidean norm is the least. This is followed by replacing the values of each cluster centroid in the chromosome by the mean of the cluster to which the cluster center belonged to, i.e., all the m_j are replaced by M_j such that

$$M_j = \frac{1}{k_j} \sum_{\text{for all } W_p \ \varepsilon \ \text{cluster } k_j} W_p \tag{1.17}$$

Then, we compute the error function considering the new centroid center M_j. The fitness function is then defined as

$$F = 1/\Delta \tag{1.18}$$

Thereafter, we do crossover as mentioned above. Now since we are dealing with real values for the genes, instead of flipping, we use a different procedure for mutation [16]. Suppose, the value of a gene is x, then for some random value μ generated using uniform distribution within the range [0,1] x is mutated (as shown in Ref. [15]) as follows

$$x = x \pm 2^*\mu^*x \quad \text{when x is not 0}$$
$$x = x \pm 2^*\mu^* \quad \text{otherwise} \tag{1.19}$$

1	2	7	8

FIGURE 1.7   Cluster chromosome.

These steps are continued till termination step is reached. We get our solution from selecting the best solution (one with the highest fitness value) from the last generation.

While implementing our GA-based clustering algorithm, we initialize the population size carefully [17]. A population size that is too large will give better results but will be too slow to be of any practical value. On the other hand, a very small population will be less accurate.

2.10 Differential evolution

Differential evolution (DE) is a stochastic, population-based metaheuristics optimization technique. It is similar in spirit to the GA besides the fact that in GA we use a chromosome to represent our solution candidates, while in DE, real vectors are considered. Let us consider the real vector W_i^G denoting data vectors along with their features (suppose there are n features), with population size as N, as

$$W_i^G = \{w_{1i}, w_{2i}, ..., w_{ni}\} \quad i = 1, 2, ..., N$$

Each W_i denotes a solution in the population. Here, G denotes the generation.

The basic DE has four steps:

❖ Initialization
❖ Mutation
❖ Recombination
❖ Selection

2.10.1 Initialization

During initialization, the upper bound and the lower bound of the vectors are determined and the initial population is taken as a random vector between these bounds.

$$W_i = W_i^L + \text{rand}() * \left(W_i^U - W_i^L\right) \tag{1.20}$$

where W_i^L and W_i^U represent the lower and upper bound, respectively.

2.10.2 Mutation

Through mutation, we bring about random changes to one/more of the parameter vectors. For each of the random vectors [18], for the purpose of mutation, three other (different from the vector selected) vectors are selected, i.e., for W_i^G, we select W_k^G, W_j^G, and W_l^G (i is not equal to j,k,l), then we take the weighted difference of two of the vectors and the difference of the third vector to find what is called the donor vector (O_i^{G+1}).

$$O_i^{G+1} = W_k^G + \varepsilon \left(W_j^G - W_l^G \right) \tag{1.21}$$

ε ranges from 0 to 1.

2.10.3 Recombination

Recombination can be of two types:

❖ Uniform (parameter values from parents are inherited with equal probability)
❖ Nonuniform

Let P_r denote the recombination probability. For the purpose of recombination, we generate a third vector say P_i^{G+1} (called the trial vector) from the donor vector O_i^{G+1} and the vector on which the donor vector is based (target vector) W_i^G by the following rule as shown in Ref. [18]:
$P_i^{G+1} = O_i^{G+1}$ if (rand $\sim$ U[0,1])$\leq P_r$ or k = vrand (vrand is a no. between 1 to n, where n is the no. of features)

$$P_i^{G+1} = W_i^G \quad \text{if (rand} \sim U[0, 1]) > P_r \text{ and k not equals vrand} \tag{1.22}$$

k determines the kth feature of P_i^{G+1}

2.10.4 Selection

The trial vector and the target vector are compared and the one with the lowest function value (fitness function) is selected for the next generation.

$$
\begin{aligned}
W_i^{G+1} &= P_i^{G+1} \text{ if } f\left(P_i^{G+1}\right) < f\left(W_i^G\right) \quad \text{(f is the fitness function)} \\
W_i^{G+1} &= W_i^{G+1} \quad \text{otherwise}
\end{aligned}
\tag{1.23}
$$

All the steps are continued till termination condition is reached.

2.11 Clustering using differential evolution

The method used is almost inherent to all different evolutionary algorithms including GA. While we used to encode the cluster centroids in a chromosome in GA, it is now encoded in the parameter vectors [19]. Each parameter vector in a population of size n represents k cluster centroids selected randomly.

Then, for each parameter vector W_i containing the k cluster centroids and corresponding to that, for each data vector Z_p, we assign it to the cluster centroid, with which it has the least Euclidean norm (as we had done in PSO clustering).Thereafter, we change the members of the population by the aforementioned DE algorithm performing the steps of initialization, mutation, recombination, and selection.

The solution is the one vector which has the best fitness function in the last generation of our algorithm.

Though the nature of the fitness function is not considered here, but intuitively it follows that we can use the same one used in our GA with a few changes of notation to adhere to the vector representation nature without loss of generality.

2.12 Semisupervised learning algorithms

2.12.1 Overview

SemiSupervised learning is based on a mixture of labeled and unlabeled data. While unlabeled data are cheap to find, labeled data on the other hand are expensive and only available in scarce amount (whether by hand or by algorithms). SemiSupervised learning is advantageous since the unlabeled data can be classified accurately from the small amount of labeled data provided [20]. There are many semisupervised algorithms among which the important ones are discussed briefly as follows:

❖ Self-Training
❖ Co-Training
❖ Mixture models, Generative methods
❖ Semisupervised SVM

2.12.2 Self-Training

Suppose $\{(x_i, y_i)\}$ denote the labeled data and $\{x_j\}$ denote the unlabeled data. Initially, the objective function f is trained from the labeled data. Subsequently, f is applied to the available unlabeled data and removes a subset of the resultant and adds it to the labeled data. This method is repeated till termination condition (Fig. 1.8).

2.12.3 Co-Training

Co-Training is used when the feature set of the data vector can be split into two subfeature set such that both of the feature sets are independent of each other and each of them can individually classify the data vectors.

Each of the two subfeatured is used to train a classifier from the labeled data giving rise to two classifiers, say C_1 and C_2. Then, each of the classifier is used to classify the unlabeled data and thereafter teach the other classifier, i.e., C_1 feeds its information to C_2 and vice versa. Both of the classifiers are retrained on the labeled as in the first step and the process is continued till termination condition occurs.

2.13 PSO-assisted semisupervised clustering

PSO has proved quite useful as far as its performance is considered for classification and clustering problems [21]. However, despite its performance, the

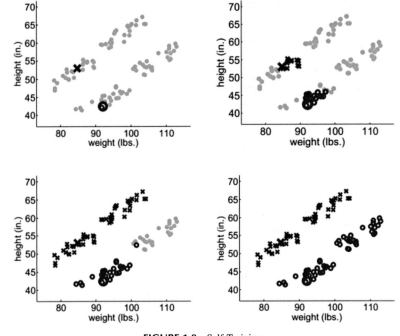

FIGURE 1.8   Self-Training.

numbers of labeled data points required to give optimal values cluster centroid values are quite high. As such, more accurate results can be found when a mixture of labeled and unlabeled data is used. The advantage of this PSO-assisted semisupervised learning algorithm is that the amount of labeled data required is quite less while also giving a better yield in performance when compared to the K nearest neighbor (KNN) and SVMs. Besides, it also has the advantage of finding and searching for new patterns faster due to the less amount of labeled data present.

Initially, the PSO step is applied to the labeled data. Preserving our notations and equations from the mainstream PSO that we have discussed earlier, the ith particle is represented by

$$X_i = \{m_{i1}, m_{i2}, ..., m_{ik}\}$$

The equation of the PSO and the fitness value remains the same. A better fitness function can also be taken which combines the structural knowledge of the unlabeled data with our previous fitness function [22].

$$\Psi(P_i) = \beta\left(\frac{1}{l}\sum_{j=1}^{l}d\big(x_j, P_{CL(j),i}\big)\right) + (1-\beta)$$

$$\times \left(\frac{1}{u}\sum_{k=1}^{u}\min\big\{d\big(X_k, P_{1,i}\big), d\big(X_k, P_{2,i}\big), ..., d\big(X_k, P_{C,i}\big)\big\}\right),$$

(1.24)

Here l is total data point, β is a value between 0 and 1, and u is the number of unlabeled data points. The first term here represents our general fitness function, i.e., $\beta = 1$ gives us the normal fitness function.

Initially, all the particles are randomly assigned with the position of the cluster centroids and then each particle is assigned with a random velocity [23]. After that, as we had already done in our aforementioned PSO algorithm, the following are repeated until some number of iterations:

1. The fitness function of each particle is calculated. After that, the best fitness value is updated. This is followed by updating the P_{best} and G_{best} as required from the PSO equations of position and velocity update.
2. The velocity and position of each particle is updated.

After this, taking the optimum centroids as found from G_{best}, the unlabeled data points are labeled using the KNN method.

2.14 Semisupervised clustering using GA

GAs excels at complex search problems due to the nature of the evolutionary stochastic search model that it follows. While labeling clusters in an unsupervised fashion, the accuracy of the clusters can be improved if some labeled data are added to the mix. For this purpose, an unsupervised clustering algorithm optimized with GA is used. The objective function is such that besides finding the clusters in the unlabeled set with the help of the Euclidean norms as discussed, the structure of the labeled data is also taken into account. For this, the GINI index [5] which is a measure of classification accuracy is used.

For some k cluster centers, the objective function to be minimized is given by

$$E = \beta * (\text{Cluster Dispersion}) + \alpha * (\text{Cluster Impurity})$$ (1.25)

Here, α and β are greater than 0. Also note that setting $\alpha = 0$ yields a result which would be produced for purely unsupervised clustering. Henceforth, the mean squared error function that we have been using before can be used as a measure of Cluster Dispersion. Another measure for this is the Davies-Bouldin index as shown in Ref. [4] which will not be dealt here.

For measuring the Cluster Impurity, the GINI index is used. In this algorithm, clustering is done with the help of GA, with objective function E as the basis.

2.14.1 GINI index

The GINI index is basically used in decision trees to figure out the impurity of a split. Drawing motivation from this, the clustering problem with k clusters can be thought of as a k-partition in decision tress corresponding to some node. The GINI index of a cluster is given as

$$G_{pi} = 1 - \sum_{j=1}^{k} \left(\frac{\text{No.of points in cluster i and class j}}{\text{total points in cluster j}} \right)^2 \tag{1.26}$$

So, the total impurity measure is given by

$$I = \left(\sum_{i=1}^{k} T_{pi} * G_{pi} \right) / \text{total no. of points} \tag{1.27}$$

3. Conclusion

The field of metaheuristics is a rich one and a hot topic among researchers. In addition to the methods discussed in this study, a lot of nature-inspired methods have been evolving lately to tackle clustering and related problems in different problem scenarios in an optimized way. Also rather than using the metaheuristics mentioned in their general form, lots of hybrid algorithms are being found and researched upon to tackle complex problems more efficiently.

References

[1]   C. Blum, A. Roli, Metaheuristics in combinatorial optimization: overview and conceptual comparison, ACM Comput. Surv. 35 (Number 3) (September 2003) 268−308.

[2]   S. Mishra, H.K. Tripathy, A.R. Panda, An improved and adaptive attribute selection technique to optimize dengue fever prediction, Int. J. Eng. Technol. 7 (2018) 480−486.

[3]   P. Arabie, L.J. Hubert, G. De Soete, Clustering and Classification, World Scientific Publishing, River Edge, Singapore, 1996.

[4]   D.L. Davies, D.W. Bouldin, A cluster separation measure, IEEE Trans. Pattern Anal. & Mach. Intell. 1 (2) (1979) 224−227.

[5]   L. Breiman, J. Friedman, R. Olshen, C. Stone, Classification and Regression Trees, Wadsworth International, California, 1984.

[6]   A. Luis Ballardini, A Tutorial on Particle Swarm Optimization Clustering, December 2016 arXiv:1809.01942 [cs].

[7] S. Mishra, P.K. Mallick, H.K. Tripathy, L. Jena, G.-S. Chae, Stacked KNN with hard voting predictive approach to assist hiring process in IT organizations, Int. J. Electr. Eng. Educ. (February 2021), https://doi.org/10.1177/0020720921989015.

[8] L. Jena, S. Mishra, S. Nayak, P. Ranjan, M.K. Mishra, Variable optimization in cervical cancer data using particle swarm optimization, in: Advances in Electronics, Communication and Computing, Springer, Singapore, 2021, pp. 147–153.

[9] R.C.E. JKennedy, Particle swarm optimization, in: Proceedings of the IEEE International Joint Conference on Neural Networks, vol. 4, 1995, pp. 1942–1948.

[10] E. Bonabeau, M. Dorigo, G. Theraulaz, Swarm intelligence, in: From Naturalto Artificial Systems, Oxford University Press, New York, 1999.

[11] N. Singh, D.P. Singh, B. Pant, ACOCA: ant colony optimization based clustering algorithm for big data preprocessing, Int. J. Math. Eng. & Manag. Sci. 4 (5) (2019) 1239–1250, https://doi.org/10.33889/IJMEMS.2019.4.5-098.

[12] S. Mishra, H.K. Tripathy, B.K. Mishra, Implementation of biologically motivated optimisation approach for tumour categorisation, Int. J. Comput. Aided Eng. Technol. 10 (3) (2018) 244–256.

[13] A. Mishra, B. Naik, S.K. Srichandan, Missing value imputation using ANN optimized by genetic algorithm, Int. J. Appl. Ind. Eng. 5 (2) (2018) 41–57.

[14] S. Mishra, P.K. Mallick, H.K. Tripathy, A.K. Bhoi, A. González-Briones, Performance evaluation of a proposed machine learning model for chronic disease datasets using an integrated attribute evaluator and an improved decision tree classifier, Appl. Sci. 10 (22) (2020) 8137.

[15] U. Maulik, S. Bandyopadhyay, Genetic algorithm-based clustering technique, Pattern Recogn. 33 (9) (2000), https://doi.org/10.1016/Soo31-3203(99)00137-5.

[16] Z. Michalewicz, Genetic Algorithms#Data Structures Evolution Programs, Springer, New York, 1992.

[17] P.K. Mallick, S. Mishra, G.S. Chae, Digital media news categorization using Bernoulli document model for web content convergence, Personal Ubiquitous Comput. (2020), https://doi.org/10.1007/s00779-020-01461-9.

[18] A. Abraham, S. Das, A. Konar, Document clustering using differential evolution, in: 2006 IEEE International Conference on Evolutionary Computation, Vancouver, BC, 2006, pp. 1784–1791, https://doi.org/10.1109/CEC.2006.1688523.

[19] S. Mishra, H.K. Tripathy, P.K. Mallick, A.K. Bhoi, P. Barsocchi, EAGA-MLP—an enhanced and adaptive hybrid classification model for diabetes diagnosis, Sensors 20 (14) (2020) 4036.

[20] S. Mishra, P.K. Mallick, L. Jena, G.S. Chae, Optimization of skewed data using sampling-based preprocessing approach, Front. Pub. Health 8 (2020) 274, https://doi.org/10.3389/fpubh.2020.00274.

[21] S. Sahoo, M. Das, S. Mishra, S. Suman, A hybrid DTNB model for heart disorders prediction, in: Advances in Electronics, Communication and Computing, Springer, Singapore, 2021, pp. 155–163.

[22] X. Zhang, L. Jiao, A. Paul, Y. Yuan, Z. Wei, Q. Song, Semisupervised particle swarm optimization for classification, Math. Probl Eng. 2014 (2014), https://doi.org/10.1155/2014/832135. Article ID 832135, 11 pages.

[23] A. Cervantes, I.M. Galván, P. Isasi, AMPSO: a new particle swarm method for nearest neighborhood classification, IEEE Trans. Syst. Man & Cybern. B: Cybern. 39 (5) (2009) 1082–1091.

Chapter 2

Metaheuristics in classification, clustering, and frequent pattern mining

Hiren Kumar Thakkar[1], Hrushikesh Shukla[2], Prasan Kumar Sahoo[3]
[1]*Department of Computer Science and Engineering, School of Engineering and Sciences, SRM University, Mangalagiri, Andhra Pradesh, India;* [2]*School of Computer Science and Engineering, Dr. Vishwanath Karad MIT World Peace University, Pune, Maharashtra, India;* [3]*Department of Computer Science and Information Engineering, Chang Gung University, Taoyuan City, Taiwan*

1. Introduction

There are multiple problems in computer science like traveling salesman problem, N-queen problem, and so on, which are computationally expensive. Most of these problems are optimization problems and belong to the category of NP problems. Optimization problems are the ones where we need to find an optimal solution from all the feasible solutions possible and the reason these problems belong to NP category of problems is that the algorithm might need to explore the entire state space for the given problem, only then there is a chance for achieving the optimal solution. There are several application-specific problems such as Skewed Data optimization [1], Virtual Network Embedding [2], Efficient Data Placement [3], where optimization theory provides a reasonable solution. Heuristic algorithms are used to solve such problems. These algorithms work on the principles of randomization and approximation, and by the use of such algorithms, we might find a suboptimal solution to the given problem in a very short duration of time. Heuristic offers a trade-off between optimality, completeness, and time for execution. However, in some cases, heuristic algorithms do not always give the best results. Metaheuristic algorithms are thus used to optimize the heuristic algorithms to give better performance.

1.1 Introduction to metaheuristics

There are some drawbacks to using heuristic algorithms. Some of them include heuristics being problem specific, meaning if a heuristic that achieves a better

Cognitive Big Data Intelligence with a Metaheuristic Approach
https://doi.org/10.1016/B978-0-323-85117-6.00005-4

result for one of the problems might not work well for other problems of the same type. On the other hand, metaheuristic algorithms act as a black box; if a metaheuristic algorithm is working well for one type of problem, then it will work well for all problems of the same type. Metaheuristics can be defined as a high-level problem-independent algorithmic framework that provides a set of guidelines to develop heuristic optimization algorithms. Metaheuristic algorithms provide a suboptimal solution for a problem even if it has incomplete or imperfect information with it. Most of the metaheuristic algorithms are inspired by nature and implement some principles of stochastic optimization; hence, the solution depends on the random variables that are generated. Researchers have proved that metaheuristic algorithms often tend to be a superior alternative to optimization problems as compared to traditional approaches like branch and bound and dynamic programming, especially when the state space is large and complex.

There are some properties which characterize metaheuristic algorithms. These properties are given below [4]:

- Metaheuristic algorithms tend to guide the search process.
- Their goal is to explore the search space to find a suboptimal solution to a given problem.
- Metaheuristic techniques may fall in the range of simple local search to complex learning procedure.
- Metaheuristic algorithms are approximate and mostly nondeterministic.
- These algorithms may have some mechanism to avoid getting trapped in some areas of search space.
- They are not problem dependent.

The key difference in heuristic and metaheuristic algorithms is that metaheuristic algorithms are problem independent. Moreover, as heuristic algorithms are problem dependent, hence, finding an appropriate heuristic that would give a better solution is a difficult task. Many heuristic algorithms are greedy and hence might get "trapped" in local optimum solution whereas metaheuristic algorithms employ certain methods to avoid getting in such local optimal. Both of the algorithms work based on approximation; however, metaheuristic algorithms tend to find a better solution than heuristic algorithms.

1.2 Classification of metaheuristic techniques

Metaheuristic algorithms can be classified based on the inspiration from which they were built [5]. Fig. 2.1 shows the classes of metaheuristic algorithms based on the inspiration. Evolution-based algorithms are inspired by nature. These algorithms take some initial set of candidate solutions. The fitness of each solution is calculated using a fitness function. This fitness function gives us the measure of the properness of our solution, and the goal is to minimize

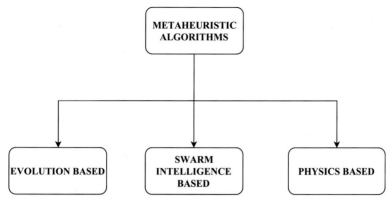

FIGURE 2.1 Classification of metaheuristic algorithms.

(or maximize) the value from this function given some solution. A set of new solutions are generated based on previous solutions. These set of new solutions are better than previous ones. Hence, as iterations increases, the set of solutions keep getting better. Genetic algorithm is the best example of evolution-based algorithms. Swarm intelligence deals with the behavior of natural or artificial systems that are decentralized and self-organized. This concept is mainly applied to artificial intelligence. However, Particle swarm optimization (PSO) is the best example of metaheuristic algorithms developed through this technique. Some algorithms are inspired by laws of physics like gravitational law, electromagnetism law, and so on [6]. Examples of physics-based algorithms are gravitational search algorithm [7], water cycle algorithm [8,9], and many more.

Other than classifying the metaheuristic algorithms based on their inspiration, they can also be classified based on other factors and parameters as the following [4,10]:

- Nature-inspired and not nature-inspired: There are multiple algorithms inspired by nature like ant colony algorithms, while some are not inspired by nature like tabu search. However, there exist some algorithms that might not belong to either of the categories; such algorithms are hybrid algorithms.
- Single point and population-based: Single point—based algorithms focus on a single solution and keep optimizing it, while population-based algorithms focus on a set of solutions and these solutions are improved. Tabu search and variable neighborhood search are examples of single point algorithms, while genetic algorithm and PSO are some examples of population-based algorithms.
- Dynamic and static objective function: Objective function is a function that calculates the completeness of the current solution. The objective of the algorithm is to minimize (or maximize) the value of this objective function.

Multiple metaheuristic algorithms keep the objective function the same during the entire execution, while some algorithms like Global Local Search modify it during the course of execution. This is done to avoid getting trapped in local optima.

- One and various neighborhood structures: Algorithms like variable neighborhood search work on multiple neighborhoods, i.e., their fitness landscape topology changes are classified as various neighborhood algorithms, while most of the algorithms are single neighborhood algorithms. An example of a single neighborhood search is Tabu search, while variable neighborhood search is an example of various neighborhood algorithms.

- Memory-based and memoryless: This is considered as an important attribute to classify the metaheuristic algorithms. The memoryless algorithms make use of Markov decision process. Hence, their next move is primarily dependent on the current move. An example of a memoryless algorithm is simulated annealing. The algorithms which use memory are genetic algorithms and tabu search. These algorithms might use short-term memory to keep track of recent moves made by the algorithm, while the use of long-term memory is for storing the parameters about the search.

1.3 Working of some metaheuristic algorithms

In this section, some common metaheuristic algorithms are discussed. The working and steps of each of the algorithm are explained for easy understanding of the further sections.

1.3.1 Genetic algorithm

The genetic algorithm is an evolution-based algorithm inspired by natural selection. They are adaptive heuristic search algorithms. These algorithms take a set of candidate solutions and then keep iteratively evolving these solutions to give optimal or near-optimal solutions. The correctness of the solution increases with iteration. The primitive components of this algorithm are the initial population, fitness function, selection, crossover, and mutation. The initial solution consists of components like gene and chromosome; each solution given in the set of initial solution is called a chromosome, while parts of the chromosome are known as a gene. Fig. 2.2 shows an example of a genetic algorithm. Here, in the initial population, there are four candidate solutions namely, S1, S2, S3, and S4, each of them is a chromosome. S1 = 0, 1, 2, 3, 2. Here, each of the numbers like 0, 1, 2, and so on is known as a gene. The value of each number in the chromosome should be between 0 and 3. The initial population given to the algorithm can be randomly generated or given by the user or can be a result of previous solutions. The calculation of fitness function is dependent on the type of problem. The objective is to maximize (or minimize) the value of fitness function for each solution. Here, the fitness

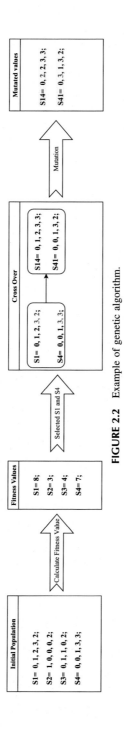

FIGURE 2.2   Example of genetic algorithm.

function just adds up the numbers in the solution and the objective is to maximize the value. Later, we perform the crossover of the candidate solutions by exchanging the genes of solutions. The genes marked red are selected for exchange. The new solutions are then mutated for better performance. The values in the mutation box are mutated values. If the fitness value of S14 and S41 is calculated, it comes out to be 10 and 9, respectively, which is comparatively better than initial solutions. These new solutions are then replaced or appended with the current set of the initial population and new iteration is started.

1.3.2 Particle swarm optimization algorithm

PSO is an algorithm based on swarm intelligence, and it is a population-based stochastic algorithm, meaning it works on a set of solutions and is random in nature. It is inspired by the behavior of birds flocking and fishes schooling. Consider several birds flying in a group, each bird in the group will be considered as a particle and the entire group will be considered as a swarm. As said previously, this algorithm takes a set of candidate solutions as an input. Here, every solution in the group is known as a particle, and the entire set of solutions is known as swarm, and the goal is to achieve an optimal solution, hence the name of the algorithm, PSO. PSO and genetic algorithm are similar as both are population based, nature inspired, and iterative, and update of the population occurs on the basis of the fitness function in both cases. The important differentiating point in genetic algorithm and PSO is that the genetic algorithm can work well with discrete variables, while PSO is computationally more efficient [11].

Fig. 2.3 shows the basic flow of the PSO algorithm. This algorithm, similar to the genetic algorithm, starts with an initial set of candidate solutions. The fitness function calculates the fitness value of each candidate solution. The goal is to maximize (or minimize) this fitness value. The term "p_{best}" indicates the personal best fitness value of a given particle in its history, while the term "g_{best}" indicates the best fitness value of all particles for that iteration. Then, based on the p_{best} and g_{best} values, the velocity for each particle is calculated

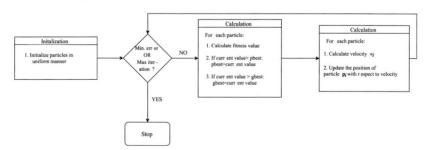

FIGURE 2.3 Flow of particle swarm optimization.

and the position of the particle is changed based on its velocity. Eq. (2.1) gives the formula to update the velocity of the particle and Eq. (2.2) gives the formula to update the position of the particle, where V_i identifies the velocity of the current particle, "rand()" is random number generator, and P_i gives the position of the current particle. The variables C1 and C2 are known as accelerating coefficients which can be adjusted by the user to modify the rate of change in position.

$$V_i = V_i + (C1 * \text{rand}()) * (p_{best} - P_i) + (C2 * \text{rand}()) * (g_{best} - P_i) \qquad (2.1)$$

$$P_i = P_i + V_i \qquad (2.2)$$

1.3.3 Ant colony optimization algorithm

Ant Colony Optimization (ACO) is a nature-inspired technique based on the behavior of ants. It is based on probability and used for finding solutions to problems that have huge state space. The ants are known for finding their food on a short path. Ants leave their trace while moving from their nest to food, and while returning, they use a pheromone to leave their trace and the other ants can sense the same. This pheromone evaporates with time. Fig. 2.4 shows an example of how ants find their shortest path. At a given time, there is a food particle on the other side of an obstacle from the nest (step 1) and none of the ants have visited in search of food. There are two ways namely path "A" and path "B" to reach food particle out of which path "A" is the shortest. Now as no ants have gone out for food, there is no deposition of pheromone on the path. The probability of an ant choosing any path is 50%. Ant "A" and ant "B" go for the search of food, ant "A" takes path "A" and ant "B" takes path "B." Both reach food and return to the nest. But, ant "A" returns earlier to nest as it took a shorter path (step 2). Hence, the following ants will follow path "A" as it will have more pheromone deposition. Eventually, there will not be any pheromone on path "B" as it evaporated and path "A" will have the most pheromone deposition and we get the shortest path from food to the nest (step3).We use multiple agents to find solution to a given problem. Each of the agents plays a role of an ant. Given below are the steps taken by ACO algorithm:

1. START
2. While (not termination) continue; else go to: 7.
3. Generate solution().
4. Compare actions().
5. Pheromone update().
6. Go to 2.
7. STOP.

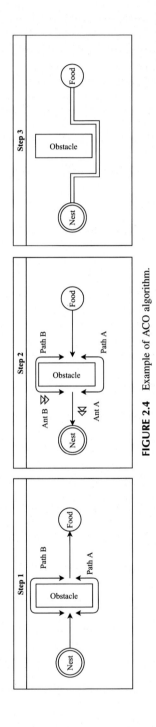

FIGURE 2.4   Example of ACO algorithm.

As the above steps show, ACO is an iterative algorithm. For each iteration, the agent forms a solution, the next step compares the solutions form all the agents, and the last step of the loop updates the pheromone levels of the best path. The ACO algorithm is probability based as the probability of an ant to take a path is dependent on the levels of pheromone on that path. The probability for a given ant "k" to follow a path starting at "x" and ending at "y" is shown in Eq. (2.3). Where τ is the attractiveness, while η is the pheromone trail level which describes the level of pheromone on a path. α and β refer to the controlling parameters and the value of α should be greater or equal to 0, while the value of β should be greater or equal to 1. Eq. (2.4) shows the equation to update the pheromones, where ρ is the coefficient of pheromone evaporation. The increasing value of $\Delta\tau_{xy}^{k}$ signifies better solution. The value of $\Delta\tau_{xy}^{k}$ can be calculated as shown in Eq. (2.5), where Q is a constant and L_k is the cost (mostly distance) for an ant to travel the path xy.

$$p_{xy}^{k} = \frac{\tau_{xy}^{\alpha} \times \eta_{xy}^{\beta}}{\sum_{x \in \text{allowed}_x} \left(\tau_{xy}^{\alpha}\right)\left(\eta_{xy}^{\beta}\right)} \tag{2.3}$$

$$\tau_{xy}^{k} \leftarrow (1-\rho)\tau_{xy}^{k} + \sum_{k} \Delta\tau_{xy}^{k} \tag{2.4}$$

$$\Delta\tau_{xy}^{k} = \begin{cases} \dfrac{Q}{L_k} & \text{if ant k travels through path xy} \\ 0 & \text{otherwise} \end{cases} \tag{2.5}$$

2. Metaheuristics in classification

Data mining is an interdisciplinary field that involves mining or extracting patterns from huge datasets. Classification is a data analytics task that involves classifying data objects in their respective classes with applications in the field of healthcare data analysis [[12−16,17], potential malware detection [18], etc. Moreover, machine learning and heuristic methods are also used prominently to investigate the healthcare issues such as lung cancer detection [19] and cardiac signal annotation [20]. For example, checking if a particular mail in the user's inbox is spam or not. Classification is a supervised learning task, meaning the algorithm needs to be trained on some amount of data. Generally, any classification algorithm has two phases namely, the training phase and testing phase. In the training phase, a classifier model is built using multiple classification algorithms. The algorithms are trained on a training dataset, from which they build the classifier. The next phase is the testing phase in which the performance of the model is evaluated by testing it on a dataset similar to the training dataset. This subchapter focuses on the use of metaheuristic algorithms for classification.

2.1 Use of ant colony optimization in classification

The basic concept of the ACO algorithm is explained in Section 1.3.3. The selection of features is an important task in classification as some irrelevant or useless features might hamper the performance of the classifier. For example, if designing a classifier to classify whether an applicant might get a job or not, the attribute of the applicant's gender would be irrelevant as the classifier might form bias if the recruiting organization has more number of female employees. ACO algorithm is mostly used in selecting a subset of features to increase the performance of an algorithm. Sreeja and Sankar developed a novel instance-based pattern matching based classification (PMC) algorithm for unlabeled samples. The PMC algorithm classifies the unlabeled sample by matching its features with features of all the instances in the dataset. In the next step, the algorithm groups all the instances with the maximum number of matching features. It then counts the occurrence of each class in this group. The class with maximum occurrence is the class of the unlabeled sample. If there is more than one maximum occurrence class, then the probabilistic approach is used. The performance of the PMC algorithm is improved by feature selection using ACO. For feature selection, the ACO has memory storage that stores the solution list and storage list as well as a global value initialized to zero. The solution list is initially empty and the storage list contains a list of all the features in the dataset. The agent has to choose two positions namely positive and negative for leaving the pheromone trace. For each position, a random number is generated; for a positive position, the random number should be in the range of 0 to n + 1 where n be the maximum number of features in storage list, and for a negative position, the random number should be in the range of 0 to q + 1 where q signifies the number of features in solution list (initially zero). Each of the random numbers generated for positive and negative positions indicates the number of features to be selected from the storage and solution list, respectively. For the first iteration, a random number is generated for a positive position as the negative position is set to zero. The algorithm selects the number of distinct features from the storage list for depositing the pheromone. The selected features are removed from the storage list. Then, the algorithm computes the energy value of agents by having average classification accuracy using the PMC algorithm for selected features and leave-one-out cross-validation. The selected features are then added to the solution list. In the next iterations, the agent again chooses two random numbers for positive and negative positions. The features selected from the storage list and the ones not selected from the solution list are grouped and the energy of the agent is calculated again. If the energy score is better than the previous iteration, then the currently chosen features are added to the solution list, while the selected features from negative positions are added back to the storage list. If the energy of agent is less than that of the previous iteration, then the currently selected features are ignored [21].

Rule R_j: If x_1 is A_{j1}, x_2 is A_{j2} ... and x_n is A_{jn}. Then class is C_j with; $CF = CF_j$.

$$(2.6)$$

Ganji and Abadeh developed a fuzzy classification system based on ACO. They named this system as FCS-ANTMINER. The use of fuzzy logic for classification problems is gaining popularity. The FCS-ANTMINER is based on a similar concept. It has two stages as any other classification algorithm namely, training stage and testing stage. In the training stage, the training dataset is sent as input to the ACO-based rule generation module. This module uses an ACO algorithm to calculate a set of rules for a class in classification. In the testing phase, the rules generated by the training phase are used by a fuzzy inference system to determine the class for each sample in the testing dataset; this process is shown in Fig. 2.5. The fuzzy rules are in form as shown in Eq. (2.6). Where R_j is the label of jth fuzzy rule, while A_{j1}, A_{j2} ..., A_{jn} denote the antecedents of the fuzzy rule. The C_j gives the class for the rule, while confidence or certainty of the rule is given by CF_j. The fuzzy rule set generated individually for each class. For the rule generation, the first ant randomly generates a rule R_j, and the following ants modify the rule according to a parameter named MAX_change, which signifies the maximum number of terms an ant can change in the rule. The fitness of rule R_j is then calculated and the pheromone levels are then updated based on the fitness value. Once all the ants have modified rules, the rule with the best modification is added to the set of learned rules. Then to learn other rules concerning the same class, the training samples which satisfy the current rule are deleted and the above process is repeated. Gupta et al. successfully developed a novel method to select features using the ACO algorithm and verified their technique using the SVM algorithm. If using a subset of features gives better accuracy, then selected features are better than others. Their feature selection mechanism involves the abstract steps like solution generation by each ant, comparison of the solution by each ant, and updation of pheromone levels using local and global rules. Initially, a heuristic is set which determines the importance of each rule. The value of heuristic for all the features can be set the same for giving equal importance to all the features. An ant selects each feature in a step-by-step manner and adds it to its solution set. Certain state transition rules are employed to select the next feature which depends on two parameters which are q and q_0, each in the range of 0–1. The value of q is generated randomly, while the value of q_0 is set by the user. If for an iteration, $q < q_0$, then the algorithm selects features based on previous knowledge, while for the condition where $q \geq q_0$, the algorithm considers unexplored features; however, the probability of selecting a feature depends on the level of pheromone and heuristic function. Once all the ants complete the selection of features, evaluation is carried out using leave-one-out cross-validation, and performance is measured using the

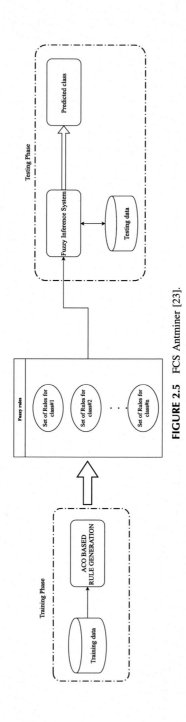

FIGURE 2.5   FCS Antminer [23].

accuracy of the SVM algorithm. The ant with maximum accuracy is called winner ant, and more pheromone is deposited on the features selected by this ant; this is a global update. While the local update reduces the pheromone levels of the features selected by other ants, this reduces the probability of selection of the features which might be irrelevant [22].

2.2 Use of genetic algorithms in classification

The basic concepts of a genetic algorithm have been explained in Section 1.3.1. Genetic algorithms have shown promising results in classification problems, and there are various works of classification using genetic algorithm; in this section, few of the works have been described. Data analysts mostly work on data from the data warehouse to derive patterns or rules or classify the given data. The size of data in a data warehouse is in several terabytes. Hence, retraining the entire classifier model after every update on the data warehouse does not seem efficient. As a result, Birant et al. came up with a solution and developed an iterative genetic algorithm model that will not require retraining the entire model. Training of genetic algorithms for classification is different from the one mentioned in previous sections; for classification purposes, different initial populations are taken into consideration for each class. Then, the encoding of each sample of the initial population is performed. The model proposed by Birant et al. is shown in Fig. 2.6. At the start, The entire data from the data warehouse are passed to the training process of genetic algorithms and it is assumed that all the hyperparameters like the technique to be used for crossover, termination criteria, and so on are set by default or by the user. After the training process is complete, the model is generated and stored. There are no frequent write operations on the data warehouse as it contains historical data and not operational data. After updates are performed on these data, the algorithm takes into consideration the previously constructed model and the entire dataset, as most of the rules in the current model are as per the previous data. Most of the data obeys the same pattern and only a few changes are needed to be done to accommodate the patterns from new data, the algorithm converges rapidly.

Motieghader et al. developed a hybrid algorithm based on metaheuristic techniques like genetic algorithms and learning automata, and they named the

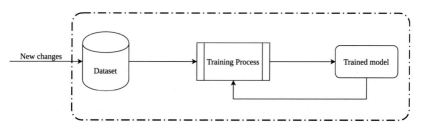

FIGURE 2.6 Iterative Genetic Algorithm for classification [24].

algorithm as GALA. They applied this algorithm for gene selection for microarray-based cancer datasets. Microarray data contain thousands of gene samples associated with some diseases. In microarray data, often the number of samples is less as compared to the number of genes; hence, the selection of particular genes is very important. This reduces the size of the dataset and also increases the accuracy of the algorithm. However, the selection of optimal genes from all the given genes is classified as an NP-hard problem. Learning automata is an abstract model that interacts with the environment through its actions. Learning automata is represented in Fig. 2.7. It selects an action from a set of actions and performs it in the environment, and the environment evaluates the actions and sends feedback to the learning automata. The learning automata then optimize or change its actions based on the feedback of the environment. Fig. 2.8 shows a flowchart of the GALA algorithm. While the initial population is generated randomly, the fitness function calculates the fitness value of each solution. For calculating the fitness value, they divided the dataset into five equal parts, then for each part, trained SVM for the other four parts, and the testing was performed on the selected part. The average accuracy of all the iterations was considered as the fitness of that solution. For a crossover, a single point method was used and an order-based method was utilized for mutation. After mutation, the system might receive a reward or penalty based on the fitness value of the selected solution. The selection mechanism would pass the chromosomes from one generation to the next; 10% of best performing chromosomes are passed to the next generation, while the remaining are selected using the roulette-wheel method. This process would repeat for a predefined maximum number of generations. GALA gene selection algorithm which gives a set of optimal features in O $(G.m.n^3)$ complexity, where G is generation number, m is size of initial population, while n corresponds to number of samples in the dataset; this complexity is less and acceptable as compared to nonpolynomial time.

Suguna and Thanushkodi proposed an algorithm by combining Genetic Algorithms and K-nearest neighbor (KNN) algorithm and named it as GKNN. The drawbacks of the KNN algorithm which include high calculation complexity, dependency on the training set, and so on were overcome by the GKNN algorithm. The flowchart of the GKNN algorithm is shown in Fig. 2.9.

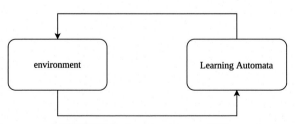

FIGURE 2.7 Learning Automata [25].

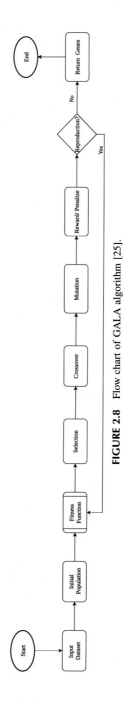

FIGURE 2.8 Flow chart of GALA algorithm [25].

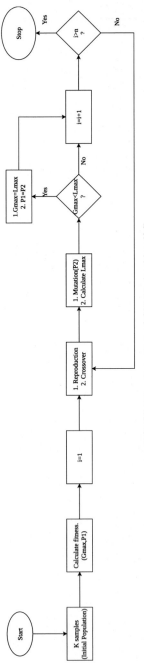

FIGURE 2.9 Flow chart of GKNN algorithm [26].

Initially, the population is generated by randomly selecting k different training samples. The samples are encoded in a string format representing the instance number. The fitness was calculated by measuring the distance between each of the k selected samples and the samples in the test dataset. Then, the selection of the chromosomes is done by having multiple copies of the chromosomes with more fitness value, whereas comparatively fewer copies of chromosomes with less fitness and using the roulette-wheel method for selection of chromosomes for crossover. The technique implemented for the crossover is a single point method. Then, a local maximum is calculated from the current population by calculating the fitness of the current population. If the current maximum is global maximum, then return the chromosomes. However, if a global maximum is not achieved, then this process halts after predefined n iterations. The experimental results show that the algorithm increases accuracy while decreasing complexity [26].

2.3 Use of particle swarm optimization in classification

PSO is a swarm-based metaheuristic algorithm. The basic concepts of PSO have been discussed in Section 1.3.2. Electrocardiogram (ECG) gives a graphical, vector representation of the electrical activity of the heart. It can be very useful to detect the medical condition of the heart, but analyzing ECG signals can be very time consuming. Korürek and Doğan figured out a way to analyze these ECG signals and classify them in six different classes namely Normal beat (N), Premature Ventricular Contraction (PVC), Fusion of the ventricular and normal beat (F), Atrial premature Beat (A), Right bundle branch block beat (R), and fusion of paced and normal beat (f). For this purpose, they used a combination of radial basis function neural network (RBFNN) and PSO algorithm. The architecture of their proposed system is shown in Fig. 2.10; the raw data required for the training and testing were obtained from the MIT-BIH arrhythmia database. The preprocessing involves filtration, baseline drift removal, and removing noise from the dataset. The denoising is done by passing data through low pass filters followed by baseline correction. The preprocessing stage is followed by the R peak detection stage which is done using Pan and Tomkins algorithm [27]. The normalization is carried out using some stored values of ECG signals which also extracts the features from the ECG signals [28].

$$\text{net} = [(c_1, \sigma_1), (c_2, \sigma_2), (c_3, \sigma_3), ..., (c_n, \sigma_n)] \qquad (2.7)$$

RBFNN are neural networks with input, hidden, and output layers but are restricted to only one hidden layer. The basis function of RBFNN used here is the Gaussian function. The hyperparameters of RBFNN are bandwidth and center of each neuron. The weights of hidden and output levels can then be calculated using the pseudoinverse method. Let "net" be a vector of parameters as shown in Eq. (2.7) where c indicates the center of the neuron, shows the

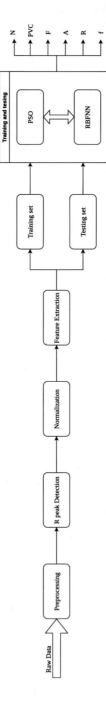

FIGURE 2.10   ECG detection using PSO and RBFNN [28].

bandwidth of the neuron, and n shows the number of neurons in a given layer. Deciding the value of each of these parameters for better performance is an optimization problem and is solved using the PSO algorithm in this case. Qin et al. performed a study that inspired the algorithm used for classification of ECG, and the flowchart of the same is given in Fig. 2.11. Initially, a count variable (i), vectors of centers, and bandwidth for each layer as shown in Eq. (2.7) and the number of maximum iterations to be performed are set. Then for each iteration, the vectors are decoded to give connections and the weights of each connection are computed followed by computation of fitness of each particle which is a single RBFNN. Then, personal best (p_i), velocity, and position for each particle are calculated along with the global best. The results show that the above method yields smaller models without compromising the performance [28,29].

$$X_i = \left[x_i^1, x_i^2, x_i^3, \ldots, x_i^n \right]; \quad \text{where } x_i^d \varepsilon \{0, 1\}. \tag{2.8}$$

Trunk and Gerard put forward an example of the curse of dimensionality. It says that if the number of dimensions (features) of the dataset is increased, then the power of prediction of classifier or regressor initially increases, but later it starts decreasing [30]. Brezočnik combined Binary Particle Swarm Optimization (BPSO) algorithm with a C.45 classifier to handle high-dimensional datasets. The key concept that differentiates binary PSO from ordinary PSO is that the search space of the BPSO algorithm is binary [31]. This is used by Brezočnik for the selection of features. For example, if a particle of six-dimensional space has a position value as 100101, then this signifies that only first, third, and sixth features are selected. Their method includes steps like initialization, calculation of fitness, calculating p_{best} and g_{best}, and updating the velocity and position. The initialization takes place in binary format as shown in Eq. (2.8), where i ranges from 1 to m and d ranges from 1 to n, m and n gives the total number of particles and features, respectively. If x_i^d is 1, then it signifies that ith particle has selected the dth feature as discussed in above example. The fitness of a particle is equal to the accuracy gained by C.45 algorithm using the features selected by the particle.

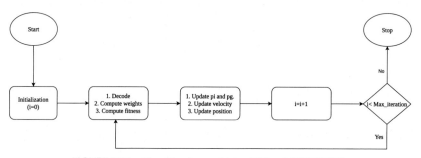

FIGURE 2.11 Algorithm for combining PSO and RBFNN [29].

This gives personal and swarm best values. The value of position is calculated with the help of sigmoid function, while the value of velocity is calculated by a formula similar to the one shown in Eq. (2.1). The experimental analysis shows that the described method gives better performance by selecting less than half of the total features [32].

$$\psi_1(i) = \frac{100 \times \sum_{j=1}^{D_{Train}} \delta\left(\overrightarrow{x_j}\right)}{D_{Train}} \tag{2.9}$$

$$\psi_2(i) = \frac{\sum_{j=1}^{D_{Train}} d\left(\overrightarrow{x_j}, \overrightarrow{p_i}^{CL_{known}\left(\overrightarrow{x_j}\right)}\right)}{D_{Train}} \tag{2.10}$$

$$\psi_3(i) = \frac{1}{2} \times \left(\frac{\psi_1(i)}{100} + \psi_2(i)\right) \tag{2.11}$$

Falco et al. studied the use of PSO for classification problems. Their study includes a comparison of performance using multiple datasets, using different fitness functions, and comparison with other classification. Consider a dataset with N features and C classes. The PSO algorithm is then made to find C centroids in an N-dimensional space. Eqs. (2.9)–(2.11) show the three fitness functions that were considered. The first fitness function is calculated in two steps: the first step assigns a class to each training instance. The second step is shown in Eq. (2.9) which calculates the percentage of samples incorrectly predicted. The second fitness function as shown in Eq. (2.10) is calculated in a single step which computes the Euclidean distance between the given instance and the centroid of the class. The feature values are normalized before the calculation of distance; hence, the distance is always between 0 and 1. This fitness function is considered more sensitive toward smaller variations in the positions of the centroid. The third fitness function is shown in Eq. (2.11) and can be computed by scaling the first fitness function in the range of 0–1 and then computing the mean with second fitness function. The results show that the performance of the third fitness function is better as compared to others. The performance of PSO with fitness function three is compared with some popular algorithms on 13 classification problems where it outperformed all the other algorithms in three classification problems [33].

3. Metaheuristics in clustering

Supervised learning is a task in machine learning where a mapping between input and output is provided. Here, the algorithm trains using these samples, and then its performance is checked on a testing set where the algorithm is given an input sample and it has to determine the corresponding output. Classification falls under the supervised learning category. On the other hand, in unsupervised learning, this input to output mapping is not provided. This type of task is mostly used to detect some unknown or undetected patterns.

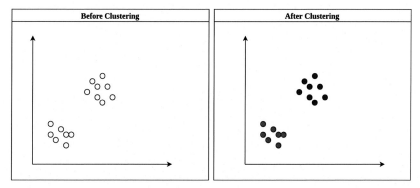

FIGURE 2.12   Clustering.

Clustering is an unsupervised learning task. Given a dataset with multiple data points, clustering algorithms tend to group these data points based on some similarities like distance as shown in Fig. 2.12. There are various types of clustering methods like hierarchical methods, partitioning methods, and so on. This subchapter presents the applications of metaheuristic algorithms in the clustering task.

3.1 Use of ant colony optimization in clustering

ACO is a metaheuristic algorithm that has multiple agents, each of which generates a partial solution in each iteration. Shelokar et al. used this property of the ACO algorithm to perform clustering. The flow of the system they proposed is shown in Fig. 2.13. In clustering, we divide N samples into K groups or clusters. Here, each ant agent contains an array of length N, while each element in the array is in range 1 to K and signifies to which cluster the element belongs. For example, consider an array [1,2], with the value of K as 2, and the value of N is 4. Here, the first and fourth element belongs to cluster number 1, while the second and third elements belong to cluster number 2. During the initialization phase, R agents are initialized by assigning clusters to every data point as per the above example. In the next step, every ant agent generates a solution either by exploitation, or by biased exploration, the method to generate a solution is decided randomly. The ant agent takes the help of pheromone levels during exploitation, while a probabilistic method is used to select a cluster for a data point during the exploration. The fitness of each solution is evaluated once all the solutions are generated. The fitness calculation includes the distance between the center of the cluster and the data points that belong to that cluster, while the centroids of each cluster are calculated considering the mean value of each attribute for all the data points that belong to the cluster. The objective is to minimize this distance. In the next step, local search is applied to best performing 20% of all the solutions. During the local search, numbers of the array are changed, i.e., a data point is assigned to different clusters using a probabilistic approach. The fitness of a solution

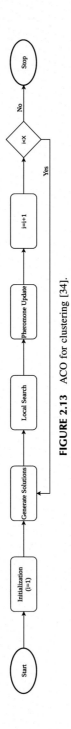

FIGURE 2.13 ACO for clustering [34].

before and after the local search is compared and the one with the least fitness value is retained. Later, the pheromone levels are updated as per the best performers. The above steps are repeated for a predefined number of times. The clusters are then shown as output. The performance of various metaheuristic algorithms was compared across nine different datasets. It was found that the performance of ACO was optimal as compared to other metaheuristic algorithms like simulated annealing, tabu search, and genetic algorithms [34].

The method discussed above is classified under centroid-based clustering. Here, the algorithm tries to cluster the points based on their distance with the center of the cluster known as centroid. However, the method is not sensitive to noise. The medoid-based clustering technique is robust to noise and is helpful when centroids cannot be easily defined. Menéndez et al. developed two medoid-based clustering algorithms namely METACOC and METACOC-K which employ the ACO algorithm for medoid selection. Fig. 2.14 shows the basic outline of both of the algorithms. In the METACOC algorithm, the user has to provide the number of clusters to be made, while the METACOC-K algorithm itself decides the number of clusters [35].

$$J^a = \sum_{i=1}^{n} \min_{j=1}^{|M_a|} d\left(x_i, m_j^a\right) \qquad (2.12)$$

$$Avg\_sil(x) = \frac{\sum\limits_{x \epsilon X} sil(x)}{|X|} \qquad (2.13)$$

In METACOC, the user defines the number of clusters (K) to be formed. Every ant agent has two records, the first record of the data points that are visited and the second record of the selected medoid data points, both of which are initially empty. Every agent has two options to select the next medoid; that is, by exploitation or exploration, that option is selected randomly. After calculating all the medoid sets, the fitness of each medoid set is evaluated using Eq. (2.12). In the proceeding step, the solutions are ranked and pheromone is updated as per and best performing r solutions are updated. These steps are repeated for T iterations. In METACOC-K, the user need not give the number of clusters as input. The value of the number of clusters is decided by each ant as any number between K_{min} and K_{max}, which are predefined. The fitness evaluation metric is also changed to the average silhouette metric for each solution as given in Eq. (2.13), where x is a single instance of entire dataset X, and sil(x) denotes the silhouette metric value for that instance of data [36]. This metric gives the value by balancing the number of clusters and cluster assignment costs. The complexities of METACOC and METACOC-K are $O(T\ Ank)$ and $O(T\ An^2k)$, respectively. The computational complexity difference is because of different fitness functions. The performance of both of these algorithms was compared with PAM and K-means and other algorithms across 20 real-world datasets and the results were positive; METACOC algorithm outperformed PAM in eight datasets, while METACOC-K was found to be better than PAMK algorithm in 15 datasets [35].

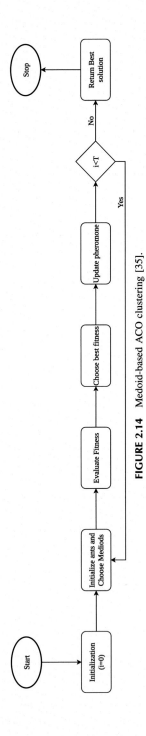

FIGURE 2.14   Medoid-based ACO clustering [35].

Ground object clustering is a task for hyperspectral remote sensing applications. However for clustering, if K-means algorithm is used, then it does not deal well with outliers, and if ACO is used, then it may deal well with outliers, but it takes a lot of time to converge as the image has multiple features and ACO might as well get stuck in a local optimal. Sun et al. proposed a system that combines ACO and K-means algorithm for hyperspectral image classification which tries to overcome the drawbacks of both K means and ACO. In the K-means–ACO algorithm, first clustering is applied using the K-means algorithm, then this clustering information is using as guiding information by ACO and further clustering takes pace using the ACO algorithm. The steps of K-means–ACO include the following [37]:

1. Cluster using K-means and obtain elicitation probability.
2. Update the initial pheromone using elicitation results.
3. Each ant generates solutions and gives elicitation set X'.
4. Calculate objective function.
5. Calculate the best path by ants and check for convergence.
6. If the path is convergent, then stop else update pheromone and go to 3.

Here, the initial pheromone levels are adjusted as per the clusters made by the K-means algorithm. Then, the ACO algorithm uses this information for clustering. As a result, the error for outliers is removed after ACO, while slow convergence issue is handled as ACO receives the clustered information from K-means. The experiments on hyperspectral images showed that the performance of K-means–ACO is better as compared to ACO and K-means [37].

3.2 Use of genetic algorithms in clustering

Genetic Algorithm is an evolutionary metaheuristic algorithm. It is based on the principle of survival of the fittest. The K-means clustering is a common clustering algorithm; however, the algorithm might not always give optimal performance. Maulik and Bandyopadhyay developed a genetic algorithm–based clustering algorithm that overcomes the drawback of the K-means clustering algorithm. The steps of the genetic algorithm for clustering include initialization, fitness calculation, selection, crossover, and mutation. The encoding of every chromosome is as a string of floating point numbers, and each chromosome in the population is of length N*K, where N indicates the number of features and K indicates the number of clusters. The first N numbers of the string indicate the center of the first cluster and the following N numbers represent the center of the second cluster and so on. For example, let N = 3 and K = 3 and a string or chromosomes are given as "10.2 11 1 11.2 12 3 15 10 8," then (10.2, 11, 1) represent the center of the first cluster, while the points (11.2, 12, 3) and (15, 10, 8) represent the centers of second and third cluster, respectively. During the initialization step, p, such chromosomes are generated randomly, where p indicates the size of the initial population.

The following step includes the clustering of data points as per their distance with the centers provided by the population. The centroids of each cluster are updated by taking the mean of each feature for all the points belonging to the same cluster. For example, consider a cluster with three data points (A, B, and C) each with two features as A = (10, 20), B = (11, 19), and C = (9, 21), then the value of centroid (Z) will be calculated as Z = ((10 + 11 + 9)/3, (20 + 19 + 21)/3), hence Z = (10, 20). The fitness value is calculated as shown in Eq. (2.14), where M is a clustering metric and can be calculated as shown in Eq. (2.15), and calculation M_i is shown in Eq. (2.16). The aim is to maximize the value of fitness function. Copies of chromosomes are generated proportional to its fitness function value. Then, the roulette-wheel method is implemented to select the chromosomes for mating. The single crossover technique is utilized for a crossover, whereas mutation is performed using random numbers. The above steps are repeated for a specified number of iterations and the best-performing chromosome is returned. The performance of the described algorithm is compared with the K-means cluster algorithm for multiple artificial and real-life datasets and it was concluded that GA-based clustering algorithm is superior to the K-means cluster algorithm [38].

$$f = 1/M \tag{2.14}$$

$$M = \sum_{i=1}^{k} M_i \tag{2.15}$$

$$M_i = \sum_{x_i \varepsilon C_i} \|x_i - z_i\| \tag{2.16}$$

Agustı et al. proposed Grouping Genetic Algorithm for clustering (GGA) which is an improvement of a similar algorithm proposed by Falkenaue [39,40]. The GGA algorithm developed by Agustı et al. does not require the number of clusters to be predefined or provided by the user, and it also allows parallel execution and using the island model the flow of the algorithm in any island is shown in Fig. 2.15. The encoding of every chromosome includes two parts, the first part shows the cluster allocated to each data point, while the second part depicts the clusters. For example, consider a data set with five data points and they are encoded as 1 1 1 2 2−1 2. The chromosome represents that the first three data points are assigned to the first cluster, while the latter points are assigned to the second cluster, and there are two clusters, cluster 1 and cluster 2. Next, determining the fitness function, the solutions are ranked such that the best solution secures the last rank and the worst solution secures the first rank. After the aforementioned, intervals in the range of 0−1 are decided for each solution such that the solution with maximum rank receives the biggest interval. Then roulette-wheel selection technique is employed to select the partners for mating. A crossover takes place with help of a unique method; the algorithm first selects two cluster numbers from each solution, later the

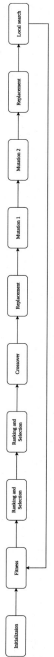

FIGURE 2.15 Process on one Island in GGA [41].

offspring receives the numbers same as a first parent and second parent if there is a conflict for a data point between two clusters, and then, it assigns the data point a cluster as per the first parent. The unassigned data points are assigned to clusters randomly; Fig. 2.16 shows an example of a crossover. Then two mutations are applied: the first one involves the splitting of clusters, while the subsequent involves merging of clusters. To gain better performance, local search is carried out. Mutation 1, mutation 2, and local search are all achieved using probabilistic methods. All these functions are carried out on one island that means there are several instances of this algorithm executing in parallel with some different initial population. Here, the solutions can also be transferred from one island to another. The performance of the algorithm was measured with the K-means cluster and DBSCAN algorithm across several real-life and artificial datasets, and it was concluded that the performance of the transformed GGA algorithm was better as compared to others [41].

Liu et al. developed a Genetic algorithm—based clustering known as automatic genetic clustering for unknown K (AGCUK). They remodeled the steps for the genetic algorithm and made it suitable for clustering where the number of clusters (K) need not be predefined or given by the user. The encoding of genes or chromosomes is given as a sequence of real numbers of length K*n where K is the number of clusters to be formed and n is the number of features or attributes for each tuple in the dataset. For example, let the chromosome be 10 12 20 19 where K = 2 and m = 2, then the centroids of the clusters are given as (10, 12) and (20, 19). The AGCUK is an iterative algorithm consisted of five steps as shown in Fig. 2.17. The algorithm begins with an initialization step in which a population of randomly created chromosomes is stored. The fitness of each solution is evaluated using the reciprocal Davies—Bouldin (DB) index [42]. Hence, if the clustering is better, the value of the DB index decreases, but the value of fitness function increases. The fitness computation is followed by the noise selection step, where the noise values are added to the variation fitness function values of each chromosome.

$$F_i^t - F_i^{t-1} + noise > 0 \qquad (2.17)$$

For selection of a chromosome of t generation represented as X_i^t, the condition shown in Eq. (2.17) should be satisfied, where F_i^t, F_i^t represents the fitness value of X_i chromosome in generations t and t−1, respectively, and noise is a random real number within a given range and the range of noise

FIGURE 2.16 Crossover in GGA [41].

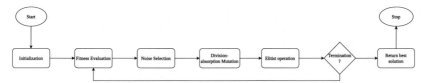

FIGURE 2.17   Flow of AGCUK algorithm [43].

decreases as the iterations increase. The next step includes mutation by division and absorption in which two operations are carried out namely division and absorption. The division operation includes splitting a large cluster in two, while the absorption includes merging of two clusters in one. The solution set is partitioned in two parts before performing these two operations, the first set contains the best solution, while the second set contains all the other solutions. Both the operations are performed on solutions in random order, while any one of the operation is performed on all the other solutions. The elitist step is carried out to keep the best-performing solution in the population. The step works by comparing the best solution in previous iteration with the best and worst solution in the current generation and keeping the best in both the comparisons. The above steps are repeated till the termination condition becomes true. The termination condition includes maximum number of iterations; once they are reached, the algorithm breaks the loop and returns the best known solution. The performance of algorithm was compared to algorithms proposed by other researchers and it seemed to outperform many of them with similar time complexity [43].

3.3 Use of particle swarm optimization in clustering

PSO is a swarm intelligence–based algorithm. Van der Merwe and Engelbrecht proposed two different ways to use PSO for clustering data vectors. The first suggestion is a basic algorithm named "g_{best}" approach, while the second method is a slightly modified version of the "g_{best}" approach known as a hybrid procedure. The "g_{best}" algorithm is evaluated in a series of steps. The steps are listed as initialization, fitness calculation, calculating global and local best, and updating position and velocity. The algorithm starts by initializing a set of particles. Each of the particles in an N-dimensional can be represented using K*N real numbers where the first N numbers determine the centroid of the first cluster and the subsequent N numbers determine the centroid of the second cluster and so on. Then, all the data vectors are clustered such that the distance between given data point and centroid of a cluster is minimum as compared to that of the centroid of any other cluster. Then, the fitness value of each particle is calculated using quantization error. In the later steps, the global and local best values are updated followed by updating the position of each particle. The hybrid algorithm is similar to the "g_{best}" algorithm discussed earlier. The only difference between the two algorithms is that in the hybrid algorithm, the clustering is first done by the K-means clustering algorithm and the centroids of the clusters developed are passed as a particle to the g_{best} algorithm. The performance of both the algorithms was compared with that of K-means cluster across different datasets. The performance is measured using quantization error, intercluster, and intracluster distance [44]. A similar approach was employed by Cui et al. while implementing document clustering. Here, first PSO algorithm is employed for a certain maximum amount of iterations, then the best solution is passed as the initial cluster centroids to the K-means clustering algorithm. The results show that this approach is useful in document clustering [45].

Fuzzy clustering is an important technique in which each data sample is associated with all the clusters using a membership function. An important fuzzy clustering algorithm is the Fuzzy c-means algorithm (FCM). It has multiple applications, but it likely ends in local optimal. Izakian et al. developed a fuzzy clustering algorithm by taking inspiration from the FCM algorithm and PSO. The PSO is used to navigate the clustering algorithm which would lead to a better quality solution. The FCM algorithm has a matrix μ of N*c where N corresponds to the number of data samples in the training dataset, while c is the number of clusters that need to be formed. The value of μ_{ij} gives the membership value of data sample i associated with cluster j. The matrix μ has some properties like every value in the matrix should be in the range of 0−1; the sum of all the values in any given row should be 1 and the sum of values in any given column should be in the range of 0−N. The flow of FCM algorithm is shown in Fig. 2.18. The initialization step includes initializing μ matrix, and cluster centers for c centers randomly. The cluster centroids are calculated by taking an average of each attribute for each data sample that belongs to the cluster. Then, the membership function matrix is updated and the algorithm checks for terminating condition; if it not met, then the above steps are repeated. There are multiple

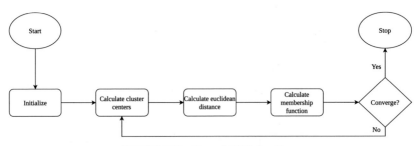

FIGURE 2.18   Flow of FCM algorithm.

terminating conditions; a simple condition might include detecting the change in the centroids; if the change is very small or there is no change, then terminate the processing [46].

$$F(x) = \frac{K}{J_m} \tag{2.18}$$

$$J_m = \sum_{j=1}^{c} \sum_{i=1}^{n} \mu_{ij}^m \times d_{ij} \tag{2.19}$$

$$d_{ij} = \left\| o_i - z_j \right\| \tag{2.20}$$

Izakian et al. modified the fuzzy-based PSO algorithm as given by Pang et al. for clustering and named it as FPSO for clustering. This algorithm maintains a matrix data structure X, similar to that used in FCM, but it represents the positions of a particle, and the velocities of particles are also stored in the same fashion. The properties of matrices μ and X are the same. However, during iterations, the position values of a particle might not add up to 1 or might be modified to not follow the properties. This is fixed by modifying the values as per formula but normalizing the entire matrix at the end of each iteration. Fig. 2.19 shows the flow of the FPSO algorithm. The initialization includes defining position and velocity matrices and other constants. Then, the fitness of each particle is calculated using Eq. (2.18), where K is a constant, while Jm is an objective function as shown in Eq. (2.19), where m is a scalar such that m is greater than 1, and d is a distance function. The distance function is shown in Eq. (2.20), where o_i is a data sample of index i, while z_j is centroid of cluster j; for calculating distance, Euclidean distance is considered. The next step includes calculating global and local best values followed by updating the position and velocity matrices. The termination condition might include no change in global best or repeating the above steps for a certain predefined number of iterations. Izakian et al. then combined both FCM and FPSO algorithms for better performance; they named this algorithm as a hybrid FCM–FPSO algorithm. This hybrid methodology includes running FPSO followed by FCM in a loop for a predefined number of iterations and

FIGURE 2.19 Flow of FPSO algorithm [46].

then returning the results of clustering. The performance of this hybrid algorithm was compared with the performance FCM and FPSO across six real-world datasets and the results show that the hybrid FCM—FPSO algorithm outperforms the others in all the six experiments [46,47].

As the quantity of data increases, the number of text documents increases, and their clustering becomes an import aspect. Document clustering is an important technique where a large number of text documents need to be clustered or grouped. Multiple features can be extracted from text documents while not all of them are useful and important for clustering and as a result feature selection becomes an important task in document clustering. Abualigah et al. used the PSO algorithm for feature selection in document clustering. The system was named as a feature selection method using PSO for text clustering (FSPSOTC) and Fig. 2.20 shows the architecture of the system. The entire FSPSOTC system is shown in three phases as preprocessing, feature selection, and clustering. In the preprocessing stage, documents are taken as input and preprocessing is performed which includes steps like tokenization, stop word removal, stemming, term weights, and vector space model (VSM). The input document is divided into sentences and then into terms or words; this process is carried out under tokenization. There are multiple words like "is," "an," " a," etc., which are high in number but do not contribute much in clustering; these words are known as stop words which are removed. In stemming, the inflectional affixes of the words are removed to extract the stem of the word. For example, the stem of the words fisher and fishing are related to the fish; while the words consultancy and consultant have the stem as consult. The algorithm used for stemming in this system is the Porter stemmer algorithm. The term weights are calculated based on the frequency of terms and inverse document frequency and these weights are stored in a format given by vector space model (VSM) [48].

The features of each document are represented as shown in Table 2.1. In the Feature selection phase, PSO is applied to each document in the dataset to extract features. The particles in PSO are represented as an array of numbers where the length of the array represents the subset, if the value at position i in the array is 0 which means the feature is not selected, if the value is 1 that means the feature is selected, while the value at position i in the array is -1 which signifies that the feature does not apply to the document under consideration. For example, $X = [0, 1, 1, 0, -1, 1, 0, 1]$ signifies that particle X has selected second, third, sixth, and eighth feature, while the fifth feature is inapplicable to the document. The PSO is programed to work document by document, meaning it would extract features from one document then move on to next. The fitness function selected for PSO is mean absolute difference which gives the relevance score to each feature by calculating the absolute difference between the value of the feature and the mean of the feature. The steps of the PSO algorithm include initialization, fitness calculation, updation of local and global best, and updation of position and velocity which are

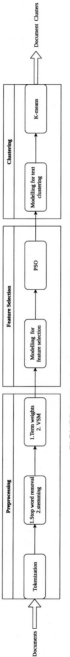

FIGURE 2.20   Architecture of FSPSOTC system [48].

TABLE 2.1 Sample features of documents.

Document no.	F1	F2	F3	F4	F5
DOC1	0.210	0.661	0	0.20	0
DOC2	0.340	0.31	0	0	0.12
DOC3	0.198	0	0.276	0.12	0.1
DOC4	0	0.123	0.3	0.139	0.121

iterated for a certain number of iteration. The feature subset selected by PSO is used for clustering using the K-means clustering algorithm. K-means algorithm has certain steps like initialization of cluster centroids, clustering the documents based on the distance measure, where the distance is calculated using cosine similarity. The cluster centroids are updated as per the feature values of members of the cluster, and the process is repeated till there is negligible difference in the cluster centroids or the members of the cluster remain the same for some iterations. The performance of this system was compared with K-means without feature selection, feature selection using genetic algorithm, and feature selection using harmony search algorithm across six different benchmark datasets, and it was found that FSPSOTC outperforms everyone [48–46].

4. Metaheuristics in frequent pattern mining

Frequent pattern mining is a data mining task that finds frequent patterns, itemsets, structures, association rules, and opinion features [51] from the given data. It is an unsupervised learning technique. Some examples of frequent pattern mining are frequent itemset mining and association rule mining. Consider a transaction dataset of a supermarket as shown in Fig. 2.21, in which each transaction shows the items purchased by a customer in his/her visit to the supermarket. The frequent itemset mining algorithm would return the list of most commonly purchased items in the dataset like milk, bread, and butter. The association rule mining algorithm would return patterns of which items in the item set are linked; for example, the association rule [milk] and [butter] → [bread] signifies that if a person buys milk and butter, then its highly probable that the person would buy bread as well. This section explains the use of metaheuristic algorithms for frequent itemset and association rule mining.

4.1 Use of ant colony optimization in frequent pattern mining

The example discussed above can be rewritten as buys(milk) and buys(butter)→buys(bread). However, here only the pattern of buying the products has been taken into account; hence, it is a one-dimensional data and the

Transaction 1: [Milk, Butter, Coffee, Bread, Detergent]

Transaction 2: [Milk, Butter, Bread, Tea,]

Transaction 3: [Milk, Butter, Detergent, Bread, Tea]

Transaction 4: [Milk, Butter, Coffee, Bread, Tea]

Transaction 5: [Milk, Butter, Coffee, Bread, Tea]

⋮

Transaction n: [Items]

FIGURE 2.21   Dataset of transactions.

dimension is "buys." Consider another example age (X; 30–60) and salary(X; 50,000–60,000) → buys(X, Car) which says that if the age of a person is in range of 30–60 years and the salary of the same individual is between 50,000 and 60,000 then the person is probable to purchase a car; this example contains multiple dimensions namely "age," "salary," and "buys." Although mining multidimensional data might uncover multiple patterns, however, many of them are not as good; hence, applying constraints to such data under guidance reveals better rules. Kuo and Shih modified the Ant Colony System algorithm to mine the frequent items from the constrained multidimensional dataset as it is considered that mining frequent pattern is computationally more expensive. The frequent patterns are later used to generate association rules [52].

The system designed by Kuo and Shih consists of four stages as shown in Fig. 2.22. The first stage includes initializing counters, initial pheromone levels, and other constants. Then, the constraints are applied to the dataset in the next stage and the only the data items satisfying the constraints are passed to the next stage. The following step includes mining the frequent items using the Ant Colony System algorithm. Here, first, the pheromone trails are set as per the support of the items received from the previous stage. Each of the ants contains a memory where it selects and keeps track of the frequent items selected by it. The ant selects an item as per biased exploration or by exploitation and the decision is made as per a random number. After selecting an item, the attractiveness of each path is updated as per the selected item and the evaporation rate. The frequent items are returned after repeating the above

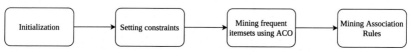

FIGURE 2.22   Mining frequent items using ACO [52].

process for a certain number of iterations and then the association rules are mined using the frequent items. The algorithm performance was compared with that of the apriori algorithm on a dataset of national health insurance research database in Taiwan. The results were compared with their efficiency and as well from reviews of multiple experts and it was found that the Ant colony approach performed better and the results were more reliable as well as computational time required for the algorithm was less as compared to apriori algorithm [52].

$$\sum_{k=1}^{nc} \sum_{i \in k} (O_i, O_{center}(T_k))^2 \qquad (2.21)$$

Kuo et al. found that if data objects are clustered and then if the association mining algorithm is applied to these data then it results in a better performance and better rule generation. The system proposed by Kuo et al. has been divided into two phases namely clustering and association rule mining as shown in Fig. 2.23. The first phase includes processing the data to convert it to a proper format for clustering followed by selecting an appropriate number of clusters using the ant system—based clustering algorithm (ASCA) algorithm and then clustering the data objects using the Ant K-means (AK) algorithm. The clustering is done in two parts: the ASCA to select the number of clusters followed by applying the AK algorithm to cluster the data. The ASCA executed in four distinct steps namely divide, agglomerate_obj, agglomerate, and remove. Initially, all the data objects are considered as the same cluster, the divide step divides the clusters into a smaller cluster and the agglomerate_obj step combines the objects that belong to the same cluster. The next is the agglomerate step in which the two clusters are merged based on their similarity, while the removing step removes the data objects which do not belong to a particular cluster. The stopping criteria include total within-cluster variance which is given in Eq. (2.21), where nc gives the number of clusters, while Oi identifies the data object "i" and Ocenter(Tk) gives the center of the selected cluster. The AK algorithm gets input as the number of clusters and their centroids from the above ASCA algorithm. The ant then goes on selecting points into the cluster as per the criteria and the pheromone is updated. This process continues for a predefined number of iterations and the clustered data are the output of this algorithm which can be then processed by

FIGURE 2.23 Mining followed by clustering [53].

the second phase of the system to mine frequent itemsets and get association rules from the same. The Ant-based association rule for the constrained dataset is used here. The algorithm mines frequent itemset from each cluster of the dataset. The first step is to initialize the constants and parameters followed by applying the constraints on the dataset. The next step includes the ant to add the data object into the frequent itemset using either exploitation technique or by biased exploration technique, the selection of which is done using a random number. The selection of an item by exploitation is by its attractiveness which is equivalent to the support of that data object. Once the ant completes the selection of the item, pheromone levels are updated as per the support of the selected objects. This process repeats for a certain number of iterations and then the association rules are generated. This two-staged system was tested on a national health insurance database of Taiwan and the results were much promising [53].

Mining frequent item subsets is a computationally expensive task and this problem was addressed by Al-Dharhani et al. Their system operates in two phases: the first phase deals with the representation of data and mining the association rules, while the second phase deals with mining frequent itemsets applying ACO algorithm. In the first phase, the transaction data are the input to the system. Then using AVL tree and sorting algorithm, all the available items in the dataset are indexed and the items are replaced as per their index as given, and this is followed by rearranging the dataset in m*n matrix where m represents the number of samples or transactions, while n indicates the number of unique items in the dataset, and each element shows whether that item is part of the transaction or not. This entire conversion is shown in Fig. 2.24. The converted data are then passed on to binary apriori algorithm which outputs multiple frequent items. The 2-frequent items are then used from the output of the apriori algorithm and the itemset is given as input to the ACO algorithm in phase 2. The apriori algorithm is used to give association rules, while the ant colony algorithm gives the output as an n-frequent itemset. Phase 2 is given 2-frequent itemset output from phase 1 and a complete connected graph is

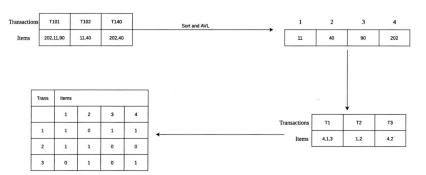

FIGURE 2.24   Converting the data in phase 1 [54].

formed to help ACO to mine n-frequent items. The initial pheromone value is set as the min. support between every two items in the 2-frequent itemset. For each of the predefined iteration, the ant adds a node into its solution followed by updating global and local pheromone levels. The next edge is added either by exploitation or by exploration which is done using a random number. After the iterations are complete, the algorithm returns the n-frequent pattern itemsets. Two experiments were carried out for this research where the first experiment shows the performance by using the apriori algorithm by using the boolean matrix, while the second experiment shows the performance of graph construction and performance of the ACO algorithm and the results of both experiments were positive [54].

4.2 Use of genetic algorithms in frequent pattern mining

The genetic algorithm is an evolutionary algorithm and accuracy of performance keeps increasing in every iteration. Ghosh and Nath used a genetic algorithm to mine association rules from the dataset and for this they used the Pareto principle of multiobjective analysis. Vilfredo Patero indicated the importance of nondominated solutions over dominated solutions. Consider two solutions "a" and "b" which are evaluated over multiple performance measures and "a" is said to be dominated by "b" only if "b" is better than "a" in at least one performance measure and solution "b" is better than or equal to solution "a" in rest of the performance measures. Ghosh and Nath measured the performance of their algorithm using three metrics namely comprehensibility (understandability), interestingness, and confidence which are shown in Eqs. (2.22)–(2.24), respectively, where C and A denote the consequent and antecedent of the association rule, while SUP(A) denotes the support of antecedent term that can be calculated as shown in Eq. (2.25) and |D| denotes the number of samples in the dataset [55].

$$\text{Comprehensiblity} = \frac{\log(1 + |C|)}{\log(1 + |A \cup C|)} \quad (2.22)$$

$$\text{Intrestingness} = \left(\frac{\text{SUP}(A \cup C)}{\text{SUP}(A)}\right) \times \left(\frac{\text{SUP}(A \cup C)}{\text{SUP}(C)}\right) \times \left(1 - \frac{\text{SUP}(A \cup C)}{|D|}\right) \quad (2.23)$$

$$\text{Confidence} = \frac{\text{SUP}(A \cup C)}{\text{SUP}(A)} \quad (2.24)$$

$$\text{SUP}(A) = \frac{\text{number of transactions that contain A}}{|D|} \quad (2.25)$$

To develop a genetic algorithm to mine association rules, the encoding of data and representing it in the form of chromosome is an important step.

Here, the encoding is done by designating one rule for one chromosome. Multiple tags are used before attributes to represent whether the attribute belongs to the antecedent or consequent part of the association rule. For example, if 00, 11, and 01 are the tags used to specify if attributes A, B, C, D are a part of the antecedent, consequent or not a part of rule, then a rule AB→D can be represented as 11A 11B 01C 00D where the tag 11 means the attribute is a part of consequent, 00 means the attribute is a part of antecedent, while the tag 01 means that the algorithm is not a part of rule at all. Similarly, other parameters like the numeric value of an attribute and different relational operators can be encoded in the chromosome to make it completely binary digits—based chromosome. Once the chromosomes are ready, genetic operations can be performed over it. The steps to apply the modified genetic algorithm include initialize, decode, compute performance, compute rank and fitness, save the best copy, select the chromosome and do a crossover, replace and perform the above steps for some iterations, and then exit and return the saved copy. The first step initializes the association rules randomly, then the chromosomes are decoded and the confidence, interestingness, and comprehensibility are calculated as per the above equations. In the subsequent step, the rank of the solution is calculated based on the performance metrics which were calculated previously and the fitness value is calculated based on the rank. The next step includes saving the best copy to another storage area, where the copies are stored in a nondominated fashion. The next step includes selecting chromosomes for multipoint crossover using a roulette-wheel selection method. The entire system was tested across multiple datasets and it gave satisfactory results [55].

$$X = \begin{bmatrix} x_{1,1} & x_{1,2} & x_{1,3} & \cdot & \cdot & \cdot & x_{1,m} \\ x_{2,1} & x_{2,2} & x_{2,3} & \cdot & \cdot & \cdot & x_{2,m} \\ & & \cdot & & & & \\ & & \cdot & & & & \\ & & \cdot & & & & \\ x_{n,1} & x_{n,2} & x_{n,3} & \cdot & \cdot & \cdot & x_{n,m} \end{bmatrix} \tag{2.26}$$

Ghosh et al. worked on genetic algorithms to give output as a set of frequent itemsets. The encoding of the transaction-based data was done in a binary format. Consider a transaction dataset with m different items and n transactions, then the dataset can be represented by the m*n matrix as shown in Eq. (2.26). Here, $x_{i,j}$ that belongs to the matrix can take value as 0 or 1, where if $x_{i,j} = 0$ it indicates that item i is not included in transaction j, while if $x_{i,j} = 1$ it indicates that item i is included in transaction j. The applied genetic algorithm includes steps like initialization followed by the fitness function, selection, recombination, and replacement. Random transactions are generated during the initialization phase. The fitness function value is calculated for each of these initial transactions. Then crossover is performed followed by mutation; the crossover points were selected randomly while mutation would flip the binary digits. The next step includes the replacement of solutions or chromosomes with new offsprings if they are better. These steps from fitness evaluation are repeated until a particular generation number is obtained. The above experiment was tested on a sample dataset first keeping initial population size as 20, mutation probability as 0.05, and minimum support as 20%. The obtained results were the same as the results obtained from the apriori algorithm. This same system was then tested on several other datasets and the results were positive. The computational complexity of the discussed system is also less as compared to that of the apriori algorithm [56].

A major problem in mining association rules is dealing with numeric attributes. In most cases, the numeric attributes are discretized by dividing them into several ranges. The problem that arises here is selecting the interval for the ranges. For example salary [30,000−40,000] → owns[car] may not have same less confidence as compared to salary [32,000−380,000] → owns[car]. Hence, selecting the appropriate interval can be a tedious task. Salleb-Aouissi et al. proposed a method to solve this problem using a genetic algorithm and named it "Quantminer." In this system, the user can guide the mining process by providing the attributes present in the antecedent and consequent part of the rule, providing the values which the categorical attributes can take and this information is called as rule template. Any dataset contains multiple attributes; a numeric attribute (X) in these rule templates can be represented as $X \in [l_i, u_i]$, while a categorical attribute (X) can be represented as $X \in v$, where l_i and u_i are lower and upper bound of the range of the numeric value which the attribute can take, while v is the value which the categorical attribute can take. The Quantminer algorithm takes these rule templates as inputs and outputs the rules with the optimal range to maximize the fitness value. As discussed earlier, Quantminer is a genetic algorithm and it has four steps namely, initial population, crossover, mutation, and fitness function. The chromosomes can be represented as a list of attributes $X \in [l_i, u_i]$, where each attribute is a part of the rule in left to right order. The initial population starts with random chromosomes with the lower and upper bound as the entire domain of the numeric attribute and the next generations keep shrinking the range until the perfect range has been found. The offspring of a parent can be developed attribute wise where the attribute can be the same as that from any of the parent or the bounds of parents mix to form the upper and lower bounds of the offsprings. The mutations involve reducing or increasing the range of an attribute by 10%. The fitness of each chromosome was calculated using the gain measure [57]. These steps were repeated for approximately 100 generations and the system was tested across several real-life and synthetic datasets. The results of the system were positive and suggested that the rules had high confidence [58].

4.3 Use of particle swarm optimization in frequent pattern mining

PSO is a swarm or population-based algorithm in which particles simulate the behavior of the crowd. In most of the association rule mining algorithms, the values of minimum support and that of minimum confidence are provided by users. The support and confidence of a sample rule $A \rightarrow C$ can be calculated as shown in Eqs. (2.27) and (2.28). The rule can be considered as a part of the final result if the values of support and confidence of the rule are greater than the given values of minimum support and minimum confidence. Selecting the appropriate value of minimum support is a challenge as if the value of minimum support is very high, then only a few rules would be shortlisted, and if the value of minimum support is low, then a huge number of rules would be shortlisted and same applies for minimum confidence value. A solution to this problem of selecting an appropriate value of minimum support and confidence is proposed by Kuo et al. by employing the PSO algorithm [59].

$$SUP(A, C) = \frac{\text{number of transactions that contain A and C}}{\text{number of transactions in the dataset}} \quad (2.27)$$

$$Confidence = \frac{SUP(A, C)}{SUP(A)} \quad (2.28)$$

$$IR = [\log(m \times TransNum(n)) + \log(n \times TransNum(m))] \frac{TransNum(m, n)}{Totaltrans} \quad (2.29)$$

The system designed by Kuo et al. is divided into two stages namely preprocessing and PSO for rule mining. In the preprocessing stage, there are two subprocesses: the first subprocess transforms the data in binary format and the second subprocess calculates the Item range and IR value. Consider there are five unique items in a transaction-based dataset, then each transaction would contain 5-bit array (T) where $T_i = 1$ would indicate that the ith element is a part of array and $T_i = 0$ otherwise. For example, consider dataset with six different items and a transaction $T = [1,2,4]$ which signifies that the transaction includes items 1, 2, and 4. After transformation, the transaction is represented as $T = [1, 1, 0, 1, 0, 0]$ which indicates the same thing. The next subprocess includes calculating the IR range and IR value. The IR range with the best IR value is used by the PSO algorithm to generate the association rules. The IR value can be calculated as shown in Eq. (2.29), where $m < n$ and $m \neq n$, while TransNum(m) and TransNum(m,n) indicate the number of transactions which contain element m and the number of transactions which contain both m and n and Totaltrans signifies the total number of transactions.

$$Fitness(x) = Confidence(x) \times \log(support(x) \times length(x) + 1) \quad (2.30)$$

The m and n in Eq. (2.29) represent the partitions; m represents minimal front partition and n represents maximal back partition. The rules can be

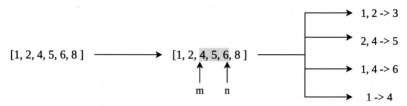

FIGURE 2.25 Generating rules from particle and IR range [59].

generated as shown in Fig. 2.25 by selecting any number of items before front partition in the antecedent part and the items between front and back partition in the consequent part. The next stage in the system includes applying the PSO algorithm to mine the value of minimum support and minimum confidence. The steps followed here include initialization, fitness value calculation, best particle search, and update. Each particle is represented in two parts namely X-itemset and Y-itemset; here, the rule is given as $X \rightarrow Y$ where the items in the antecedent part are given in X-itemset and the items in consequent part are given in Y-itemset, and the rules are generated IR range as discussed above. The fitness value of a particle x is calculated by using Eq. (2.30) and the objective is to maximize the fitness value. The next step includes calculating the local and global best values of particles and updating the position of particles based on global and local best values. The position of particles includes the X and Y itemset values. These steps are continued till a termination condition is reached. The termination condition includes either reaching maximum iterations or till positions of particles do not change. Then, the particle is found and its support and confidence are used for mining the association rules. The performance of the algorithm was evaluated for two datasets and a comparison was done with a genetic algorithm. The results show that the performance of the algorithm was better and the system can also be used to find some associations [59].

Mining high-utility itemset (HUI) is a recent concept and it is different from mining frequent itemsets. In a frequent itemset mining, we mine only those items which are frequent and support of the item set is above the threshold, i.e., minimum support. Though it's not the same case with mining HUIs as here, we are searching for a set of items that provide maximum profit or utility, and infrequent items can have high utility. Statistical methods to mine HUIs have high computational complexity. Lin et al. proposed HUIM-BPSO$_{sig}$ which is a binary PSO-based HUI mining system. The HUIM-BPSO$_{sig}$ system is divided into two stages namely the preprocessing stage and PSO stage as shown in Fig. 2.26. Each item in the dataset is represented as a tuple (i, T_q) where i represents the label of the item, and T_q represents the quantity of purchase, and there also exists a profit table which gives the profit for each unique item label in the dataset [60].

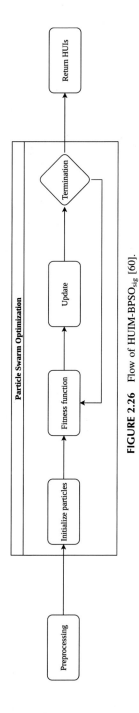

FIGURE 2.26 Flow of HUIM-BPSO$_{sig}$ [60].

In the preprocessing stage, the high-transaction—weighted utilization 1-itemsets (1-HTWUIs) are mined using the traditional algorithm. For achieving this, first, the transaction utility (tu) is calculated. Consider a sample dataset as shown in Fig. 2.27, the transaction utility of transaction T2 is given as $(2*5 + 3*1) = 13$. In the same way, transaction utility of all transactions is calculated and added to get total utility (TU). Then, a threshold or minimum utility value is calculated as a fraction of total utility. The next step includes calculating transaction-weighted utility (TWU) for each item. The transaction-weighted utility for each item can be calculated as the sum of transaction utility of all the transactions which contain the item; for example, the transaction weighted utility for item "c" is given as TWU(c) = tu(T1)+ tu(T3). If TWU of any item is greater or equal to minimum utility, then the item is added in 1-HTWUIs. This completes the preprocessing step and output of the step, i.e., 1-HTWUIs are supplied to the PSO algorithm. The items in the 1-HTWUIs are arranged in alphabetical order and a binary array of the same length is created for each particle. For example, consider items [s, r, q, p] are the part of 1-HTWUIs, they will be sorted in alphabetical order as [p, q, r, s]. A particle is represented by a binary array where if the value of the index i is 1, then the item at ith index of the sorted array is considered else the item is not considered. The sorted array in the above example was [p, q, r, s], a particle represented as $X = [1, 0, 0, 1]$ signifies that particle X identifies item p and s as high-utility items. Similarly, the other particles are initialized based on sorted items from 1-HTWUIs. The fitness of each particle is calculated using the sum of utility value (u(X)) of the particles in all the transactions. For example, in Fig. 2.27, u(c) = utility(c,T1)+utility(c,T3) which is equivalent to $u(C)=(5*3)+(5*2) = 25$. If the fitness value of the particle is greater than the minimum utility value, then the item is added in HUI. Then, the velocity of the particle is calculated and the position is updated as per the local and global best values of particle's fitness function. The position of the particle is updated as per the sigmoid function and hence the position update is also in a binary format. These steps are repeated until a termination condition is reached.

Dataset	
Transaction id	**Items**
T1	(a, 2), (c, 3), (d, 1)
T2	(a, 5), (b, 1)
T3	(c, 2), (d, 3)

Profit Table	
Items	
	Profit
a	2
b	3
c	5
d	1

FIGURE 2.27   Example of dataset required for High-Utility Itemset mining [60].

The complexity of the algorithm is O(N*M*m), where N gives the number of iterations, M indicates the number of particles in the swarm, and m gives the size of 1-HTWUIs. The results show that HUIM-BPSO$_{sig}$ outperforms the genetic algorithm—based on HUI mining algorithm [60].

Metaheuristic algorithms can be helpful in mining association rules as most of these algorithms directly mine association rules from the dataset and skip the usual two-step approach of mining the frequent itemsets first than mining the association rules. Sarath and Ravi proposed a similar association rule mining system based on BPSO. In the proposed system, the number of rules to be mined is decided first and then the BPSO is employed to mine one rule per iteration as shown in Fig. 2.28. The transactional data which are an input to the system need to be preprocessed to convert them into a defined form. Here, each transaction is converted to a binary form such as each transaction contains a list of an array of length equal to the number of all unique items in the dataset. If an element in the array is one, then the item is part of the transaction, and if the element in the array is 0, then the element is not a part of the array. For example, if there are five unique items in the transaction database, and a transaction T is represented as $T = [I_1, I_3]$, then as per above description, the binary form of transaction $T = [0, 1, 0, 1, 0]$ where 1s at index 1 and 3 represent that the items I_1 and I_3 are selected. The BPSO algorithm mines one rule per run; hence, "m" runs are required to mine m rules. Each particle in the proposed BPSO algorithm consists of one rule and each rule consist of two parts. The first part indicates whether an element is part of the rule or not if ith element is 1, then the item is part of the rule, while the second part of rule shows that if the element is part of the rule, then it belongs to antecedent or consequent part of rule by value 1 and 0, respectively. Therefore, if a particle that has $I_i = 11$ signifies that item i is part of the rule and it is an antecedent, while $I_i = 01$ indicates that the item i does not belong to the rule. The fitness function is calculated as the product of support and confidence of the rule. If only support was used, then the rare item problem arises, while if confidence was used as a sole measure, then there would have been more items on the consequent side which would have led to less efficient rules. After calculating the fitness function, the local and global best values of each particle are updated. The velocities of the particle are updates as per the previous values, while the positions of particles are updated using the velocity and sigmoid function as each particle has positions that are in binary. The above described BPSO process is repeated for T times, and the best rule is returned, and in a similar manner m, different rules are mined. The complexity of the algorithm is comparable to that of the apriori algorithm. The performance of BPSO-based association rule mining algorithm is compared with that of FP growth and apriori algorithm and it was found that better rules are mined by the BPSO-based association rule mining algorithm [61].

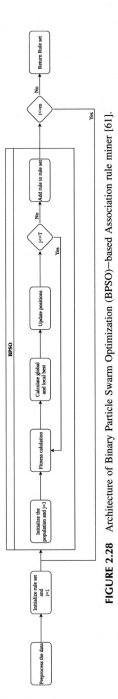

FIGURE 2.28 Architecture of Binary Particle Swarm Optimization (BPSO)—based Association rule miner [61].

5. Conclusion

Classification, clustering, and frequent pattern mining are the most common tasks in data mining. Almost all of these tasks can be completed using machine learning algorithms, but sometimes even these algorithms will not perform better. Deep learning is currently used in solving these data mining problems which very high accuracy. However, a recent report from the Massachusetts Institute of Technology states that computational limits of deep learning have reached. The report also stated that improvements can be achieved by using some optimization framework [62]. Metaheuristic algorithms provide a framework for solving optimization problems and it is shown in this chapter sometimes metaheuristic algorithms outperform these machine learning algorithms and with less complexity. This chapter discusses different methods by which some common metaheuristic algorithms like ACO, Genetic Algorithms, and PSO can be used to perform the different data mining tasks effectively.

References

[1] S. Mishra, P.K. Mallick, L. Jena, G.-S. Chae, Optimization of skewed data using sampling-based preprocessing approach, Front. Public Health 8 (2020).

[2] H.K. Thakkar, C.K. Dehury, P.K. Sahoo, Muvine: multi-stage virtual network embedding in cloud data centers using reinforcement learning-based predictions, IEEE J. Sel. Area. Commun. 38 (6) (2020) 1058–1074.

[3] H.K. Thakkar, P.K. Sahoo, B. Veeravalli, RENDA: Resource and network aware data placement algorithm for periodic workloads in cloud, IEEE Trans. Parallel Distrib. Syst. 32 (12) (2021) 2906–2920.

[4] C. Blum, A. Roli, Metaheuristics in combinatorial optimization: overview and conceptual comparison, ACM Comput. Surv. 35 (01 2001) 268–308.

[5] A. Hegazy, M. Makhlouf, G. Eltaweel, Dimensionality reduction using an improved whale optimization algorithm for data classification, Int. J. Mod. Educ. Comput. Sci. 10 (7) (2018) 37–49.

[6] B. Alatas, U. Can, Physics based metaheuristic optimization algorithms for global optimization, Am. J. Inform. Sci. Comput. Eng. 1 (2015).

[7] E. Rashedi, H. Nezamabadi-Pour, S. Saryazdi, GSA: a gravitational search algorithm, Inf. Sci. 179 (13) (2009) 2232–2248.

[8] H. Eskandar, A. Sadollah, A. Bahreininejad, M. Hamdi, "Water cycle algorithm—a novel metaheuristic optimization method for solving constrained engineering optimization problems, Comput. Struct. 110 (2012) 151–166.

[9] A. Sadollah, H. Eskandar, A. Bahreininejad, J.H. Kim, Water cycle algorithm with evaporation rate for solving constrained and unconstrained optimization problems, Appl. Soft Comput. 30 (2015) 58–71.

[10] M. Birattari, L. Paquete, T. Stützle, K. Varrentrapp, Classification of Metaheuristics and Design of Experiments for the Analysis of Components, Teknik Rapor, AIDA-01-05, 2001.

[11] R. Hassan, B. Cohanim, O. de Weck, 04, A Comparison of Particle Swarm Optimization and the Genetic Algorithm, vol. 2, 2005.

[12] H. Kumar Thakkar, H. Shukla, S. Patil, A comparative analysis of machine learning classifiers for robust heart disease prediction, in: 2020 IEEE 17th India Council International Conference (INDICON), 2020, pp. 1−6.

[13] S. Mishra, H.K. Tripathy, P.K. Mallick, A.K. Bhoi, P. Barsocchi, EAGA-MLP an enhanced and adaptive hybrid classification model for diabetes diagnosis, Sensors 20 (14) (2020) 4036.

[14] H.K. Thakkar, P.K. Sahoo, Towards automatic and fast annotation of seismocardiogram signals using machine learning, IEEE Sens. J. 20 (5) (2019) 2578−2589.

[15] S. Mishra, H.K. Tripathy, B.K. Mishra, Implementation of biologically motivated optimisation approach for tumour categorisation, Int. J. Comput. Aided Eng. Technol. 10 (3) (2018) 244−256.

[16] D. Rai, H.K. Thakkar, D. Singh, H.V. Bathala, Machine learning assisted automatic annotation of isovolumic movement and aortic valve closure using seismocardiogram signals, in: 2020 IEEE 17th India Council International Conference (INDICON), 2020, pp. 1−6.

[17] H.K. Thakkar, W.W. Liao, C.Y. Wu, Y.W. Hsieh, T.H. Lee, Predicting clinically significant motor function improvement after contemporary task-oriented interventions using machine learning approaches, J. NeuroEng. Rehabil. 17 (1) (2020) 1−10.

[18] H. Shukla, S. Patil, D. Solanki, L. Singh, M. Swarnkar, H.K. Thakkar, On the design of supervised binary classifiers for malware detection using portable executable files, in: 2019 IEEE 9th International Conference on Advanced Computing (IACC), IEEE, 2019, pp. 141−146.

[19] S. Mishra, H. Thakkar, P.K. Mallick, P. Tiwari, A. Alamri. A Sustainable IoHT Based Computationally Intelligent Healthcare Monitoring System for Lung Cancer Risk Detection, Sustainable Cities and Society, Elsevier, 2021, p. 103079.

[20] D. Rai, H.K. Thakkar, S.S. Rajput, Performance characterization of binary classifiers for automatic annotation of aortic valve opening in seismocardiogram signals. In 2020 9th International Conference on Bioinformatics and Biomedical Science, 2020, pp. 77−82.

[21] N. Sreeja, A. Sankar, Pattern matching based classification using ant colony optimization based feature selection, Appl. Soft Comput. 31 (2015) 91−102.

[22] A. Gupta, V.K. Jayaraman, B.D. Kulkarni, Feature selection for cancer classification using ant colony optimization and support vector machines, in: Analysis of Biological Data: A Soft Computing Approach, World Scientific, 2007, pp. 259−280.

[23] M.F. Ganji, M.S. Abadeh, A fuzzy classification system based on ant colony optimization for diabetes disease diagnosis, Expert Syst. Appl. 38 (12) (2011) 14650−14659.

[24] G. Bakırlı, D. Birant, A. Kut, An incremental genetic algorithm for classification and sensitivity analysis of its parameters, Expert Syst. Appl. 38 (3) (2011) 2609−2620.

[25] H. Motieghader, A. Najafi, B. Sadeghi, A. Masoudi-Nejad, A hybrid gene selection algorithm for microarray cancer classification using genetic algorithm and learning automata, Inf. Med. Unlocked 9 (2017) 246−254.

[26] N. Suguna, K. Thanushkodi, An improved k-nearest neighbor classification using genetic algorithm, Int. J. Comput. Sci. Issues 7 (2) (2010) 18−21.

[27] J. Pan, W.J. Tompkins, A real-time QRS detection algorithm, IEEE Trans. Biomed. Eng. (3) (1985) 230−236.

[28] M. Korürek, B. Doğan, ECG beat classification using particle swarm optimization and radial basis function neural network, Expert Syst. Appl. 37 (12) (2010) 7563−7569.

[29] Z. Qin, J. Chen, Y. Liu, J. Lu, Evolving RBF neural networks for pattern classification, in: International Conference on Computational and Information Science, Springer, 2005, pp. 957−964.

[30] G.V. Trunk, A problem of dimensionality: a simple example, IEEE Trans. Pattern Anal. Mach. Intell. (3) (1979) 306–307.

[31] J. Kennedy, R.C. Eberhart, A discrete binary version of the particle swarm algorithm, in: 1997 IEEE International Conference on Systems, Man, and Cybernetics. Computational Cybernetics and Simulation, vol. 5, IEEE, 1997, pp. 4104–4108.

[32] L. Brezočnik, Feature selection for classification using particle swarm optimization, in: IEEE EUROCON 2017-17th International Conference on Smart Technologies, IEEE, 2017, pp. 966–971.

[33] I. De Falco, A. Della Cioppa, E. Tarantino, Facing classification problems with particle swarm optimization, Appl. Soft Comput. 7 (3) (2007) 652–658.

[34] P. Shelokar, V.K. Jayaraman, B.D. Kulkarni, An ant colony approach for clustering, Anal. Chim. Acta 509 (2) (2004) 187–195.

[35] H.D. Menéndez, F.E. Otero, D. Camacho, Medoid-based clustering using ant colony optimization, Swarm Intell. 10 (2) (2016) 123–145.

[36] L. Kaufman, P.J. Rousseeuw, Finding Groups in Data: An Introduction to Cluster Analysis, vol. 344, John Wiley & Sons, 2009.

[37] S. Xu, Z. Bing, Y. Lina, L. Shanshan, G. Lianru, Hyperspectal image clustering using ant colony optimization (ACO) improved by k-means algorithm, in: 2010 3rd International Conference on Advanced Computer Theory and Engineering (ICACTE), vol. 2, IEEE, 2010, pp. V2–V474.

[38] U. Maulik, S. Bandyopadhyay, Genetic algorithm-based clustering technique, Pattern Recognit. 33 (9) (2000) 1455–1465.

[39] E. Falkenauer, The grouping genetic algorithms: widening the scope of the GA's, Belg. J. Operat. Res. Stat. Comput. Sci. 33 (1–2) (1993) 79–102.

[40] E. Falkenauer, Genetic Algorithms and Grouping Problems, John Wiley & Sons, Inc., 1998.

[41] L. Agustı, S. Salcedo-Sanz, S. Jiménez-Fernández, L. Carro-Calvo, J. Del Ser, J.A. Portilla-Figueras, et al., A new grouping genetic algorithm for clustering problems, Expert Syst. Appl. 39 (10) (2012) 9695–9703.

[42] D.L. Davies, D.W. Bouldin, A cluster separation measure, IEEE Trans. Pattern Anal. Mach. Intell. (2) (1979) 224–227.

[43] Y. Liu, X. Wu, Y. Shen, Automatic clustering using genetic algorithms, Appl. Math. Comput. 218 (4) (2011) 1267–1279.

[44] D. Van der Merwe, A.P. Engelbrecht, Data clustering using particle swarm optimization, in: The 2003 Congress on Evolutionary Computation, 2003. CEC'03, vol. 1, IEEE, 2003, pp. 215–220.

[45] X. Cui, T.E. Potok, P. Palathingal, Document clustering using particle swarm optimization, in: Proceedings 2005 IEEE Swarm Intelligence Symposium, 2005. SIS 2005, IEEE, 2005, pp. 185–191.

[46] H. Izakian, A. Abraham, V. Snášel, Fuzzy clustering using hybrid fuzzy c-means and fuzzy particle swarm optimization, in: 2009 World Congress on Nature & Biologically Inspired Computing (NaBIC), IEEE, 2009, pp. 1690–1694.

[47] W. Pang, K.-p. Wang, C.-g. Zhou, L.-j. Dong, Fuzzy discrete particle swarm optimization for solving traveling salesman problem, in: The Fourth International Conference on Computer and Information Technology, 2004. CIT'04, IEEE, 2004, pp. 796–800.

[48] L.M. Abualigah, A.T. Khader, E.S. Hanandeh, A new feature selection method to improve the document clustering using particle swarm optimization algorithm, J. Comput. Sci. 25 (2018) 456–466.

[49]   L.M. Abualigah, A.T. Khader, M.A. Al-Betar, Unsupervised feature selection technique based on harmony search, in: 2016 7th International Conference on Computer Science and Information Technology (CSIT), IEEE, 2016.

[50]   L.M. Abualigah, A.T. Khader, M.A. Al-Betar, Unsupervised feature selection technique based on genetic algorithm for improving the text clustering, in: 2016 7th International Conference on Computer Science and Information Technology (CSIT), IEEE, 2016, pp. 1–6.

[51]   H.K. Thakkar, P.K. Sahoo, P. Mohanty, DOFM: domain feature miner for robust extractive summarization, Inf. Process. Manage. 58 (3) (2021) 102474.

[52]   R. Kuo, C. Shih, Association rule mining through the ant colony system for national health insurance research database in taiwan, Comput. Math. Appl. 54 (11–12) (2007) 1303–1318.

[53]   R. Kuo, S. Lin, C. Shih, Mining association rules through integration of clustering analysis and ant colony system for health insurance database in taiwan, Expert Syst. Appl. 33 (3) (2007) 794–808.

[54]   G.S. Al-Dharhani, Z.A. Othman, A.A. Bakar, A graph-based ant colony optimization for association rule mining, Arabian J. Sci. Eng. 39 (6) (2014) 4651–4665.

[55]   A. Ghosh, B. Nath, Multi-objective rule mining using genetic algorithms, Inf. Sci. 163 (1–3) (2004) 123–133.

[56]   S. Ghosh, S. Biswas, D. Sarkar, P.P. Sarkar, Mining Frequent Itemsets Using Genetic Algorithm, arXiv preprint arXiv:1011.0328, 2010.

[57]   T. Fukuda, Y. Morimoto, S. Morishita, T. Tokuyama, Data mining using two-dimensional optimized association rules: scheme, algorithms, and visualization, ACM SIGMOD Rec. 25 (2) (1996) 13–23.

[58]   A. Salleb-Aouissi, C. Vrain, C. Nortet, Quantminer: a genetic algorithm for mining quantitative association rules, in: IJCAI, vol. 7, 2007, pp. 1035–1040.

[59]   R.J. Kuo, C.M. Chao, Y. Chiu, Application of particle swarm optimization to association rule mining, Appl. Soft Comput. 11 (1) (2011) 326–336.

[60]   J.C.-W. Lin, L. Yang, P. Fournier-Viger, J.M.-T. Wu, T.-P. Hong, L.S.-L. Wang, J. Zhan, Mining high-utility itemsets based on particle swarm optimization, Eng. Appl. Artif. Intell. 55 (2016) 320–330.

[61]   K. Sarath, V. Ravi, Association rule mining using binary particle swarm optimization, Eng. Appl. Artif. Intell. 26 (8) (2013) 1832–1840.

[62]   N.C. Thompson, K. Greenewald, K. Lee, G.F. Manso, The Computational Limits of Deep Learning, arXiv preprint arXiv:2007.05558, 2020.

Chapter 3

Impacts of metaheuristic and swarm intelligence approach in optimization

Abhishek Banerjee[1], Dharmpal Singh[2], Sudipta Sahana[2], Ira Nath[2]
[1]*Pailan College of Management and Technology, Pailan, Joka, Kolkata, West Bengal, India;* [2]*JIS College of Engineering, Kalyani, West Bengal, India*

1. Introduction

1.1 Introduction of metaheuristic

Glover [57] coined the term Metaheuristic, which is formed by combining the Greek prefix "meta" which means beyond in the sense of high-level and "heuristic" from the Greek heuriskein or euriskein which means to search. A metaheuristic is an elevated level issue free algorithmic structure that gives a lot of rules or methodologies to create heuristic enhancement calculations. Variable neighborhood search, tabu search (TS), ant colony optimization (ACO), genetic/evolutionary algorithms (adaptive), large neighborhood search, and simulated annealing (SA) are some of the notable examples of metaheuristics. An issue has occurred due to explicit usage of heuristic improvement calculation as indicated by the rules which is communicated in a metaheuristic system is additionally alluded to as a metaheuristic.

Metaheuristic calculations, i.e., streamlining techniques structured by the systems spread out in a metaheuristic system, are—as the name recommends—consistently heuristic in nature. This reality recognizes them from definite techniques that do accompany a proof that the ideal arrangement will be found in a limited (albeit regularly restrictively enormous) measure of time. Metaheuristics are accordingly grown explicitly to discover an answer that is good enough in a registering time that is small enough. This helps it to be not a subject of combinatorial explosion, i.e., the condition where the optimal solution of NP-hard problems takes huge computing time.

Metaheuristics have been exhibited by established researchers to be a reasonable, and frequently unrivaled, option in contrast to more conventional

Cognitive Big Data Intelligence with a Metaheuristic Approach
https://doi.org/10.1016/B978-0-323-85117-6.00008-X

(accurate) strategies for mixed-integer optimization, for example, branch and bound and dynamic programming. Particularly for convoluted issues or enormous issue cases, metaheuristics are regularly ready to offer a superior compromise between arrangement quality and figuring time. Additionally, metaheuristics are more adaptable than accurate strategies in two significant manners. To start with, on the grounds that metaheuristic systems are characterized when all is said in done terms, metaheuristic calculations can be adjusted to fit the necessities of most genuine streamlining issues as far as anticipated arrangement quality and permitted processing time, which can shift extraordinarily across various issues and various circumstances.

Also, metaheuristics do not put any requests on the definition of the improvement issue (like requiring requirements or target capacities to be communicated as straight elements of the choice factors). In any case, this adaptability comes at the expense of requiring extensive issue explicit variation to accomplish great execution.

The exploration fields of metaheuristics are not complete without its fault finders, the greater part of the apparent absence of generally material structure strategy, the absence of logical meticulousness in testing and looking at changed executions, and the inclination to make excessively mind boggling techniques with various administrators. A few creators have likewise condemned the way by which metaphors are utilized by certain creators to persuade the improvement of "novel" techniques. Despite this analysis, it is difficult to contend with progress. The capacity to get great arrangements where different techniques fall flat has settled on metaheuristics, the strategy for decision for illuminating a dominant part of huge genuine advancement issues, both in scholarly examination and in common sense applications. Therefore, a few business programming sellers have actualized metaheuristics as their essential enhancement engines, both in general-purpose optimization and simulation packages as well as in specialized software packages for production scheduling, vehicle routing, and nurse rostering.

Despite of the fact that some completely deterministic strategies have been proposed, the metaheuristics frameworks, in general, rely heavily on the use of randomness. The basic foundation of different metaheuristics varies significantly. Some methods do not use such an intermediary level of explanation, but rather focus on exploiting the problem structure to improve the search for good solutions, like TS. On the other hand, some develop the optimization process by using a metaphor seemingly unrelated to optimization, such as the cooling of a crystalline solid (SA), natural evolution (genetic/evolutionary algorithms), or the behavior of animal swarms (e.g., ACO).

Since the early 80's, the metaheuristic frameworks have come up with a steady rise in both popularity and use. Although some root cases have been traced from back 60's and 70's. A great number of journals and conferences have made the metaheuristics field to focus on. EU/ME—the metaheuristics community—is one of such great examples.

1.2 Introduction of swarm intelligence

Swarm intelligence (SI) is simply the aggregate conduct of decentralized, sorted out frameworks, regular or fake. The idea is utilized in chipping away at man-made consciousness. The articulation was presented by Gerado Beni and Jing Wang in 1989, with regards to cell mechanical frameworks.

SI frameworks comprise commonly of a population of straightforward specialists or boids interfacing locally with each other and with their condition. The motivation frequently originates from nature, particularly organic frameworks. The specialists observe exceptionally straightforward standards, and in spite of the fact that there is no unified control structure directing how singular operators ought to carry on, nearby, and in a specific way arbitrary, associations between such operators lead to the rise of "intelligent" worldwide conduct, obscure to the individual operators. Instances of multitude insight in normal frameworks incorporate insect settlements, winged creature rushing, birds of prey chasing, creature crowding, bacterial development, fish tutoring, and microbial intelligence.

The utilization of swarm principles to robots is called swarm robotics, while "swarm intelligence" refers to the more broad arrangement of calculations. "Swarm prediction" has been utilized with regards to anticipating issues. Comparative ways to deal with those proposed for swarm mechanical technology are considered for hereditarily adjusted living beings in engineered aggregate insight.

2. Concepts of Metaheuristic

2.1 Optimization problems

Metaheuristic optimization manages optimization issues utilizing metaheuristic calculations. Optimization is basically all over, manufacturing design to finances and from occasion celebrating to Internet of Things. As cash, assets, and time are restricted, the ideal utility of these accessible assets is expressively significant.

Most genuine optimizations are exceptionally nonlinear and multimodal, under different complex boundaries. It is very much conflicting when dealing with different objectives. In any event, for a solitary goal, once in a while, ideal arrangements may not exist by any stretch of the imagination. All in all, finding an ideal arrangement or even problematic arrangements is not a simple undertaking. This chapter intends to present the basics of metaheuristic optimization, just as some mainstream metaheuristic calculations.

From a diverse perception, optimization algorithms can be categorized into trajectory based and population based. A single agent or one solution at a time is classically used in a trajectory-based algorithm which will trace out a path as the iterations continue. For example, Hill-climbing is trajectory based that connects the opening point with the closing point via a piecewise zigzag path.

Another significant illustration is SA that is extensively used in metaheuristic algorithm. Alternatively, use multiple agents which will interact and trace out multiple paths, i.e., population-based algorithms such as particle swarm optimization (PSO) [55].

Furthermore, optimization algorithms can be categorized as deterministic or stochastic. It is called deterministic when an algorithm performs in a mechanical deterministic manner without any random nature. For such an algorithm, it will reach the same final solution if we start with the same initial point. Some good examples of deterministic algorithms are hill-climbing and downhill simplex. Conversely, if there is some randomness in the algorithm, the algorithm will usually reach a different point every time the algorithm is executed, even though the same initial point is used. Genetic algorithms (GAs) and PSO are good examples of stochastic algorithms.

Search capability can also be a basis for algorithm classification. In this case, algorithms can be divided into local and global search algorithms. Local search algorithms typically converge toward a local optimum, not necessarily (often not) the global optimum, and such an algorithm is often deterministic and has no ability to escape from local optima. We can take Simple hill-climbing as such an example. As an alternative, for global optimization, local search algorithms are not suitable, and global search algorithms should be used. Modern metaheuristic algorithms in most cases tend to be suitable for global optimization, though not always successful or efficient. A simple strategy such as hill-climbing with random restarts can turn a local search algorithm into an algorithm with global search capability. In essence, randomization is an efficient component for global search algorithms.

2.2 Classification of metaheuristic techniques

Metaheuristics can be classified based on the following properties:

2.2.1 Local search versus global search

One methodology is to portray the sort of search system. One kind of search procedure is an enhancement for straightforward neighborhood search calculations. A notable nearby hunt calculation is the slope climbing strategy which is utilized to discover neighborhood desired states. Notwithstanding, hill-climbing does not ensure finding global optimum solutions.

Numerous metaheuristic thoughts were proposed to improve nearby inquiry heuristic so as to discover better arrangements. Such metaheuristics incorporate iterated local search, simulated annealing, tabu search, variable neighborhood search, and GRASP. These metaheuristics can both be named nearby hunt based or worldwide pursuit metaheuristics.

Other worldwide hunt metaheuristics that are not neighborhood search based are generally population-based metaheuristics. Such metaheuristics incorporate ACO, evolutionary computation, particle swarm optimization, and genetic algorithms.

2.2.2 Single-solution versus population based

Another grouping measurement is single arrangement versus population-based searches. Single arrangement approaches center around changing and improving a solitary competitor arrangement; single arrangement metaheuristics incorporate reenacted strengthening, iterated nearby inquiry, variable neighborhood search, and guided nearby pursuit. Populace-based methodologies keep up and improve numerous up-and-coming arrangements, frequently utilizing populace attributes to manage the pursuit; population-based metaheuristics incorporate developmental calculation, hereditary calculations, and molecule swarm advancement. Another class of metaheuristics is SI which is an aggregate conduct of decentralized, self-composed specialists in a populace or swarm. Ant colony optimization, PSO, and social cognitive optimization are instances of this class.

2.2.2.1 Hybridization and memetic algorithms

A hybrid metaheuristic approachconsolidates a metaheuristic with other optimization methods, for example, calculations from mathematical programming, constraint programming, and machine learning. The two parts of a hybrid metaheuristic may run simultaneously and trade data to direct the pursuit.

Then again, Memetic algorithms speak to the collaboration of evolutionary or any populace-based methodology with discrete individual learning or local improvement techniques for issue search. A case of memetic algorithm is the utilization of a local search algorithm rather than a basic mutation operator in evolutionary algorithms.

2.2.3 Parallel metaheuristics

A parallel metaheuristic is one which utilizes the strategies of parallel programming to run multiple metaheuristic searches in parallel; these may extend from straightforward disseminated plans to simultaneous pursuit runs that communicate to improve the general arrangement.

2.2.4 Nature-inspired and metaphor-based metaheuristics

A functioning region of exploration is the plan of nature-inspired metaheuristics. Numerous ongoing metaheuristics, particularly evolutionary calculation-based algorithms, are inspired by natural systems. Nature goes about as a wellspring of ideas, instruments, and standards for planning of fake figuring systems to manage complex computational issues. Such metaheuristics incorporate SA, evolutionary algorithms, ACO, and PSO. An enormous number of later representation inspired metaheuristics have begun to draw in analysis in the examination network for concealing their absence of oddity behind a detailed allegory.

2.3 A generic metaheuristic framework

Recent times have seen significant advances to approximate the solution of complex optimization problems in both the theory and application of metaheuristics. In order to state and solve combinatorial problems in Ref. [56]; to describe TS in Refs. [57] and [58]; and to classify recent approaches such as evolutionary methods, adaptive memory programming, greedy randomized adaptive search procedures, ants systems, genetics algorithm, guided local search, neural networks, problem-space search, SA, scatter search, TS, threshold algorithms, and their hybrids in Refs. [59–62] and as a title for the biennial series of the metaheuristics international conferences (MIC-95, MIC-97, MIC-99, and MIC-01), the metaheuristic term was used as a language and a program.

A metaheuristic was characterized in Refs. [62,63] as an iterative ace cycle that guides and changes the tasks of subordinate heuristics to productively create excellent arrangements. It might join cleverly various ideas for investigating the search space and use learning systems to structure data. It might control a total (or deficient) single arrangement or an assortment of arrangements at each iteration. The subordinate heuristics might be high (or low) level methods, or a simple local search, or only a development strategy.

Metaheuristics furnish chiefs with hearty apparatuses that get top-notch arrangements, in a sensible computational effort, to significant applications in business, building, financial aspects, and the sciences. Finding accurate answers for these applications despite everything represents a genuine test notwithstanding the effect of ongoing advances in computer technology and the incredible association between computer science, management science/ operations research, and mathematics. For additional subtleties on hypothesis and applications, we allude to the comprehensive bibliography on metaheuristics in Ref. [60] and the books in Refs. [61–63].

A metaheuristic may have four segments: initial space of solutions; management of information structures; search engines; and learning and guideline strategies. In the accompanying setting, the most effective metaheuristics and their related segments are quickly portrayed. The bound together metaheuristic framework introduced [59] is stretched out into a broader one to show how the current metaheuristics can fit into it. The overall framework welcomes additional research into designing new imaginative and unexplored metaheuristics. At last, we finish up by featuring ebb and flow patterns and future research headings in this dynamic territory of the study of heuristics.

3. Metaheuristic techniques

The metaheuristic techniques are useful for searching the near-optimal solutions which are very close to the optimal one of a real-world problem. These searching techniques guide the search processes to solve real-world problems which vary from easy to complex one. Some real-world problems cannot be solved in linear time. Their complexities are nonlinear in nature. The well-known mathematical heuristics are not able to solve and produce optimal results for these types of problems in a finite amount of time. To find out a near-optimal solution of these types of problems, the metaheuristics are most suitable. These metaheuristics can solve these problems in a finite amount of time using a finite number of steps.

The metaheuristics are not applicable for finding optimal solutions of a real-world problem, but they are capable for finding near-optimal or approximate solutions of a problem using a simple and comparatively easy number of steps. Due to the ease of implementation, these metaheuristics are becoming popular nowadays for solving various types of complicated real-world problems.

In this section, a number of metaheuristics such as SA, GAs, ACO, Bee Algorithms (BAs), PSO, Harmony Search Algorithm (HSA), and TS techniques are discussed below. New metaheuristic algorithms are being developed by scientists on a regular basis. So, it is very important to classify various metaheuristics depending upon their dissimilar features and also recognize their similar characteristics. This comparison and discussion of various metaheuristics will permit the future researchers to select the most accurate metaheuristic technique for the required problem solving.

3.1 Simulated annealing

SA is a technique for solving unconstrained and bound-constrained optimization problems. The technique is based upon the logic of heating an object and then gradually decreasing the temperature to lower imperfections. In this way, we can lower the system's energy. SA heuristic is one of the most popular and well-known heuristic techniques for solving the problems related with optimization. The SA heuristic takes a travel iteratively according to the variable temperature parameter which initiates the annealing contract of the objects.

3.2 Genetic algorithms

The GAs are the search algorithms which were based on survival of the fittest of natural evolution. This metaheuristic is based on the method of natural choice of the best one for producing the children of the next generation. GAs are the metaheuristics based on the random search technique. These heuristics depend upon the method of natural selection and natural genetics. These metaheuristics work on biological string structures. These biological structures are developing in time maintaining the law of Darwin's theory. These biological structures share the data in random fashion but in a structured manner. So, in each generation, a new set of offspring is generated, utilizing portions of the fittest individuals of the previous generations. The main features of GA are given below. The GA can be applied with a coding of the parameter set. The GA starts its execution from a group of points not from a single point. The GA applies payoff data and transition rules based on probability.

3.3 Ant colony optimization

ACO is a population-based metaheuristic that can be utilized to search near-optimal solutions for hard optimization problems. In ACO, a set of software agents known as artificial ants finds out best solutions for a particular real-world problem. The general method to find out the solution of the optimization problem using ACO is to convert the real-world problem into the problem of searching the best path on the weighted graph. The main purpose of the artificial ants is to develop an optimal or near-optimal solution of the problem by traveling on the weighted graph. The method of development of the optimal solution is stochastic and depends upon a pheromone model. The artificial ants are responsible to change the values of the graph components while traveling on the weighted graph. The graph components of a weighted graph indicate the node or edge values associated with the weighted graph.

3.4 Bee Algorithms

The BA was invented in the year 2005. It is a very well-known metaheuristic to solve various problems related with Computer Science and Operations Research. The main logic behind the development of this metaheuristic is the food searching nature of honey bee colonies in the real world. This metaheuristic is basically a neighbor searching technique which is associated with global search. This metaheuristic can be applied for optimization in both combinatorial and continuous. The simulation results of various research papers show its effectiveness and efficiency.

3.5 Particle swarm optimization

PSO is a very popular metaheuristic. It was invented in the year 1995a.b. This heuristic is developed on the concept of nature and motion of the flock of birds in the real world. PSO is the most well-known metaheuristic which is basically used for solving research problems known as swarm intelligence. This metaheuristic is the most popular one due to its simplicity and ease of implementation. In PSO metaheuristic, the present location of each particle is calculated by a velocity term associated with each particle. In the figure below, g_b represents the attraction of global best and o_b is its own best which are measured by the past movement of the particle and coefficients generated randomly (Fig. 3.1).

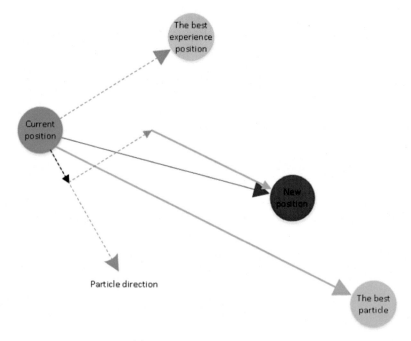

FIGURE 3.1 The motion of particles in PSO. https://www.nature.com/articles/s41598-021-81111-z.

3.6 Harmony search

Nowadays, the HSA is popular because of its simplicity and ease of implementation. It was first invented in the year 2001. The HSA has three operators: random search, rule based on harmony memory consideration, and rule based on pitch adjusting. These three operators make the HAS a unique one which is able to solve problems with the process of exploration and exploitation with the three operators which make the HSA a unique one. Some researchers have demanded that the performance of HSA is very close to an evolution strategy (ES). The ES has been developed based on two operators. Those are recombination and mutation. The similarity between the ES and HSA is that both metaheuristic algorithms create a single new solution at each stage. The main advantage of creation of a single new solution at each stage is that it can exchange the worst solution in the population. The main dissimilarity between ES and HSA is that the syntax of the exploration and exploitation operators is not the same at all.

3.7 Tabu search

TS is a metaheuristic which is utilized to solve optimization problems. The performance of TS has been improved over local search technique by escaping from the already visited solutions of the problem and their neighbors. This stops the searching of local optimal solutions. TS creates candidates which are basically a set of various integer variables. These candidates vary by one or more bits from the present optimal solution and are discarded from the list created by TS. The subproblems of the original problem are then solved for each candidate by the gradient-based technique. To create the seed for the next generation, the one present candidate with the best objective value is selected.

4. Swarm intelligence techniques

One of the types of metaheuristic algorithm is SI that is working on the base of artificial intelligence. It is the collective behavior of distributed and self-organized systems which is natural or artificial. It focuses on the collective behaviors from the local interactions of the individuals with each other and their environment. There are two research areas based on SI. One is natural SI research where we are doing research on biological systems and another is artificial SI where we are doing research based on human objects. Natural SI and artificial SI are opposite based on their nature where one could modify the behavior or the characteristics in a biological swarm and another is working on the modification of human objects. Metaheuristic algorithms have been classified into many groups as depicted below (Fig. 3.2).

4.1 Bat Algorithm

We know that the Bat Algorithm is based on the echolocation of microbats. Echolocation is a fascinating sonar wave emitted by the microbats which helps them to find prey by some magical ways where they are able to differentiate the different kinds of obstacles or danger on the way or toward their target in whole darkness. There are different types of areas where Bat Algorithms are applied. Different types of areas are scheduling, energy systems, solving the numerical optimization problem, mathematical problems, data mining

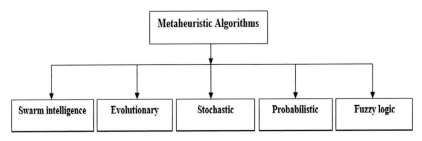

FIGURE 3.2 Different types of metaheuristic algorithms.

problems, networking problems, and image processing problems. The detection of hairline bone fracture in Medical X-ray Images is discussed by the authors [1] using the BAT Algorithm concept where they have applied BAT algorithm in preprocessing stage to enhance the image, self-organizing map K-means clustering. After that authors have been used these techniques to produce the objective image and opined the effectiveness of the BAT algorithm as an image enhancer was effective. A new algorithm based on the echolocation behavior of bats to know the initial value to overcome the K-Medoids issues is proposed by Ref. [2]. The authors have used a combination of K-Medoids clustering algorithm and Bat Algorithm to achieve better results. The authors showed the difference between K-Medoid Clustering Technique with BAT Algorithm and K-Medoid itself. A hybrid algorithm ABATA (accelerated bat algorithm) to solve integer-programming problems by combining the bat algorithm with the Nelder–Mead method is proposed by Ref. [3]. The authors have tested the performance of ABATA on seven integer-programming problems and compared against four benchmark algorithms. They have proposed that the performance of ABATA was very good for a global optimal solution. The localization problem in WSN using the BAT algorithm was proposed by Ref. [4] to solve the localization problem. The authors have shown that the localization accuracy was very high and BA can achieve higher accurate position estimation than existing algorithm. BAT algorithm–based approaches were used by Ref. [5] to solve various types of Unit Commitment problems. The authors opined that the proposed method has superior features, including stable convergence characteristic and avoids premature convergence characteristic. The authors further opined that the proposed method was capable of reaching the optimum solution in less computational time than that required for other algorithms. A new optimization of BAT algorithm to solve CEED problems with three and six generating units has been proposed by Ref. [6]. The authors have opined that the BAT algorithm had superior features, including quality of solution, stable convergence characteristics, and good computational efficiency as compared to other used algorithms. A new SI optimization algorithm, DBA (Discrete Bat Algorithm), for community detection was proposed by authors [7] to identify automatically the number of communities easily for search the global optimal solution to overcome the shortcomings of traditional algorithms. A comparative Bacterial Foraging Optimization Algorithm and Bat Algorithm (BAT) using the 12 selected benchmark functions have been proposed by authors [8] to get more accurate solution faster convergence rate as compared to BA. Bat algorithm [9] is also used for handwritten digit recognition on standard MNIST dataset to achieve global accuracy. The authors have shown that the proposed method gave 95.60% results as compared to other algorithms. A hybrid method is used [10] for improving the dynamic stability of the power system using UPFC for

---

Algorithm Standard Bat Algorithm

Input: Bat population $x_i = (x_{i1}, x_{i2}, ..., x_{id})^T$, for $i = 1, 2, ..., NP$,
velocity v_i, pulse rates r_i, loudness L_i, pulse frequency q_i at x_i, and
maximum number of generations Max_Gen.

Output: The best solution x_{GBest} and its corresponding fitness value $f(x_{GBest})$

1: Initial bat x_i, $i = 1, 2, ..., NP$
2: Evaluate fitness for each bat $f(x_i)$
3: **while** $(t < Max\_Gen)$
4:    Generate new solutions by adjusting frequency, and updating
5:    velocities and locations/solutions
6:    **if** (rand $> r_i$)
7:       Select a solution among the best solutions
8:       Generate a local solution around the selected best solution
9:    **end if**
10:   Generate a new solution by flying randomly
11:   **if** (rand $< L_i$ and $f(x_i) < f(x_{GBest})$)
12:      Accept the new solutions
13:      Increase r_i and decrease L_i
14:   **end if**
15:   Rank the bats and update the current best solution x_{GBest}
16:   Increase the generation number t
17: **end while**

FIGURE 3.3 Pseudo code of standard Bat Algorithm. https://www.thaiscience.info/Journals/Article/SONG/10988015.pdf.

optimizing the maximum power loss and optimum capacity of UPFC with minimum cost in another side a novel bat algorithm (NBA) [11] which is implemented to improve the optimization problems of original bat algorithm on 20 benchmark problems and 4 real-world engineering designs with better performance of NBA as compared to BA (Figs. 3.3 and 3.4).

4.2 Firefly algorithm

It is a metaheuristic optimization algorithm which is based on the social behavior of fireflies or lightning bugs in the summer sky in the tropical temperature regions. It was developed by Dr. Xin-She Yang at Cambridge University in 2007. It is based on the swarm behavior like fish, insects, and bird training in nature. Firefly algorithm has a lot of similarities with SI algorithms like PSO, Artificial Bee Colony optimization, and Bacterial Foraging algorithms. Firefly algorithm uses real random numbers. It is based on the global communication among the swarming particles (i.e., the fireflies). It appears to be more effective in multiobjective optimization.

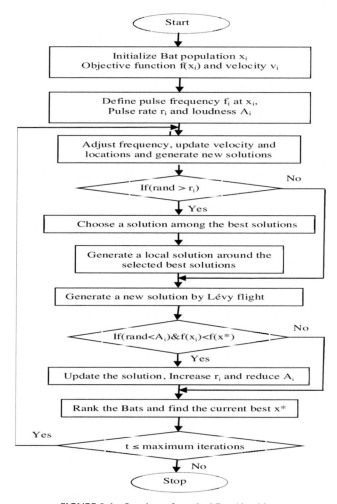

FIGURE 3.4 flowchart of standard Bat Algorithm.

The firefly algorithm has three rules which are based on flashing characteristics of real fireflies. These are as follows:

1. All fireflies are unisex, and they will move toward more attractive and
   brighter ones regardless their sex.
2. The degree of attraction of a firefly is proportional to its brightness which
   cuts as the distance from the other firefly increases due to the fact that the
   air absorbs light. If there is not a brighter or more attractive firefly than a
   particular one, it will then move randomly.
3. The brightness or light intensity of a firefly is determined by the value of
   the objective function of a given problem.

There are different types of areas where firefly algorithms are applied. Different types of areas are optimization problem, benchmark problem, Networking problems, and Image Processing problems. We know that queuing theory is used for analyzing complex service systems in transportation, networks, and manufacturing. In paper [12], authors have presented how firefly algorithm has been used for optimization of queuing systems where authors [13] have shown that firefly algorithm evaluates the performance of different algorithms for nonlinear benchmark problems. In another paper [14], firefly algorithm with mutation is checked by the author and measured for performance for solving optimization problems. Experiment results focused that firefly with mutation is more useful for solving most of the benchmark functions. And the firefly algorithm with mutation has superior performance to the compared method on all 10 standard benchmark functions. School location allocation optimization problem is solved by the Firefly Algorithms [15] such that the total of students' travel distance is minimized (Fig. 3.5).

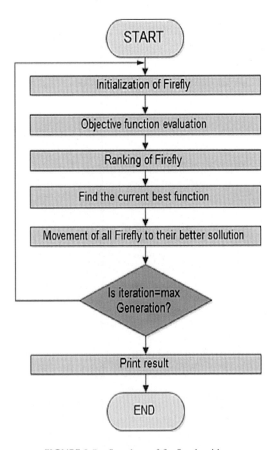

FIGURE 3.5   flowchart of firefly algorithm.

Lion Optimization Algorithm pseudo code

1. Generate random sample of Lions N_{pop}(N_{pop} is number of initial population).
2. Initiate prides and nomad lions

   i. Randomly select %N (Percent of lions that are nomad) of initial population as nomad lion. Partition remained lions into P (P is number of prides) prides randomly, and formed each pride's territory.
   ii. In each pride %S (Sex rate) of entire population are known as females and the rest as males. This rate in nomad lions is inversed.

3. For each pride do

   i. Some randomly selected female lion go hunting.
   ii. Each of remained female lion in pride go toward one of the best selected position from territory.
   iii. In pride, for each resident male; %R (Roaming percent) of territory randomly are selected and checked. %Ma (Mating probability) of females in pride mate with one or several resident male. → *New cubs become mature.*
   iv. Weakest male drive out from pride and become nomad.

4. For Nomad do

   i. Nomad lion (both male and female) moving randomly in search space. %Ma (Mating probability) of nomad Female mate with one of the best nomad male. → *New cubs become mature.*
   ii. Prides randomly attacked by nomad male.

5. For each pride do

   i. Some female with I rate ((Immigrate rate)) immigrate from pride and become nomad.

6. Do

   i. First, based on their fitness value each gender of the nomad lions are sorted. After that, the best females among them are selected and distributed to prides filling empty places of migrated females.
   ii. With respect to the maximum permitted number of each gender, nomad lions with the least fitness value will be removed.

If termination criterion is not satisfied, then go to step 3

FIGURE 3.6   Pseudo code of Lion Optimization Algorithm.

4.3 Lion Optimization Algorithm

Lion Optimization Algorithm (LOA) is a nature inspired optimization, SI-based algorithm which is used to solve a variety of optimization problems. It is formed by a set of randomly generated solutions called Lions. It appears more effective in multiobjective optimization. Cloud computing is a new technology which reduces storage and maintenance cost of the data. Authors have proposed how the LOA optimized [16] centrality measures fragmentation and replication of data in the cloud environment for optimum performance and security. Here, Territorial Defense and Territorial Takeover are intended to find and replace the worst solution by new the best solution. In paper [17], authors have presented how LOA has been used in different experiment, how it is behaved, and how it is better than other optimization algorithms (Fig. 3.6).

4.4 Chicken swarm optimization algorithm

Chicken swarm optimization (CSO) algorithm can categorize the hierarchical order in the chicken swarm and the behaviors of the chicken swarm, including roosters, hens, and chicks. It extracts the chickens' SI for problem optimization and simulates the relationship between swarm and the food search behavior between groups. It is also a mathematical model where attributes are few parameters, fast convergence speed, and high convergence precision. There are different types of areas where CSO algorithms are applied. Different types of areas are optimization, job scheduling, reservoir optimization scheduling, environment and disaster assessment, social network construction and detection, image recognition processing, process control and orbit optimization, and communication optimization. Authors have shown that how CSO algorithm [17] has been used to solve nonconvex economic load dispatch (ELD) problem with valve point loading effect, prohibited operating zones, ramp-rate limits, and transmission losses involving variations of consumer load patterns, whereas in another paper, authors have used [18] CSO algorithm for solving optimization problem. CSO algorithm is also used to solve the problem of reentry trajectory optimization [19]. In this paper, improved chicken swarm optimization (ICSO) method has been proposed by the author considering CSO method which is easy to fall into local optimum when solving high-dimensional optimization problem. The control variables are discretized as a set of Chebyshev collocation points and the angle of attack is set to fit with the flight velocity to make the optimization efficient. Based on those operations, the process of ICSO method is portrayed. Authors have presented ICSO-RHC [20] for solving constrained optimization where ICSO-RHC has four aspects, namely, cock position update mode, hen position update mode, chick position update mode, and population update strategy. ICSO-RHC is inspired by CSO. The results of the test functions and the actual engineering problems show that the performance of ICSO-RHC proposed in this paper is better than other algorithms. How CSO algorithm has been used for detecting methane gas that has shown in paper [21]. In this paper, improved chicken swarm algorithm optimized support vector machine (ICSO-SVM) was proposed to predict the concentration of methane. The ICSO algorithm had the best convergence effect, relative error percentage, and average mean squared error, when the four models were applied to predict methane concentration. The results showed that the average mean squared error values of the ICSO-SVM model were smaller than the other three models which have been portrayed in this paper. Authors have also proved that the ICSO-SVM model has better stability and the average recovery rate of the ICSO-SVM is much closer to 100%.

In another paper [22], authors have proposed the CSO algorithm as multistep CSO for global optimization. Modification of reducing the CSO algorithm's steps eliminates the parameter roosters, hens, and chicks. Multistep CSO are more efficient than CSO algorithms to solve optimization problems (Fig. 3.7).

4.5 Social Spider Algorithm

Social Spider Algorithm (SSA) is used to solve a global optimization problem which is based on the seeking strategy of social spiders, utilizing the vibrations on the spider web to determine the positions of prey. The SSA is evaluated by a series of functions. The SSO algorithm is based on the simulation of

Chicken Swarm Optimization (CSO)

Algorithm

Chicken Swarm Optimization. Framework of the CSO
Initialize a population of N chickens and define the related parameters;
Evaluate the N chickens' fitness values, $t=0$;
While (t < Max_Generation)
If ($t \% G == 0$)
Rank the chickens' fitness values and establish a hierarchal order in the swarm;
Divide the swarm into different groups, and determine the relationship between the chicks and mother hens in a group; End if
For $i = 1 : N$
If $i ==$ rooster   Update its solution/location using equation (1); End if
If $i ==$ hen   Update its solution/location using equation (3); End if
If $i ==$ chick   Update its solution/location using equation (6); End if
Evaluate the new solution;
If the new solution is better than its previous one, update it;
End for
End while

FIGURE 3.7   Pseudo code of chicken swarm optimization algorithm.

cooperative behavior of social spiders. In this algorithm, individuals match a group of spiders which interact to each other based on the biological laws of the cooperative colony. There are two types of search agents (spiders), males and females. Depending on gender, each individual is conducted by a set of different evolutionary operators which mimic different cooperative behaviors that are typically found in the colony. There are different types of areas where SSAs are applied. Different types of areas are optimization, load dispatch problem, nonconvex ELD problems, image recognition processing, process control and orbit optimization, and communication optimization. Authors have proposed in paper [23] a modified version of the SSA and studies of the application of this version for solving the nonconvex ELD problem which improves the performance of the SSA, whereas in another paper [24], authors have used the SSA as an optimization algorithm. SSA has also been used for global optimization purposes [25]. This algorithm performs preliminary parameter sensitivity analysis by choosing the parameter values which is evaluated by a series of widely used benchmark functions. ELD is an important component in power system control and operation. To solve nonconvex ELD problems, authors have proposed [26] a new approach based on the SSA where originally SSA is modified and improved to adapt to the unique characteristics of ELD problems like valve-point effects, multifuel operations, prohibited operating zones, and line losses. To demonstrate the superiority, widely adopted test systems are employed and the simulation results are compared with the state-of-the-art algorithms. Here, the parameter sensitivity is demonstrated by a series of simulations where the simulation results show that SSA can solve ELD problems efficiently. How Spectrum Allocation is optimized for Cognitive Radio Networks with the help of an SSA has been described in paper [27]. Here, the numerical results showed that the result by using the SSA is more accepted with comparison to other methods. In paper [28], authors have discussed the theory and application of SSAs, whereas in another paper [29], authors have shown how SSA has applied for the 0/1 knapsack problem. SSA has also applied for finding optimal operation of energy storage units in distributed systems [30]. Three points have been considered by the authors. They are Cost reduction, losses reduction, and voltage profile. The proposed method is applied to a 33-bus standard distribution system and results show that this novel method is simple and creates a better result compared to another method (Fig. 3.8).

4.6 Spider monkey optimization algorithm

A metaheuristic algorithm, Spider monkey optimization, is inspired by social behavior of spider monkeys. It is based on Fission—Fusion social (FFS) structure of spider monkeys throughout their foraging behavior. Key features are as follows:

1. FFS is based on animals that are social and live in groups of 40—50 individuals. FFS may reduce the group into more than one subgroup for searching their food.
2. A female monkey leads the group and is responsible for searching food sources. If she is not able to get enough food for the group, she divides the group into smaller subgroups (size varies from three to eight members) that forage independently.
3. Subgroups are led by a female (local leader) who is the decision-maker for planning an efficient foraging route each day.
4. The group members communicate among themselves and with other group members to maintain social bonds and territorial boundaries.

This algorithm is applied in different types of areas like optimization, numerical problems, image recognition processing, local search problem, traffic delay problem, energy-efficient clustering, and communication optimization. Proportional—derivative with filter cascaded with a proportional—integral controller has been proposed by the author in paper [31] which is inspired by spider social monkey optimization algorithm for load frequency control. There are two system which has been considered to authenticate the performance of SMO based proportional-integral (PI) controller PI controller designed with teaching learning-based optimization, differential evolution, hybrid bacterial foraging optimization-particle swarm optimization, BFOA, GA, and conventional Ziegler Nichols. For verification of system performance, authors have prolonged to a hybrid one by incorporating distributed generation unit and diesel unit in area-1 and area-2, respectively, along with thermal generating unit. Combination of redox flow battery energy storage system and high voltage-DC is used to improve the dynamic performance of the overall system and finally

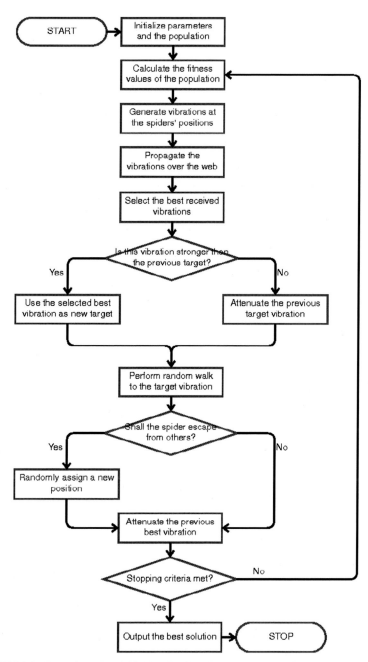

FIGURE 3.8   Flow chart of Social Spider algorithm. https://www.semanticscholar.org/paper/A-social-spider-algorithm-for-global-optimization-Yu-Li/93492ff6d4cee8865c41ef77eba0c52e1c8 9fb9f.

checked by the author that the proposed systems are working or not, whereas spider monkey optimization algorithm is used to solve traffic delay problem in paper [32]. Authors have chosen spider monkey optimization algorithm because it is decentralized, stochastic, and self-organizational which makes it appropriate for the nature of traffic networks. In paper [33], authors have used spider monkey optimization algorithms for analyzing spectrum sensing in cognitive radio networks. Authors have also used GAs for comparing results with spider monkey optimization. The results of spider monkey optimization algorithms are showing better than GAs. For numerical optimization, spider monkey optimization algorithm is used [34], whereas in another paper, authors have used this algorithm only for optimization purpose [35]. Authors have proposed an improved spider monkey optimization (ISMO) algorithm which is developed to improve the rate of convergence. Proposed algorithm is tested for standard problems and its advantages are recognized with the help of statistical results. In another paper [36], authors have made a survey about spider monkey optimization. In this paper, authors have shown its different types, applications, and relative performance with other algorithms. In paper [37], authors have proposed to implement energy-efficient clustering based on spider monkey optimization for wireless sensor networks, whereas in another paper [38], authors have used ISMO algorithm for improving the local search using automatic modified position. The result of the proposed algorithm is satisfactory compared to other optimization algorithms. Authors have designed a fuzzy rule base [39] using spider monkey optimization algorithm for cooperative framework (Fig. 3.9).

4.7 African buffalo optimization algorithm

Another kind of metaheuristic algorithm, African buffalo optimization, is based on movement of African buffalos from one place to another place across the African forests, deserts, and grassland in search of food. This algorithm is applied in different types of areas like optimization, numerical problems, image recognition processing, local search problem, team formation, scheduling problems, and combinatorial optimization problem. Solution to traveling salesman problem by African buffalo optimization algorithm clearly been mentioned in paper [40].The result of this experiment is better compared with other algorithms, whereas in paper [41], authors have discussed this algorithm. In another paper [42], African buffalo optimization is used to solve global optimization problems. This is based on artificial representation of different search techniques ranging from unimodal to multimodal, separable to non-separable, and constrained to unconstrained search landscapes. Authors have reached to a conclusion that the result of the experiment is better compared to other optimization problems. In paper [43], authors have used African buffalo algorithms to solve traveling salesman problems, whereas in another paper [44], an improved African buffalo optimization algorithm is used for collective

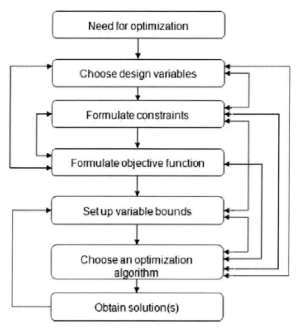

FIGURE 3.9   Flow chart of spider monkey optimization algorithm. https://www.semantic-scholar.org/.

team formation in the social network. In this paper, authors have introduced swap sequence to improve the performance by generating better team members that cover all the required skills. The results are showing better compared with the other optimization techniques. In paper [45], African buffalo optimization algorithm and hybrid GA is used to solve scheduling problems in zigBee network. In this paper, authors have proposed HGAABO which is the combination of the GA and African buffalo optimization. HGAABO is used to optimize the path selection in the network and to identify a set of routes which can satisfy the delay constraints and then select a reasonably good route through the proposed algorithm. The proposed approach is showing better results compared with another approach, i.e., GA and African buffalo optimization. In another paper [46], authors have used African buffalo optimization for parameters-tuning of PID controllers for automatic voltage regulators. Result was better compared to other optimization techniques like GA pid, particle swarm optimization pid, ACO pid, pid, bacteria-foraging optimization pid, etc. (Fig. 3.10).

4.8 Flower pollination algorithm

Flower pollination is an optimization algorithm which is inspired by the pollination process of flowers. This algorithm has applied in different types of

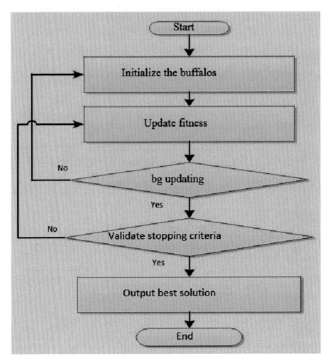

FIGURE 3.10 Flow chart of African buffalo optimization algorithm. https://www.semanticscholar. org/paper/Convergence-Analysis-of-the-African-Buffalo-Odili-KaharM.N./8a119240b60745eed3-fe3d453ac0e002285346cd/figure/0.

areas like optimization, numerical problems, image recognition, local search problem, economic and emission dispatch problems, Power System, scheduling problems, and combinatorial optimization problem. In paper [47], authors have applied flower pollination algorithms (FPAs) for three-area power systems. Here, the fractional order PID (FOPID) controller is considered for the three-area load frequency control. FOPID controller parameters are used FPA for the minimize error. The result of FOPID controller parameters using FPA is better than other results. For solving combined economic and emission dispatch problems, FPA is used [48], whereas in paper [49], authors have used this algorithm for DNA cryptography. Authors have used this algorithm because it helps to find the optimal solution, whereas DNA cryptography helps to encrypt a large number of data in few grams of DNA. This paper has been done to achieve optimized technique and to enhance cloud security. In paper [50], improved version of FPA is used for node localization optimization in wireless sensor network, whereas in paper [51], authors have used FPA for making short-term load forecasting model which was made by using artificial intelligence—based optimization technique. Authors have also proposed five different experimental models which were optimized using FPA. Results of proposed load forecasting model are satisfactory compared to other models for short-term load forecasting. In paper [52], authors have used FPAs for solving optimization problems. FPA is used to solve initial value problems in paper [53], whereas in another paper, this algorithm is used by the author to identify the essential protein [54] (Fig. 3.11).

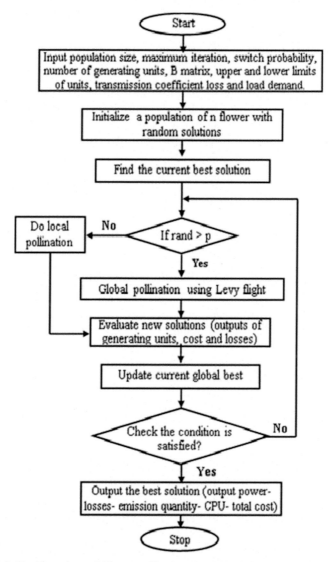

FIGURE 3.11 Flow chart of Flower pollination algorithm. https://www.sciencedirect.com/science/article/abs/pii/S0360544216300846.

5. Impacts of metaheuristic and swarm intelligence approach in optimization

5.1 Implication of the metaheuristic techniques in optimization

A wide range of metaheuristic algorithms are flattering a vital part of modern optimization in the last 2 decades, and many metaheuristics are becoming even more popular too. Despite their popularity, the mathematical part present in these algorithms kept them lacking behind as compared to others. Moreover, Convergence analysis in these algorithms still remains unsolved, while efficiency analysis is also equally challenging. But, it has been observed that many researchers have done the researchers' work and try to provide an overview of convergence and efficiency studies of metaheuristics. They tried to provide a framework which can do the analysis on metaheuristics convergence and efficiency factor, respectively. This effort has provided the great help of metaheuristic algorithm in the field of optimization. The convergence and efficiency is the basis for analyzing other algorithms too.

5.2 Implication of the swarm intelligence techniques in optimization

SI algorithms are inspired by biologically approaches that have been applied in optimization very fast in recent years. The application SI algorithms has been successfully applied to a variety of real-world applications like controlling nanobots tfor killing tumors and etc.

The main reason of the popularity of these above mentioned algorithms are that these are not only flexible and adaptive to the problems but also have strong global search ability and robust performance. Therefore, SI algorithms are significant and promising to improve the performance of optimization. SI is a new technology because it is inspired by behavior of social insects and flocking animals. The algorithms of SI are used to solve the portfolio optimization problem, small-scale and large-scale portfolio, and medium-scale portfolio, respectively. SI algorithms are also used in many real-world problems to optimize them and provide the way for hybrid structure of algorithms for optimization also.

6. Conclusion

Metaheuristics optimization deals with optimization problems using different algorithms. It is a high-level procedure which is used to produce a good solution to an optimization problem. Different types of metaheuristics algorithm are used in different areas like engineering, agriculture, medicine, and in others. In the above discussion, we have discussed about impacts of metaheuristic and SI approach in the optimization. Optimization is essentially everywhere, from engineering design to economics and from holiday planning to Internet routing. As money, resources, and time are always limited, the optimal utility of these available resources is crucially important. Most real-world optimizations are highly nonlinear and multimodal, under various complex constraints. Different objectives are often conflicting. Even for a single objective, sometimes, optimal solutions may not exist at all. We have discussed about how different algorithms have used, how they react, and how they are used to solve different problems.

References

[1] G. Das, Bat algorithm based softcomputing approach to perceive hairline bone fracture in medical X-ray images, Int. J. Comput. Sci. Eng. Technol. 4 (04) (2013) 435.

[2] M. Sood, K-medoids clustering technique using bat algorithm, Int. J. Appl. Inf. Syst. (IJAIS) 5 (8) (2013) 535–560 (USA).

[3] F.A. Ahmed, Accelerated bat algorithm for solving integer programming problems, Egypt. Comput. Sci. J. 39 (1) (2015).

[4] S. Goyal, M. Singh Patterh, Wireless sensor network localization based on BAT algorithm, Int. J. Emerg. Technol. Comput. & Appl. Sci. (IJETCAS) (2013) 507–518.

[5] R. Anand, A. Azeezur Rahman, Solution of unit commitment problem using BAT algorithm, IJETI Int. J. Eng. & Technol. Innov. 1 (2) (2014).

[6] B. Ramesh, V. Chandra Jagan Mohan, V.C. Veera Reddy, Application of bat algorithm for combined economic load and emission dispatch, Int. J. Elec. & Electr. Eng. & Telecoms. 13 (2013).

[7] A. Song, M. Li, X. Ding, W. Cao, K. Pu, Community detection using discrete bat algorithm, IAENG Int. J. Comput. Sci. 20 (2014).

[8] Y.A. Alsariera, H.S. Alamri, A.M. Nasser, M.A. Majid, K.Z. Zamli, Comparative performance analysis of bat algorithm and bacterial foraging optimization algorithm using standard benchmark functions, in: 8th. Malaysian Software Engineering Conference (MySEC), Langkawi, 2014, pp. 295–300.

[9] E. Tuba, M. Tuba, S. Dana, Handwritten digit recognition by support vector machine optimized by bat algorithm, in: GECCO'17 Proceedings of the Genetic and Evolutionary Computation Conference Companion, 2017, pp. 125–126.

[10] B. Vijay Kumar, N.V. Srikanth, Bat algorithm and firefly algorithm for improving dynamic stability of power systems using UPFC, Int. J. Elec. Eng. & Inf. 8 (Number 1) (2016).

[11] X.B. Meng, X.Z. Gao, Y. Liu, Z. Hengzhen, A novel bat algorithm with habitat selection and doppler effect in echoes for optimization, Expert Syst. Appl. (n.d.). Elsevier Ltd. https://doi.org/10.1016/j.eswa.2015.04.026 0957-4174/_ 2015.

[12] J. Kwiecień, b. Filipowicz, Firefly algorithm in optimization of queueing systems, Bull. Pol. Acad. Sci. Tech. Sci. 60 (2) (2012), https://doi.org/10.2478/v10175-012-0049-y.

[13] A.J. Umbarkar, U.T Balanade, P.D Seth, Performance evaluation of firefly algorithm with variation in sorting for non-linear benchmark problems, Appl. Math. & Comput. Sci., AIP Conf. Proc. 1836, 020032-1–020032-9 (n.d.), https://doi.org/10.1063/1.4981972, Published by AIP Publishing. 978-0-7354-1506-5/$30.00.

[14] S. Arora, S. Singh, Performance research on firefly optimization algorithm with mutation, International Conference on Communication, Computing & Systems (ICCCS–2014).

[15] P. Prima, A. Aniati Murni, Optimization of school location-allocation using firey algorithm, in: The 3rd International Conference on Computing and Applied Informatics 2018, IOP Conf. Series: Journal of Physics: Conf. Series 1235, IOP Publishing, 2019, p. 012002, https://doi.org/10.1088/1742-6596/1235/1/012002.

[16] S. Periyanatchi, K. Chitra, A lion optimization algorithm for an efficient cloud computing with high security, J. Sci. Res. 64 (1) (2020) 378–384, https://doi.org/10.37398/JSR.2020.640152. Institute of Science, BHU Varanasi, India.

[17] P.K. Mallick, S. Mishra, G.S. Chae, Digital media news categorization using Bernoulli document model for web content convergence, Personal Ubiquitous Comput. (2020), https://doi.org/10.1007/s00779-020-01461-9.

[18] S.K. Mohapatra, P. Nayak, S. Mishra, S.K. Bisoy, Green computing: a step towards eco-friendly computing, in: Emerging Trends and Applications in Cognitive Computing, IGI Global, 2019, pp. 124–149.

[19] S. Mishra, P.K. Mallick, H.K. Tripathy, L. Jena, G.-S. Chae, Stacked KNN with hard voting predictive approach to assist hiring process in IT organizations, Int. J. Electr. Eng. Educ. (February 2021), https://doi.org/10.1177/0020720921989015.

[20] J. wang, Z. Cheng, K.E. Okan, Z. Mingxin, S. Kexin, B. Yusheng, Improvement and application of chicken swarm optimization for constrained optimization, in: IEEE. Translations and Content Mining Are Permitted for Academic Research only vol. 7, 2019, pp. 2169–3536. Personal use is also permitted, but republication/redistribution requires IEE, permission. See, http://www.ieee.org/publications_standards/publications/rights/index.html for more information.58053-58072.

[21] Z. Wang, S. Wang, D. Kong, S. Liu, Methane detection based on improved chicken algorithm optimization support vector machine, Appl. Sci. 9 (2019) 1761, https://doi.org/10.3390/app9091761. www.mdpi.com/journal/applsci.

[22] N. Irsalinda, A. Thobirin, W. Dian Eka, Chicken swarm as a multi-step algorithm for global optimization, Int. J. Eng. Sci. Invent 6 (1) (January 2017) 08–14. ISSN (Online): 2319 – 6734, ISSN (Print): 2319 – 6726, www.ijesi.org.

[23] W.T. Elsayed,Y.G. Hegazy, F.M. Bendary, M.S. El-bages, Modified social spider algorithm for solving the economic dispatch problem, Eng. Sci. & Technol., Internat. J. (n.d.). https://doi.org/10.1016/j.jestch.2016.09.0022215-0986/_2016. Karabuk University. Publishing services by Elsevier B.V.This is an open access article under the CC BY-NC-ND license. http://creativecommons.org/licenses/by-nc-nd/4.0/. Journal homepag'e: www.elsevier.com/locate/jestch.

[24] E. Cuevas1, M. Cienfuegos, D. Zaldívar, M. Pérez-Cisneros, A swarm optimization algorithm inspired in the behavior of the social-spider, Expert Syst. Appl. 40 (16) (2013) 6374–6384.

[25] J.Q.Y. James, O.K.L. Victor, A Social Spider Algorithm for Global Optimization, arXiv:1502.02407v1 [cs.NE], February 9, 2015.

[26] L. Tutica, K.S.K. Vineel, S. Mishra, M.K. Mishra, S. Suman, Invoice deduction classification using LGBM prediction model, in: Advances in Electronics, Communication and Computing, Springer, Singapore, 2021, pp. 127–137.

[27] T.D. Binh, C.V. Minh, K.T. Tung, Social spider algorithm-based spectrum allocation optimization for cognitive radio networks, ISSN 0973-4562, Int. J. Appl. Eng. Res. 12 (Number 13) (2017) 3879–3887. © Research India Publications, http://www.ripublication.com.

[28] D. Evangeline, T. Abirami, Social spider optimization algorithm: theory and its applications, Int. J. Innov. Technol. & Expl. Eng. (IJITEE) 8 (10) (August 2019). ISSN: 2278-3075.

[29] P.H. Nguyen, D. Wang, K.T. Tung, A novel binary social spider algorithm for 0-1 knapsack problem, Int. J. Innov. Comput. Inf. & Control ICIC Int. Conf. 13 (Number 6) (December 2017) 2039−2049. ISSN 1349-4198.

[30] M. Tabasi, P. Asgharian, Optimal operation of energy storage units in distributed system using social spider optimization algorithm, AIMS Electr. & Electr. Eng., 3(4) (n.d). 309−327. doi: 10.3934/ElectrEng.2019.4.309 Received: 18 July 2019 Accepted: 24 September 2019 Published: 08 October 2019,http://www.aimspress.com/journal/ElectrEng.

[31] D. Tripathy, B.K. Sahu, N.B.D. Choudhury, D. Subhojit, Spider monkey optimization based cascade controller for LFC of a hybrid power system., in: Proceedings of International Conference on Computational Intelligence & IoT (ICCIIoT), ELSEVIER-SSRN, 2018, pp. 747−753. ISSN: 1556-5068, https://www.ssrn.com/link/ijciiot-pip.html.

[32] S.E. Ezekwere, V.I.E. Anireh, M. Daniel, Application of the spider monkey optimization algorithm in a class of traffic delay problem, SSRG Int. J. Comput. Sci. & Eng. (SSRG-IJCSE) 7 (2) (February 2020) 48−55. ISSN: 2348 − 8387, www.internationaljournalssrg.org.

[33] H. kaur, A. kumargeol, Spectrum sensing analysis in cognitive radio network using spider monkey optimization algorithm compare with genetic algorithm, Int. J. Innov. Eng. & Technol. (IJIET) 14 (2) (n.d). https://doi.org/10.21172/ijiet.142.02/volume.

[34] J. Chand Bansal, H. Sharma, S. Singh Jadon, M. Clerc, Spider monkey optimization algorithm for numerical optimization, Memetic Comp. 6 (2014) 31−47, https://doi.org/10.1007/s12293-013-0128-0.

[35] V. Swami, S. Kumar, S. Jain, An improved spider monkey optimization algorithm, Soft Comput. Theor. & Appl. (n.d). https://www.researchgate.net/publication/321294231, doi: 10.1007/978-981-10-5687-1_7.

[36] V. Agrawal, R. Rastogi, D.C. Tiwari, Spider monkey optimization: a survey, Int. J. Syst. Assur. Eng. Manag. (n.d). doi: 10.1007/s13198-017-0685-6.

[37] N. Mittal, U. Singh, R. Salgotra, B. Singh Sohi, A boolean spider monkey optimization based energy efficient clustering approach for WSNs, Wirel. Netw. 24 (2018) 2093−2109, https://doi.org/10.1007/s11276-017-1459-4.

[38] A. Bhuguna, V. Prasad Tamta, Improve the local search using automatic modified position in improved spider monkey optimization algorithm, Int. J. Eng. & Adv. Technol. (IJEAT) 8 (6) (August 2019). ISSN: 2249 − 8958.

[39] J. Dhar, Designing fuzzy rule base using Spider Monkey Optimization Algorithm in cooperative framework, Future Comput. & Inf. J. 2 (1) (2017).

[40] J.B. Odili, M.N. Mohmad Kahar, S. Anwar, African buffalo optimization: a swarm-intelligence technique, in: 2015 IEEE International Symposium on Robotics and Intelligent Sensors (IRIS 2015), Julius Beneoluchi Odili et al./Procedia Computer Science vol. 76, 2015, pp. 443−448.

[41] J.B. Odili, M.N. Mohmad Kahar, African buffalo optimization, ISSN: 2289-8522, Int. J. Soft. Eng. & Comput. Syst. (IJSECS) 2 (February 2016) 28−50, https://doi.org/10.15282/ijsecs.2.2016.1.0014. ©Universiti Malaysia Pahang.

[42] J.B. Odili, A. Noraziah, African buffalo optimization for global optimization, Curr. Sci. 114 (No. 3) (February 10, 2018) 627−636.

[43] J.B. Odili, M.N. Mohmad Kahar, Solving the Traveling Salesman's Problem Using the African Buffalo Optimization, Hindawi Publishing Corporation Computational Intelligence and Neuroscience vol. 2016, Article ID 1510256 12. https://doi.org/10.1155/2016/1510256.

[44] W.H. El-Ashmawi, An improved African buffalo optimization algorithm for collaborative team formation in social network, I.J. Inf. Technol. & Comput. Sci. 5 (2018) 16−29, https://doi.org/10.5815/ijitcs.2018.05.02. Published Online May 2018 in MECS, http://www.mecs-press.org/.

[45] N.R. Solomon Jebaraj, D.H.R. Keshavan, Hybrid genetic algorithm and african buffalo optimization (HGAABO) based scheduling in ZigBee network, ISSN 0973-4562, Int. J. Appl. Eng. Res. 13 (Number 5) (2018) 2197−2206. © Research India Publications, http://www.ripublication.com.

[46] J. Beneoluchi Odili, M. Nizam, M. Kahar, A. Noraziah, Parameters-tuning of PID controller for automatic voltage regulators using the African buffalo optimization, PloS One (April 25, 2017) 1−17, https://doi.org/10.1371/journal.pone.0175901.

[47] D.K. Sambariya, O. Nagar, A.K. Sharma, Application of FOPID design for LFC using flower pollination algorithm for three-area power system, Univ. J. Contr. & Automa. 8 (1) (2020) 1−8, https://doi.org/10.13189/ujca.2020.080101. http://www.hrpub.org.

[48] A.Y. Abdelaziz, E.S. Ali, S.M. Abd Elazim, Flower pollination algorithm to solve combined economic and emission dispatch problems, Eng. Sci. & Technol. Int. J. 19 (2016) 980−990, https://doi.org/10.1016/j.jestch.2015.11.0052215-0986/c 2016, Karabuk University. Publishishing services by Elsevier B.V. Journal homepage: http://www.elsevier.com/locate/jestch.

[49] M. Popli, Gagandeep, DNA cryptography: a novel approach for data security using flower pollination algorithm, International Conference on Sustainable Computing in Science, Technology & Management (SUSCOM-2019), February 26−28, 2019, Amity University Rajasthan, Jaipur, India, 2069−2076.

[50] J.-S. Pan, T.-K. Dao, T.-S. Pan, T.-T. Nguyen, C. Shu-Chuan, J.F. Roddick, An improvement of flower pollination algorithm for node localization optimization in WSN, J. Inf. Hiding & Multimed. Sig. Process. C vol. 8 (Number 2) (March 2017). ISSN 2073-4212 Ubiquitous International.

[51] A. Volkan, B. Necaattin, Short-term load forecasting model using flower pollination algorithm, Int. Sci. & Vocation. J. (ISVOS J) 1 (1) (December 2017) 22−29. Received: 20.12.2017 Accepted: 30.12.2017 Final Version: 31.12.2017.

[52] X.S. Yang, M. Karamanoglu, X. He, Flower Pollination Algorithm: A Novel Approach for Multi Objective Optimization, Publisher: Taylor & Francis, (n.d). Informa Ltd Registered in England and Wales Registered Number: 1072954 Registered,office: Mortimer House, 37-41 Mortimer Street, London W1T 3JH, UK, https://doi.org/10.1080/0305215X.2013.832237.

[53] F. Ouaar, N. Khelil, Solving initial value problems by flower pollination algorithm, Am. J. Electr. & Comput. Eng. 2 (2) (2018) 31−36. ISSN: 2640-0480 (Print); ISSN: 2640-0502 (Online), http://www.sciencepublishinggroup.com/j/ajece. https://doi.org/10.11648/j.ajece.20180202.14.

[54] X. Lei, M. Fang, W. Fang-Xiang, L. Chen, Improved flower pollination algorithm for identifying essential proteins, BMC Syst. Biol. 12 (Suppl. 4) (2018) 46, https://doi.org/10.1186/s12918-018-0573-y.

[55] J. Kennedy, R.C. Eberhart, Particle swarm optimization, in: Proc. of IEEE International Conference on Neural Networks, Piscataway, NJ, 1995, pp. 1942−1948.

[56] J.L. Lauriere, Language and a program for stating and solving combinatorial problems, Artif. Intell. 10 (1) (1978) 29−127.

[57] F. Glover, Future paths for integer programming and links to artificial intelligence, Comput. Oper. Res. 13 (1986) 533−549.

[58] A. Hertz, D. de Werra, The tabu search metaheuristic: how we used it, Ann. Math. Artif. Intell. 1 (1991) 111−121.

[59] I.H. Osman, An introduction to metaheuristics, in: M. Lawrence, C. Wilsdon (Eds.), Operational Research Tutorial Papers, Operational Research Society Press, Birmingham, 1995, pp. 92−122.

[60] I.H. Osman, G. Laporte, Metaheuristics: a bibliography, Ann. Operat. Res. 63 (1996) 513−628.

[61] C. Ray, H.K. Tripathy, S. Mishra, Assessment of autistic disorder using machine learning approach, in: International Conference on Intelligent Computing and Communication, Springer, Singapore, June 2019, pp. 209−219.

[62] I.H. Osman, J.P. Kelly, Metaheuristics Theory and Applications, Kluwer, Boston, 1996.

[63] K.C. Jena, S. Mishra, S. Sahoo, B.K. Mishra, Principles, techniques and evaluation of recommendation systems, in: 2017 International Conference on Inventive Systems and Control (ICISC), IEEE, January 2017, pp. 1−6.

Further reading

[1] M. Yazdani, Fariborz J., Lion Optimization Algorithm (LOA): A Nature-Inspired Meta-heuristic Algorithm, (n.d). https://doi.org/10.1016/j.jcde.2015.06.0032288-4300/. & 2015 Society of CAD/CAM Engineers. Production and hosting by Elsevier. All rights reserved. This is an open access article under the CC BY-NCND, license. http://creativecommons.org/licenses/by-nc-nd/4.0/.

Chapter 4

A perspective depiction of heuristics in virtual reality

Moushita Patnaik[1], Angelia Melani Adrian[2]

[1]*School of Computer Engineering, KIIT University, Bhubaneswar, Odisha, India;* [2]*Informatics Engineering Department, De La Salle Catholic University, Manado City, Indonesia*

1. Introduction to virtual reality

Virtual Reality (VR) is a computer machine—generated artificial world in which the user feels as if he is part of that world. The user can navigate the surroundings and manipulate the objects in the environment just as he would do in the real world. The social and geographical barriers are seemed to be removed ever since it has been increasingly used by everyday people. The virtual environments are computer-simulated environments that can simulate physical presence in imaginary worlds [1]. A VR interface stimulates the human senses. In simpler systems like a PC monitor or a headphone, the visual and auditory senses are stimulated. These two interfaces are therefore commonly used as interfaces for VR [2]. Simulated reality, as the name suggests, is an innovative, illusionistic environment that creates the impression that you are within the simulated world generated by simulations using computer software. VR environments are configured in a three-dimensional (3D) model, which allows the subject or the user to move in X,Y, and Z directions. It is on the immersive medium, which means that it can transport the user in the virtual medium [3]. To construct a simulated world, VR helps [4]. Haptic interfaces are also available that allow the user to feel. Haptic displays produce forces and movements that are perceived both by touch and by kinaesthesia [5]. Two major types of haptic interfaces exist, the off-body interface and the on-body interface.

Depending on the application criteria, the reason for this technology varies, but often it gives the user intricate knowledge that he can never acquire by only utilizing his imagination, senses, and 2D resources. Augmented Reality (AR) has the ability to solve a wide range of issues, and therefore, numerous technology giants such as Google, HP, IBM, Sony as well as various universities have made efforts to improve it. In nearly every current field of work,

Cognitive Big Data Intelligence with a Metaheuristic Approach
https://doi.org/10.1016/B978-0-323-85117-6.00006-6

especially chemistry, medicine, physics, astronomy, mathematics, biology, history, and even, music and art, AR can be applied. These major corporations are trying to create effective technology devices that can handle all of these themes and that can eventually affect the life of the consumer.

VR has been extensively used in various fields, such as follows:

1. Scientific Visualizations: VR helps the scientists and their audience to interact with the visuals of the concepts and thus improves understanding.
2. Education: VR is the most useful when it comes to education. Virtual university trips help students visit their dream campus without actually being there. 3D classes keep the students intrigued in the course syllabus.
3. Military: VR is used for various training purposes like, Aviation Combat Training Systems, Dismounted Soldier Training Systems, and Operation Planning Tool which are some of the VR technologies currently in use.
4. Health care: VR is used in medical training, treatment of patients, medical marketing, and recognition of diseases.
5. Media: Better transmission, better viewing experience is what VR does in media. It lets the audience live in the movies, with the characters, in the breathtaking locations. It makes the audience feel more involved by broadcasting the normal content in 3D mode.

2. Heuristics in brief

Heuristics are a method of problem solving which uses shortcuts in a given limited time frame to produce almost perfect solutions. It is a versatile technique for rapid decisions. In particular, heuristics are helpful when dealing with complex data. Decisions taken using a heuristic technique are not always optimal. These algorithms find solutions among all possible solutions. But there is no certainty that the solution given is the best one available. Heuristic algorithms are also commonly known as approximate and not precise algorithms. Typically, heuristics find an answer similar to the right one and they efficiently and simply find it.

The following are important features of the heuristic algorithm:

➤ Complete: The heuristic algorithm must find every existent solution.
➤ Optimal: The heuristic will find only optimal solutions even if there are many valid solutions.
➤ Understandable: The algorithm must be understandable to the user.
➤ Approach: The heuristics should be designed such that they can be quickly taught to a nonexperienced user.
➤ Validation: The heuristics must have been validated by facts and practical examples.

Some commonly used heuristics algorithms are listed below:

Swarm Intelligence: It refers to autonomous systems' collective actions. Swarm Intelligence networks employ large numbers of agents who communicate both with each other and with the world locally. Both natural and artificial systems can be represented using it.

Tabu Search: Tabu search is a heuristic approach that uses dynamically generated taboos to direct optimum solutions to the solution search. In order to find an improved solution, it explores possible solutions to a problem and tests immediate nearby neighbors.

Simulated Annealing: Simulated Annealing is used in global optimization. This approach converges into a solution in a way similar to how, by increasing grain size, metals are brought to minimum energy configurations. For a function with a broad search space, it can provide a rational approximation of a global optimum.

Genetic algorithms: Genetic Algorithms belong to evolutionary algorithms that define a set of methods inspired by natural selection such as mutation, inheritance, and crossover. To evaluate the solution domain, these algorithms require a genetic representation of the solution domain as well as a fitness function. By iterating the fitness function for each generation, the technique produces a population of candidate solutions and then selects the optimal solution. The termination criterion is met either when the population has achieved an optimal fitness level or the maximum generations have been reached.

Support Vector Machines: These are models used by artificial intelligence to identify patterns and assess information from training data. For the purposes of regression analysis and classification, SVM algorithms are used.

Heuristic-based algorithms find scope in various application domains particularly where searching and sorting operations are involved. Recent developments have led to the use of heuristics in VR.

Heuristic evaluation can be integrated as an informal way of evaluating the usability of User Interfaces (UIs). Evaluating a UI can be described heuristically as the process of the practitioner looking at the UI and judging its quality based on their own knowledge and experience.

The method of using heuristics in VR consists of three basic steps:

❖ Evaluators individually go through the interface first time to become familiar with the interface.
❖ Evaluators individually go through the interface second time where they focus on individual elements and check if they comply with basic heuristics principles.
❖ The findings from the evaluators are combined.

As new technology, applications, and domains emerge, researchers have seen a need for more specific heuristics, more suited to specific interfaces. Domain- and technology-specific heuristics have been developed for a variety of domains and technologies, and commonly the studies find the specific heuristics more effective than general purpose heuristics. Heuristics should be refined and synthesized to establish core principles. Then, the specific and individualized principles can be applied to different mediums. Even though many studies find specific heuristics to be effective than general purpose heuristics, some others raise concerns that many specific heuristics sets are developed and published rapidly. As a result, many of them lack follow-up studies and extensive research on their effectiveness.

Heuristics in VR offer some potential benefits which are discussed here:

➢ It gives quicker feedback, and early in the process, making the designing easy.
➢ The best corrective steps are recommended by the heuristics. A usability test can also be performed to evaluate possible problems.
➢ A single cue or a familiar sequence of signs is used by the recognition heuristic to quickly size up a situation or shape a conclusion.
➢ A short sequence of cues is evaluated by the one-good-reason heuristic. When we experience a powerful or persuasive signal, it ceases.
➢ The heuristic tallying helps us to arrange cues to decide between competing alternatives.

3. Virtual reality—enabled case studies

Numerous real-time scenarios exist in reality depicting and analyzing the role of VR concept. In this section, few such relevant case studies are discussed.

3.1 Virtual reality in crime scene evaluation

A sample depiction of VR in a crime scene is shown in Fig. 4.1. There was a completely immersive application that used an HMD, and an interacting 3D mouse was the VE application used in this review. This provided a simulated atmosphere of a crime scene in the garage premises. Here, the user can move around and take a look at the layout of the garage and collect minute details present in the crime scene. True life photographs were incorporated at various points within the simulated world to help solve crime scenes. The purpose of this analysis was to inspect the office in the garage where the offense was committed, enter the office, and record data relevant to the prosecutor (for instance, blood stains, objects riotous, door or window unlatched, etc.). Various test cases are illustrated in Fig. 4.2.

FIGURE 4.1   Illustration of virtual reality in a crime scene.

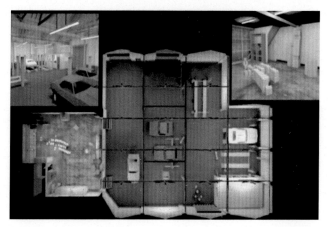

FIGURE 4.2   Illustration of different test cases in crime scene using virtual reality.

The evaluators' role was to navigate through the VE several times, examining information in the space adjacent to the garage, and discovering the real life photos embedded in the VE.

The evaluator went through the application and developed the following technology audit while familiarizing himself with the VE:

User presence operation: The movement and viewpoint of the user regulated all the area displayed, so the presence of the user was minimal. An avatar presence may be required to examine physical gestures; for example, an escape from a compact opening.

Haptic Input: Haptic feedback was not necessary because manipulation of entities in the environment was not needed for the application.

Interactive techniques: The interactive facilities were not necessary due to the reduced scale of the VE and the absence of digital objects.

Realistic graphics: The request required an in-depth inspection of the area, so high fidelity graphics were required.

Ranking and analysis of heuristics concerning the case study is highlighted in Table 4.1.

In Table 4.2, the classification of problems experienced with severity ratings and potential design changes is mentioned.

TABLE 4.1 Heuristics ranking and analysis of issues experienced.

Heuristic	Score	Issues
Natural involvement	3	Most objects seem to float. The original photos of environment cause the VE to appear perhaps less realistic.
User objective compatibility	3	It should not float through the air and move through solid objects, such as floors and walls. It does, however.
Natural expression of action	2	There has been no opportunity to explore the environment with objects (e.g. displacing the furniture).
Close coordination	3	During navigation, some delays in graphic rendering interfered with engagement. The persistent slow navigation speed was frustrating.
Realistic feedback	N/A	It did not support contact with objects.
Faithful viewpoints	4	Generally decent
Navigation and orientation support	3	Disorientation caused by the ability to walk through walls.
Clear points for entry and exit	N/A	In Desktop VR, exit from VE not applicable to immersive VR except for modified environments.
Consistent departures	3	Incongruent practical images
Learning assistance	N/A	Not needed for concise navigation
Taking distinct turn	N/A	No avatars, VE single user
Perception of presence	4	Reduced by visual jerkiness and distinction between real-world photos and VE graphics

TABLE 4.2 Problem classification with score level.

Feature	Problem addressed	Score	Design issue
Illustration (graphics)	Delays in rendering, Floating artifacts	Unsuitable, difficult	Faster speed hardware
Interaction operation	Examine items, components	Bothersome, disturbing	Clarification of requirements
Controls	Conflicting photos	Bothersome, disturbing	Software upgrade: Offer photo controls
Environmental issues	Moving through surfaces	Irritating	In application design, introduce movement limitations

3.2 Virtual reality in assessing a chess game

A chess game with an entirely submerged CAVE system with shutter glasses was designed to allow users to take a holographic view and have pinch controlled grips. To control the CAVE view area according to the movements of the body and head of the user, compatible devices monitored the hands of the users and the head tracking devices were placed in the shutter glasses. A small context was used by the app to show 12 chess pieces on the board. The evaluators' task was to organize the chess pieces, which had been shattered initially, for a standard chess game. Fig. 4.3 depicts a sample demonstration of chess game using VR.

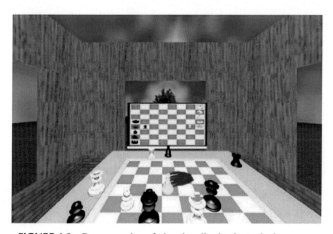

FIGURE 4.3 Demonstration of virtual reality in chess playing game.

Two different aspects of the VE application were used to complete the tasks:

➢ with the virtual hand present.
➢ without the virtual hand present.

The haptic reaction of the selection of the parts was assisted by a color adjustment, so that when the user manipulated the globe, the piece shifted color from white/black to yellow when picked. Then, the selected piece moved along with the hand movements of the user until it was released. Once released, the piece switched back to black/white, whichever was its color before selection. When a chosen piece of chess (yellow) was gripped by the other hand, which was already in its correct position, it changed color to blue, meaning that both hands chose it. The chess piece changed its color back to yellow when the piece was released from one hand, showing that it was still picked by the other. It changed back to its original color when the other hand released it. A simple step sequence is denoted in Fig. 4.4.

The technology audit is discussed below:

❖ *Functioning of the presence of the user:* The user was present in the environment through a virtual hand. Minimal visual feedback was provided as only pinch operations from thumb and forefinger were supported.
❖ *Missing haptic feedback:* Haptic feedback was followed by shifts in color to indicate that chess pieces have been selected. Color shifts were introduced when the user's hand was near the piece with a collision detection algorithm.

FIGURE 4.4 Depiction of steps in chess playing game with virtual reality.

TABLE 4.3 Heuristics ranking and analysis of issues experienced.

Heuristic	Score	Problems faced
Natural involvement	3	Passing the chess piece around the chessboard was possible. It was difficult to move pieces between hands.
Task compatibility	2	In moving chess pieces from one hand to the other, ambiguous color changes were noticed.
Natural expression of action	3	Because of a lack of haptic input, glove pinch behavior and subsequent color changes had to be taught.
Close coordination	4	Occasional delays in graphics rendering irritating
Realistic feedback	3	Haptic feedback was not substituted by any visible color differences.
Faithful perspectives	4	Usually decent, though it might leave off the VE at times
Navigation for orientation	4	Minor dissonance caused by the ability to walk through walls
Clear points for entry and exit	N/A	Move out of CAVE
Coherent divergences	0	No upgrade in technology. Consistent changes in color for manipulating pieces.
Learning assistance	4	Clear optical indicators supported learning about manipulation of objects.
Taking distinct turns	N/A	No avatars, VE single user
Perception of presence	4	Most lowered by the waits and the average scarce presentation.

❖ *Immersive methods:* Hand gestures and pinch actions manipulated and shifted the interactive objects. The location of the hand and body of the user was independently monitored by sonic equipment. The VE needed little to no help with navigation as it was a small VE.

❖ *Realistic graphics:* The program had a minimal environment, as the chess pieces were minimally depicted.

Ranking level of heuristics and its concerning issues are summarized in Table 4.3.

Classification and improved design for the exclusion of the problems faced along with their seriousness ratings is highlighted in Table 4.4.

TABLE 4.4 Classification of problems with its score level.

Feature	Problem in hand	Score	Design issue
Illustration (graphics)	Delays in rendering, Floating artifacts	Unsuitable, difficult	Faster speed hardware
Interaction operation	Manipulating artifacts	Bothersome, disturbing	Hardware: Provide haptic feedback
Presence in environment	Grasping, operating problems	Irritating, tiresome	Software upgrade: Enhance changes in color
Environmental issues	Moves through solid surfaces	Irritating, tiresome	Software upgrade: Introduce movement limitations

3.3 Virtual reality in client assignment problem

This case study sought to establish a relevant and accurate way to distribute clients to servers while substantially enhancing communication between the DVEs [6]. The DVE is a distributed network allowing several users to be distributed geographically in a shared, 3D virtual space. This allows consumers to search and connect with other consumers on the network in actual time. A multiserver networking architecture is generally used to support the heavy resource needs of DVEs [7]. The mirrored cloud architecture is a common technique to distribute the simulated universe across the server network. The entire virtual world is represented on all servers on the system and a client may choose to connect to the closest node to avoid connection delays [8].

In general, the artificial realm is split into many independent regions dimensionally and only one server manages each region. Here, the approach followed is zone based.

Clients communicate only with other clients in the same zone in a zone-based strategy and can switch to other zones. In order to make the device more scalable, the server has to handle one or so zones instead of the whole globe. Here, the same server is linked to all clients in a region. However, since clients are geographically dispersed, there may be different network delays for clients in the same zone to the server in that zone. If a client's round-trip (client-to-server) latency in a zone is high, for all customers in this zone, DVE interactivity may be damaged. The interactivity of the entire zone will be degraded because of a single device that is far from its destination server.

Model and descriptions of the system framework [9]:

❖ Communication Server: This client has a server directly linked to it.
❖ Domain Node: The server hosting the region is the client's target server.
❖ Zone (Region) Contact Delay (DiZ): It checks every customers' inter-activity in the DVE zi region.
❖ Device Contact Delay (DS): Measures the cumulative overall delay in zone contact for all system regions.
❖ Delay bound: Signifies the DS prerequisite to retain interactivity.
❖ Server load: This is the load in the DVE of a server. It can be split into the load associated with the network and the load associated with the program.

3.4 Client assignment algorithms

We describe some basic but impactful server assignment algorithms. These techniques are based on the greedy algorithm initially proposed to overcome the issue of the terminal allotment in the architecture of communication networks. Generally, TA is an NP-complete problem [10]. TA's principal objective is to discover the lowest cost network connections via the link between the terminal collection and the center collection.

Concentrators may have different capability and terminals may have different resource specifications; for example, weights. The expense of connecting the terminal to the hub shall be the gap between the terminal and the hub. Each terminal is attached to a single concentrator, and the total weight of its allocated terminals must not overload any concentrator.

3.4.1 Virtual assignment algorithm

We are implementing virtual assignment (VA) algorithms with a first-pass heuristics, one of the most simple and powerful bin packaging algorithms [11]. In the figure below, we can see the pseudocode. 3.1. The VA algorithm first classifies the zone list in descending by the total client weight in each location. The current zone (and its users) is then transmitted with adequate intensity to the current node. VA has the same destination server and communication server for all clients in the region. Fig. 4.5 denotes the pseudocode.

3.4.2 Greedy assignment algorithm 1

The suggested greedy assignment 1 (GDA-1) algorithm benefits from the fact that the delays in connecting servers are usually much lower than for connecting clients and servers. If a client does not explicitly submit requests to his target server, we can even obtain a smaller response delay. Rather, clients choose the closest server for their contact server, transferring their requests to their target server through a short-term connection between their contact server and the target server. Fig. 4.6 represents the GDA-1.

Algorithm :

begin

 sort list of zones L^Z in descending order by total weight of each zone;

 while L^Z is not empty **do**

  pick the first zone z^i in L^Z;

  find a server sj such that capacity is sufficient;

  set contact server and target server of all clients ck $\in$ z_i to s_j ;

  remove z_i from L^Z;

 end

end

FIGURE 4.5 Pseudocode for virtual assignment problem.

Algorithm :

 begin

 find list L^C of delay-exceeding clients c_i ;

 sort L^C in descending order by $d(c_i s_k)$,

  where sk is the target server of ci $\in$ LC ;

  while LC is not empty **do**

   pick the first $c^i \in L^C$;

   find a server s_j such that

   $d(c_i s_j) + d(s_j s_k) \leq D$ **and** $L(s_j) + \beta(c_i) \leq T(s_j)$;

   if such sj can't be found **then**

    select a non-saturated server sj with $\min(d(c_i s_j) + d$

   $(s_j s_k))$;

   end

   change the contact server of c_i to s_j ;

   remove c_i from L^C ;

  end

 end

FIGURE 4.6 Pseudocode for greedy assignment problem (GDA-1).

3.4.3 Greedy assignment algorithm 2

For the greedy assignment 2 (GDA-2) algorithm, we are attempting to maximize the original allocation of the GDA-1 algorithm to minimize the reassignment in the optimized allotment (this ensures that the additional network burden for contact servers to be handled due to reassignment would be reduced) [12]. Fig. 4.7 represents the GDA-2 algorithm.

Algorithm :

begin

 sort the list of zones L^Z in descending order by

 the total weight of each zone;

 while L^Z is not empty **do**

  pick the first zone z_i in L^Z;

  find a server s_j such that the number of

  delay-exceeding clients in z_i is minimized and s_j is not

 saturated;

   set the contact server and target server of all clients $c_k \in z_i$

 to s_j ;

  remove z_i from L^Z;

 end

end

FIGURE 4.7 Pseudocode for greedy assignment problem (GDA-2).

4. Performance evaluation and discussion

This section discusses the results obtained through simulation of the discussed algorithmic models. Performance of VA, GDA-1 and GDA-2 are analyzed and discussed here [13−17].

 The system latency period of the discussed algorithms are done as shown in Fig. 4.8. As a sample example, 10s-15z-204c denotes servers−zones−clients

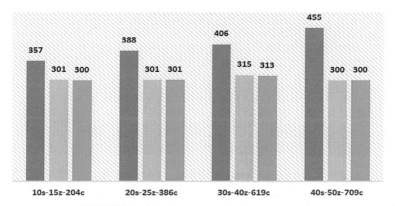

SYSTEM COMMUNICATION LATENCY

■ VA ■ GDA I ■ GDA II

FIGURE 4.8 System communication latency analysis.

notation. The simulation outcome indicates that GDA-1 and GDA-2 provide better efficiency thereby reducing the system communication latency delay when compared to VA algorithm.

The system mean utilization throughput analysis is shown in Fig. 4.9. It shows that the overall utilization of GDA-1 and GDA-3 is comparatively better than VA model.

It can be noted in Fig. 4.10 as relative to GDA-1 and VA algorithms, the GDA-2 algorithm is also less time consuming than clients. This is because GDA-2 undergoes an initial phase of assignment. It greedily searches for an original assignment that reduces the number of late customers. The GDA-2 algorithm must reassign a minor number of customers relative to GDA-1 and thereby obtain a comparable or increased DS with a lower system use than GDA-1.

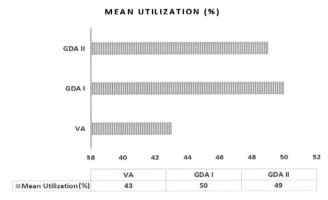

FIGURE 4.9   System mean utilization analysis.

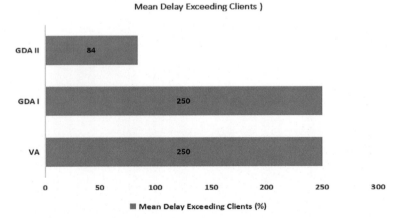

FIGURE 4.10   System mean delay analysis.

5. Conclusion

VR has opened doors to what was unimaginable a few decades ago. Traveling through an artificial environment, experiencing the world of simulation is helpful in numerous ways. Be it practical tests, or crime scene investigation, or just a visit to some place you have always wanted to visit, VR makes the experience easier and better. And this is just the start of the applications of this realm. Heuristics are now being implemented into the VR techniques to make the experience even better [18–20]. Various heuristic algorithms have also been suggested to make the VR implementation more efficient and impactful. VR is a sea of openings which no one knows will lead us where. Along with the heuristic algorithms, AR is bound to be the next big milestone to be achieved in the digital world.

References

[1] Y.S. Hsu, Y.H. Lin, B. Yang, Impact of augmented reality lessons on students' STEM interest, Res. Pract. Technol. Enhanc. Learn. (RPTEL) 12 (1) (2017) 1–14.
[2] J. Novak-Marcincin, Prof.dr.ing, Hardware Devices Used in Virtual Reality Echnologies, Technical University of Kosice, ISSN 1224-3264.
[3] S. Manjrekar, et al., CAVE: An Emerging Immersive Technology - A Review, UKSim-AMSS 16th International Conference on Computer Modelling and Simulation, IEEE computer society, 2014, pp. 130–135.
[4] J. Fox, et al., Virtual reality: a survival guide for the social scientist, J. Media Psychol. 21 (3) (2009) 95–113.
[5] D. Sharma, A review paper on virtual reality oculus rift and augment reality, Int. J. Curr. Res. 8 (09) (2016) 37941–37945.
[6] Zona Inc. and Executive Summary Consulting Inc., State of Massive Multiplayer Online Games 2002: A New World in Electronic Gaming", 2002. Available at: http://www.zona.net.
[7] T. Nitta, K. Fujita, S. Cono, An Application of Distributed Virtual Environment to Foreign Language, IEEE Education Society, 2000.
[8] J. Dias, R. Galli, A. Almeida, C. Belo, J. Rebordao, mWorld: a multiuser 3D virtual environment, IEEE Comput. Graph. 17 (2) (1997).
[9] S. Khuri, T. Chiu, Heuristic algorithms for the terminal assignment problem, Proc. of ACM Appl. Comput. (1997) 247–251.
[10] S. Salcedo-Sanz, X. Yao, A hybrid hop-field network-genetic algorithm approach for the terminal assignment problem, IEEE Trans. Syst. Man & Cybernet. 34 (6) (2004).
[11] N.B.T. Duong, S. Zhou, A dynamic load sharing algorithm for massively multi-player online games, in: Proc. Of the 11th IEEE International Conference on Networks, 2003.
[12] J. Lui, M. Chan, An effiffifficient partitioning algorithm for distributed virtual environment systems, IEEE Trans. Parallel Distr. Syst. 13 (3) (2002).
[13] W. Cai, P. Xavier, S. Turner, B.S. Lee, A scalable architecture for supporting interactive games on the internet, in: Proc. Of the 16th Workshop on Parallel and Distributed Simulation, 2002.

[14] S. Mishra, P.K. Mallick, L. Jena, G.S. Chae, Optimization of skewed data using sampling-based preprocessing approach, Front. Pub. Health 8 (2020) 274, https://doi.org/10.3389/fpubh.2020.00274.

[15] S. Mishra, H.K. Tripathy, B.K. Mishra, Implementation of biologically motivated optimisation approach for tumour categorisation, Int. J. Comput. Aided Eng. Technol. 10 (3) (2018) 244–256.

[16] S. Mishra, P.K. Mallick, H.K. Tripathy, L. Jena, G.-S. Chae, Stacked KNN with hard voting predictive approach to assist hiring process in IT organizations, Int. J. Electr. Eng. Educ. (February 2021), https://doi.org/10.1177/0020720921989015.

[17] S. Mishra, P.K. Mallick, H.K. Tripathy, A.K. Bhoi, A. González-Briones, Performance evaluation of a proposed machine learning model for chronic disease datasets using an integrated attribute evaluator and an improved decision tree classifier, Appl. Sci. 10 (22) (2020) 8137.

[18] P.K. Mallick, S. Mishra, G.S. Chae, Digital media news categorization using Bernoulli document model for web content convergence, Personal Ubiquitous Comput. (2020), https://doi.org/10.1007/s00779-020-01461-9.

[19] S. Mishra, H.K. Tripathy, P.K. Mallick, A.K. Bhoi, P. Barsocchi, EAGA-MLP—an enhanced and adaptive hybrid classification model for diabetes diagnosis, Sensors 20 (14) (2020) 4036.

[20] S. Sahoo, M. Das, S. Mishra, S. Suman, A hybrid DTNB model for heart disorders prediction, in: Advances in Electronics, Communication and Computing, Springer, Singapore, 2021, pp. 155–163.

Chapter 5

A heuristic approach of web users decision-making using deep learning models

Vaisnav Roy[1], Ankit Desai[2]
[1]*School of Computer Engineering, KIIT University, Bhubaneswar, Odisha, India;* [2]*Embibe, Bengaluru, Karnataka, India*

1. Introduction

Decision-making systems are one of the most imperative and promising fields today in decision-making software supported by artificial intelligence technologies [1]. Decision-making does the very job it claims to do for you, that is, selection among various alternatives. Various practices like contemporary management, trading systems, bargain, and financial arrangements use this concept widely. E-Commerce is a place where a user gets a wide spectrum of choices of items, therefore making this field a testing application of making decisions. In such a scenario, having an online artificial intelligence agent greatly improves their experience where the selection part is done by the agent which suggests various items perfectly fitting their preference based on their searches, click-on, add-to-carts keywords, and previously bought items [2]. Therefore, multinational companies like Google and Amazon, in order to get the best of techniques to integrate artificial intelligence in decision-making, have provided open access to the decision-making support platforms.

Retargeting, online form of advertising, can keep your product in front of the bounced traffic even after you leave the website, would become a lot more easier, and efficient if users' intentions toward buying a product or interest in a particular category could be predicted. Better understanding of the user behavior and interest could only be achieved by recording a track of the search patterns of the user [3]. Mobile e-commerce have millions of enumerable users form a rich set of data from which available information about online merchant's potential search patterns regarding a transaction decision can be extracted, which in turn can be processed to reflect customer's purchase intentions. Search patterns can be quantified as different functions,

Cognitive Big Data Intelligence with a Metaheuristic Approach
https://doi.org/10.1016/B978-0-323-85117-6.00015-7

i.e., time spent on a particular item, frequent searches, and recurring visits to a particular item [4]. Clickstream data, focusing on purchase records, can be quantified using machine learning techniques [5]. Not only purchasing records indicate a user's preference in a particular category but are also a quintessential component about his intentions toward a particular category in the website. Here, we are introducing a latent context variable which captures the simultaneous influence from watching location and time that will be used in a probabilistic and generative process to create a model using customer's exploration and purchase history. During the time of shopping, we can identify the search pattern of the consumer and recommend the right product by predicting their click decisions. Known models including logistic regressions (LR) and boosted decision tree have been used by modern search engines for prediction of user activity within the web. Decision trees, despite being popular in this domain, face difficulties when data become highly dimensional and sparse [6]. While linear relations can be formulated using LR models, networks have an upper hand in capturing nonlinear relationships. The multiple layered architecture and deep learning abilities give them greater modeling strength. The beneficial factor of the probabilistic generative model, who's point of inspiration was deep neural network, is that here it mimics the consumer's purchase process thus capturing a latent variable that explains the data.

User behavior is one of the most complex structures which consist of large collection of defining elements including three elements called actions, activities, and behavior. While on one hand when actions are described by the simplest conscious movement, on the other hand, behavior years defined the complex conduct of the person. Various elements of user's behavior are shown in Fig. 5.1.

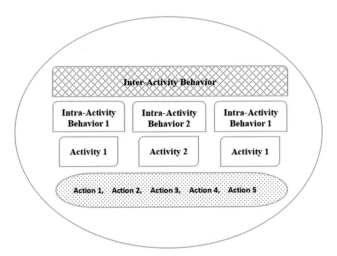

FIGURE 5.1 Elements of the user behavior.

The various components included in user behavior are as follows:

❖ Short conscious and temporary movements of the muscle made by the user to perform a task are called actions. (For example, picking up a mug, looking at the watch, opening the fridge)

❖ Several actions when combined together to perform a particular task are called activities. Activities are temporarily longer but finite (for example, preparing dinner, watching a movie, bathing).

❖ Explanation of complex conduct of user behavior describing how these activities are performed by the user at different times. There are namely two types of behaviors: Interactivity behavior and Intraactivity behavior. The intraactivity behavior describes the manner in which an activity is performed at different point of times which is describing the time pattern of the activities. For example, while preparing dinner, a user might decide to gather the ingredients first or he may gather them while performing the cooking. The interactivity behavior on the other hand describes how the user changes different behavior, i.e., the sequential pattern.

In the new digital era, mimicking human behavior and reasoning to solve complex problems is possible with the help of cognitive computing. Various patterns can be extracted by wading through massive collection of heterogeneous information that is generated by the vast masses of users and can be used to create a machine-assisted model with the help of cognitive computing. Heuristics on the other hand when applied to algorithms gives an optimal solution. Heuristic problem does not guarantee the best solution but various experimentation and observations have led to the conclusion that looking into the most cost-efficient direction eventually will lead you to the most efficient path to the goal. By combining these two technologies, heuristics and cognitive computing, the process of wedding true to the diverse information to find patterns will be much shorter and time and space efficient. It is the human nature to look for the optimum path when struck with the problem; similarly, cognitive computing's general characteristic is to act like a human. For cognitive computation, all the local cues are processed in symbol structures to access and integrate distal knowledge to generate a responsive model. In this local-to-distal processing, heuristic searches are performed to locate and integrate the most optimum set of distal structures. The efficiency of the heuristic search is critically the deciding factor of the intelligence of the system. For a bounded rationality system, the level of intelligence is measured by the amount of search it needs to do. One instance that can be used to describe this is when a machine plays tic-tac-toe or chess, it strongly realized on the efficiency of the heuristics search algorithm, clearly demonstrating the heuristics and intelligence relations. Similarly, humans while searching for information over the internet improve their performance of extraction and use full data over time as they learn the optimum path leading to an improved rationality system to perform their tasks. These two examples clearly show

how using these two technologies will eventually lead to better results. Whenever huge amount of data are to be processed and computed which can neither be easily done by humans nor be accessible for feasible solutions, we opt for cognitive computing technology which has a vast amount of computing power and shall also be able to perceive patterns much more easily than humans. To train a model using adaptive and adoptive cognitive computing, using heuristics approach will eventually help the technologies a lot.

In this chapter, you will discover the possibility and advantage of integrating the greedy algorithm as a crucial step of a deep learning neural network model for the support of online user decision-making.

2. Analysis of user online behavior using deep learning models

Techniques of machine learning and AI have explored a new level of accurately and effectively tackling problems where machine learns to accomplish task by human brains' neural networks. The ground-breaking innovations and relegation using these technologies have affected the whole digital community of the world. In addition to that, integrating human brains' neural networks in deep learning algorithms has given a new perspective to the whole model making procedures.

2.1 Classic neural networks

Designed in 1958, by Fran Rosenblatt, an American psychologist, classic neural networks use the concept of connecting a well-defined neuron into continuous layers to form a multilayered perceptron structure. Three functions of the model are as follows:

a. Linear function: A constant multiplier is multiplied with its input and represented as a single line.
b. NonLinear Function: These are of three types:
 ❖ Sigmoid curve: A mathematical function which has a characteristic "S"-shaped sigmoid which has a curve range from 0 to 1.
 ❖ Hyperbolic tangent (tanh) is "S" shaped which has a curve range from −1 to 1.
 ❖ Rectified Linear Unit (ReLU): In this, a set value is decided and the single point function gives us 0 if input is lesser than the set value, whereas if the input exceeds the set value, it gives us a linear multiple.

 Best used in the following:

➢ *Any CSV format table dataset consisting of rows and columns.*
➢ *Regression and Classification problems with real value inputs.*
➢ *Any highly flexible model like ANNS.*

2.2 Convolutional Neural Networks

Convolutional Neural Networks (CNNs) are advanced and high-potential classical artificial neural network model which can tackle and handle higher complexity data, difficult compilation, and preprocessing of data. It takes reference from the neuron arrangements in the visual cortex of an animal's brain and is one of the most efficient and powerful models to process image and nonimage data. The CNNs have four different organizations:

➢ A 2D neuron arrangement which is a single input layered structure and is used for analyzing primary image data which shows similarity to photo pixels.
➢ With the help of scattered and connected convolutional layers, some of these neural networks process images on their inputs and thus these contain a single-dimensional neuron output layer.
➢ CNN also consists of a third layer called the sampling layer that helps in limiting the neuron numbers in the corresponding layers.
➢ To sum up, in order to connect the sampling to the output layer, CNNs may have single or multiple connected layers.

For relevant image data processing, in smaller units or chunks, this network model is used. The neuron clusters in the previous layer are held accountable with respect to the neurons present in the convolution layer. After being imported into the convolution layer, the input data go through four stages in modeling the CNN:

➢ Convolution: Deriving feature maps from the input data and applying a function to these maps.
➢ Max Pooling: CNNs detect images with respect to the given modifications.
➢ Flattening: The generated data are flattened for the CNN to analyze.
➢ Full connection: The loss function is compiled for the model by this layer, which is often described as a hidden layer.

The CNNs are most frequently and efficiently used for image processing tasks that involve image analyzing, image recognition, video analysis, segmentation of image, and NLP. In addition to that, the other places where CNN can be used are as follows:

❖ Image data sets which contain OCR document analysis.
❖ For the purpose of quicker analysis, a 2D input data that can be additionally transformed to 1D.
❖ In order to yield output, involvement of the model in its architecture is required.

2.3 Recurrent neural networks

These kind of neural networks were designed for the purpose of sequence prediction. The long short-term memory algorithm, which works completely on sequences of data of varying input length is mostly known for multiple functions, uses recurrent neural networks (RNNs). The previously gained knowledge of the state is given as input for the next prediction by the RNN. This particular function of the RNN helps in achieving short-term memory which leads to efficient management of various time-based data systems and changes in stock price. RNN designs are of two types:

- ❖ LSTMs (Long Short-Term Memory networks): they are used in the prediction of time sequence data, through memory. They consist of three gates: input gate, output gate, and forget gate.
- ❖ Gated RNNs: They are useful in the prediction of time sequence data, through memory. They consist of two gates—Update gate and Reset gate.

Best used in the following:

- ➢ 1 to 1: One element of the input is only connected to one element of the output, like image classification.
- ➢ 1 to many: One element of the input is only connected to many output sequences like image captioning which require several words from a single image.
- ➢ Many to 1: More than one number of inputs generating a single output; for example, sentiment analysis.
- ➢ Many to many: More than one number of multiple input yields a series of multiple outputs like video classification.
- ➢ Language translation conversation modeling are some other places where RNN is used.

2.4 Self-organizing maps

The self-organizing maps (SOMs) make use of unsupervised data that help in reduction of random number variables within a model. As each synapse is connected to its input node and output node, the output dimension is fixed as a two-dimensional model. Every data point in the model is competing for model representation; therefore, the Best Matching Units (BMUs) or weight of the closest nodes of the SOM gets updated. The value of the weights changes based on the BMU proximity. The value represents the location of the node in the network which itself is considered as load characteristics.

Best used in the following:

- ❖ In datasets that do not come with a y-axis.
- ❖ Exploration of projects for data set analyzation framework.
- ❖ Creative and innovative projects in Videos, Music, and Text with the help of Artificial Intelligence.

2.5 Boltzmann machines

In this network, the nodes are connected in a circular arrangement and it does not come with any predefined directions. This unique feature of this network helps in producing model parameters. This network is different from the previous deterministic network model and therefore referred as stochastic.

Best used in the following:

❖ *System monitoring*
❖ *A binary recommendation platform setup*
❖ *Analyzation of particular and specific data sets*

2.6 Deep reinforcement learning

In Reinforcement learning, the agent requires interaction with its environment in order to change its state. This agent may observe, and appropriate actions may be taken accordingly and it helps the network to attain an objective by interacting with the situation. Here, the model of network contains an output, input, and many hidden layers, when the state of environment is an input layer itself. Continuous attempts are made by the model for prediction of the future reward of every action that is taken in the provided state of the situation.

Top use in the following:

❖ *Poker, chess, or similar board games*
❖ *Self-Driving Car*
❖ *Robotics*
❖ *Inventory Management*
❖ *Financial tasks for ex, asset pricing*

3. Greedy algorithm as the heuristic

Greedy search algorithm is an effectual tool, which is generally used for optimization problems. The important steps of all greedy algorithms are as follows:

1. Choosing a candidate set and dividing the main problem into a finite set of subproblems. For the first subproblem, arbitrarily a candidate set is to be chosen. This set will be the solution of this subproblem, so the solution of remaining subproblems can be obtained based on this candidate set.
2. Choosing a selection function. In order to test which is the best candidate to be added to the solution of selection function is chosen.
3. Choosing a feasibility function. The selection function previously chose also has a feasibility function that helps to determine the candidate set which has probable contribution toward the solution.

4. Choosing an objective function. This function will let you to choose a candidate at every step in some optimal sense.
5. Finally choosing a solution function. This function is chosen in accordance to establishing a desired precision in which approximation of solution is achieved.

Greedy algorithms are specially competent when one works with the set of huge data sets. If the universally agreed optimal solution of a problem contains optimal solutions of locally optimal subproblem, the nonperforming greedy search global solutions will be obtained in a reasonable time. However, in some special cases, like the traveling salesman problem, using this algorithm may also result in a unique worst achievable solution [7]. The failure in this particular problem occurs as greedy algorithm that does not make use of the entire data in the problem. Any globally optimal solution also contains optimal subsolutions therefore in order to have a successful application of the algorithm which one needs to have success at every partial step. In addition to that, as the selection function varies from identity, a particular candidate can only be invoked at one single step of the algorithm, i.e., neither of the previous steps, except for the direct previous one, plays a role in proceeding computations/searches. This is called the greedy choice property of the algorithm which helps to save a lot of computational cost.

4. Background study

For the purpose of monitoring automatic human behavior and evaluation of its activities, there are two main modern monitoring method called, respectively, vision- and sensor-based monitoring. For understanding the first approach, Ref. [8] may be referred. Privacy is of utmost importance to most of the users and therefore vision-based approaches may lead to various security concerns; therefore, in order to approach behavior and activity evaluation within an intelligent environment [9], approach based on sensor is mostly preferred [10]. Sensor-based approaches work on the principle of networks emerging from sensors in order to monitor activities and behavior in the active environment. The sensor monitored data that are generated are mostly series of time, generated by changes in state and different parameters and values that are normally processed using union or fusion of the data, also including statistical analysis methods or probabilistic methods and formal knowledge technologies for identification of activities. That is to say, there are two important ways of approaching the sensor-based behavior and evaluation of activities: data-driven approaches and knowledge-driven approaches. Data-driven approach generally uses machine learning techniques and data mining to train activity models and learn behavior from the sensor collected data for supervised learning. In order to train different kinds of classifiers, data-driven procedure requires big data sets of labeled activities. This approach has a broad spectrum of learning techniques, from naive Bayes classifier [11] to dynamic Bayesian networks [12], Markov hidden models [13], support vector machine [14], and online (or instrumental) classifiers [15]. While on one hand where data-driven approaches require data sets which are properly labeled, on the other hand, an approach which is driven by knowledge tries to make use of the existing knowledge of the domain for training the models. To tackle the problems faced by manually labeled activity data sets, Cook and Rashidi [16] tried to extract activity clusters with the help of unsupervised learning technologies. These clusters were utilized to train and develop a boosted hidden Markov model, which is proved to be able to recognize various activities. Chen et al. [17] used logic-based approach for recognizing activity, based on prior knowledge that was gained from the domain specialists or experts. To agree on an explicit presentation of activity definition which is algorithmic choices independent, ontology-based approach have been adopted by others, which facilitate portability, interoperability, and reusability [18–20]. In the presence of an intelligent environment, user behavior is built on activities of the user to describe the user's conduct. These behavior models mainly describe how accurate user performance activities are and what activities constitute their day-to-day living. Predicting user behavior is an imperative task in an intelligent environment. Predicting these behaviors will help us in anticipating users' need and the variations on the behavior can be related to health perils later. The MavHome project [21] was a set of an algorithm that predicts the user's device usage mobility patterns. With their algorithm, the intelligent environment could then adapt to the user's needs, as it was mainly based on compression, sequence matching, and Markov models [22]. A detailed review of the importance of making these predictions can be referred from Ref. [23]. Intelligent environment predictions have also been used for controlled artificial illumination [24] with the help of neuro-fuzzy systems and for controlling climate parameter based on user behavior [25]. A detailed analysis of comfort management prediction within an intelligent environment based on user's behavior can be found in Ref. [26]. As discussed earlier, we identified behavior to be of two types: firstly intraactivity behavior and secondly interactivity behavior. The former describes how the activity is performed by the user, while the latter describes the activity sequences and actions that compose the user's day-to-day life. For predicting interactivity behavior and generating a model, action sequences are used, which permit fine and detailed user conduct description while drawing out the model from a specific sensor technology.

5. Description of the dataset

The dataset used here is the record of a user's interaction, for a time period of 6 months, with an e-commerce website. There are almost 25,000 different

TABLE 5.1 Various data samples used in model validation and evaluation.

Data samples	Data size	Information
Sample 1	3,000	Weekly gathered sales data
Sample 2	10,000	Weekly gathered sales data with more quantity
Sample 3	30,000	Weekly gathered sales data with even more quantity
Sample 4	10,000	Weekly gathered semiaggregated sales data with more quantity
Sample 5	10,000	Weekly gathered sales data with more quantity with more attributes
Sample 6	30,000	Weekly gathered sales data with even more quantity with more attributes

types of products and five categories of events namely: page view of a product, basket view, buy, add click, and add view. The events of buy or basket view contain information about the price and extra details of the product. The data are categorized into two classes which are considered as buy or not buy. The data set is about 10 GB of memory which makes it very difficult to load the data directly, so initially a sample of the first most 100,000 events behaves as a snapshot of the interactions. Table 5.1 shows the dataset details.

6. Implementation and discussion

This section presents the implementation outcomes discussion of the work. Primarily the comparison analysis is performed with and without using greedy search heuristics. Classification accuracy rate is the parameter considered for the comparative evaluation [27–29].

In Fig. 5.2, the data set extracted from the record of user's interaction with an e-commerce website is fed to a deep learning neural network without the use of involving a greedy search in any of the steps of the algorithm. The sales data set is divided into six samples which were obtained weekly and each sample had the tendency of gathering even more quantity of sales data than the previous sample. On feeding the data to different deep learning neural networks, we observe that the acquired amount of accuracy is fair.

Classic neural networks give a lowest of 89.2 accuracy with the first sample and an accuracy of 90.5 with sample 6 which consists of large quantity of sales data with varied attributes. This signifies that with increase of attributes and data in the sample, the tendency of the deep learning algorithm to create a more accurate model increases.

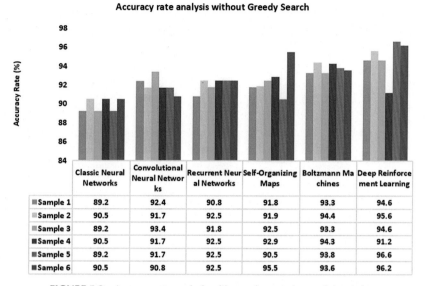

Accuracy rate analysis without Greedy Search

	Classic Neural Networks	Convolutional Neural Networks	Recurrent Neural Networks	Self-Organizing Maps	Boltzmann Machines	Deep Reinforcement Learning
Sample 1	89.2	92.4	90.8	91.8	93.3	94.6
Sample 2	90.5	91.7	92.5	91.9	94.4	95.6
Sample 3	89.2	93.4	91.8	92.5	93.3	94.6
Sample 4	90.5	91.7	92.5	92.9	94.3	91.2
Sample 5	89.2	91.7	92.5	90.5	93.8	96.6
Sample 6	90.5	90.8	92.5	95.5	93.6	96.2

FIGURE 5.2   Accuracy rate analysis without using greedy search heuristics.

Similarly, the data are also fed to CNN, SOMs, RNNs, and Boltzmann Machines. But it is observed that the maximum level of accuracy is obtained on feeding the data to a deep learning reinforcement model. This model gives the highest accuracy of 96.2 with the lowest accuracy of 91.2. Even without the use of greedy search, this algorithm gives a fair amount of accuracy in predicting user behavior.

In Fig. 5.3, the user interaction data extracted are fed into some deep learning models, but in this case, the use of greedy search heuristic is made. As we have read before, every next sample fed to model contains more and more relevant information and attributes. And therefore it is observed that the classic neural network gave lowest efficiency of 89.8 which is 0.6 more than the lowest accuracy given by CNN without the use of greedy search. Even the highest accuracy rate in the classic neural network using greedy search is 1.9 greater than the one without greedy search.

A general trend of increased accuracy is seen across all the deep learning algorithms used with greedy search. Lastly, it shows a very high accuracy of 97.2 when used with a deep reinforcement learning model. Deep reinforcement learning is that category of machine learning where intelligent machines can learn from their actions which are similar to the ways humans learn. When paired with heuristics, the results have been very promising. Even the lowest accuracy with this model has gone only to 91.9.

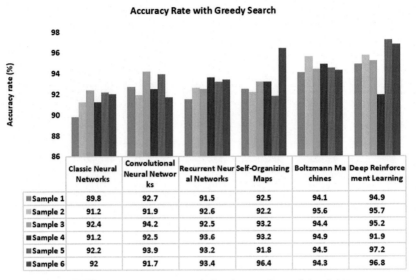

Accuracy Rate with Greedy Search

	Classic Neural Networks	Convolutional Neural Networks	Recurrent Neural Networks	Self-Organizing Maps	Boltzmann Machines	Deep Reinforcement Learning
▪ Sample 1	89.8	92.7	91.5	92.5	94.1	94.9
▪ Sample 2	91.2	91.9	92.6	92.2	95.6	95.7
▪ Sample 3	92.4	94.2	92.5	93.2	94.4	95.2
▪ Sample 4	91.2	92.5	93.6	93.2	94.9	91.9
▪ Sample 5	92.2	93.9	93.2	91.8	94.5	97.2
▪ Sample 6	92	91.7	93.4	96.4	94.3	96.8

FIGURE 5.3   Accuracy rate analysis using greedy search heuristics.

7. Conclusion

In order to reduce the computational complexity of user behavior prediction on the basis of users' online behavior, we found that incorporating a heuristic greedy algorithm helps us attain that aim. User behavior data extracted can be of nonlinear nature, thus giving multilayered deep learning architecture and upper hand in generating probabilistic decision support for better user experience. In this chapter, various deep learning models were discussed to perform cognitive computing on a dataset which consisted user's interaction with an e-commerce website for a duration of 6 months. The data are then categorized into six samples each consisting of different data size gathered weekly.

After choosing candidates set heuristically and making a choice of selection function, we apply a feasibility function. The output is used for constructing a solution function to get the desired precision of approximation of the solution. On performing detailed numerical analysis of the obtained data, we find that the deep learning algorithms using the greedy algorithm show an increase in the accuracy rate as compared to the accuracy rate analysis performed without greedy search. Thus concluding, taking a heuristic approach to deep learning predictive model may give better and improved accuracy and efficiency.

References

[1]   J. Crunk, M.M. North, Decision support system and AI technologies in aid of information based marketing, Int. Manag. Rev. 3 (2007) 61−86.

[2] G. Phillips-Wren, L. Jain, Artificial intelligence for decision making, in: B. Gabrys, R.J. Howlett, L.C. Jain (Eds.), Knowledge-Based Intelligent Information and Engineering Systems, Lecture Notes in Computer Science, vol. 4252, Springer, Berlin, Heidelberg, 2006, pp. 531–536.

[3] P.K. Mallick, S. Mishra, G.S. Chae, Digital media news categorization using Bernoulli document model for web content convergence, Personal Ubiquitous Comput. (2020), https://doi.org/10.1007/s00779-020-01461-9.

[4] S. Mishra, H.K. Tripathy, P.K. Mallick, A.K. Bhoi, P. Barsocchi, EAGA-MLP—an enhanced and adaptive hybrid classification model for diabetes diagnosis, Sensors 20 (14) (2020) 4036.

[5] J.B. Kim, P. Albuquerque, B.J. Bronnenberg, Online demand under limited consumer search, Market. Sci. 29 (6) (2010) 1001–1023.

[6] S. Mishra, P.K. Mallick, H.K. Tripathy, A.K. Bhoi, A. González-Briones, Performance evaluation of a proposed machine learning model for chronic disease datasets using an integrated attribute evaluator and an improved decision tree classifier, Appl. Sci. 10 (22) (2020) 8137.

[7] M. Zhang, G. Chen, Q. Wei, Discovering consumers' purchase intentions based on mobile search behaviors, Adv. Intell. Syst. & Comput. 400 (2015) 15–28.

[8] S. Mishra, P.K. Mallick, H.K. Tripathy, L. Jena, G.-S. Chae, Stacked KNN with hard voting predictive approach to assist hiring process in IT organizations, Int. J. Electr. Eng. Educ. (February 2021), https://doi.org/10.1177/0020720921989015.

[9] A. Yilmaz, O. Javed, M. Shah, Object tracking: a survey, ACM Comput. Surv. 38 (2006) 13, https://doi.org/10.1145/1177352.1177355.

[10] L. Chen, J. Hoey, C.D. Nugent, D.J. Cook, Z. Yu, Sensor-based activity recognition, IEEE Trans. Syst. Man Cybern. Part C (Appl. Rev.) 42 (2012) 790–808.

[11] L. Bao, S.S. Intille, Activity recognition from user-annotated acceleration data, in: Proceedings of the International Conference on Pervasive Computing, Linz and Vienna, Austria, 21–23 April 2004, Springer, Berlin/Heidelberg, Germany, 2004, pp. 1–17.

[12] N. Oliver, A. Garg, E. Horvitz, Layered representations for learning and inferring office activity from multiple sensory channels, Comput. Vis. Image Understand. 96 (2004) 163–180.

[13] T. Van Kasteren, A. Noulas, G. Englebienne, B. Kröse, Accurate activity recognition in a home setting, in: Proceedings of the 10th International Conference on Ubiquitous Computing, Seoul, Korea, 21–24 September 2008, ACM, New York, NY, USA, 2008, pp. 1–9.

[14] I. Fatima, M. Fahim, Y.K. Lee, S. Lee, A unified framework for activity recognition-based behavior analysis and action prediction in smart homes, Sensors 13 (2013) 2682–2699.

[15] F.J. Ordóñez, J.A. Iglesias, P. De Toledo, A. Ledezma, A. Sanchis, Online activity recognition using evolving classifiers, Expert Syst. Appl. 40 (2013) 1248–1255.

[16] P. Rashidi, D.J. Cook, COM: a method for mining and monitoring human activity patterns in home-based health monitoring systems, ACM Trans. Intell. Syst. Technol. (TIST) 4 (2013) 64, https://doi.org/10.1145/2508037.2508045.

[17] L. Chen, C.D. Nugent, M. Mulvenna, D. Finlay, X. Hong, M. Poland, A logical framework for behaviour reasoning and assistance in a smart home, Int. J. Assist. Robot. Mechatron. 9 (2008) 20–34.

[18] D. Riboni, C. Bettini, COSAR: hybrid reasoning for context-aware activity recognition, Personal Ubiquitous Comput. 15 (2011) 271–289.

[19] L. Chen, C.D. Nugent, H. Wang, A knowledge-driven approach to activity recognition in smart homes, IEEE Trans. Knowl. Data Eng. 24 (2012) 961−974.

[20] H. Aloulou, M. Mokhtari, T. Tiberghien, J. Biswas, P. Yap, An adaptable and flexible framework for assistive living of cognitively impaired people, IEEE J. Biomed. Health Inform. 18 (2014) 353−360.

[21] S.K. Das, D.J. Cook, A. Battacharya, E.O. Heierman, T.Y. Lin, The role of prediction algorithms in the MavHome smart home architecture, IEEE Wirel. Commun. 9 (2002) 77−84.

[22] D.J. Cook, M. Youngblood, E.O. Heierman, K. Gopalratnam, S. Rao, A. Litvin, F. Khawaja, MavHome: an agent-based smart home, in: Proceedings of the First IEEE International Conference on Pervasive Computing and Communications, (PerCom 2003), Fort Worth, TX, USA, 26 March 2003, IEEE, Piscataway, NJ, USA, 2003, pp. 521−524.

[23] D.J. Cook, S.K. Das, How smart are our environments? An updated look at the state of the art, Pervasive Mob. Comput. 3 (2007) 53−73.

[24] C.P. Kurian, S. Kuriachan, J. Bhat, R.S. Aithal, An adaptive neuro-fuzzy model for the prediction and control of light in integrated lighting schemes, Light. Res. Technol. 37 (2005) 343−351.

[25] N. Morel, M. Bauer, M. El-Khoury, J. Krauss, Neurobat, a predictive and adaptive heating control system using artificial neural networks, Int. J. Sol. Energy 21 (2001) 161−201.

[26] A.I. Dounis, C. Caraiscos, Advanced control systems engineering for energy and comfort management in a building environment—a review, Renew. Sustain. Energy Rev. 13 (2009) 1246−1261.

[27] S.N. Roy, S. Mishra, S.M. Yusof, Emergence of Drug Discovery in Machine Learning, vol. 119, Technical Advancements of Machine Learning in Healthcare, 2021.

[28] C. Ray, H.K. Tripathy, S. Mishra, Assessment of autistic disorder using machine learning approach, in: Proceedings of the International Conference on Intelligent Computing and Communication, Hyderabad, India, 9−11 January 2019, pp. 209−219.

[29] P. Chaudhury, S. Mishra, H.K. Tripathy, B. Kishore, Enhancing the capabilities of student result prediction system, in: Proceedings of the 2nd International Conference on Information and Communication Technology for Competitive Strategies, Uidapur, India, 4−5 March 2016, pp. 1−6, 88.

Chapter 6

Inertia weight strategies for task allocation using metaheuristic algorithm

Arabinda Pradhan, Sukant Kishoro Bisoy
Department of Computer Science and Engineering, C.V. Raman Global University, Bhubaneswar, Odisha, India

1. Introduction

Nowadays, cloud computing has become a well-known business processing paradigm. It can offer different measuring services to clients with virtual machine (VM) as the resource unit such as storage, applications, networks, and servers over the Internet [1]. Users or clients can get these resources on request according to the Service Level Agreement and user pay for which they expend the services for explicit span of time [2]. In cloud environment, each data center consists of number of hosts and each physical host can stack at least one VM with the goal that clients can run the applications freely [3]. When the number of requests increases at a particular time, then it becomes difficult to manage enire request with a minimum execution time and maitain quality of service. Work of Cloud Service Provider (CSP) is to allocate the task into suitable VM so that no machine is overloaded and manage these resources appropriately to keep the load as balanced in between these resources. Resources are handled by the incoming task that depends on the property of resource information, task information, and proper scheduling algorithm [4]. Therefore, a better load balancing and task scheduling technique is required to avoid the allocation problem in cloud system.

Balancing the load is a challenging concept in cloud computing [5]. It is hard work to arrange these resources in the cloud because the task load may change from time to time according to client necessity in the cloud [6]. Load balancing is a process to distribute the request between different machines through task scheduling so that numbers of jobs are executing with less time (reduce makespan) and monitors the performance of VMs [7,8].

Cognitive Big Data Intelligence with a Metaheuristic Approach
https://doi.org/10.1016/B978-0-323-85117-6.00004-2

131

In task scheduling, the virtualized resources can be assigned to the specific assignment for a particular time period. Due to increase of number of task as well as its length the task scheduling problem becomes an NP-hard issue. It is difficult to establish the mappings between task and resources. Hence, we need a proficient technique which can better deal with the task and tackle NP-hard issue. For such issue, many researchers focused their researching work on heuristic, metaheuristic, and hybrid scheduling strategies. Ref [9] shows that most metaheuristics accomplish preferred outcomes over conventional heuristics. In current situations, metaheuristic calculations have increased gigantic fame because of their viability in tackling huge computational and complex issues. Metaheuristic calculations are issue free. Some of the helpful properties of metaheuristic algorithms are as follows:

(i) These algorithms can easily handle dynamic behavior of system.
(ii) Solve NP Complete problems.
(iii) Investigate the search space to discover ideal arrangements.

A number of metaheuristic algorithms are available, such as Artificial Bee Colony, Particle Swarm Optimization (PSO), Ant Colony Optimization (ACO), Differential Evolution Algorithm, Genetic Algorithm, Simulated Annealing, Bacteria Foraging Optimization, BAT optimization, Cat optimization, Firefly optimization, Cuckoo search, and so on. Above algorithms are used to deal with the optimization issue. PSO is a famous metaheuristic technique to solve optimization issue. PSO is appropriate for dynamic task scheduling but fewer changes are required in its parameter. PSO has a strong worldwide searching capability toward the start of the run and a nearby pursuit close to the furthest limit of the run. Therefore, it has been generally utilized in different applications and has made incredible progress. But when the load is high, dynamic, and heterogeneous, then most particles unite to a nearby outrageous point in searching region. Therefore, the biggest drawback of PSO algorithm is easily trapped into local optimal solution. Due to this reason, we focused modified PSO algorithm [10] that progressively acts as indicated by the load and nature in the cloud. PSO has number of diverse controlled parameters such as inertia weight, velocity, position, coefficient of acceleration, and so on. But we have focused inertia weight parameter to control the deviation of particles movement from whole population. In [11] proposed the idea of inertia weight, through which large values of inertia weight show worldwide best arrangement and smaller values show neighborhood best. In this chapter, we focused 10 different inertia weights that are proposed by different researchers and compare their result to found the best inertia weight [6,12].

The rest of this chapter is mentioned as follows: Section 2 shows the related work and Section 3 shows Standard PSO algorithm. Section 4 shows model of task allocation in VM. Section 5 depicts inertia weight strategy. Section 6 shows performance evaluation and final Section 7 shows conclusion and future work.

2. Related work

In ongoing time, a number of VM allocation, load balancing, and task scheduling approaches have been proposed to diminish makespan time and balance the load among different machine. Researchers proposed various heuristic, metaheuristic, and hybrid scheduling strategies for the cloud environment to solve the above issue. Here, we talked about a portion of various heuristic, metaheuristic, and hybrid algorithms. Table 6.1 shows some advantages and limitations of task and load balancing scheduling.

TABLE 6.1 Load balancing and task scheduling algorithm with their merits and drawbacks.

Article	Algorithm	Scheduling	Merit	Drawback
[1]	PTS	Metaheuristic	Overall execution time is minimized.	Less scalability, network latency, and task transfer time are not flexible.
[2]	PSO-SC	Heuristic	Reduces completion time of tasks and cost.	Not suitable in high dimension.
[4]	DLBA	Heuristic	Increases resource utilization, decreases makespan, and provides elasticity.	Does not consider priority of task, deadline of task.
[5]	QMPSO	Hybrid	Maximizes the throughput of VMs and maintains the load between VMs.	Migration is costly and time consuming.
[6]	PSO-ALBA	Heuristic	Reduces makespan, increases throughput, and balances the load of virtual machine.	Significance degree of the metrics is not used.
[8]	MR-PSO	Hybrid	Better host utilization and decreases the energy consumption.	Less scalability.
[13]	L-PSO	Metaheuristic	Reduces makespan, cost, and increasing resource utilization.	Load is not balanced between VMs.
[14]	M-PSO	Metaheuristic	Reduces execution and transmission cost.	Does not balance between local and global search.

Continued

TABLE 6.1 Load balancing and task scheduling algorithm with their merits and drawbacks.—cont'd

Article	Algorithm	Scheduling	Merit	Drawback
[15]	K–PSO	Metaheuristic	Minimizes execution time and increases resource utilization.	Cost factors and bandwidth are ignored.
[16]	RTPSO-B	Hybrid	Reduces both makespan and cost and also increases resource utilization.	Complexity issue.
[17]	PSOBTS	Metaheuristic	Reduces makespan and increases the resource utilization.	High response time.
[18]	PSOTS	Metaheuristic	Increases of resource utilization and decrease makespan.	Not satisfies all QoS criteria.
[19]	CPSO	Hybrid	Reduces the makespan and cost.	Requires more focus on deadline constraint.
[20]	IPSO	Metaheuristic	Reduces makespan and increases resource utilization.	Slow convergence rate.
[21]	Hybrid algorithm	Hybrid	Reduces makespan and energy consumption.	Higher possibility of overloaded and underutilization of resources.
[22]	IWRR	Heuristic	Improves response time and resource utilization ratio.	Algorithm failed to balance the workload among the resources.
[23]	PSO-BOOST	Metaheuristic	Balances the workload among all the VMs with elastic resource provisioning and reduces makespan.	Does not consider QoS parameters like reliability, availability, etc.
[24]	Hybrid	Hybrid	Reduces makespan, cost, and increases the utilization of VMs.	Time consuming and complex.
[25]	HLBZID	Heuristic	Optimizes completion time and balances the load.	More energy consumed.

Different task scheduling mechanisms are proposed by Refs. [1,2,6,13−21]. Various load balancing algorithms are developed by Refs. [4,5,8,22−25].

Ref. [1] proposed PTS algorithm to compute the rent time among the tasks in two different groups (i.e., G1 to G2) and minimize the layover time. Ref. [2] proposed Service Cost Optimization dependent on PSO algorithm that decreases completion time of task and allocates it based on the computing power of the VMs. Ref. [6] proposed PSO-ALBA task scheduling algorithm to minimize the makespan and maximize the throughput. By using adaptive load balancing approach, it balances the load among VMs. Ref. [13] proposed Logarithm-PSO (L-PSO) task scheduling algorithm, which is focused logarithm decreasing inertia weight (LOGDIW) strategy to diminish makespan and increase the convergence rate. Ref. [14] proposed M-PSO task scheduling approach to deal with minimum transmission and execution cost of the controller by taking modified inertia weight (MIW) method. Ref. [15] proposed improved Kubernetes-based PSO that shows faster convergence rate and improved the resource utilization also minimize run time of all executing tasks by applying nonlinear inertia weight (NLIW) method. Ref. [16] proposed a hybrid algorithm named as ranging and tuning function−based PSO with bat algorithm (RTPSO-B) which is used to avoid the scheduling issues in cloud computing environment. It improves resource utilization and reduces both makespan and cost by applying range and tuning function inertia weight (RTFIW) method. Ref. [17] proposed PSO-based task scheduling (PSOBTS) mechanism to reduce 30% in makespan and expand the asset use by 20% by applying global−local best inertia weight (GLBIW) method. Ref. [18] introduced PSO-based method that enhanced the efficiency of the PSO standard method using the concept of load balancing technique. Ref. [19] proposed hybrid algorithm known as Cuckoo Search and PSO algorithm to decrease both cost and makespan value. Ref. [20] has introduced IPSO algorithm allocating huge number of tasks in cloud computing environment, achieved by clustering approach. After receiving the most desirable solution of every cluster, the algorithm gets final allocation map. Ref. [21] proposed Hybrid algorithm combining both ACO and cuckoo search algorithm to optimize energy and makespan time.

Ref. [4] proposed DLB algorithm to reduce makespan time of tasks and keeping balance the load among VMs by using task migration approach instead of VM migration approach. Ref. [5] proposed QMPSO algorithm which combines both modified PSO and improved Q-learning algorithm. This algorithm is used to increase the machine performance and maximize the throughput of VMs. Ref. [8] proposed Multiple Regression PSO to detect resource utilization and decrease energy consumption. Ref. [22] proposed Improved Weighted Round Robin algorithm to minimize completion time of task and deduct any idle time of the participating VMs. Ref. [23] has introduced PSO-BOOST algorithm that improved various performance metrics such as processing time, processing cost, and throughput. Ref. [24] proposed

HDD-PLB framework to enhance the use of VMs with uniform load distribution and reduce makespan and cost. Ref. [25] proposed HLBZID algorithm to optimize completion time and earliest finish time by considering task transfer time to handle load balancing.

3. Standard PSO

PSO is affected by social conduct of creatures like flock of birds discovering nourishment source, which is an intelligent evolutionary computing technology. It was developed by Kennedy and Eberhart [26]. The fundamental thought of PSO is to look through the ideal arrangement through the collaboration and data sharing among particles in a gathering which can be considered as a population. In this technique, particles are flown to search the food in hyperdimensional search space. The position of every particle is changed by its own comprehension and its neighbors. Let $P_i(k)$ indicate the position of particle ith task, at iteration k. The position of $P_i(k)$ is including a speed $V_i(k+1)$ to it that is shown in Eq. (6.1). Velocity of each particle shows socially exchanged information as shown in Eq. (6.2). Table 6.2 shows the term and meaning of PSO algorithm.

$$P_i(k+1) = P_i(k) + V_i(k+1) \ldots \tag{6.1}$$

$$V_i(k+1) = \omega V_i(k) + c_1 r_1(P_{best} - P_i(k)) + c_2 r_2(G_{best} - P_i(k)) \ldots \tag{6.2}$$

PSO begins work after the initialization of the task and VM. It finds the suitable VM, then assigned the task to it, and calculated the total time of

TABLE 6.2 Denote term and meaning of PSO.

Terms	Meaning
i	Particle
m	Dimension
t	Iteration
ω	Inertia weight factor
P_{best}	Personal best
G_{best}	Global best
P	Position
V	Velocity
c_1 and c_2	Cognitive and social learning factor
r_1 and r_2	Random number

Pseudocode of SPSO Algorithm
1. Initialize number of tasks and VMs.
2. Initialize population of PSO with p number of tasks allocated to q number of VM, inertia weight, random number andconstant acceleration factors.
3. Initialize position and velocity of each particle.
4. Set iteration (k) =1.
5. Compute fitness (F) value as P_{best} of each particle.

6. Compare current F value with P_{best}
    6.1.If current F value is better than P_{best} then select F value
    6.2. Otherwise, P_{best} is set as F value.

7. Compute G_{best} from all P_{best}.
8. Update position and velocity.
9. Then k= k + 1.

10. Set G_{best} is our optimum result
    10.1.   If no, then go to step 3.
    10.2.   Otherwise, compute all iteration.

11. stop

FIGURE 6.1   Pseudocode of SPSO algorithm.

execution as well as utilization of resource [27]. In this procedure, each particle acts like a solution at their individual position. Then, the velocity of particle is changed and the position of every particle is recomputed. At that point, we find a new position of every particle. This procedure proceeds until the advanced optimized solution is not found. Fig. 6.1 shows the pseudocode of SPSO algorithm.

4. Model of task allocation in VM

Fig. 6.2 shows the model structure of task allocation in VM. This model gives the basic idea for allocating huge amount of task in a suitable VM by applying different PSO-based metaheuristic approach. In this model, numbers of tasks are going into CSP getting their services. By applying different PSO metaheuristic algorithms, it can be found that available VM is used for assigning the incoming request with minimum allocating time and provides the services with minimum time. Therefore, it can reduce makespan as well as balance the load.

Fig. 6.3 shows if we achieve the optimal result in cloud scenario, then we gather all required information about incoming tasks and VMs such as task length or size, bandwidth capacity, number of processor and processing speed, etc. The whole model is partitioned into different buffer which contains the various sorts of task and resource information so that makespan and resource allocation strategies can be optimized.

5. Inertia weight strategy

Global search and local search are the important stages in every population-based swarm intelligence algorithm. Keeping up a balance between these two stages permits the calculation to locate the best situation in a sensible

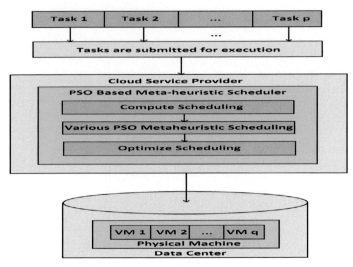

FIGURE 6.2   Model of PSO-based metaheuristic algorithm.

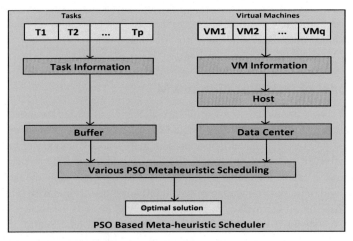

FIGURE 6.3   Collect necessary information.

measure of time. Also, these two stages permit the calculation to investigate more regions in the search space and get the global optima. In PSO algorithm, there is a single parameter named as inertia weight (ω) to achieve best optimum result. The inertia weight is used to alter the impact of the past speed on the current speed and to adjust among worldwide and nearby investigation capacities of the particle. As huge estimation of inertia weight parameter, it shows better global search capacity and the output is taken as final result in the whole solution. Similarly, when its value is little, then PSO has better local search capacity. In Standard PSO [26], no inertia weight is defined. It was first introducing by Shi and Eberhart [11] and suggested that an enormous inertia weight encourages a worldwide pursuit, while a little inertia weight encourages a neighborhood search. In traditional PSO, toward the finish of an improvement technique, the diversity of the population is small and the velocities of particles bit by bit diminished over the iteration. It shows the slow convergence rate and local optimum problem due to lack of diversity in population. Then different researcher has proposed number of inertia weight value to overcome this issue in PSO. But in this chapter, we focused on 10 different inertia weights such as Constant Inertia Weight, Random Inertia Weight, Chaotic Random Inertia Weight, Chaotic Inertia Weight, Linearly decreasing Inertia Weight, GLBIW, LOGDIW, MIW, RTFIW, and NLIW. Tables 6.3 and 6.4 represent the value and notation of inertia weight.

TABLE 6.3 Different inertia weight.

Name	Value	Eqs. No.	Refs.
Constant inertia weight	$\omega = 0.7$	(3)	[11]
Modified inertia weight	$\omega = \left(\dfrac{\alpha \times k_{max}}{k^{\gamma} + k_{max}} \right) + \beta$	(4)	[14]
Nonlinear inertia weight	$\omega(k+1) = w_{min} + (w_{max} - w_{min}) \exp\left[-\dfrac{\theta \times k^2}{k^2_{max}} \right]$	(5)	[15]
Range and tuning function inertia weight	$\omega = w_{min} + \alpha_t \beta_t (w_{max} - w_{min})$	(6)	[16]
Random inertia weight	$\omega = 0.5 + \dfrac{rand()}{2}$	(7)	[28]
Chaotic random inertia weight	$\omega = 0.5 \times rand() + 0.5 \times z$	(8)	[29]
Chaotic inertia weight	$\omega = (\omega_{max} - \omega_{min}) \times \dfrac{k_{max} - k}{k_{max}} + \omega_{min} \times z$	(9)	[29]
Linearly decreasing inertia weight	$\omega = w_{max} - \dfrac{w_{max} - w_{min}}{k_{max}} \times k$	(10)	[30]
Global–local best inertia weight	$\omega = \left(1.1 - \dfrac{G_{best_i}}{P_{best_i}} \right)$	(11)	[31]
Logarithm decreasing inertia weight	$\omega = w_{max} + (w_{min} - w_{max}) \times \log_{10}\left(a + \dfrac{10k}{k_{max}} \right)$	(10)	[32]

TABLE 6.4 Denote notation and meaning.

Notation	Meaning
ω	Inertia weight
rand()	Random function
z	Random number in between [0,1]
ω_{max}	Maximum inertia weight values having 0.9
ω_{min}	Minimum inertia weight values having 0.4
k_{max}	Most extreme number of iterations
k	Current number of iterations
G_{best_i}	Global best position of particle i
P_{best_i}	Local best position of particle i
a and β	Constant parameter.
α_t	Range function at time t
β_t	Tuning function at time t
γ	Acceleration factor
θ	Control factor having value 3.4

6. Performance evaluation

In this chapter, we evaluated and compared different PSO-based algorithms. The simulation is executed on Eclipse Java Programming Environment and CloudSim toolkit. We have used our PC having the following configurations: Intel (R) Core (TM) i3-7100 Processor (2.40 GHz) and 4 GB of RAM. The operating system was 64 bits with Windows 10. The parameters used for the simulation is shown below.

6.1 Experiment setup

The inspiration driving this work is to find suitable inertia weight parameter and diminish the makespan in dynamic environment. For the test, we have considered the nonpreemptive tasks which are free in nature as shown in Table 6.5. Tasks are allocated number of heterogeneous VMs in a datacenter as appeared in Table 6.6. Table 6.7 shows various properties of PSO algorithm. In this section, we compared various inertia weight strategies and compare the makespan in between three PSO techniques such as RTPSO-B, PSOBTS, and L-PSO. For simulation, we take two different testing scales: (1) three VMs with 10–50 tasks and (2) five VMs with 100–500 tasks.

TABLE 6.5 Task properties.

Task range	10–500
Length	1000–6000
File size	300

TABLE 6.6 VM properties.

VM range	3–5
Processing speed (MIPS)	250–300
Memory	256–512
Processing unit (CPU)	1–5
Bandwidth	1000
VMM	XEN

TABLE 6.7 PSO properties.

Number of particle	30
Maximum iteration	1000
$c_1 \& c_2$	2
$r_1 \& r_2$	[0,1]
ω	[0,1]
Stopping criterion	k_{max}

6.2 Result and analysis

Simulation results are shown in Figs. 6.4–6.7. Figs. 6.4 and 6.5 compare the fitness of different inertia weight strategy by taking the tasks range from 10 to 100. The convergence of all inertia weight is almost similar. But the fitness of the NLIW is marginally better than other strategy. It is on the grounds that the NLIW updates the current best answer for picking the VMs with the minimum allocation time and reducing execution time to execute tasks.

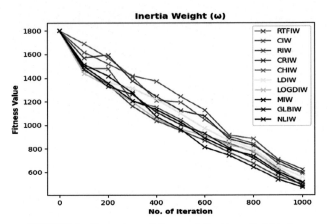

FIGURE 6.4 Comparison of fitness and iteration with 10 tasks.

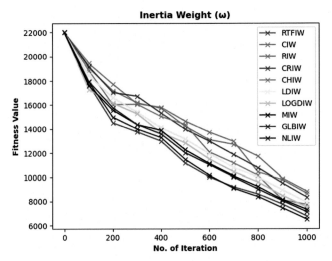

FIGURE 6.5 Comparison of fitness and iteration with 100 tasks.

Fig. 6.6 is obtained for the task scheduling with three VMs having 10 to 50 tasks. From this figure, it is clear that RTPSO-B technique takes less makespan than other metaheuristic PSO algorithms and is shown in Table 6.8.

Fig. 6.7 shows the outcomes got for the task scheduling with five VMs and 100−500 tasks. In this figure, it is clear that RTPSO-B technique also takes less makespan than other metaheuristic PSO algorithms and is shown in Table 6.9.

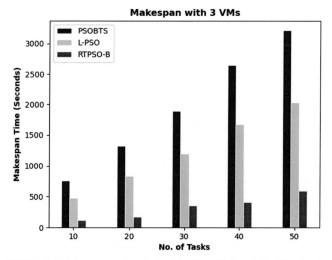

FIGURE 6.6 Makespan value obtained for three VMs and 10−50 task sets.

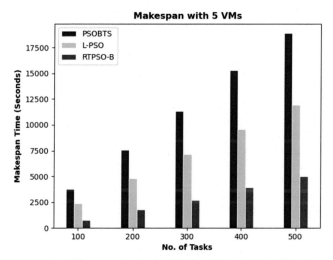

FIGURE 6.7 Makespan value obtained for five VMs and 100−500 task sets.

TABLE 6.8 Minimum and maximum makespan for different scheduling algorithms for three VMs.

Scheduling algorithm	Minimum makespan	Maximum makespan
RTPSO-B	119.24	593.26
PSOBTS	757.3	3214.3
L-PSO	477.42	2028.41

TABLE 6.9 Minimum and maximum makespan for different scheduling algorithms for five VMs.

Scheduling algorithm	Minimum makespan	Maximum makespan
RTPSO-B	748.29	5,011.71
PSOBTS	3,781.4	18,901.4
L-PSO	2.389.65	11,952.09

7. Conclusion and future work

This chapter presents impact of inertia weight in PSO algorithm. A set of three most popular PSO-based optimization algorithms and a single criterion for comparison have been considered. As compared to other PSO-based algorithms, NLIW has a faster convergence rate and a better search capability during the period of iteration and RTPSO-B technique is used to reduce makespan that improves the system performance. In this approach, a huge amount of task can be handled by suitable VM to minimize the allocation time, execution time, waiting time and balance the load among all VMs. In future, a technique can be proposed which can improve the quality of service parameters.

References

[1] S.K. Panda, S.S. Nanda, S.K. Bhoi, A pair-based task scheduling algorithm for cloud computing environment, J. King Saud Uni. Comput. & Inf. Sci. (2018) 1−10, https://doi.org/10.1016/j.jksuci.2018.10.001. Elsevier.

[2] S. Xue, W. Shi, X. Xu, A heuristic scheduling algorithm based on PSO in the cloud computing environment, Int. J. u- and e- Serv. Sci. & Technol. IJUNESST 9 (1) (2016) 349−362, https://doi.org/10.14257/ijunesst.2016.9.1.36.

[3] Z. Liu, X. Wang, A PSO-Based Algorithm for Load Balancing in Virtual Machines of Cloud Computing Environment, ICS. Part I, LNCS 7331, Springer, 2012, pp. 142−147.

[4] S. Mishra, H.K. Tripathy, P.K. Mallick, A.K. Bhoi, P. Barsocchi, EAGA-MLP—an enhanced and adaptive hybrid classification model for diabetes diagnosis, Sensors 20 (14) (2020) 4036.

[5] U.K. Jena, P.K. Das, M.R. Kabat, Hybridization of meta-heuristic algorithm for load balancing in cloud computing environment, J. King Saud Univ. Comput. & Inf. Sci. (2020) 1−11, https://doi.org/10.1016/j.jksuci.2020.01.012. Elsevier.

[6] S. Mishra, P.K. Mallick, H.K. Tripathy, A.K. Bhoi, A. González-Briones, Performance evaluation of a proposed machine learning model for chronic disease datasets using an integrated attribute evaluator and an improved decision tree classifier, Appl. Sci. 10 (22) (2020) 8137.

[7] M. Kumar, S.C. Sharma, Deadline constrained based dynamic load balancing algorithm with elasticity in cloud environment, Comput. & Electr. Eng. (2017) 1−17. Elsevier.

[8] A.S.A. Alhammadi, V. Vasanthi, Multiple Regression Particle Swarm Optimization for Host Overload and Under-load Detection, Test Engineering and Management, 2020, pp. 10253−10261. ISSN: 0193-4120.

[9] M. Xu, W. Tian, R. Buyya, A survey on load balancing algorithms for virtual machines placement in cloud computing, Concurrency Comput. Pract. Ex. 29 (12) (2017) 1−16, e4123.

[10] P.K. Mallick, S. Mishra, G.S. Chae, Digital media news categorization using Bernoulli document model for web content convergence, Personal Ubiquitous Comput. (2020), https://doi.org/10.1007/s00779-020-01461-9.

[11] Y. Shi, R. Eberhart, A modified particle swarm optimizer, in: Evolutionary Computation Proceedings, 1998. IEEE World Congresson Computational Intelligence. IEEE International Conference, 1998, pp. 69−73.

[12] N. Kumar, S.K. Sharma, Inertia weight controlled PSO for task scheduling in cloud computing, Int. Conf. Comput. Power & Commun. Technol. (2018) 155−160.

[13] X. Huang, C. Li, H. Chen, D. An, Task scheduling in cloud computing using particle swarm optimization with time varying inertia weight strategies, Clust. Comput. (2019), https://doi.org/10.1007/s10586-019-02983-5. Springer.

[14] Z. Zhou, J. Chang, Z. Hu, J. Yu, F. Li, A modified PSO algorithm for task scheduling optimization incloud computing, Concurr. Comput. Pract. Exper. (2018) 1−11. Wiley.

[15] B. Liu, J. Li, W. Lin, W. Bai, P. Li, Q. Gao, K-PSO: An Improved PSO-Based Container Schedulingalgorithm for Big Data Applications, Wiley, 2020, pp. 1−16.

[16] R. Valarmathi, T. Sheela, Ranging and tuning based particle swarm optimization with bat algorithm for task scheduling in cloud computing, Clust. Comput. (2017), https://doi.org/10.1007/s10586-017-1534-8.

[17] M. Agarwal, G.M.S. Srivastava, A PSO algorithm based task scheduling in cloud computing, Int. J. Appl. Metaheuristic Comput. (IJAMC) 10 (4) (2019) 1−17, https://doi.org/10.4018/IJAMC.2019100101.

[18] F. Ebadifard, S.M. Babamir, A PSO based task scheduling algorithm improved using a load balancing technique for the cloud computing environment, Concurr. Comput. Pract. Exper. (2017) 1−16, https://doi.org/10.1002/cpe.4368. Wiley.

[19] C. Ray, H.K. Tripathy, S. Mishra, Assessment of autistic disorder using machine learning approach, in: International Conference on Intelligent Computing and Communication, Springer, Singapore, June 2019, pp. 209−219.

[20] S.N. Roy, S. Mishra, S.M. Yusof, Emergence of drug discovery in machine learning, Tech. Adv. Mach. Learn. Healthc. 119 (2021).

[21] N. Moganarangan, R.G. Babukarthik, S. Bhuvaneswari, M.S.S. Basha, P. Dhavachelvan, A novel algorithm for reducing energy-consumption in cloud computing environment: web service computing approach, J. King Saud Univ. Comput. & Inf. Sci. (2014) 1−13, https://doi.org/10.1016/j.jksuci.2014.04.007. Elsevier.

[22] D.C. Devi, V.R. Uthariaraj, Load balancing in cloud computing environment using improved weighted round Robin algorithm for nonpreemptive dependent tasks, Hindawi Publishing Corporation, The Sci. Word J. 2016 (2016) 14. Article ID 3896065.

[23] M. Kumar, S.C. Sharma, PSO-based novel resource scheduling technique to improve QoS parameters in cloud computing, Neur. Comput. & Appl. (2019), https://doi.org/10.1007/s00521-019-04266-x. Springer.

[24] A. Kaur, B. Kaur, Load balancing optimization based on hybrid heuristic- metaheuristic techniques in cloud environment, J. King Saud Univ. Comput. & Inf. Sci. (2019) 1−12, https://doi.org/10.1016/jksuci.2019.02.010. Elsevier.

[25] L. Kong, J.P.B. Mapetu, Z. Chen, Heuristic load balancing based zero imbalance mechanism in cloud computing, J Grid Comput. (2019), https://doi.org/10.1007/s10723-019-09486-y. Springer.

[26] J. Kennedy, R.C. Eberhart, Particle swarm optimization, in: Proceedings of the IEEE International Conference on Neural Networks. Piscataway, NJ, USA, 1995, pp. 1942−1948.

[27] R. Goddu, K.R. Reddi, Swarm-inspired task scheduling strategy in cloud computing, innovative product design and intelligent manufacturing systems, Lectur. Notes Mech. Eng. (2020) 743−751, https://doi.org/10.1007/978-981-15-2696-1_71. Springer.

[28] R.C. Eberhart, Y. Shi, Tracking and optimizing dynamic systems with particle swarms, in: Evolutionary Computation, Proceedings of the Congress, vol. 1, 2002, pp. 94−100.

[29] Y. Feng, G.F. Teng, A.X. Wang, Y.M. Yao, Chaotic inertiaweight in particle swarm optimization, in: International Conference on Innovative Computing, Information and Control (ICICIC), 2007, 475−475.

[30] J. Xin, G. Chen, Y. Hai, A particle swarm optimizer with multistage linearly-decreasing inertia weight, Int. Conf. Comput. Sci. & Optimizat. 1 (2009) 505−508.

[31] S.M. Muthukumaraswamy, M.V.C. Rao, On the performance of the particle swarm optimization algorithm withvarious inertia weight variants for computing optimal control of a class of hybrid Systems, Hindawi Publishing Corporation, Discret. Dyn. Nat. & Soc. 2006 (2006) 1−17. Article ID 79295.

[32] Y.L. Gao, X.H. An, J.M. Liu, A particle swarm optimizationalgorithm with logarithm decreasing inertia weight and chaos mutation, Int. Conf. Comput. Intell. & Secur. 1 (2008) 61−65.

Chapter 7

Big data classification with IoT-based application for e-health care

Saumendra Kumar Mohapatra, Mihir Narayan Mohanty
ITER, Siksha 'O' Anusandhan (Deemed to be University), Bhubaneswar, Odisha, India

1. Introduction

Different facts and figures accessed and stored by computers are generally referred to as data. In one report, it was estimated that five exabytes of data were generated by humankind from the start of civilization until 2003. However, nowadays, five exabytes of data are produced every 2 days, and this amount is also accelerating daily. These data are of different types, such as human activity data, image and video data, multiple sensor-generated data, conversion data, and data generated through different Internet of Things (IoT)-enabled devices [1]. Processing and storing of these data is a challenging task in the current scenario, and research on large-scale data processing is growing constantly [2]. Big data has been considered to be a breakthrough technological development over a few years. However, there remains a constrained understanding of how its potential can be turned into real social and financial worth. Big data has increased the urgency of a leap forward for innovative advancements in scholarly and business networks. Big data in this way alludes to our capacity to utilize ever-expanding volumes of information [3,4].

The definition of big data can be derived from the dimension of data. A data set can is considered as "big data" if it satisfies the following three high-degree discrete dimensions: volume, velocity, and variety. Also, there are two other V dimensions, value and veracity, which have been recently added to the big data definition [5]. The definition of big data can be defined through the 5 V as follows:

- Velocity: data generation speed
- Volume: generated data size
- Variety: an assorted variety of various sorts of data

- Value: data worth
- Veracity: quality, precision, or reliability of the data.

Generally, these large data sets are available in two kinds of format: structured data and unstructured data. The data generated from machines or humans having a specific size, shape, and model are referred to as structured data. These data are defined by well-structured data types. Integer, float, and string-type data are examples of structured data stored in database columns. Data that do not have any specific structure, shape, or model are referred to as unstructured data. Different text files, social media posts, mobile phone data, media data, and log files are basic examples of unstructured data. Nowadays, all organizations produce huge amounts of data, and this is increasing constantly, and so it is essential to adopt different advanced technologies to manage these high volumes of data. In the field of data analysis, big data technology is a revolution. For obtaining important information and hidden patterns from large quantities of data, big data technology plays a significant role. This can be helpful for understanding different information more accurately. Organizations can collate their data and new opportunities can be identified. It can help organizations in securing more proficient operations, adopting smart business moves, and generating increased profit and customer satisfaction [6,7].

In a smart business system, big data plays an important role in identifying new opportunities. A number of organizations are adopting this technology to improve their business processes. This can help in boosting the business process, with minimum complexity in the operation. It also can increase business efficiency, which can help in increasing both profit and customer satisfaction. The following factors are the main ones behind the popularity of big data.

Reduced cost: This advanced data-processing technique is more cost-effective for handling a large quantity of data and can be useful for effective business processing.

Quick decision-making: Big data technology is a combination of high-power memory and the capability to analyze different types of data. These features help in making decisions much faster than was possible previously. Also, organizations can make smart decisions with the help of an analytical learning strategy.

New products and features: Big data technology can identify customers' needs and satisfaction levels. Some organizations also use this technology for creating new products that better meet customer requirements.

A basic structure of factors for adopting big data technology is presented in Fig. 7.1. Due to the aforementioned factors of the big data concept, numerous organizations are increasing their sale, operation, efficiency, customer service, and risk management Fig. 7.1.

FIGURE 7.1 Factors behind adopting big data technology.

Data are not just about discovering answers, they are the place where ideas start. Each huge organization faces multiple challenges in obtaining tremendous amounts of data and effectively utilizing them for business profitability. Data are put away into various frameworks and storehouses that make it difficult for them to get to that information and upgrade their daily activities with appropriate measures. Examination of this large amount of data by utilizing the intensity of the cloud can transform it into very useful bits of knowledge. Utilizing progressive diagnostic procedures for broad, differing informational collections enables transformation of the information into new experiences assisting in improving business forms alongside a dynamic system. These large information examination capacities assist in enabling everybody in an association to have better and more useful experiences to settle on information-driven choices. According to industry experts, academicians, and other entrepreneurs, big data has been acting as a great game-changer in many sectors in the last few years. Big data has been at the forefront of industry's thoughts for a long time. Also, the truth of the matter is that big data has spread out rapidly, and is spreading to almost all parts of the modern world. Huge data, on account of the advantages it presents the different enterprises with, is presently turning into a fundamental asset. Large data, on the other hand, is step-by-step replacing the more established out-of-date systems and is a major area of concern for those experts who are currently dealing with it. The purposes of big data applications include assisting organizations with making increasingly informed business choices by examining enormous volumes of information. It can integrate web server logs, Internet click stream information, online life substance and action reports, content from client messages, cell phone call subtleties, and machine information caught by different sensors. In Fig. 7.2, a framework for big data application in various sectors is presented.

Associations from various areas are putting resources into big data applications, for analyzing huge informational collections to reveal concealed examples, ambiguous relationships, advertising patterns, client tendencies, and other cooperative business information. The basic application areas of big data technology include retail organizations, the healthcare sector, finance, telecoms, automobiles, media and entertainment, e-commerce, and education.

The healthcare sector is a complex and coordinating organization of various departments in financial support, providing goods and procedures to treat patients with considerations of treatment, prevention, rehabilitation, and analysis The term healthcare big data refers to the assembly, dissection, and exploitation of customer, patient, physical, and clinical information that is too large or complex to be understood by conventional techniques for biomedical data processing and analysis.

FIGURE 7.2 Major application of big data analytics.

2. State of the art

The size of data has increased in numerous fields over the last 2 decades; hence, the term "big data" has been introduced. It has been generally foreseen that the size of data will continue to expand enormously for the foreseeable future, where tremendous amounts of information are continually being produced from a number of sources. The entirety of this information creates new opportunities. In this way, the term "big data" could be characterized as a quickly developing source of information from different areas that represents a test to mechanical associations and presents them with unpredictable scope for significant use, stockpiling, and examination issues. Research into big data is becoming increasingly popular and has a major role in the processing and analyzing of a large amount of data.

Due to the rise in population and constant urbanization, people in urban areas face numerous daily difficulties. To tackle these difficulties, governments and leaders have embraced smart city projects focusing on sustainable financial development and improved personal satisfaction. Data and communication technology is a key empowering innovation for smart city development which will also generate a huge amount of data. Finding important information and patterns from data is an advanced data analysis technology which will also help in introducing smart systems. From the literature, it can be observed that numerous works have been conducted using big data technology in smart city development.

A novel big data analytics-based smart city framework to provide the solutions to multiple data enable projects was introduced by the authors in Ref. [8]. In the initial stage of their work, they conducted a literature review of works related to the application of big data in smart city development. They then proposed a novel system to analyze different kinds of large data sets generated from various technologies installed in smart cities. The assessment of their proposed structure was conducted to analyze recent customer activities in different business organizations. Different administrative authorities are now planning to implement numerous smart city concepts in their urban areas and analyzing a massive amount of related data that will help in the maintenance and execution of different advanced concepts. Various novel smart innovations are currently used in urban communities to improve quality of life, transportation, vitality, and also water and energy supplies. This includes reducing expenses and asset utilization. One of the ongoing developments that has huge potential to upgrade smart city management is analyzing a large amount of related data. As digitization has become a main aspect of daily life, the diversity of information has led to the accumulation of a large amount of information, which can be used in different productive application fields. Convincing research and the use of vast amounts of data are key factors in achieving success in numerous commercial and administrative fields, including smart cities. A review of the application of big data in smart cities was discussed by the authors in Ref. [9]. In their review, smart cities and the application of big data were analyzed to examine the potential challenges and advantages of big data-enabled smart cities. In addition, it also strives to achieve the prerequisites that enable the use of big data applications for smart city governance. A big data-enabled novel background image analysis technique for urban surveillance systems was introduced in Ref. [10]. In their proposed automatic system, a computer was enabled for renewing an image with a new background at a time when there was no object in the image. Their proposed method was designed with simple and robust properties concerning changes in light conditions. Innovations increasingly help catch rich and abundant information on customer actions. To obtain better performance by using this advanced technology on multiple applications, another novel approach was discussed in Ref. [11] for organizing the data generated from smart systems. The recognition of uncommon traffic designs, including blockages, is a critical research issue in data analytics research. In Ref. [12], the authors presented a work that builds a novel system to avoid traffic issues in smart cities. Their proposed system detected road-blocking problems in smart cities by gathering the recorded data in urban areas. Connected machines and tools within the smart home create a great deal of information about customers and how they carry out their day-to-day activities. The IoT can help in developing a more advanced system that will help in the planning of daily activities. The application of big data on IoT-based data collected from smart homes was presented in Ref. [13]. In this system, fog nodes and cloud systems were considered to be data-driven and addressed different challenges of online and offline data processing and analysis. Smart agriculture is another development that emphasizes the use of data and communication modernization in substantive digital farms. Advanced innovations such as the IoT and cloud computing are needed to take advantage of this improvement and may help to solve the problems in various fields. This was combined with the miracle of big data, with a wide variety and wealth of information, which can be dynamically captured, analyzed, and used. Some authors have also proposed that big data will be used for major changes to the work and power relationships of different participants in the current food production network system [14].

To extend the business strategy, the analysis of data is an important asset. It can be useful for analyzing and further processing the data generated from different sectors. An overview of big data technology in the manufacturing sector was given in Ref. [15] using the IoT. Also, the authors discussed some challenges and necessities of big data technology for manufacturing industries. Due to the prevalence of the Internet and the focus of Web 2.0 progress, the analysis of large amounts of information has recently developed into an important research field. Furthermore, the rise and acceptance of web-based social media applications have brought about a wide range of opportunities and challenges to scientists and researchers working in this area. This vast volume of produced information, known as "big data," has become increasingly important. A review of the role of big data for social media data was discussed by the authors in Ref. [16] and was classified based on different useful aspects. Big data is progressively turning into a significant hierarchical endeavor to deal with all sizes of business enterprises. It is a framework or stage for new pending endeavors, which provides more opportunities to acquire, collate, and research a large amount of information created from different sources, thus gaining an advantage [17]. The fast predominance and potential effect of big data analysis have created a great deal of enthusiasm among various experts [18]. With the rapid expansion of the analysis of monetary activity, a great deal of financial information is being collected. Although this information provides an open door for currency surveys, its low quality, high dimensionality, and large quantity have brought about great difficulties for the effective survey of massive amounts of financial information.

3. Big data in health care

In the present era of smartphones and wearable gadgets, huge amounts of patient well-being information records framed within big data are being sent to enormous databases where they can be accessed by various entities including specialists, parents and other guardians, and patients. In Fig. 7.3, the application of big data in the healthcare domain is displayed. The aim of this work is to survey the use of big data in the human services field and the related results. Big data is for the most part described by the volume, speed, assortment, and veracity of complex information. Numerous emergency clinics examine huge amounts of information from different sources, including health

FIGURE 7.3 Big data applications in the healthcare sector.

records, to accomplish a significant improvement in the services offered. The investigation of big data in medical services can enable an improvement in care combined with significant cost savings. Simultaneous difficulties to be addressed include the availability, protection, security, ease of use, usage costs, transportability, interoperability, and normalization of data. To sum this up, utilizing effective and streamlined investigation for big data sources will enable rapid and precise conclusions, suitable treatments, reduced expenses, and generally improved medical services quality [8].

Nowadays, the healthcare sector is one of the leading areas adopting advanced technologies in different units, which is causing a huge increase in data generation. A proper analysis of such massive amounts of biomedical data is required for an effective hospital management system. Currently, the main focus of biomedical research has been shifted from data generation to knowledge discovery, which is particularly true for biomedical data mining. Analysis of such data types has proved to be a major challenge as these data are complex, unstructured, and enormous. The application of data mining in biomedical data analysis will be very helpful for both physicians and patients as it results in early detection and diagnosis, drug discovery, and clinical decision-making with minimum manpower. Data mining-based disease classification can also be an encouraging approach for doctors and will be a constructive approach for medical personnel. Classification techniques in the area of data mining and machine learning help to diagnose disease. It is still an ongoing research field aiming for further accuracy and reduced time. Researchers are trying to develop a model that can accurately classify disease with minimum errors and reduced computational complexity.

Data mining is a process of knowledge discovery in databases (KDD) where useful, valid, understandable, and novel patterns can be discovered from the high volume of data. The important steps in the KDD process are selection, preprocessing, transformation, data mining, and evaluation. The processed data are passed through a data-mining algorithm that generates an output in the form of a rule or some kind of pattern. Most of the algorithms used for this approach are related to machine learning, pattern recognition, and statistics. The volatile growth in the database has formed a need to adopt different intelligent data-mining techniques. Research into developing novel systems has also become more popular. Association, characterization, classification, clustering, outlier detection, pattern recognition, prediction, regression, and visualization are the basic data-mining techniques that allow for identifying useful patterns for real-world application.

Some data-mining applications that include medical data are anomaly detection, audience prediction, banking, bioinformatics, crime investigation, customer segmentation, disease diagnosis, electric load prediction, financial data forecasting, fraud detection, lie detection, product design and manufacturing, product marketing, research and analysis, satellite image analysis, scientific experiments, student performance analysis, text mining, valuation of real estate, and weather forecasting.

The size of the data in medical sectors is increasing exponentially day-by-day due to the identification of various diseases and their relevant research. The data types include electronic patient records, pathological reports, biomedical images and signals, hospital staff records, and visitor details. The analysis of such types of data is one of the essential tasks for a flexible hospital management system. Before starting the diagnosis process, physicians analyze the various pathological reports of the specific patient. This is a time-consuming process and sometimes the patient fails to get the treatment in a timely fashion [2]. Data mining has the ability to deal with such issues. The role of this advanced technique in biomedical data analysis is discussed in the next subsection.

3.1 Biomedical data mining

In data mining research and development, demonstrating the important applications is a challenging task. Automation in disease diagnosis is an ongoing research field. Researchers are working in this domain to obtain a model that can detect disease and suggest the diagnosis process at an early stage with minimum error. Most of the clinical applications of data-mining approaches are predictive in nature, attempting to find a model by analyzing different types of patient-specific information. Research on biomedical data mining is also gaining popularity and numerous works have been carried out by applying various techniques in the different data sets, as presented in Table 7.1.

Diabetes, cardiovascular disease, and cancer are the leading causes of death worldwide. These diseases significantly impact human health, reduce the life span, and cause a great deal of suffering, disability, and economic costs [25]. In addition to these diseases, COVID-19 is a recent major cause of death globally, with the death rate increasing due to the spread of this novel

TABLE 7.1 Application of biomedical data mining in various data sets.

Data	References
Diabetic	[3–8]
Cardiac	[3,9–11]
Cancer	[10,12–17]
Coronary artery	[18,19]
Cancer chemotherapy	[20–22]
Asthma	[20,23,24]

coronavirus. The global economy has also been greatly affected by COVID-19. Early detection and diagnosis of these aforementioned diseases is a challenging task. The application of data mining in the detection and diagnosis of these diseases will be very useful for physicians and patients. Different techniques can be used for this purpose that can analyze and classify the related data. The data may include different pathological reports, ECGs, X-rays, and symptoms.

4. Classification techniques

Classification is a data analysis process where a model is designed to predict and distinguish the class labels of the data set. From the literature, it can be observed that there are numerous machine learning and data mining classifiers used for classifying data.

A decision tree-based classifier has major applications in data classification where a tree-based model distinguishes the class labels of the data. This classifier can be used for classifying various multidimensional data. Random forest is another type of tree-based classifier where multiple decision tree classifiers are combined to classify a specific type of input data. It attempts to construct a set of assumptions and combine them for further decision-making. The final outcome is measured by a voting scheme. A Bayesian classifier is another type of statistical model that works on Bayes' theorem. The probabilistic features are made in it to discover the class label of an input set. The performance of these types of classifiers can be improved by adopting some other types of models that can handle greater amounts of data with improved accuracy.

An artificial neural network (ANN) is a generalized mathematical model which is based on biological nervous systems. The fundamental elements of the neural network are artificial neurons interconnected with each other. ANN and its variants have been widely used for classifying the data. Multilayer perceptron (MLP), radial basis function network (RBFN), probabilistic neural network (PNN), generalized regression neural network (GRNN), and block-based neural network (BBNN) are the most commonly used data classification models. These classifiers consist of an input layer, hidden layer, and output layer. The performance of these models was found to be good for both binary and multiclass problems but was not enough capable of handling a large amount of data.

Deep learning is another advanced machine learning model with the ability to process high-dimension raw data [26]. The term deep refers to the use of many layers in the neural network. These layers help the model to discover high-level features from the raw input data. There are different types of deep learning-based classifiers such as deep neural network (DNN), deep belief network (DBN), recurrent neural network (RNN), and convolutional neural network (CNN), which have been applied in different fields including biomedical data classification. The performance of these types of classifiers was found to be better for a large amount of data. For further accuracy, the aforesaid classifiers can be combined to form a single model with the capability to handle a large data set and avoid statistical and computational problems.

Ensemble learning is one of the most recent research findings in the machine learning and data mining field. This is useful because of its capability to integrate data fusion, data modeling, and data mining into a combined framework. To process unstructured, complex, noisy high-dimension data, this model is very useful. In an ensemble learning-based classifier, the performance of a single model can be improved by combining multiple models for a single classifier. Stacking, bagging, boosting, and blending are the most common ensemble techniques. Several classifiers can be found in the literature that work on the ensemble technique and the performance of these classifiers is found to be better than that of traditional methods.

Modern health care is well equipped in terms of analysis, diagnosis, and research. This motivates researchers to work in diversified fields with the application of recent engineering techniques wherever necessary. of the numbers of diseases are constantly increasing, and this is matched by increasing numbers of patients due to population growth. The mortality rate therefore increases also, producing data on a huge scale. This includes patients and their characteristics, diseases and their characteristics, and causes of mortality and their characteristics. This results in medical data mining and helps researchers to carry out analysis, diagnosis, prevention, and treatment [1]. The modern lifestyle generates many different types of diseases that spread through the generations. Therefore gene analysis is extremely important for current and future generations. In this work, a deep learning approach is used for microarray data classification. For effective cancer treatment, early diagnosis is one of the most important factors. Deoxyribonucleic acid (DNA) microarray is used for cancer detection due to gene sequence disorder. Machine learning algorithms are capable of handling high-dimensional data [2]. Typically, these types of data contain more features for each sample and a typical classification task is to distinguish healthy and cancerous patients based on their gene expression profile [3]. Human hereditary information is generally stored in the genes. A genetic disease is a type of disease that is caused by any disorder in gene expression. This can happen due to the mutation in a single gene, multiple gene mutations, gene mutation combination, several environmental factors, and/or damage to chromosomes. Some genetic disorders or mutations can be the cause of cancer. Also, the mutation of genes leads to a variety newly generated viruses. This type of change is referred to as the hereditary cancer syndromes and it can be passed on from parent to child. Leukemia is a type of bone marrow cancer that occurs due to a genetic disorder [9]. Lifestyle and environmental factors increase the risk of leukemia, although it may occur with no known contributory factors. At the initial stage of leukemia, a stem cell turns into a cancerous cell and gradually multiplies uncontrollably. These cancerous cells do not do their job well and they crowd out healthy cells in the bone marrow and bloodstream. The basic factor that develops leukemia in the body is the mutation of cells in the bone marrow. Sometimes it may stop bone marrow from developing healthy cells. It is a complicated task to detect the DNA mutation for early diagnosis of various genetic diseases because most of genes have many regions where mutations can take place. DNA microarray is one of the advanced technologies that is used to measure the expression level of a large number of genes. This technology has the capability to determine whether the DNA of an individual has a genetic mutation or not. Microarray technology is widely used for the analysis and prediction of different types of leukemia [10].

Early prediction of leukemia is a challenging task for physicians which can be helped by adopting computer-aided automated disease diagnosis systems. Different machine learning techniques have been applied to medical data sets for the development of an intelligent diagnosis system. Due to the digital revolution and advances in information technology, a huge amount of data is generating from the medical sectors. Machine learning techniques are well suited for the analysis of these large amounts of data and also several techniques have been adopted for the diagnosis of different diseases [11,12]. To successfully run any machine learning algorithms, different diagnosis data are available in the form of medical records. Due to microarray technology, a large amount of DNA expression data is also generated in medical settings. Automatic analysis and classification of these data are essential for the early diagnosis and decision-making around genetic diseases. Research into gene expression data is one of the most popular areas in machine learning-based biomedical data analysis. Different machine learning algorithms have been also used for the analysis of these data.

Due to the greater number of features and small sample size, microarray data classification is a challenging task for machine learning researchers. To deal with this high-feature set, numerous feature selection algorithms have been adopted in the literature including wrappers and embedded methods [4]. Along with these feature selection algorithms, different machine learning classifiers have been also adopted for classifying the microarray data. These methods include support vector machine (SVM) [5], multilayer perceptron [5], fuzzy neural network [6−8], k-nearest neighbor [9−11], naive Bayes [12,13], decision tree [14,15], and radial basis function network (RBFN) [16−18]. Most of these aforementioned works are two-step processes, including feature selection and classification. In some cases, the authors have also adopted clustering techniques [19−21] to obtain the relevant gene patterns. To select the optimal gene subset, numerous optimization algorithms have been adopted by researchers, including genetic algorithm [8,22,23], heuristic algorithm [15], artificial bee colony [12], particle swarm optimization [24], harmony search [25], and mimetic algorithm [26].

The major drawbacks to these microarray data analysis models are as follows: most of these algorithms fail to provide better results due to high-dimensional data, overfitting problems also occur due to the traditional architecture of the classifier, due to the presence of various uncertainties during data generation, the conventional machine learning models fail to provide a reliable classification model, and the computational time is greater due to the number of steps.

To avoid such issues, deep learning-based approaches have been adopted to classify the high-dimensional microarray data [27–31]. The performance of the deep learning models was also improved by providing optimized features to the classifier [32,33], and it has been observed that the deep learning models provide better performance than the traditional machine learning-based classifiers in high-dimensional data [34,35].

Most of the deep neural network classifiers are more specific to the training data and sometimes they may locate a dissimilar set of weights at each training epoch. This problem is generally referred to as a neural network having maximum variance and it creates the possibility of misclassification. Instead of training a single model, a combination of multiple models can be a successful approach to reduce the neural network variance. This combined model is known as the ensemble model and, from the literature, it is observed that the performance of this model is better than that of a single model [36–38].

In ensemble techniques, multiple submodels statistically contribute to a combined prediction problem. This approach is generally referred to as the model averaging technique. Most of the ensemble models are classified into three categories: bagging, boosting, and stacking. Generally, the usual ensemble learning models consist of bagging and boosting in the random subspace of data [39,40].

The limitation of these approaches is that the contribution of each model remains equal to the ensemble prediction, despite how well the model performed. To improve the performance in terms of model averaging, weighted average ensemble techniques can be considered where a model is used to combine the predictions of submodels with the learning algorithm. This approach is referred to as stacking or stacked generalization. Numerous microarray data classification works have been done by adopting the stacked ensemble classifiers [41–44]. However, these ensemble methods are still dependent on the manual feature selection step. Deep learning can find relevant features from the raw data and this happens due to the presence of a number of hidden layers. Motivated by the power of deep learning and stacked ensemble learning techniques, we have proposed a deep-stacked dual ensemble model for classifying the high dimensional microarray data. Generally, the ensemble models work on the bagging, boosting, and stacked approach [45,46].

5. IoT-based smart biomedical data acquisition and processing system

The ECG is one of the most important references for the diagnosis of many types of cardiac problems. Doctors can identify disorders in the heart by visually analyzing the ECG recordings of patients. Sometimes its acquisition directly affects the treatment of cardiac patients. In a traditional 12-lead ECG recording system, the electrodes are attached to different parts of the body, as presented in Fig. 7.4. The signal is recorded by a machine placed external to the human body. Generally, there are five major deflections in a cardiac signal which correspond to the amplitude, shape, location, and duration. These are generally called the P, Q, R, S, and T waves. The U wave is a small deflection in signal as displayed in Fig. 7.5.

The P wave corresponds to the atrial systole. This is a diminutive low-voltage deflection missing from the baseline. It wave is related to the right and left atrial depolarization. The Q wave is the starting element in the QRS complex which is situated at the downward deflection after the P wave. The R wave is another part of the QRS complex which is the first upward deflection after the P wave. The S wave is the downward deflection after the R wave and is also a component of the QRS complex [13]. The Q, R, and S waves are considered as the QRS complex of the ECG signal, and this QRS feature is considered to be the most powerful feature for ECG analysis. It represents the depolarization of both the left and right ventricles together. The T wave represents the ventricular repolarization. Repolarization occurs in the opposite direction to depolarization and begins on the surface epicardium of the heart,

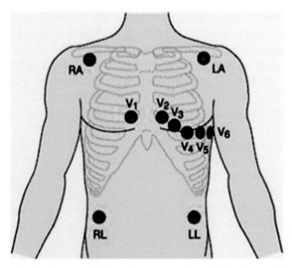

FIGURE 7.4   Electrode placement in the body during ECG recording in the traditional method [47].

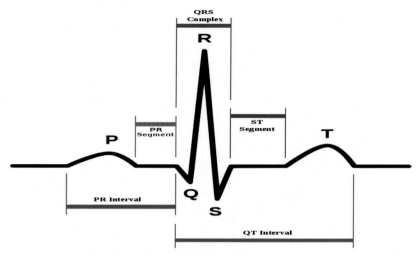

FIGURE 7.5 ECG signal with standard fiducial points.

extending toward the endocardium. The U wave typically follows the T wave on the ECG and is always in the direction of the T wave itself [14]. The QRS complex feature is one of the most used features for ECG signal analysis Fig. 7.5.

These traditional types of equipment are not portable and sometimes these systems are not suitable for analyzing a long-duration ECG. It cannot be used at the home due to being so expensive and so patients are required to visit hospitals repeatedly. To overcome this problem, a portable long-term ECG recording machine is required which can easily record cardiac function with minimum time, and the data can be transmitted to the hospital. A framework for a smart ECG system is presented in Fig. 7.6 [15]. Other devices can be deployed for measuring different parameters of the human body such as heartbeat-measuring sensors, pulse rate, and devices for measuring SpO_2 as an alternative. These portable devices can be used for home-care patients. Doctors can also verify and analyze these data without patients having to visit hospital. Different smart devices for measuring these parameters are presented in Figs. 7.7 and 7.8. In heartbeat-measuring sensors, the amount of blood flow to the fingers over time can be recorded. For calculating the heart rate, a sensor is assembled with LM358 OP-AMP that monitors the heartbeat.

5.1 IoT-based data communication framework

This is another important task to monitor and analyze the data collected by smart devices. Several sensors and other instruments are required for this advanced healthcare system. These devices include specialized devices or smartphones. Data transmission can be performed by applying the body area network concept [16]. An Arduino-based ECG data-recording machine is

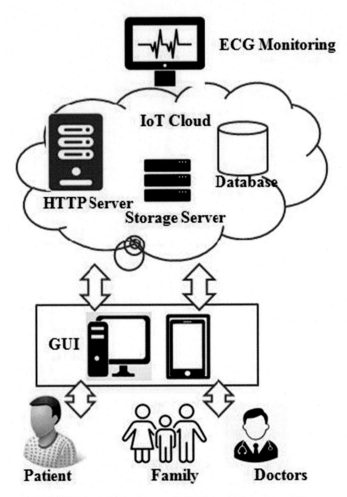

FIGURE 7.6 IoT-based automatic ECG monitoring system [13].

proposed which is monitored by a portable computer. ECG data are collected from patients and sent to the cloud. The overall process is performed using an Arduino board. It will be helpful for mobile devices also Fig. 7.9 shows the setup for the communication system and the corresponding output is shown in Fig. 7.10.

6. Multiagent system for biomedical data processing

A multiagent system for processing cardiac data is proposed that can classify different cardiac abnormalities. This approach is designed for the application of big data in the cardiac data analysis system. Different blocks in the

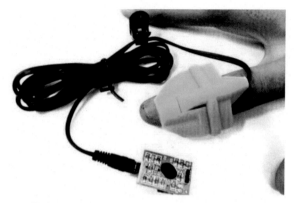

FIGURE 7.7 A smart device for measuring the heartbeat.

FIGURE 7.8 Smart SpO$_2$-measuring device.

proposed multiagent system are presented in Fig. 7.11. The multiagent system consists of the intelligent module for automatic disease detection along with the communication module with the blood bank. Once the abnormalities are detected they are communicated to the physician and patient. If the patient requires blood then the diagnosis center will send a request to the blood bank [17,18].

Patient agent: A patient, who suffers from any disease, consults a hospital. Different pathological tests will be performing on the physicians' advice. Test result data will communicate with the server.

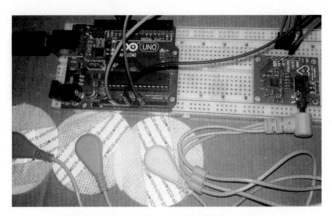

FIGURE 7.9   Arduino setup for ECG recording.

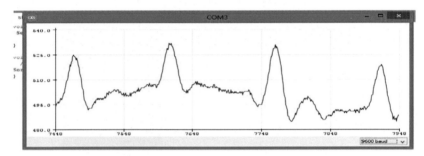

FIGURE 7.10   ECG signals recorded by Arduino setup.

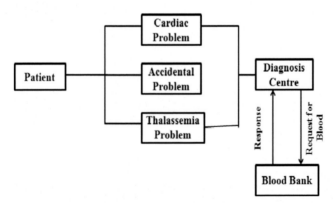

FIGURE 7.11   Proposed multiagent intelligent system.

Physician agent: This agent will communicate with the doctors. After diagnosis, the decision will be sent to patients by email or SMS.

Diagnostic center agent: Data generated from the pathological tests will be sent to the diagnosis center for analysis and future diagnosis.

Blood bank agent: This agent controls the blood bank and responses to the diagnosis center.

7. Detection of cardiac abnormalities

The proposed multiagent framework is considered for the detection of heart abnormalities. Human services research recommends that cardiovascular variations from the norm starts with harm to the inward layers of the heart arteries. Harm may be caused by the following factors:

1. High blood pressure
2. High cholesterol
3. High blood sugar
4. Inflammation of the blood vessel.

Coronary illness is currently the most widely recognized type of cardio-vascular illness. Diverse related tests can be attempted to make a precise analysis. Normally, doctors endorse the accompanying insignificant tests for heart patients. A blood test is required to obtain the levels of various factors such as electrolytes, blood cells, hormones in the blood, and clotting factors; also, the blood sugar level can be verified. An electrocardiogram (ECG) may show changes that indicate the heart muscle is not receiving sufficient oxygen.

7.1 Classification algorithm

SVM is one of the most popular linear machine learning classifiers with some attractive properties. This technique is mostly based on the structural risk minimization method where a hyperplane/decision boundary is created in such a manner that the positive and negative class separation margins can be maximized. Let us consider $\left\{ \left(\mathbf{x}_j, o_j \right) \right\}_{j=1}^{N}$ as the training data set for the SVM classifier where $\mathbf{x}_j$ is the input feature for the j-th example and o_j is the corresponding output (target). Before beginning the classification process, let us assume that the output classes are linearly separable and are represented by $+1$ (positive class) and -1 (negative class). The output pattern separation process in the hyperplane or decision boundary can be represented by

$$\mathbf{w}^*\mathbf{x} + d = 0 \tag{7.1}$$

The output of the SVM classifier can be defined by

$$\begin{aligned} \mathbf{w}^* + d \geq 0 \quad \text{for } o_j = +1 \\ \mathbf{w}^* + d \leq 0 \quad \text{for } o_j = -1 \end{aligned} \tag{7.2}$$

where $\mathbf{x}$ is the input feature vector, $\mathbf{w}^*$ is the corresponding adjustable weight vector, and d is the bias or threshold. In linear SVM the separation between two classes $\mathbf{x}$ is done by maximizing the separation margin in the optimal hyperplane. In the case of nonlinear SVM, the two classes are first mapped with the kernel function in feature space with a high dimension [19,20]. The representation is presented in Fig. 7.12. The mathematical representation for nonlinear SVM is

$$\sum_{j=1}^{N} \mathbf{w}_j^* \phi_j(\mathbf{x}) + d \tag{7.3}$$

where $\phi(.)$ is the mapping function. The main goal is to develop an efficient classifier using a set of training data $\left\{ (\mathbf{x}_j, o_j) \right\}_{j=1}^{N}$. The optimized value of the weight vector $\mathbf{w}^*$ and bias d can be stated as

$$o_j \left(\mathbf{w}^* \mathbf{x}_j + d \right) \quad \geq 1 - \xi_j \quad \text{for } j = 1, 2, 3, \ldots, N \tag{7.4}$$

where ξ is the slack variable for all j [21]. The weight vector $\mathbf{w}^*$ and the slack variable minimize the cost function which can be represented by

$$\varphi(\mathbf{w}^*, \xi) = \frac{1}{2} \|\mathbf{w}^*\|^2 + R \sum_{j=1}^{N} \xi_j \tag{7.5}$$

where R is a regularized parameter, that is, it is used to control the discriminant function size. The final output of the SVM classifier is represented as

$$o(x) = \sum_{j=1}^{N} K(\mathbf{x}_j, \mathbf{x}) \tag{7.6}$$

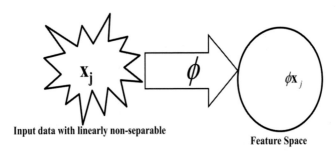

Input data with linearly non-separable

Feature Space

FIGURE 7.12 Transformation of linearly nonseparable data to feature space.

The kernel function $K(\mathbf{x}_j, \mathbf{x})$ is a special case of Mercer's theorem which arises at the time of functional analysis. In the proposed work the performance of the SVM is measured for four types of kernels: polynomial, linear, sigmoid, and linear. The polynomial kernel is one type of nonstationary kernel and it performs well for normalized training data. It can be represented as

$$K(\mathbf{x}_j, \mathbf{x}) = (\mathbf{x}_j \cdot \mathbf{x} + 1)^b \tag{7.7}$$

where b is the degree of the polynomial and is specified a priori by the user. Linear kernel is another type of kernel in which the training of the SVM classifier is much faster than for other kernels. The mathematical equation of the linear kernel is

$$K(\mathbf{x}_j, \mathbf{x}) = \mathbf{x}_j \cdot \mathbf{x} \tag{7.8}$$

Sigmoid is another type of kernel function of SVM which is also used as the proxy for neural network classifiers. It is represented as

$$K(\mathbf{x}_j, \mathbf{x}) = \tan h(\beta \mathbf{x}_j \mathbf{x} + A) \tag{7.9}$$

where β is the slope and A is the intercept constant, respectively. An RBF kernel is one of the most general kernels used in many neural network problems. The performance of this kernel is better when there is no earlier knowledge about the data. It is represented as

$$K(\mathbf{x}_j, \mathbf{x}) = \exp\left(-\delta \|\mathbf{x}_j - \mathbf{x}\|^2\right) \tag{7.10}$$

where δ is a parameter inversely proportional to the width of the Gaussian kernel.

8. Results and discussion

After collecting the data, the classification is done using an SVM classifier. These 13 features are considered as the input to the proposed SVM classifier, whereas attribute number 14 is considered as the target class of the classifier. The original data set is divided into training and testing sets. Ninety per cent of the data (272 samples) are considered as the training set and the remaining 10% (31 samples) data is kept for testing purposes. For measuring the performance of the classifier, different measuring parameters are considered such as precision, recall, accuracy, and F-1 score. The formulas for calculating these parameters are

$$\text{Precision} = \frac{TP}{TP + FP} \tag{7.11}$$

$$\text{Recall} = \frac{TP}{TP + FN} \tag{7.12}$$

$$F - 1 \; \text{Score} = 2 * \frac{\text{Precision} * \text{Recall}}{\text{Precision} + \text{Recal}} \qquad (7.13)$$

$$\text{Accuracy} = \frac{TP + TN}{N} \qquad (7.14)$$

The corresponding confusion matrices generated from the SVM classifier with different kernels are shown in Fig. 7.13. In Table 7.2 the performance-measuring parameters calculated from the confusion matrix are presented.

It can be observed that the classification performance of SVM with the polynomial kernel is better than for the other three types of kernels. The classification accuracy is around 87.5% for SVM with a polynomial kernel function.

The proposed classifier is then applied in a multiagent system that can classify the cardiac abnormalities. In Fig. 7.14, the screenshot of the output screen of the multiagent system for cardiac abnormalities detection is

Confusion matrix SVM with Polynomial Kernel

	Normal	Cardiac
Normal	18	2
Cardiac	1	10

Confusion matrix SVM with Linear Kernel

	Normal	Cardiac
Normal	16	2
Cardiac	3	10

Confusion matrix SVM with Sigmoid Kernel

	Normal	Cardiac
Normal	12	5
Cardiac	5	9

Confusion matrix withRBF Kernel

	Normal	Cardiac
Normal	11	7
Cardiac	5	8

FIGURE 7.13   Confusion matrix obtained from the SVM classifier.

TABLE 7.2 SVM classification result.

Kernel types	Precession (%)	Recall (%)	F1 score (%)	Accuracy (%)
SVM with polynomial kernel	83.33	96.90	86.26	87.5
SVM with linear kernel	83.33	76.92	79.99	83.87
SVM with sigmoid kernel	64.28	64.25	62.27	67.74
SVM with RBF kernel	53.33	61.53	57.13	61.26

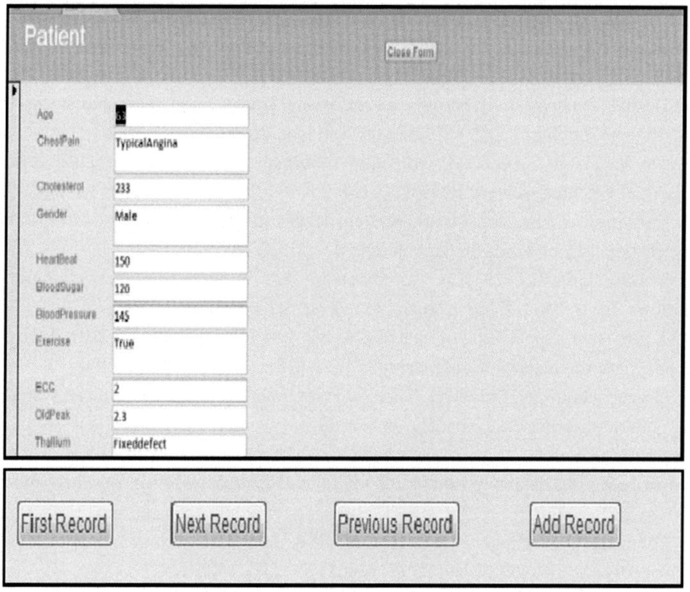

FIGURE 7.14 Screenshot of the proposed multivalent system for cardiac abnormalities detection.

displayed. After providing the required information this system displays the cardiac risk factors and classes to the patients and also the doctors. The proposed multiagent system is also connected with the blood bank system in case of an urgent requirement for blood for patients admitted due to cardiac illness.

9. Conclusion

Big data has a major role in the healthcare domain, with hospitals gaining increased benefits by adopting this technology. It can help with disease diagnosis and different electronic health records (EHR)-handling in the inpatient service sector. A case study on big data application in cardiac data analysis has been provided in this chapter. Classification of different cardiac abnormalities with the application of a multiagent system is provided also. The proposed system provides a better classification result with the SVM classifier. In the future, other machine learning classifiers could be used for the processing of different biomedical data to improve the performance of the classifier.

References

[1] P. Russom, Big data analytics. TDWI best practices report, Fourth Quarter 19 (4) (2011) 1–34.
[2] C. Ji, et al., Big data processing: big challenges and opportunities, J. Interconnect. Netw. 13 (03n04) (2012) 1250009.

[3] H.K. Gupta, R. Parveen, Comparative study of big data frameworks, in: 2019 International Conference on Issues and Challenges in Intelligent Computing Techniques (ICICT), IEEE, 2019.

[4] N. Deshai, et al., A study on big data processing frameworks: spark and storm, in: Smart Intelligent Computing and Applications, Springer, 2020, pp. 415−424.

[5] A. De Mauro, M. Greco, M. Grimaldi, A Formal Definition of Big Data Based on its Essential Features, Library Review, 2016.

[6] S. Kaisler, et al., Big data: issues and challenges moving forward, in: 2013 46th Hawaii International Conference on System Sciences, IEEE, 2013.

[7] M.S. Hajirahimova, A.S. Aliyeva, About big data measurement methodologies and indicators, Int. J. Mod. Educ. Comput. Sci. 9 (10) (2017) 1.

[8] S.M. Krishnan, Application of analytics to big data in healthcare, in: 2016 32nd Southern Biomedical Engineering Conference (SBEC), IEEE, 2016.

[9] M. Bracher-Smith, K. Crawford, V. Escott-Price, Machine learning for genetic prediction of psychiatric disorders: a systematic review, Mol. Psychiatr. (2020) 1−10.

[10] S.E. Bibri, The IoT for smart sustainable cities of the future: an analytical framework for sensor-based big data applications for environmental sustainability, Sustain. Cities Soc. 38 (2018) 230−253.

[11] I. Kononenko, Machine learning for medical diagnosis: history, state of the art and perspective, Artif. Intell. Med. 23 (1) (2001) 89−109.

[12] N. Mahmood, et al., Identification of significant risks in pediatric acute lymphoblastic leukemia (ALL) through machine learning (ML) approach, Med. Biol. Eng. Comput. (2020) 1−10.

[13] A. Karimipour, M.R. Homaeinezhad, Real-time electrocardiogram P-QRS-T detection−delineation algorithm based on quality-supported analysis of characteristic templates, Comput. Biol. Med. 52 (2014) 153−165.

[14] G. Bognár, S. Fridli, Heartbeat classification of ECG signals using rational function systems, in: International Conference on Computer Aided Systems Theory, Springer, 2017.

[15] Z. Yang, et al., An IoT-cloud based wearable ECG monitoring system for smart healthcare, J. Med. Syst. 40 (12) (2016) 286.

[16] S.K. Dhar, S.S. Bhunia, N. Mukherjee, Interference aware scheduling of sensors in IoT enabled health-care monitoring system, in: 2014 Fourth International Conference of Emerging Applications of Information Technology, IEEE, 2014.

[17] L. Sarangi, M.N. Mohanty, S. Patnaik, Design of ANFIS based e-health care system for cardio vascular disease detection, in: International Conference on Intelligent and Interactive Systems and Applications, Springer, 2016.

[18] L. Sarangi, M.N. Mohanty, S. Pattnaik, Design of diagnosis and monitoring system of heart related diseases using fuzzy inference system, Ann. Comput. Sci. Inf. Syst. 10 (2017) 321−327.

[19] V. Vapnik, I. Guyon, T. Hastie, Support vector machines, Mach. Learn. 20 (3) (1995) 273−297.

[20] S. Haykin, Neural Networks: A Comprehensive Foundation, Prentice Hall PTR, 1994.

[21] M.N. Mohanty, et al., Power quality disturbances classification using support vector machines with optimised time-frequency kernels, Int. J. Power Electron. 4 (2) (2012) 181−196.

[22] K. Baker, et al., Process mining routinely collected electronic health records to define real-life clinical pathways during chemotherapy, Int. J. Med. Inf. 103 (2017) 32−41, https://doi.org/10.1016/j.ijmedinf.2017.03.011.

[23] B. Alizadeh, R. Safdari, M. Zolnoori, A. Bashiri, Developing an intelligent system for diagnosis of asthma based on artificial neural network, Acta Inf. Med. 23 (4) (2015) 220−223, https://doi.org/10.5455/aim.2015.23.220-223.

[24] V.S. Tseng, C.H. Lee, J.C.Y. Chen, An integrated data mining system for patient monitoring with applications on asthma care, Proc. - IEEE Symp. Comput. Med. Syst. (2008) 290−292, https://doi.org/10.1109/CBMS.2008.111.

[25] A.G. Renehan, A. Howell, Preventing cancer, cardiovascular disease, and diabetes, Lancet 365 (9469) (2005) 1449−1451, https://doi.org/10.1016/S0140-6736(05)66399-4.

[26] Y. Lecun, Y. Bengio, G. Hinton, Deep learning, Nature 521 (7553) (2015) 436−444, https://doi.org/10.1038/nature14539.

[27] Z. Wu, Q. Xu, J. Li, C. Fu, Q. Xuan, Y. Xiang, Passive indoor localization based on CSI and naive bayes classification, IEEE Trans. Syst. Man, Cybern. Syst. 48 (9) (2018) 1566−1577, https://doi.org/10.1109/TSMC.2017.2679725.

[28] Y.F. Safri, R. Arifudin, M.A. Muslim, K-nearest neighbor and naive bayes classifier algorithm in determining the classification of healthy card Indonesia giving to the poor, Sci. J. Inform. 5 (1) (2018) 18, https://doi.org/10.15294/sji.v5i1.12057.

[29] M.O. Mughal, S. Kim, Signal classification and jamming detection in wide-band radios using naïve bayes classifier, IEEE Commun. Lett. 22 (7) (2018) 1398−1401, https://doi.org/10.1109/LCOMM.2018.2830769.

[30] D.L. Naik, R. Kiran, Naïve Bayes classifier, multivariate linear regression and experimental testing for classification and characterization of wheat straw based on mechanical properties, Ind. Crop. Prod. 112 (2018) 434−448, https://doi.org/10.1016/j.indcrop.2017.12.034. November 2017.

[31] S.R. Gomes, et al., A comparative approach to email classification using Naive Bayes classifier and hidden Markov model, in: 4th Int. Conf. Adv. Electr. Eng. ICAEE 2017, vol. 2018-January, 2017, pp. 482−487, https://doi.org/10.1109/ICAEE.2017.8255404.

[32] A. Kumar Sharma, S. Kumar Prajapat Assistant Professor, M. Aslam, A comparative study between naïve bayes and neural network (MLP) classifier for spam email detection, Int. J. Comput. Appl. (2014) 975−8887.

[33] H. Parvin, H. Alizadeh, B. Minati, A modification on K-nearest neighbor classifier, Global J. Comput. Sci. Technol. 10 (14) (2010) 37−41.

[34] N.S. Altman, An introduction to kernel and nearest neighbor nonparametric regression, Am. Statistician 46 (June) (1992) 3.

[35] Y. Liao, V.R. Vemuri, Classifier for intrusion, Comput. Secur. 21 (5) (2002) 439−448.

[36] L.Y. Hu, M.W. Huang, S.W. Ke, C.F. Tsai, The distance function effect on k-nearest neighbor classification for medical datasets, SpringerPlus 5 (1) (2016), https://doi.org/10.1186/s40064-016-2941-7.

[37] W.A. Chaovalitwongse, Y.J. Fan, R.C. Sachdeo, On the time series K-nearest neighbor classification of abnormal brain activity, IEEE Trans. Syst. Man, Cybern. Part A Systems Humans 37 (6) (2007) 1005−1016, https://doi.org/10.1109/TSMCA.2007.897589.

[38] Y. Lei, M.J. Zuo, Gear crack level identification based on weighted K nearest neighbor classification algorithm, Mech. Syst. Signal Process. 23 (5) (2009) 1535−1547, https://doi.org/10.1016/j.ymssp.2009.01.009.

[39] S.E. Buttrey, C. Karo, Using k-nearest-neighbor classification in the leaves of a tree, Comput. Stat. Data Anal. 40 (1) (2002) 27−37, https://doi.org/10.1016/S0167-9473(01)00098-6.

[40] J. Zhan, L.W. Chang, S. Matwin, Privacy preserving K-nearest neighbor classification, Int. J. Netw. Secur. 1 (1) (2005) 46−51.

[41] S.Y. Ho, C.C. Liu, S. Liu, J.W. Jou, Design of an optimal nearest neighbor classifier using an intelligent genetic algorithm, in: Proc. 2002 Congr. Evol. Comput. CEC 2002, vol. 1, 2002, pp. 594—599, https://doi.org/10.1109/CEC.2002.1006993.

[42] K. Sasirekha, K. Thangavel, Optimization of K-nearest neighbor using particle swarm optimization for face recognition, Neural Comput. Appl. 31 (11) (2019) 7935—7944, https://doi.org/10.1007/s00521-018-3624-9.

[43] S. Chen, K-nearest neighbor algorithm optimization in text categorization, IOP Conf. Ser. Earth Environ. Sci. 108 (5) (2018), https://doi.org/10.1088/1755-1315/108/5/052074.

[44] T. Kaur, B.S. Saini, S. Gupta, An adaptive fuzzy K-nearest neighbor approach for MR brain tumor image classification using parameter free bat optimization algorithm, Multimed. Tool. Appl. 78 (15) (2019) 21853—21890, https://doi.org/10.1007/s11042-019-7498-3.

[45] D.Y. Liu, H.L. Chen, B. Yang, X.E. Lv, L.N. Li, J. Liu, Design of an enhanced Fuzzy k-nearest neighbor classifier based computer aided diagnostic system for thyroid disease, J. Med. Syst. 36 (5) (2012) 3243—3254, https://doi.org/10.1007/s10916-011-9815-x.

[46] L. Breiman, J. Friedman, C.J. Stone, R.A. Olshen, Classification and Regression Trees, CRC press, 1984.

[47] A.S. Karthiga, M.S. Mary, M. Yogasini, Early prediction of heart disease using decision tree algorithm, Int. Jounral Adv. Res. Basic Eng. Sci. Technol. 3 (3) (2017) 1—16.

Chapter 8

Study of bio-inspired neural networks for the prediction of liquid flow in a process control system

Pijush Dutta[1], Korhan Cengiz[2], Asok Kumar[3]

[1]*Department of Electronics and Communication Engineering, Global Institute of Management and Technology, Krishnagar, West Bengal, India;* [2]*Department of Telecommunication, Trakya University, Edirne, Turkey;* [3]*Dean of Student Welfare Department, Vidyasagar University, Medinipur, West Bengal, India*

1. Introduction

In the process control industry, to achieve the optimum output, we need to calculate the input parameters. Also, inaccurate input parameter settings can affect the system seriously. The application of the traditional approach to discovering the optimum potential input variables in a multivariable process control is inconsistent, tedious, and expensive. In the traditional advancement approach, when a dependent variable is estimated regarding the impact of a specific variable, at that point, distinct factors need to be kept consistent. In the process model, intuitiveness between the potential independent variables is missing. Subsequently, there is consistently an opportunity to obtain a response variable, affected by singular free factors. The number of experimental dataset need to be increased so that it can overcome this inconvenience. However, it also increases the expense of production and the time requirement. Another optional methodology is computational algorithm where numerical relations are formed between input & output variables utilizing diverse computational insights. When testing datasets are available then a model is implemented by the computational algorithm such that dependable variables are functions of independent variables with higher degree of precision. Typically, in most liquid flow process models, the flow rate relies on a few significant elements such as sensor yield, pipe width, liquid conductivity, viscosity, etc. In those cases, numerical models are created with the help of

Cognitive Big Data Intelligence with a Metaheuristic Approach
https://doi.org/10.1016/B978-0-323-85117-6.00009-1

previously mentioned independent factors and finally different computational models are utilized which can carry out the process measurement efficiently.

Employing high measuring accuracy, linearity, and a very short response time in the process control industry, there are a number of flow sensors used, such as: piezoresistive flow sensor [1], hot film flow sensor [2], turbine flow sensor [3], calorimetric flow sensor, microelectromechanical flow sensor [4], electrochemical thermal flow sensor [5], ultrasonic flow sensor [6], optical flow sensor [7], Coriolis mass flow sensor [8], orifice flow sensor [9], low thermal air flow sensor [10], vortex flow sensor [11], low-cost anemometer thermal flow sensor [12], and semiconductor-based anemometer [13], which have been widely utilized in aviation, petroleum treatment facilities, flammable gas, etc., for standard estimation.

In a nonlinear process industry, it is a challenge to improve the performance of a flow sensor whenever any potential input parameters are changed and so an efficient algorithm is required to upgrade the process model in such a way that it best fits the actual system. Several studies have been performed in this field, including an enhanced artificial neural network (ANN) model [14] proposed to calculate the speed of gas using test information such as sensor voltage and liquid temperature, and an enhanced neural system model for an ultrasonic sensor where the flow rate depends upon the potential input parameters [15]. In addition to the ANN nonlinear model, a few nonlinear models such as regression analysis [16], response surface methods [17], analysis of variance (ANOVA) [18], etc. are well known, where polynomial, strategic, quadratic, exponential, logarithmic, power and so forth also used in the field of process control industry to make a connection between process output, flow rate and independent input process variables such as pipe diameter and liquid nature, etc. conditions can be utilized to express the framework behavior [19]. During a mathematical extraction strategy, a proficient improvement procedure is needed to streamline the model boundaries to such an extent that exploratory yield fits best with the reenacted yield. Thus, precise demonstration of the fluid stream control measure is a typical example of nonlinear improvement issues where we ideal estimations of the model boundaries have to be distinguished. The accuracy of the separated boundaries depends upon the choice of an appropriate streamlining method.

A metaheuristic is one of the most mainstream subclass enhancement strategies where advancement measures are normally motivated by physical wonders, animal behavior, or developmental ideas [20,21]. Swarm intelligence (SI)-based strategies are one of best known and most effective subclasses of metaheuristic optimization. SI follows the social behavior of multitudes, groups, runs, or schools of insects and other creatures where the inquiry operators utilize the group behavior and social aspects of animals [22]. Straightforwardness, adaptability, inference free component, and neighborhood optima evasion capacity are the principal explanations for the prevalence of metaheuristics. These qualities make metaheuristics fit extremely well for genuine enhancement issues. There have been several researches conducted on the basis of swarm intelligence, such as particle swarm improvement (PSO) [23], bat algorithm (BA) [24], artificial bee colony (ABC) [25], firefly algorithm (FA) [26], flower pollination algorithm (FPA) [27], ant colony optimization (ACO) [28], cuckoo search optimization (CSO) [29], elephant swarm water search algorithm (ESWSA) [30], etc. To improve the computational time, precision, intermingling speed, investigation, proper parameter tuning, and misuse capacity a single metaheuristic is not capable of addressing all the factors, therefore a metaheuristics is used, which is known as the No Free Lunch hypothesis [31].

In the combinational computational model, several soft computing techniques that analyze the mathematical model have been used in modern research fields. In this area, several metaheuristics algorithms have been used to optimize the synaptic weights of the neural network model so that the present model fits with the desired process system; there have been several researches conducted in this area. A comparative study of different bio-inspired optimization techniques has been done to tune the neural network parameters and so improve the accuracy of the gene expression analysis [32]. A spiking neural network is integrated with evolutionary algorithms to optimize the structure and size of the neural network, and is thus able to control dynamic systems [33]. A genetic algorithm and a direct search algorithm were used to tune the backpropagation neural network to develop an efficient predictive model for monthly rainfall in Thailand [34]. An investigation into improved versions of artificial neural network models was done with the help of metaheuristic algorithms [35], genetic algorithm (GA) and harmony search (HS) and for the forecasting of the stockmarket performance. In Ref. [36] the proposed hybrid artificial neural network models include: particle swarm optimization, cuckoo search, genetic algorithm, and improved cuckoo search to predict stock prices according to statistical performances by considering 28 dominant independent variables of stock indices. In Ref. [37]. PSO and DE optimized best synaptic weighted ANN models were proposed to solve different nonlinear problems In Ref. [38], a multiobjective evolutionary algorithm was designed to train an ANN for the classification of samples from two different biomedical data sets.

Because of the more credible possibility of being stuck in the neighborhood least arrangement, they are presently being replaced by the use of different metaheuristic calculations which would give the close to ideal or worldwide ideal arrangements in a shorter time due to their high convergence speed. In this study, we propose two different swarm intelligence techniques, PSO and FA, to optimize the weighted values of neural network modeling for liquid flow process control. The chapter is organized as follows: Sections 2 and 3 briefly describe previous work and the experimental set up of the process. The preliminaries of the algorithm are followed by the proposed approach in Sections 4 and 5. The analysis of the results and conclusion of the project are described in Sections 6 and 7.

2. Related work

Notable intelligent techniques in liquid flow control process are listed in Table 8.1.

TABLE 8.1 Notable intelligent techniques for prediction of flow rate.

Sl no.	Year of publishing	References	Algorithm used
1	2017	[6]	Fuzzy logic controller with different nature and number of membership functions are used for the modeling of an ultrasonic flow sensor-based liquid flow process
2	2018	[39]	Here the authors used supervised machine learning k-nearest neighbor and support vector machine for data classification purposes
3	2018	[40]	An artificial neural network model used with a varied number of nodes and activation functions
4	2018	[41]	Modeling of adaptive neuro fuzzy inference system
5	2018	[18]	A bio-inspired flower pollination algorithm was used to optimize the neural network model
6	2018	[17]	A bio-inspired flower pollination algorithm was used to optimize the empirical model of analysis of variance (ANOVA) and response surface methodology (RSM)
7	2017	[42]	An evolutionary, genetic algorithm was used to optimize the synaptic weight of a neural network model
8	2020	[43]	An evolutionary genetic algorithm was used to optimize the empirical model of analysis of variance (ANOVA) and response surface methodology (RSM)
9	2019	[44]	An improved form of metaheuristic advancement, elephant swarm water search calculation, was utilized to streamline the observational model of ANOVA and RSM
10	2019	[18]	A bio-inspired flower pollination algorithm was used to optimize the empirical model of analysis of variance (ANOVA)
11	2015	[15]	An artificial neural network model was used and an ultrasonic sensor was used as a flow sensor

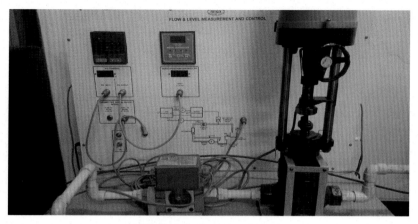

FIGURE 8.1 Experimental setup.

3. Experimental setup

The experimental setup for the present research is shown in Fig. 8.1. In this experiment, the liquid velocities measured were in the range 0−600 liquid per minute (lpm). When this liquid passes through the semiconductor-based flow sensor it provides a voltage in the range of a millivolt. The sensor output voltage range is also affected by the pipe diameter and other liquid properties. Tables 8.2 and 8.3 shows the experimental setup and miscellaneous components, along with the range of potential independent input variables.

4. Preliminary details of the algorithm

4.1 Preliminary details of the neural network (NN)

An ANN is a subclass of artificial intelligence which is a replica of human neuron geology applied in a nonlinear problem formulation [18] (Fig. 8.2).

TABLE 8.2 Experimental setup [43].

Machine/tools	Specification/description
Flow and level measurement and control	Model no. WFT -20-I
Flow sensor	Constructed by SL 100 transistor
Diameter of PVC pipe	20, 25, 30 mm
Digital multimeter	$3\frac{1}{2}$ volt /ohm meter
Rota meter	Taking the reading of the flow rate ranging between 0−600 lpm

TABLE 8.3 Ranges of the process parameters [43].

Process parameter	Range
Output of the sensor	210–285 mV
Pipe diameter (mm)	20, 25, 30 mm
Water conductivity (W/m.k)	606, 615, 622(W/m.k)
Water viscosity	725.4, 779.7, 898.2 μpas.s
Water density	993.9, 995.6, 996.9 kg/m³

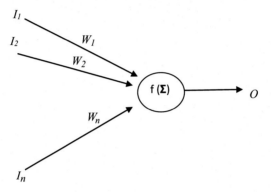

FIGURE 8.2 A simple architecture of neuron.

This model helps to discover the output from the data sets which contained obscure input variable data. ANN has an extraordinary potential to foresee and resolve a more reasonable outcome than the usual strategies. The sole objective of ANN is to cause a PC to pick up something with the goal that the system can acclimate to a target data set. Like other AI, ANN can learn through a model and can be applied to predict the test dataset with greater accuracy. For this reason it makes appropriate for design acknowledgment, information clustering, or information grouping issues [45–47].

In most modern process control systems, three distinct layered feedforward neural systems are more effective. Input attributes along with vector information are carried out by input layer. A hidden layer, similar to output layer contains a number of neurons connecting with whole system. Finally output from output layer sends back to the input layer for a given set of input attributes.

Let us consider I an input vector and W as the weights of each synapse of the neural model where $I = [I_1, I_2, ... I_n]^T$ and $W = [W_1, W_2, ... W_n]$. Each input is multiplied by the associated weights of the neuron to produce $I^T W$. Positive and negative weights of the neural network model excite and reduce the strength of node output.

$$I = I^T W = I_1 W_1 + I_2 W_2 + \dots + I_n W_n = \sum_{i=1}^{n} I_i W_i \qquad (8.1)$$

Output O is obtained at the yield layer represent by the following expression:

$$O = f(I) = f\left\{ \sum_{i=1}^{n} I_i W_i - \phi_k \right\} \qquad (8.2)$$

where ϕ is the magnitude offset.

During the training of the model, training datasets are taken care of the synaptic weight & bias value by means of learning algorithm. The target of a neural system framework is to give desired output through some information signals. Before the preparation of the neural system, the framework is set at its default or other settings. While the system is being prepared, the synaptic weights are updated depending on the input and output values, utilizing a regular learning algorithm such as the backpropagation algorithm [48]. Nonetheless, extraordinary transformative improvement procedures or meta-heuristics [32,36] have been effectively used to gain proficiency with neural network loads.

4.2 Preliminaries of the firefly algorithm

The firefly count (FA), described in Ref. [26], is used for solving ideal force stream issues and to achieve better overall ideal game plans. The flashing or blinking of the light at night is done to attract the mates or prey, igestion, and mutual interest. This estimation uses a lower number of managers and can be successfully realized for any any optimization problems. Layout of the proposed Firefly algorithm minimized the true objective function. The firefly calculation is applied in various areas such as shading picture division [49], heat exchangers [50], versatile robot route [51], appropriated advancement [52], consonant identification in a power framework [53], and remote sensor organization [54].

The rules include:

1. Fireflies will be pulled in by various fireflies paying little notice to their sex;
2. Allure relates to their quality and reduces as the space between them increases;
3. The brillance of a Firefly is chosen for generating the optumum value of target objective function.

4.3 Preliminaries of particle swarm optimization (PSO)

PSO is a metaheuristic search calculation used to locate an ideal arrangement in a field of examination [23]. Its activity is dependent on swarm speculations where singular particles commonly attempt to discover the optimum search space. After every time interval, each particle pushes toward the best arrangement by P_{best} and G_{best}. The best aspect of PSO is that it is able to identify the ideal arrangement in a wide area of inquiry. Moreover, PSO can be utilized in the issues needing improvement, such as unpredictable, and violent [55,56]. In PSO calculation, each group of travels strolls through the n-dimensional pursuit space of an n level of freedom. Finally, the value of P_{best} and G_{best} should be updated at after every complete cycle v_i^{m+1} and x_i^{m+1}. The updated velocity and position vector in the $(m+1)$ iteration are defined as:

$$v_i^{m+1} = w, \ v_i^m + c_1 r_1^n \left(p_{best_i}^m - x_i^m \right) + c_2 r_2^n \left(g_{best_i}^m - x_i^m \right) \qquad (8.3)$$

$$x_i^{m+1} = x_i^m + v_i^{m+1} \qquad (8.4)$$

where, v_i^m and x_i^m are the speed and position after m-th iteration, respectively. c_1 and c_2 are steady qualities and characterized as the speeding up factors, r_1 and r_2 are haphazardly created loads with values somewhere in the range of $0-1$, ω is a dormancy weight that controls the effect of speed from the past cycle on the recently processed speed, and $p_{best_i}^m$ and $g_{best_i}^m$ are the personal and global best solutions in the m-th iteration [57]. P_{best} and G_{best} are dependent on the tuning and preliminary false perceptions in PSO.

5. Proposed model

The main objective of this research is to discover the predicted model that had the best fit with the actual result. From Section 2 it can be seen that the process output and the flow rate depend on potential input variables, such as pipe diameter and liquid properties. The overall process is defined in two stages. In the first stage, the process response, flow rate, is defined by the potential input variables using a neural network model where each of the nodes is considered to be the input variables of the present process. In the second stage, two metaheuristic optimization methods, PSO and FA, are applied to the neural network linear model to discover the optimal node weight to give the proposed best fit to the actual flow rate of the process shown in Fig. 8.3 (Table 8.4).

5.1 Modeling of the flow rate using a neural network

In this subsection, the neural network model is used to design a linear model where the process response, flow rate (F), is a function of the potential in-dependent input variables: liquid properties (k, n), sensor voltage (E), and pipe

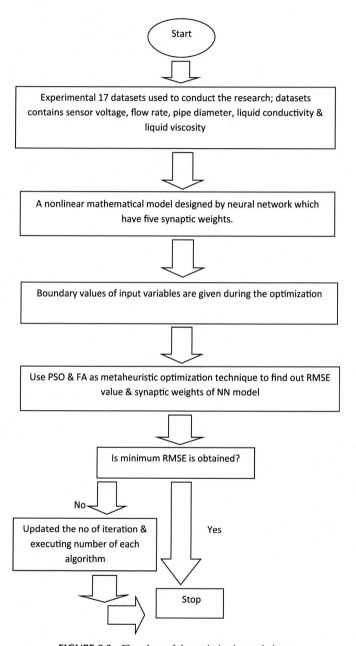

FIGURE 8.3 Flowchart of the optimization technique.

diameter (D). That is, the flow rate is the function of the other four input variables represented as:

$$F = f(E, D, k, n) \qquad (8.5)$$

TABLE 8.4 Parameter settings for the algorithm.

PSO	FA
Inertia weight $(w) = 1$	No of number fireflies = population size = 50
Inertia weight damping ratio $W_{damp} = .99$	Light absorption coefficient $(\gamma) = 1$
Personal learning coefficient $(c_1) = 1.5$	Attraction coefficient base value $(\beta) = 2$
Global learning coefficient $(c_2) = 1$	Mutation coefficient $(\alpha) = 0.2$
Population size = 50	Mutation coefficient damping ratio = 0.98
Maximum iteration = 5000	Maximum iteration = 5000

When presenting the neural network model pipe diameter, liquid properties and sensor output voltages are considered as a node of the input layer, while the flow rate is a node of the output layer of the linear neural network model. Four weights, W_1, W_2, W_3 and W_4, are multiplied with each input node and finally added to the constant β to correlate with the output node. For simplification of the neural model, we do not need any activation function. Hence, Eq. (8.5) can be further modified as follows:

$$F = E * W_1 + D * W_2 + k * W_3 + n * W_4 + \beta \qquad (8.6)$$

In Eq. (8.6), both the weights and bias values are unknown, in finding the optimum values of these coefficient two different metaheuristic optimization techniques (PSO and FA) are applied. For NN learning, a given set of input process variables was used to find the calculated flow rate which had the best fit with the actual flow rate of the present process. However, in this research, we used 17 data sets to test the model and we verified the model by using the error parameter squared error, which can be given as:

$$E = \sum_{i=1}^{n} (E_t - E_o)^2 \qquad (8.7)$$

where E_t and E_o represents the target output and calculated output from after the optimization and metaheuristic optimization techniques: FA and PSO are used to optimize the objective function E.

6. Results and discussion

In the previous section, we discussed the neural network model used to make a linear relation between the process responses and the flow rate using four potential input variables. In the next stage, two optimization techniques, PSO and FA, are used to discover the weights of the neural network model in such a manner that the calculated flow rate best fits with the experimental flow rate. During optimization of the synaptic weights of the NN model, we used 17 experimental data sets. For all the algorithms, maximum iteration and population are set to 5000 and 50, respectively. For the NN model, the quantity of weightage factors is 5, that is, $\{w_1, w_2, w_3, w_4, w_5\}$, with the search range set to $[-75, 75]$ for the entirety of the coefficients for both types of modeling. All the metaheuristic improvements were reenacted utilizing Matlab 2015b in a PC with 4 GB RAM, Intel I core I3 processor, and Windows7 Working Framework. Because of the stochastic idea of bio-inspired enhancement, every calculation is executed multiple times for each case and every algorithm executed several times to get the optimum & repeated value. Each algorithm is carried out 20 times to enable result analysis from the simulated results.

6.1 Computational efficiency test

The computational efficiency test is one of the major factors for the identification of bio-inspired algorithm efficiency. For this, computational efficiency is determined by the average execution time taken by each algorithm. From Table 8.5, it can be seen that the average execution time is better for PSO-NN than for the FA-ANN model.

6.1.1 Flowchart

Fig. 8.3 shows a flowchart of the overall process where 17 data sets are considered for testing the model. Each of the algorithms is used to find the optimum synaptic weight of the neural network model. In this research we used RMSE as an error function to predict the best model.

6.2 Convergence test

The convergence test was observed by finding the best (minimum) fitness values of the objective function applied in an algorithm at each iteration index. In this research, we executed each algorithm for 20 runs, where the number of populations and maximum iterations are set to 50 and 5000, respectively. To graphically represent the convergence test we made a comparative study between PSO-NN and FA-NN for up to 500 iterations. From Fig. 8.4 it can be seen that PSO-NN has better convergence ability than FA-ANN.

TABLE 8.5 Comparative study based on execution time.

Algorithm	Average computational time
FA-NN	315.4467 s
PSO-NN	281.192 s

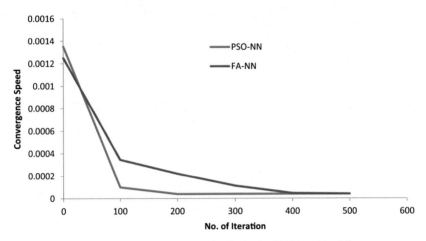

FIGURE 8.4 Convergence speed for bio-inspired NN-based modeling.

6.3 Accuracy test

The accuracy test is a statistical measurement that is used to calculate the flow rate following experimental data sets under various exploratory conditions. For measuring the accurateness of the model two records are used in the current research, as defined in Eqs. (8.8) and (8.9)

$$IAE = |F_{\text{measured}} - F_{\text{calculated}}| \tag{8.8}$$

$$\text{Mean absolute percentage error (MAPE)} = \frac{1}{n}\sum_{i=1}^{n}\frac{IAE}{F_{\text{measured}}} \tag{8.9}$$

$$\text{And mean absolute error (MAE)} = \frac{\sum_{i=1}^{n}IAE_i}{n} \tag{8.10}$$

where n is the number of estimations in the trial data set, Fmeasured is the exploratory estimation of the flow rate and Fcalculated is the estimation of the flow rate. The coefficient of the linear model of the neural network is obtained after applying each algorithm when the objective function gives the lowest RMSE among all the possible runs. The coefficient of the models is acquired from the PSO-NN and FA-NN Matlab codes appearing in Table 8.6.

The model root mean square error (RMSE) and accuracy are expressed in Eqs. (8.11) and (8.12).

$$RMSE = \sqrt{\frac{1}{m}\sum_{i=1}^{m}\left(\frac{X_{\text{exp}} - X_{\text{Cal}}}{X_{\text{exp}}}\right)^2} * 100\% \tag{8.11}$$

$$\text{Accuracy} = (100 - RMSE)\% \tag{8.12}$$

where X_{exp} and X_{cal} indicate the experimental and calculated flow rates obtained after optimization of the linear model of NN. Determining worth and m

TABLE 8.6 Estimated optimal parameters using PSO-NN- and FA-NN-based modeling.

Method	W_1	W_2	W_3	W_4	β
FA-NN	0.1371	0.0218	0.0085	0.0011	−0.0363
PSO-NN	0.1310	0.0072	0.02822	0.00172	−0.04714

TABLE 8.7 Comparative study based on the mean absolute error (MAE) in FA-NN and PSO-NN.

Method	Mean absolute percentage error (MAPE)	Mean absolute error(MAE)
FA-NN	0.159816	0.000377
PSO-NN	0.134061	0.000382

TABLE 8.8 Comparative study based on RMSE and accuracy.

Method	RMSE	Accuracy
FA-ANN	0.0426	99.957
PSO-ANN	0.0459	99.954

is the number of testing datasets. Table 8.7 illustrates that PSO-NN offers the lowest MAPE, while FA-NN gives the lowest MAE. It has been additionally seen from Table 8.8 that FA-NN enhancement has the lowest RMSE and greatest accuracy. Fig. 8.5 shows the relative error (RE) versus distinctive fluid stream rate estimation cases for PSO-NN and FA-NN displayed separately. It can be seen clearly that the proposed FA-NN has a lower RE than the PSO-NN model. Therefore FA-NN is considered as best model by means of RE in present control framework.

Fig. 8.6 shows a relative comparison among the trial and determined estimations of the flow rate, with the result expanded relative to the cases.

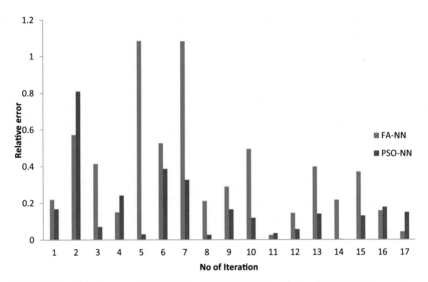

FIGURE 8.5 Relative errors for PSO-NN- and FA-NN-based modeling of the liquid flow control process.

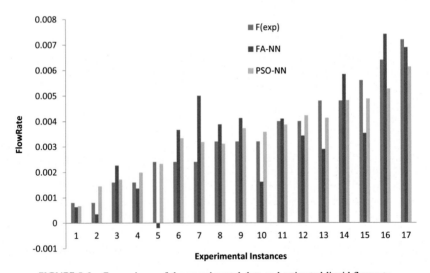

FIGURE 8.6 Comparisons of the experimental data and estimated liquid flow rate.

FA-NN streamlining gives a better determined flow rate for the exploratory stream rate. Fig. 8.7 explain that deviation of flow rate is optimum when flow rate ranges from 300–400 lpm. PSO-NN has the lowest deviation from the stream rate.

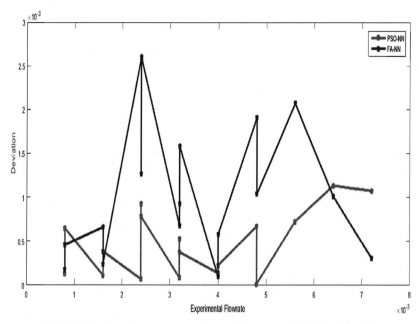

FIGURE 8.7 Deviation versus experimental flow rate in PSO-NN and FA-NN.

7. Conclusions and future work

Proper modeling of the process system is an important task for researchers. In the present model, flow rate is the function of four potential independent process variables: pipe diameter, sensor output voltages, and liquid properties (conductivity and viscosity). A linear model neural network is used to create a relation between the process response, flow rate, and input variables. Two metaheuristic optimization methods, PSO and FA, are applied to find the optimum values of weights of the neural network so that the RMSE of the objective function is at a minimum. For the model prediction, we used 17 experimental data sets containing process response and independent input variables.

Mathematical activities are performed and the measurable examination of the outcomes is also given. All the outcomes show that the results of the proposed FA-NN outperformed PSO-NN in most instances demonstrating fluid stream control measurement, however a significant drawback was its computational time. Although both algorithms can predict the process response, the flow rates achieved were 99.957% by FA-NN and 99.954% by PSO-NN.

Table 8.9 shows that the present study provides greater accuracy than previously applied intelligent techniques for the same flow control model.

TABLE 8.9 Comparison between the present study and previous research.

Sl. No.	Model analysis (with reference)	RMSE
1	FLC	8%
2	Neural network model	2.294
3	GA-ANN	1.58%
4	GA-RSM	1.03%
5	GA-ANOVA	7.4423%
6	ANFIS	2.143%

A more advanced model could be implemented by measuring the experimental liquid density as another input process variable. In addition, to give greater accuracy, convergence speed and stability tunings of metaheuristics algorithm are still a challenge.

References

[1] R. Hagihghi, A. Razmjou, Y. Orooji, M.E. Warkiani, M. Asadnia, A miniaturized piezoresistive flow sensor for real-time monitoring of intravenous infusion, J. Biomed. Mater. Res. B Appl. Biomater. 108 (2020) 568–576.
[2] T. Dinh, H.-P. Phan, T.-K. Nguyen, A. Qamar, P. Woodfield, Y. Zhu, et al., Solvent-free fabrication of biodegradable hot-film flow sensor for noninvasive respiratory monitoring, J. Phys. Appl. Phys. 50 (2017) 215401.
[3] S.I. Abdullahi, N.A. Malik, M.H. Habaebi, A.B. Salami, Miniaturized turbine flow sensor: design and simulation, in: 2018 7th International Conference on Computer and Communication Engineering (ICCCE), IEEE, 2018, pp. 38–43.
[4] M. Bora, A.G.P. Kottapalli, J.M. Miao, M.S. Triantafyllou, Fish-inspired self-powered microelectromechanical flow sensor with biomimetic hydrogel cupula, Apl. Mater. 5 (2017) 104902.
[5] A. Baldwin, L. Yu, E. Meng, An electrochemical impedance-based thermal flow sensor for physiological fluids, J. Microelectromech. Syst. 25 (2016) 1015–1024.
[6] P. Dutta, A. Kumar, Intelligent calibration technique using optimized fuzzy logic controller for ultrasonic flow sensor, Math. Modell. Eng. Prob. 4 (2017) 91–94.
[7] S.-E. Tsai, S.-H. Zhuang, Optical flow sensor integrated navigation system for quadrotor in GPS-denied environment, in: 2016 International Conference on Robotics and Automation Engineering (ICRAE), IEEE, 2016, pp. 87–91.
[8] D. Alveringh, T.V.P. Schut, R.J. Wiegerink, W. Sparreboom, J.C. Lötters, Resistive pressure sensors integrated with a coriolis mass flow sensor, in: 2017 19th International Conference on Solid-State Sensors, Actuators and Microsystems (TRANSDUCERS), IEEE, 2017, pp. 1167–1170.
[9] J.N. Mashak, Variable Orifice Flow Sensor, 2016.

[10] F. Wenig, C. Heschl, T. Glatzl, T. Sauter, Numerical and experimental characterization of a novel low-cost thermal air flow sensor, in: IECON 2017-43rd Annual Conference of the IEEE Industrial Electronics Society, IEEE, 2017, pp. 3633−3637.

[11] C.-L. Shao, K.-J. Xu, Z.-P. Shu, A. Li, A frequency correcting method combining bilateral correction with weighted average for vortex flow sensor signal, IEEE Trans. Instrument. & Measur. 66 (2017) 2711−2724.

[12] A. Leoni, V. Stornelli, L. Pantoli, A low-cost portable spherical directional anemometer for fixed points measurement, Sensor Actuator Phys. 280 (2018) 543−551.

[13] S.C. Bera, B. Chakraborty, D.N. Kole, Study of a modified anemometer type flow meter, Sensors & Transduc. J. 83 (2007) 1521−1526.

[14] A. Al-Salaymeh, Optimization of hot-wire thermal flow sensor based on a neural net model, Appl. Therm. Eng. 26 (2006) 948−955.

[15] K.V. Santhosh, B.K. Roy, A practically validated intelligent calibration technique using optimized ANN for ultrasonic flow meter, Int. J. Electr. Eng. & Inf. 7 (2015) 379.

[16] N.G. Waller, A. Tellegen, R.P. McDonald, D.T. Lykken, Exploring nonlinear models in personality assessment: development and preliminary validation of a negative emotionality scale, J. Pers. 64 (1996) 545−576.

[17] P. Dutta, S. Mandal, A. Kumar, Comparative study: FPA based response surface methodology and ANOVA for the parameter Optimization in Process Control, Adv. Model. Anal. C 73 (2018) 23−27, https://doi.org/10.18280/ama_c.730104.

[18] P. Dutta, S. Mandal, A. Kumar, Application of FPA and ANOVA in the optimization of liquid flow control process, RCES 5 (2019) 7−11, https://doi.org/10.18280/rces.050102.

[19] T. Amemiya, Non-linear regression models, Handb. Econom. 1 (1983) 333−389.

[20] L. Bianchi, M. Dorigo, L.M. Gambardella, W.J. Gutjahr, A survey on metaheuristics for stochastic combinatorial optimization, Nat. Comput. 8 (2009) 239−287.

[21] A.H. Gandomi, X.-S. Yang, S. Talatahari, A.H. Alavi, Metaheuristic Applications in Structures and Infrastructures, Newnes, 2013.

[22] E. Bonabeau, M. Dorigo, D. de RDF. Marco, G. Theraulaz, G. Théraulaz, Swarm Intelligence: From Natural to Artificial Systems, Oxford university press, 1999.

[23] R.C. Eberhart, Y. Shi, Comparing inertia weights and constriction factors in particle swarm optimization, in: Proceedings of the 2000 Congress on Evolutionary Computation. CEC00 (Cat. No. 00TH8512), vol. 1, IEEE, 2000, pp. 84−88.

[24] P. Dutta, R. Agarwala, M. Majumder, A. Kumar, Parameters extraction of a single diode solar cell model using bat algorithm, firefly algorithm & cuckoo search optimization, Ann. Facul. Eng. Hunedoara 18 (2020) 147−156.

[25] D. Karaboga, B. Basturk, A powerful and efficient algorithm for numerical function optimization: artificial bee colony (ABC) algorithm, J. Glob. Optim. 39 (2007) 459−471.

[26] X.-S. Yang, Firefly algorithm, stochastic test functions and design optimisation, Int. J. Bio-Inspired Comput. 2 (2010) 78−84.

[27] X.-S. Yang, Flower Pollination Algorithm for Global Optimization. International Conference on Unconventional Computing and Natural Computation, Springer, 2012, pp. 240−249.

[28] M. Dorigo, V. Maniezzo, A. Colorni, Ant system: optimization by a colony of cooperating agents, IEEE Trans. Syst. Man, & Cybernet. Part B (Cybernetics) 26 (1996) 29−41.

[29] X.-S. Yang, S. Deb, Engineering optimisation by cuckoo search, Int. J. Math. Model. Numer. Optim. 1 (2010) 330−343.

[30] P. Dutta, S.K. Biswas, S. Biswas, M. Majumder, Parametric optimization of solar parabolic collector using metaheuristic optimization, Comput. Intell. & Mach. Learn. 2 (2021) 26−32.

[31] D.H. Wolpert, W.G. Macready, No free lunch theorems for optimization, IEEE Trans. Evol. Comput. 1 (1997) 67–82.

[32] A.L.D. Rossi, A.C.P.L.F. Carvalho, C. Soares, Bio-inspired parameter tunning of MLP networks for gene expression analysis, in: 2008 Eighth International Conference on Hybrid Intelligent Systems, Barcelona, Spain: IEEE, 2008, pp. 435–440, https://doi.org/10.1109/HIS.2008.152.

[33] J. Pérez, J.A. Cabrera, J.J. Castillo, J.M. Velasco, Bio-inspired spiking neural network for nonlinear systems control, Neural Netw. 104 (2018) 15–25, https://doi.org/10.1016/j.neunet.2018.04.002.

[34] J. Kajornrit, A comparative study of optimization methods for improving artificial neural network performance, in: 2015 7th International Conference on Information Technology and Electrical Engineering (ICITEE), Chiang Mai, Thailand: IEEE, 2015, pp. 35–40, https://doi.org/10.1109/ICITEED.2015.7408908.

[35] M. Göçken, M. Özçalıcı, A. Boru, A.T. Dosdoğru, Integrating metaheuristics and Artificial Neural Networks for improved stock price prediction, Expert Syst. Appl. 44 (2016) 320–331, https://doi.org/10.1016/j.eswa.2015.09.029.

[36] R. Ghasemiyeh, R. Moghdani, S.S. Sana, A hybrid artificial neural network with metaheuristic algorithms for predicting stock price, Cybern. Syst. 48 (2017) 365–392, https://doi.org/10.1080/01969722.2017.1285162.

[37] B.A. Garro, H. Sossa, R.A. Vazquez, Design of artificial neural networks using a modified Particle Swarm Optimization algorithm, in: 2009 International Joint Conference on Neural Networks, Atlanta, Ga, USA: IEEE, 2009, pp. 938–945, https://doi.org/10.1109/IJCNN.2009.5178918.

[38] V. Bevilacqua, F. Cassano, E. Mininno, G. Iacca, Optimizing feed-forward neural network topology by multi-objective evolutionary algorithms: a comparative study on biomedical datasets, in: F. Rossi, F. Mavelli, P. Stano, D. Caivano (Eds.), Advances in Artificial Life, Evolutionary Computation and Systems Chemistry, vol. 587, Springer International Publishing, Cham, 2016, pp. 53–64, https://doi.org/10.1007/978-3-319-32695-5_5.

[39] P. Dutta, A. Kumar, Flow Sensor Analogue: Realtime Prediction Analysis Using SVM & KNN, 2018.

[40] P. Dutta, A. Kumar, Study of optimized NN model for liquid flow sensor based on different parameters, in: Proceeding of International Conference on Materials, Applied Physics and Engineering, 2018.

[41] P. Dutta, A. Kumar, Application of an ANFIS model to optimize the liquid flow rate of a process control system, Chem. Eng. Trans. 71 (2018) 991–996, https://doi.org/10.3303/CET1871166.

[42] P. Dutta, A. Kumar, Design an intelligent calibration technique using optimized GA-ANN for liquid flow control system, J. Eur. Systèmes Automatisés 50 (2017) 449–470, https://doi.org/10.3166/jesa.50.449-470.

[43] P. Dutta, A. Kumar, Modelling of liquid flow control system using optimized genetic algorithm, Stat. Optimiz. & Inf. Comput. 8 (2020) 565–582, https://doi.org/10.19139/soic-2310-5070-618.

[44] S. Mandal, P. Dutta, A. Kumar, Modeling of liquid flow control process using improved versions of elephant swarm water search algorithm, SN Appl. Sci. 1 (2019) 886, https://doi.org/10.1007/s42452-019-0914-5.

[45] S. Lokesh, P.M. Kumar, M.R. Devi, P. Parthasarathy, C. Gokulnath, An automatic Tamil speech recognition system by using bidirectional recurrent neural network with self-organizing map, Neural Comput. Appl. 31 (2019) 1521–1531.

[46] M.M. Saritas, A. Yasar, Performance analysis of ANN and Naive Bayes classification algorithm for data classification, Int. J. Intell. Syst. & Appl. Eng. 7 (2019) 88−91.
[47] T. Zan, Z. Liu, H. Wang, M. Wang, X. Gao, Control chart pattern recognition using the convolutional neural network, J. Intell. Manuf. 31 (2020) 703−716.
[48] Y.-R. Zeng, Y. Zeng, B. Choi, L. Wang, Multifactor-influenced energy consumption forecasting using enhanced back-propagation neural network, Energy 127 (2017) 381−396.
[49] D. Giuliani, Colour image segmentation based on principal component analysis with application of firefly algorithm and Gaussian mixture model, Int. J. Image Process. 12 (2018).
[50] D.K. Mohanty, Application of firefly algorithm for design optimization of a shell and tube heat exchanger from economic point of view, Int. J. Therm. Sci. 102 (2016) 228−238.
[51] S. Swain, P. Patel, S. Nandi, A multiple linear regression model for precipitation forecasting over Cuttack district, Odisha, India, in: 2017 2nd International Conference for Convergence in Technology (I2CT), IEEE, 2017, pp. 355−357.
[52] N.I. Manik, Y. Nursalim, D. Suhartono, Design of distribution optimization application using firefly algorithm, Comtech: Comput. Mathe. & Eng. Appl. 8 (2017) 155−162, https://doi.org/10.21512/comtech.v8i3.2567.
[53] X. Du, Z. Liu, Application of firefly algorithm intelligent optimization particle filter in dynamic harmonic detection of power system, IOP Conf. Ser. Mater. Sci. Eng. 439 (2018) 032015, https://doi.org/10.1088/1757-899X/439/3/032015.
[54] A. Nadeem, T. Shankar, R.K. Sharma, S.K. Roy, An application of firefly algorithm for clustering in wireless sensor networks, in: Proceedings of the International Conference on Recent Cognizance in Wireless Communication & Image Processing, Springer, 2016, pp. 869−878.
[55] G. Mühürcü, E. Kose, A. Muhurcu, A. Kuyumcu, Parameter optimization of PI controller by PSO for optimal controlling of a buck converter's output, in: 2017 International Artificial Intelligence and Data Processing Symposium (IDAP), IEEE, 2017, pp. 1−6.
[56] I. Soesanti, R. Syahputra, Batik production process optimization using particle swarm optimization method, J. Theor. Appl. Inf. Technol. 86 (2016) 272.
[57] X. Zhang, X. Zheng, R. Cheng, J. Qiu, Y. Jin, A competitive mechanism based multiobjective particle swarm optimizer with fast convergence, Inf. Sci. 427 (2018) 63−76, https://doi.org/10.1016/j.ins.2017.10.037.

Chapter 9

Affordable energy-intensive routing using metaheuristics

Priyom Dutta[1], B.S. Mahanand[2]
[1]*School of Computer Engineering, KIIT University, Bhubaneswar, Odisha, India;* [2]*Department of Information Science and Engineering, Sri Jayachamarajendra College of Engineering, JSS Science and Technology University, Mysuru, Karnataka, India*

1. Introduction

With the advancement of the Internet, various Internet of Things (IoT) devices have been connected at the same time. As home automation has increased, connecting those devices has become challenging because both fast data packet transfer and reduced energy consumption are important. various control algorithms have been proposed to manage this scenario. We propose an algorithm to easily route data packets to devices with less power consumption while maintaining the scalability and privacy of the data packet information as it travels the network. Therefore, the techniques are implemented at the routing level, as explained in this chapter. Metaheuristics and cognitive science have responsible roles in this kind of efficient routing. Metaheuristics are algorithms that help find solutions to problems at a higher level or are designed for heuristics; we could say that they generate, select, and provide optimized solutions. Metaheuristics and cognitive science allow us to design computer models focused on the study of intelligence, and that computational intelligence is used in techniques for efficient routing. In this chapter, routing and various routing techniques are explained, and metaheuristics and cognitive science are discussed. Efficiency based on various scenarios is addressed as well.

2. Literature survey

Xzhang et al. [1] proposed a model using energy-aware routing algorithms that include ad hoc networks, called reliable energy, that incur minimal cost. Energy-efficient routing has three main aspects: network reliability, network energy efficiency, and prolonged network life. They proposed reliable minimum energy routing and reliable minimum energy cost routing for networks

Cognitive Big Data Intelligence with a Metaheuristic Approach
https://doi.org/10.1016/B978-0-323-85117-6.00013-3
193

that include energy-efficient routing strategies mainly focused on the restricted transactions and transmissions allowed per packet as well as the impact of acknowledgment packets. Tai Hieng Tie et al. [2] discussed the important aspect of energy consumption of wireless ad hoc networks. They proposed an ad hoc on-demand distance vector routing protocol to improve energy conservation. The concept of an energy metric for improving the communication life span of ad hoc networks was investigated by Xang et al. [3], whose research described nodes of the sensor draining power. Low-energy adaptive clustering hierarchy (LEACH) is considered direct communication from source to destination, so they developed an efficient edge computation. Their simulation, energy-efficient least edge computation LEACH (ELEC-LEACH), resulted in lifetime enhancement, node failure reduction, and reduced packet drop. Ashwani Kumar Dubey et al. [4] proposed an energy-efficient, static model that includes a multihop routing protocol that has been deployed in agriculture. The model was evaluated based on energy efficiency and packet loss compared with those of existing models, and the simulation achieved a better throughput and lifetime. Research by Yiming Shen et al. [5] described a wireless transmission power and communication radius that would result in a change in communication distance. Their research also proved that fewer hops should not be considered reduced energy consumption, and the choice of communication node should be considered lower energy consumption over the entire network. Xiaoning Zhang et al. [6] described a reduction in energy use for various Internet applications to reduce energy consumption. They proposed a crisis and emergency risk communication (CERC) strategy for energy management based on dynamic traffic control, so their CERC model performs well under load balancing and for energy efficiency. Renu Yadav et al. [7] developed a model to adjust energy consumption and modify sleep or active nodes, thereby increasing the network's life span. A simulation was performed with MATLAB and showed higher efficiency. Rana E. Ahmed et al. [8] developed a fault-tolerance method to enhance energy efficiency by finding two ideal routing paths, i.e., from the source node to the destination node. Hence, the model achieves high throughput and network delivery. Fang Junli et al. [9] developed a software-defined wireless sensor network with an efficient algorithm. They simulated the routing algorithm and found that for network extension and increased network lifetime, the algorithm works perfectly well and handles network traffic. Min Wan et al. [10] proposed a new energy-efficient routing protocol for wireless sensor construction and found that the cluster radius is reduced with reductions among the clusters, hence balancing reduced energy consumption and the lifetime of the network improvement. V Jaya Lakshmy et al. [11] focused on reducing energy consumption and concluded that less energy consumption results in a longer network lifetime. Their model focuses on developing clustering that is more energy efficient and scalable. Kartik Chawda et al. [12] performed a survey and found energy-aware routing protocols based on functionalities, benefits, and limitations that also focus on ad hoc networks and application developers. Fatma Almajadub et al. [13] researched detection of node locations comprised in the mobile sensor node based on dynamic location. They proposed a model that tracks network nodes based on signal strength. Their results showed 12.5% less energy consumption. Ziaur Rahman et al. [14] proposed a theoretical framework model based on clusters called zigzag routing inside cluster (ZRIC). The reduction in power consumption and the distance calculation between sender and receiver are based on the spanning-tree path and data transmission. Rana E. Ahmed et al. [15] describe a new way of reducing power consumption by proposing a model that finds the best routes to choose for improved fault tolerance and cost reduction. I Hameem Shanavas et al. [16] describe a new model and algorithm, called the memetic algorithm, that works with a combination of evolutionary and local search algorithms. Their approach focuses on minimizing wire length as well as channel capacity reduction and traffic congestion estimation that are priorities in global routing. Xiaoning Zhang et al. [17] describe a new energy-saving routing algorithm, described as a centralized energy-efficient algorithm control strategy for the Internet and an energy management controller for network links. Quan Li et al. [18] discuss cognitive radios that use spatially unused wireless channels for data transmission. They proposed a geographical routing process meant for large-scale heterogeneous cognitive radio on cognitive mesh networks and traditional cognitive radio systems. Xuefeng Wang et al. [19] describe a logistics system for delivering goods and propose a formulation to determine optimal solutions or strong lower bounds in investigating the effectiveness of the heuristic approach. Petac Eugen et al. [20] described Cisco routing techniques to determine routing tables.

3. Problem description

According to the latest research objectives, the growing needs of the Internet have resulted in the manufacture of an extraordinary number of IoT devices that need to be connected to the Internet [21−23]. But connecting such large devices leads to two main issues:

Too many devices may lead to congestion, and increased congestion indicates enormous network traffic. As a result, routers sometimes crash; other times, avoiding network traffic may require a long path, thereby increasing network latency.

With increased network traffic, routing costs also increase—the number of IoT devices, degree of network congestion, and router energy consumption become greater. When we consider the scenario at a larger scale, this energy use becomes enormous and reduces efficiency among routers. Even when routers sometimes reroute across the network to bypass it, that energy use must be considered. Energy demand tolerance increases dramatically, and delay is increased despite having the latest network capabilities such as 4G, 5G, 6G, and so on.

4. Routing

When a network device wants to communicate with another device at the same or a different location, a communication path is selected for network traffic across different networks. This process of communication across various devices is called routing [24].

In simple words, routing means selecting a path to transfer data from a source location to a desired destination location. The device that performs this selection process is called a router.

Routing takes place in the third layer of the open systems interconnection model network layer. Devices ask the router to deliver packets to a destination by choosing an optimal path or the most efficient and fastest path from one network to another to perform data transfer [25]. A diagram of devices communicating through routing can be seen in Fig. 9.1, which shows how devices connect through routers to connect to the Internet.

4.1 Routers

The device that forwards a network packet across the network is called a router—basically, it sends data from source to destination with advanced features and control mechanisms based on its routing table. We can call it a traffic controller of routes, where it decides the flow of packets from one location to another—this is similar to a real-life traffic controller for roads,

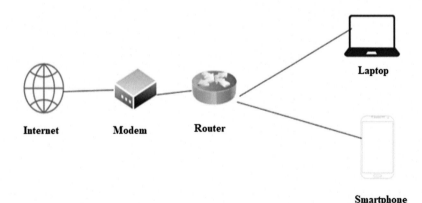

FIGURE 9.1 Devices connected to the Internet.

except in this case, the controller handles packet transfers. The router looks at the sender's IP address to determine the recipient and location to which the data should be sent; it then forwards the data packet to the next network.

4.2 Router paths

Suppose a packet wants to communicate with a computer that requested it. At that moment, the router will discover all the connected devices. Regardless of whether the packet is coming from the same or a different network, the router forwards the packet to the computer that expects to receive the packet. Hence, routers act as network watch guards. Thus, routers handle both incoming and outgoing packets, and the paths they select for data travel are called router paths.

4.3 Router transmission

Further, the router must perform the work of sending data packets and must decide the path over which the data will be sent [26]. While obtaining the next host address over the Internet, it must transmit the incoming packet it receives from the modem to the computer or vice versa, which in turn sends the information across the Internet.

Fig. 9.2 shows a mesh network consisting of communicating devices: laptops, routers, etc. The router chooses the best possible connection to the Internet and forwards incoming and outgoing data packets across the network. It uses a table that keeps track of all the packet forwarding information. The

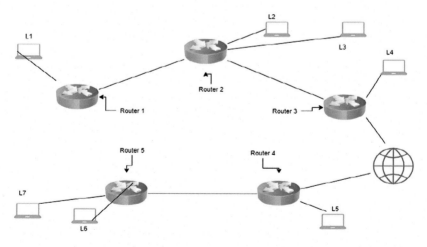

NETWORK CONSISTING OF ROUTER AND DEVICE COMPONENTS

FIGURE 9.2 Mesh networking system consisting of router and device components.

table is prepared using routing algorithms, so we first see routing algorithms, followed by the routing table. Fig. 9.2 displays connected devices within a mesh network. This setup is called nested routing, wherein each router is connected to another and forwards packets to another router as part of the routing process. The setup is like a bridge network carrying the signal strength forward to another router, hence sharing the network and network energy resources from the sender to the destination port. The network shown is a mesh network of five routers sharing energy and network resources.

5. Routing algorithms

The process of forwarding a packet is called routing, wherein data packets are forwarded from one router to another [27]. Various routing algorithms are available and can be categorized as follows:

1. Adaptive algorithms
2. Nonadaptive algorithms
1. Adaptive algorithms

Adaptive algorithms adapt to routing decisions when needed. When the traffic load or network topology changes, adaptive algorithms change their routing decisions for data packet forwarding. Hence, network algorithms with the capability to change their routes based on priorities and deal with sharing constraints are called adaptive algorithms.

Adaptive algorithms are further classified as follows:

(a) Isolated—with this method, each node makes its own routing decisions using existing information rather than seeking it from another node. The sending node does not have information about the overall route. As a result, the packet may be sent through the most congested route, and this is a disadvantage of this algorithm. Examples of routing using this algorithm are hot potato routing and backward learning routing.

(b) Centralized—in this system, the central node has all the network information and decides all routing protocols on its own. The sole merit of this system is that the central node contains the information of all the other nodes. The demerit is that system delay or failure can arise if the central node is disturbed or goes down.

(c) Distributed—in the distributed algorithm, nodes fetch information from adjacent nodes and uses that information to make routing decisions. The single demerit is the time required to fetch information, while decision-making is performed with packet forwarding.

2. Nonadaptive algorithms

Nonadaptive algorithms do not change the routing decisions of the selected routing path. Thus, nonadaptive algorithms use a static routing path; the routing table is computed in advance, and the routers are rebooted when the routing information has been downloaded to them [28].

Classifications are as follows:

(a) Flooding: in the flooding technique, a router sends an incoming packet to every node except the outgoing node where it was received. The only issue is with the sequence numbers, which can be resolved by sequence numbers, spanning trees, and hop count.

(b) Random walk: in the random walk method, data packets are sent by the router to the next adjacent node. This process is considered the most robust and is implemented by sending the data packets to the link that is in the queue

6. Routing table

The routing table consists of predefined rules derived by a tabular method to determine packet forwarding between senders and receivers over an IP address. Every IP address accessed by an enabled device uses a routing table. Fig. 9.3 shows a routing table that defines the forwarding of packets from one router to another or to a destination.

7. Metaheuristics

A high-level problem-independent algorithmic framework for providing a set of guidelines is known as a metaheuristic. Well-defined examples of heuristics are evolutionary algorithms, genetic algorithms, tabulated optimized search, optimized ant colony, neighborhood search, and many others. A problem-

Interfaces and Connections

Create Connection | **Edit Interface/Connection**

Edit | Add ▾ | Delete | Summary | Details | Test Connection

Interface	IP	Type	Slot	Status	Desc
FastEthernet0/0	192.168.1.1	10/100Ethernet	0	Up	
FastEthernet0/1	172.16.1.1	10/100Ethernet	0	Up	
FastEthernet0/3/0	not applicable	Ethernet Switch Port	0	Up	
FastEthernet0/3/1	not applicable	Ethernet Switch Port	0	Up	
FastEthernet0/3/2	not applicable	Ethernet Switch Port	0	Up	
FastEthernet0/3/3	not applicable	Ethernet Switch Port	0	Up	
Vlan1	no IP address	Vlan		Up	

FIGURE 9.3 Routing table of a Cisco router, showing packet forwarding.

based implementation of an optimized in accord with the guidelines of an algorithmic metaheuristic framework is also called a metaheuristic, as proposed by Glover, which "heuristic" with the Greek prefix "meta."

The optimization methods of these algorithms are formulated based on strategies involved in the framework and are hence known as a metaheuristics framework, i.e., heuristic in nature [29–31]. Finding an optimum solution within the set of guidelines is the sole reason to develop a metaheuristic, which is differentiated from exacted methodologies that provide a proof of the optimum solution. Computing a solution within the framework takes less relative time than required for an exact method, and the efficient solution is good enough. An optimum metaheuristics solution is preferable for NP-hard problems in which computing time increases exponentially with problem size. For complex problems and those with large instances, metaheuristics is better at finding an optimum solution with less time complexity. Metaheuristics frameworks are formulated in general terms, and metaheuristic algorithms can be adopted that fit well with optimized problems in real life, resulting in acceptable computation time and quality solutions even for platform-variant optimization, and hence for optimization problems that would typically consider constraints or use a linear function for decision variables. Thus, the chosen adaptation must be problem-specific and achieve good performance. The metaheuristic research field lacks a universal design methodology and rigorous testing and design implementations, creating intricate methods across various operators.

The various types of metaheuristics are as follows:

1. Constructive metaheuristics
2. Population-based metaheuristics
3. Hybrid metaheuristics

7.1 Constructive metaheuristics

Constructive metaheuristics develop solutions from their own elements rather than improving the overall solution, and hence are performed by adding one element at a time to partial solutions. This approach is adapted from greedy algorithms that add all the elements at each iteration [32]. Hence, to improve the quality of the final solution, constructive metaheuristics may include a local phase after the construction phase. Processes can be constructed without restoring them to random solutions by using memory. Hence, metaheuristics are notable because they can be the element that can be added by the effect and not by the possible next move. For example, we consider a look-ahead method using a constructive metaheuristic to determine the potential element value by obtaining a solution complete with added elements from the current or partial solution.

7.2 Population-based metaheuristics

Population metrics based on metaheuristics always obtain an optimal solution by selecting solutions iteratively and combining the solutions, and the collected set is termed the population. The set or class has several important members, one of which is the evolutionary algorithm for retrieving the natural evolution process. When applied to combinatory problems, these are also called "pure" algorithms, which are evolutionary and unique and include an operator for improvement, such as local search.

7.3 Hybrid metaheuristics

In recent decades, the tendency has been to visualize metaheuristics frameworks that provide concepts and ideas as well as components that can be built for optimization rather than to blindly follow. Algorithms for metaheuristics collect ideas from different classes. The hybrid form of metaheuristics has substantial disciplinary powers, and for this reason, many sorts of metaheuristics are used, including specialized metaheuristics that solve the subproblems produced by metaheuristic methods.

8. Metaheuristics for efficient routing

In networking, metaheuristics optimization can include uncertain, dynamic information in routing information according to routing parameters and functional objectives and constraint violations of the problem and the random variables. The feasible value of the objective approximation and solution is determined by approximation or Monte Carlo simulation [33]. Different stochastic problems are meant to be solved using metaheuristics with each possibility. In routing, this approach can help in making efficient routing decisions to reduce traffic and costs. The next step is explaining about the energy and cost efficiency in networks. Using metaheuristics and cognitive science, we can efficiently reduce costs, and the dynamic prediction used in adaptive routing helps reduce traffic and provides faster communication. An enormous number of IoT devices existed in 2020, and routing among them was a challenging task; thus, faster and cost-effective communication is needed.

Cognitive science helps metaheuristic algorithms work efficiently. In networking, cognitive science allows better connectivity of IoT devices with routers. Thus, the router must prioritize routing to devices requiring immediate response rather than those that can tolerate or adjust to a bit of latency.

9. Proposed solution using metaheuristics

The network consists of various nodes, and energy is spent by them to transmit data packets. Some problem solutions are intended to stop the use of maximum nodes and to save energy at the node level, which can improve node energy levels and improve the life spans of routing devices. Assumptions are made that the node can measure the energy level at the time of packet transmission. In that case, the network will try to make two routes that are possible for the sender and receiver.

The above solution modifies existing routing algorithms, such as dynamic source routing, to facilitate energy-efficient routing. Here, we take

E_k (t): node "K", the percentage of remaining energy at time t

Thr: percentage energy threshold in the system

A node remains active only when E(t) > Thr, and is dormant in all other cases. Hence, a node in active mode can also deal with the direct server return (DSR) mode for all data packets for a node in a dormant stage—i.e., a dormant node that cannot work as a node that is intermediate in the path of two adjacent nodes. he sending source must send a packet to the receiver or the destination address but does not have a valid routing algorithm, or it has invalid routing information, and then it starts the route finding, i.e., the route discovery process.

The sender node is the source node that makes out the route request packet (RREQ) and adds the remaining energy level E_s (t), which is one of the header files, so the request data packet, RREQ, receives too many within the network and has only the active nodes and the network that arrives at the receiver or destination node. We consider the case of one or more data routes through the active nodes. The protocol has a defined interval of time, and the receiver node must wait until the first RREQ is received from the node and the next packets arriving from the sender node. So the receiver node, while receiving one or more packets during the predefined time interval, must choose the best among two nodes. The first priority route, which is the best route, is called the primary route, and the other route is called the secondary route. The proposed solution provides the error tolerance and cost of energy efficiency for the network, and hence for the chosen data path, a node again sends the route reply (RREP) for both the primary and the secondary data path. Hence, if the primary route for a sender and receiver fails, the next secondary node will be used. This way, computation of less energy will be calculated.

The figure below shows the basic dynamic source routing. Here, we consider six nodes, A—H, connected by solid lines. We consider that the A node has no route and no routing information to reach node D. Node A starts the finding process by route discovery by sending RREQ packets to neighbor nodes and includes its own identification with it. It can reach D by an RREQ request through a path called [A,B,C,D] along with an RREQ request traveling across that path [A,F,E,D]. The destination node will send an RREP message that RREQ has received. The remaining percentage of energy at any node k is denoted as E_k. We will assume the value threshold, i.e., Thr, is 40% in this scenario. The source node fetches the broadcast to request RREQ packets to its adjacent node, (B,G,E) and receives the packet. Node G has only 10% of its total energy remaining, so it is not the destination or the source node involved in route discovery and will not broadcast the process of route discovery. Here the first packet RREQ received by node D involves path [A,B,C,D], and the second packet RREQ involves path [A,F,E,D], and the primary path according to the algorithm choosing the path is the average remaining path. Hence, in Fig. 9.4, node D will broadcast an RREP [A,B,C,D][A,F,E,D] message for node A, and the router cache is updated as the new path shown in the diagram.

The previous diagram was the basic DSR model for achieving less energy consumption. In Fig. 9.5, we have proposed an advanced DSR model that is more energy-efficient than the previous model.

9.1 Probability estimation of congestion

Routing process demand can be estimated by the end points of each terminal; here, we consider the wire for the source and destination. Hence, the demand can be generated by the need for the generated routing-based graph based on the total number for maximum routes and the number that use the router using the graph edge.

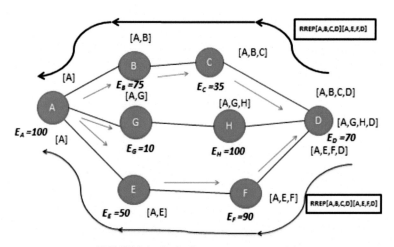

FIGURE 9.4   Basic direct server return model.

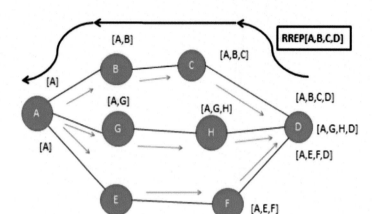

FIGURE 9.5 Our proposed energy-efficient model.

9.2 Memetic algorithms

Memetic algorithms (MAs) are evolutionary algorithms that use another local search rather than global search algorithms. MAs are evolutionary algorithms that use local search processes to refine individuals. When we combine global and local search, it becomes a global optimization process. Thus, a powerful algorithm is required for efficient routing. Fig. 9.6 shows the memetic algorithm developed by the researcher.

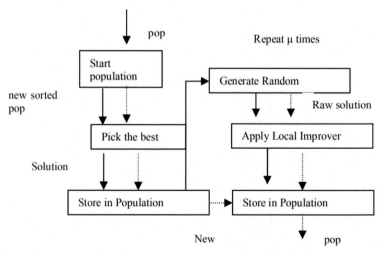

FIGURE 9.6 Memetic algorithm from combining global and local search.

Link sleeping procedure

Input:
A network topology *G* with traffic distribution, a group of link metrics, the set *S* of alternative sleeping link set based on two selection methods.

Output:
The links turned into the sleeping, and the routing of traffic switched from the sleeping links.

Procedure Description:
1. Sort all of the links in the set *S* according to the selection standard value (i.e., link utilization or link traffic number) and put them into a new set *S'* in ascending order;
2. Select the first link *l* in *S'*;
3. Assuming link *l* turns into sleeping, detect *G* whether is a connected graph:
    > **if** (*G* is connected)
    >> Go to the next step;
    > **else**
    >> Go to Step 5.
4. Assuming link *l* turn into sleeping, calculate new shortest path for the traffic on link *l* without changing the other link's metric, detect the network whether occurs congestion:
    > **if** (no congestion in the network)
    >> Sleep link *l*, and update the new graph *G*;
    > **else**
    >> Go to Step 5.
5. Delete the connection request *c* from *S'*;
6. If *S'* is not empty, go back to step 2; otherwise the link sleeping procedure ends.

FIGURE 9.7   Link-sleeping algorithm.

We now develop the optimization structure used in a centralized energy-efficient structure with the direct algorithms shown in the paper. Fig. 9.7 shows the link-sleeping algorithm for energy efficiency and cost-effective routing.

A working illustration of the algorithm discussed above is shown in Fig. 9.8 and shows the bidirectional forwarding of packets based on the link-sleeping algorithm. The unused links for the process of routing are put to sleep. If a link is not interconnected, that link is put to sleep as shown in the figure, the new link is updated, and the packet is forwarded using that link. This process also applies to congestion.

The basic functions of the link-sleeping algorithm are to awaken the network when congestion is reduced and update the link [34,35]. The process is the reverse of the link-sleeping algorithm described above. Fig. 9.9 shows the link-awakening algorithm. To reduce network congestion and improve energy efficiency, the algorithm is more suitable for application over a network that can wake links and put them to sleep, which allows it to use the algorithm to reduce costs, improve efficiency, and hence increase network life. Fig. 9.10 illustrates the link-awakening algorithm described above.

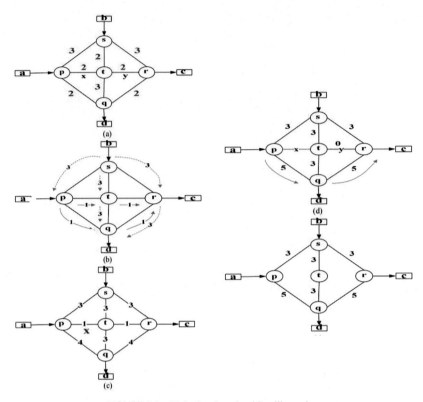

FIGURE 9.8   Link-sleeping algorithm illustration.

Link awaking procedure

Input:
A network topology **G** with traffic distribution, a group of link metrics, the set **S** of sleeping link in the network, the link congestion information uploading to the controller.

Output:
The links turned into awaking, and the load-balancing routing of traffic.

Procedure Description:
1. Copy set **S** to **S'**;
2. Randomly select the first sleeping link *l* in **S'**;
3. Assuming link *l* turn into awaking, calculate new shortest path in the network, detect the network link congestion:

    if (link congestion is alleviated)
    　Awake link *l*, and update the new graph **G**;
    else
    　Do null.
4. Delete the connection request *c* from **S'**;
5. If **S'** is not empty, go back to step 2; otherwise go to the next step;
6. Detect the network link congestion:

    if (link congestion disappear)
    　The procedure ends;
    else
    　Awake all sleeping link in set **S'** once time and the procedure ends.

FIGURE 9.9   Link-awakening algorithm.

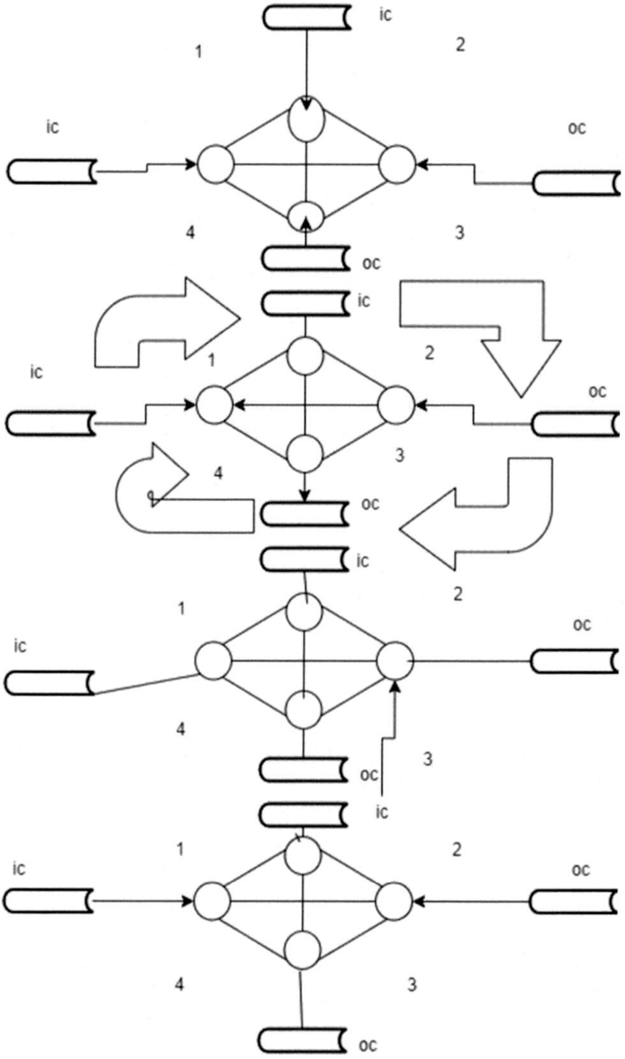

FIGURE 9.10 Link-awakening illustration.

10. Conclusion

A routing protocol design that includes metaheuristics and cognitive science while reducing errors and providing energy efficiency for IoT devices is challenging. Some approaches have been proposed using metaheuristics and cognitive science. This paper has focused on two types of routing paths by modifying dynamic source routing and managing the remaining energy at intermediate nodes. Compared with traditional dynamic source routing, the results provide less overhead, and control messages are reduced. The result obtained from the simulation is a higher packet delivery ratio and reduced overhead in obtaining control messages.

References

[1] X. Zhang, H. Wang, Centralised Energy Efficient Routing Control for Greener Internet, n.d.

[2] Q. Li, Link Quality Aware Geographical Routing in Hybrid Cognitive Radio Mesh networks, n.d.

[3] X. Wang, Multi Objective Metaheuristics for a Location Routing Problem with a Simultaneous Pickup and Delivery, n.d.

[4] P. Eugen, Packet Tracer as a Supportive Tool Dedicated to Gain Practical Networking Skills, n.d.

[5] J. Vazifehdan, et al., Energy-efficient reliable routing considering residual energy in wireless ad hoc networks, IEEE Trans. Mobile Comput. 13 (2) (2014) 434−447.

[6] T.H. Tie, et al., Maximum energy level ad hoc distance vector scheme for energy efficient ad hoc networks routing, 2009 IEEE 9th Malaysia International Conference on Communications (MICC), n.d.

[7] N.U. Sama, et al., Energy efficient least edge computation LEACH in wireless sensor network, 2020 2nd International Conference on Computer and Information Sciences (ICCIS), n.d.

[8] A.K. Dubey, et al., An energy-efficient static multi-hop (ESM) routing protocol for wireless sensor network in agriculture, 2018 2nd International Conference on Micro-electronics and Telecommunication Engineering (ICMETE), n.d.

[9] Y. Shen, et al., Wireless sensor network energy-efficient routing techniques based on improved GEAR, 2009 IEEE International Conference on Network Infrastructure and Digital Content, n.d.

[10] X. Zhang, et al., Centralized energy-efficient routing control for greener internet, 2013 8th International Conference on Communications and Networking in China (CHINACOM), n.d.

[11] R. Yadav, et al., Energy efficient content based routing with cluster based scheduling mechanism, 2019 International Conference on Machine Learning, Big Data, Cloud and Parallel Computing (COMITCon), n.d.

[12] R.E. Ahmed, et al., A fault-tolerant, energy-efficient routing protocol for wireless sensor networks, 2015 International Conference on Information and Communication Technology Research (ICTRC), n.d.

[13] F. Junli, et al., An improved energy-efficient routing algorithm in software define wireless sensor network, 2017 IEEE International Conference on Signal Processing, Communications and Computing (ICSPCC), n.d.

[14] M. Wan, et al., An energy-efficient routing protocol for wireless sensor networks, 2012 Fourth International Conference on Computational Intelligence and Communication Networks, n.d.

[15] V. Jaya Lakshmy, et al., A structural analysis of few energy efficient hierarchical routing protocols in wireless sensor networks, 2017 International Conference on Innovations in Information, Embedded and Communication Systems (ICIIECS), n.d.

[16] K. Chawda, A survey of energy efficient routing protocol in MANET, 2015 2nd International Conference on Electronics and Communication Systems (ICECS), n.d.

[17] F. Almajadub, et al., Novel location tracking energy efficient model for robust routing over wireless sensor networks, 2014 2nd International Conference on Artificial Intelligence, Modelling and Simulation, n.d.

[18] Z. Rahman, et al., ZRIC (Zigzag routing inside cluster) energy efficient routing protocol for wireless sensor networks, 2011 IEEE Conference on Open Systems, n.d.

[19] R.E. Ahmed, A Fault Tolerant Energy Efficient Routing Protocol for Wireless Sensor Networks, n.d.

[20] I.H. Shanavas, R.K. Gnanamurthy, Application Metaheuristic Technique for Solving VLSI Global Routing Problem, n.d.

[21] S. Mishra, H.K. Tripathy, P.K. Mallick, A.K. Bhoi, P. Barsocchi, EAGA-MLP—an enhanced and adaptive hybrid classification model for diabetes diagnosis, Sensors 20 (14) (2020) 4036.

[22] S. Mishra, P.K. Mallick, H.K. Tripathy, A.K. Bhoi, A. González-Briones, Performance evaluation of a proposed machine learning model for chronic disease datasets using an integrated attribute evaluator and an improved decision tree classifier, Appl. Sci. 10 (22) (2020) 8137.

[23] S. Mishra, H.K. Tripathy, B.K. Mishra, Implementation of biologically motivated optimisation approach for tumour categorisation, Int. J. Comput. Aided Eng. Technol. 10 (3) (2018) 244–256.

[24] L. Jena, S. Mishra, S. Nayak, P. Ranjan, M.K. Mishra, Variable optimization in cervical cancer data using particle swarm optimization, in: Advances in Electronics, Communication and Computing, Springer, Singapore, 2021, pp. 147–153.

[25] S. Mishra, P.K. Mallick, L. Jena, G.S. Chae, Optimization of skewed data using sampling-based preprocessing approach, Front. Pub. Health 8 (2020) 274, https://doi.org/10.3389/fpubh.2020.00274.

[26] P.K. Mallick, S. Mishra, G.S. Chae, Digital media news categorization using Bernoulli document model for web content convergence, Personal Ubiquitous Comput. (2020), https://doi.org/10.1007/s00779-020-01461-9.

[27] S. Mishra, P.K. Mallick, D. Koner, Significance of IoT in the agricultural sector, in: Smart Sensors for Industrial Internet of Things, Springer, Cham, 2021, pp. 173–194.

[28] S. Mishra, H.K. Tripathy, A.R. Panda, An improved and adaptive attribute selection technique to optimize dengue fever prediction, Int. J. Eng. Technol. 7 (2018) 480–486.

[29] S. Sahoo, M. Das, S. Mishra, S. Suman, A hybrid DTNB model for heart disorders prediction, in: Advances in Electronics, Communication and Computing, Springer, Singapore, 2021, pp. 155–163.

[30] S. Mishra, H.K. Tripathy, B. Acharya, A precise analysis of deep learning for medical image processing, in: Bio-inspired Neurocomputing, Springer, Singapore, 2021, pp. 25–41.

[31] S. Mishra, Y. Tadesse, A. Dash, L. Jena, P. Ranjan, Thyroid disorder analysis using random forest classifier, in: Intelligent and Cloud Computing, Springer, Singapore, 2019, pp. 385–390.

[32] S. Mishra, P. Chaudhury, B.K. Mishra, H.K. Tripathy, An implementation of feature ranking using machine learning techniques for diabetes disease prediction, in: Proceedings of the Second International Conference on Information and Communication Technology for Competitive Strategies, Udaipur India, 4–5 March 2016, pp. 1–3.

[33] L. Jena, B. Patra, S. Nayak, S. Mishra, S. Tripathy, Risk prediction of kidney disease using machine learning strategies, in: Intelligent and Cloud Computing, Springer, Singapore, 2019, pp. 485–494.

[34]   C. Ray, H.K. Tripathy, S. Mishra, Assessment of autistic disorder using machine learning approach, in: Proceedings of the International Conference on Intelligent Computing and Communication, Hyderabad, India, 9−11 January 2019, pp. 209−219.

[35]   S. Sahoo, S. Mishra, B.K.K. Mishra, M. Mishra, Analysis and implementation of artificial bee colony optimization in constrained optimization problems, in: Handbook of Research on Modeling, Analysis, and Application of Nature-Inspired Metaheuristic Algorithms, IGI Global, Pennsylvania, PA, USA, 2018, pp. 413−432.

Chapter 10

Semantic segmentation for self-driving cars using deep learning: a survey

Qusay Sellat[1], Sukant Kishoro Bisoy[1], Rojanlina Priyadarshini[2]
[1]*Department of Computer Science and Engineering, C.V. Raman Global University, Bhubaneswar, Odisha, India;* [2]*Department of Computer Science and Information Technology, C.V. Raman Global University, Bhubaneswar, Odisha, India*

1. Introduction

The advancements in technology, especially the amazing improvements of computing methods, artificial intelligence, and hardware capabilities, have allowed us to expand our horizon regarding what possible things we can improve or create. Because of that, one particular application that was considered somehow dreamy one time that is autonomous driving now seems to come true soon. Being able to move efficiently and safely in vehicles that are driverless has been a hot research topic in recent years due to its expected benefits such as ease of use, reduction of accidents, less traffic jams, and better energy efficiency [1]. In general, each autonomous driving system comprises two main stages. The first one is the perception and localization stage that derives features representing the driving situation so that the autonomous vehicle understands the surrounding scene. The second stage is responsible for decision-making, which is in turn divided into motion planner and trajectory controller [2].

When speaking about self-driving systems, road scene understanding is a priority in order to make the right decision every moment. For a scene understanding mission to complete, a self-driving car has to know the segment label under which each pixel of the received image signal is classified. This problem is known as "**semantic segmentation.**" The semantic segmentation research has achieved very little success before the development of advanced machine learning (ML) techniques such as deep learning (DL). Initially, traditional algorithms were aimed at designing useful techniques for independently detecting traffic visual components such as roads, cars, buildings, or pedestrians. However, recent developments in DL algorithms have allowed the

Cognitive Big Data Intelligence with a Metaheuristic Approach
https://doi.org/10.1016/B978-0-323-85117-6.00002-9
211

researchers to study these recognition tasks under one single label: semantic segmentation [3].

So, in the era of DL, a lot of things that one day were very hard or impossible to achieve have become possible or even easy. These developments caused the research in many areas to flourish. Semantic segmentation is one of these areas that achieved very little success until recently when a lot of research has been conducted and good results have been reached. A lot of fields that need semantic segmentation, such as autonomous driving, are expected to benefit from the efficient pixel-wise classification.

2. Semantic segmentation for autonomous driving

2.1 Autonomous driving

Many companies and research centers are trying to come up with the first completely practical driverless car model. This is a very promising field with a lot of possible benefits:

- **Increase of safety:** Experts predict a dramatic decrease of traffic accident rates after the full application of autonomous driving. The number of accidents caused by human error will be extensively reduced due to the full automation [4].
- **Less costs:** Autonomous driving limits the need for vehicle insurance [5].
- **Comfortable travel:** Driverless cars provide smoother traveling experience along with higher speed limits [6].
- **Increased mobility:** The young, elderly, and disabled will significantly benefit from the development of self-driving vehicles [7].
- **Reduced environmental footprint:** high fuel efficiency will be achieved by optimizing the drive cycle and improving the traffic flow [8].

An autonomous driving system comprises two main stages, namely **Perception and Localization** and **Decision-Making** [2]. The Perception and Localization stage is responsible for receiving the signals from the surrounding environment by using sensors (lidar, radar, camera, etc.) and then processing this information in order to come up with a full understanding of the driving situation. In the Decision-Making stage, the driverless car plans and follows the best trajectory that participates in making the car reach its target place safely and fast. This stage is divided into two tasks:

- **Motion planning:** This module benefits from the situation understanding in order to generate the high-level behavior of the ego car. It generates a candidate trajectory according to the selected behavior.
- **Trajectory control:** This module tries to follow the trajectory produced by the motion planner as closely as possible with full consideration of safety and efficiency. Accordingly, it generates steering and acceleration commands.

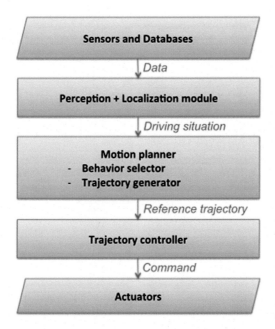

FIGURE 10.1   Standard architecture of an automated ground vehicle. *Image is taken from Ref. S. Lefèvre, A. Carvalho, F. Borrelli, A learning-based framework for velocity control in autonomous driving, IEEE Trans. Autom. Sci. Eng. 13 (1) (2016) 32–42.*

Finally, actuators respond to the commands generated by the trajectory controller. The described system is shown in Fig. 10.1.

However, reaching complete autonomy is not that easy due to the many obstacles faced by the parties responsible for developing this technology. This is related to many technical challenges related to the internal systems of the driverless car that need to be improved. These systems include the perception systems (laser, radar, and visual), the navigation system, the location system, the control system, etc. Because of the recent improvements of hardware capabilities, artificial intelligence, control algorithms, material science, physics, etc., these obstacles are gradually solved [1].

2.2 Semantic segmentation

Semantic segmentation is the process of assigning each pixel of the received image into one of the predefined classes. These classes represent the segment labels of the image, e.g., roads, cars, signs, traffic lights, or pedestrians [3]. Therefore, semantic segmentation is sometimes referred to as **"pixel-wise classification."** Fig. 10.2 illustrates examples of images that are labeled at the pixel level. We can notice how each pixel in the original images is assigned to one predefined class. There are many classes such as road, sky, building, car, etc.

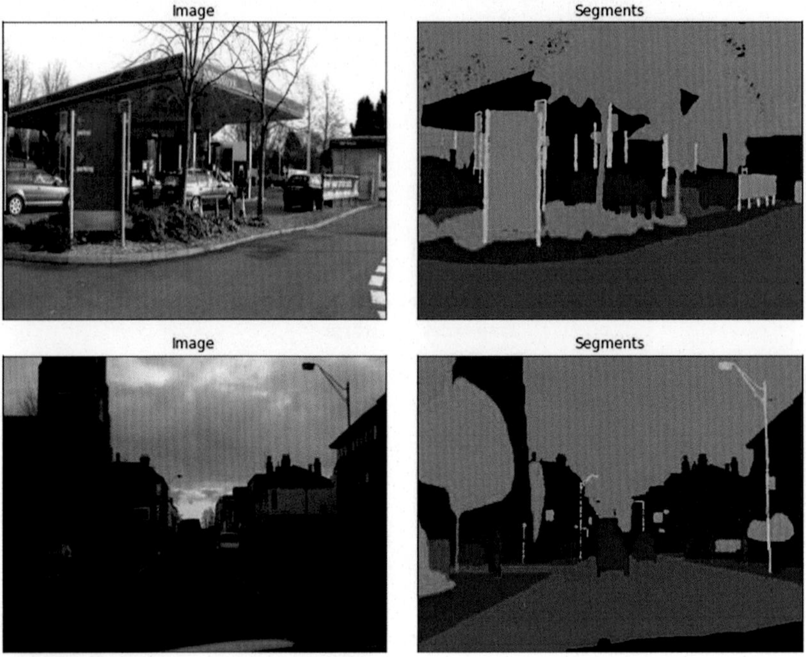

FIGURE 10.2 Images labeled at the pixel level. The examples are taken from the CamVid dataset [10].

The main benefit of semantic segmentation is situation understanding. It is therefore used in many fields such as autonomous driving, robotics, medical images, satellite images, precision agriculture, and facial images as a first step to achieving visual perception. As mentioned earlier, autonomous driving depends on the information received by sensors of the surrounding environment in order to form a complete picture of the driving situation. Because the visual signal is very rich in such information, doing semantic segmentation correctly is crucial for scene understanding [9]. The more we perform semantic segmentation with a high accuracy and a short time, the more correctly the ego car understands the surrounding environment and accordingly makes the right decision every moment.

However, semantic segmentation is challenging due to the complicated relationship between pixels in each image frame and also between successive frames. Even with the fast development of new technologies such as DL which have made the mission of semantic segmentation more and more efficient, doing accurate semantic segmentation in real time is still a hot topic in current research as is shown in detail later.

To summarize, semantic segmentation describes the process of linking each pixel in an image to a class label. These labels could include a person, car, flower, piece of furniture, etc. Therefore, we can think of semantic segmentation as image classification at a pixel level. Of course, there are a lot of fields that benefit from the pixel-wise classification of images. Apart from autonomous driving, robotics, medical images, satellite images, precision agriculture, facial images, etc., are all examples of fields where semantic segmentation is crucial.

3. Deep learning

3.1 Machine learning

ML is a subset of artificial intelligence. According to Tom Mitchell, it can be summarized in the following sentence: "A computer program is said to learn from experience E with respect to some class of tasks T and performance measure P, if its performance at tasks in T, as measured by P, improves with experience E" [11]. As we can see from the previous definition, ML aims at learning a mathematical model from the samples (also called the training set) in order to be able to make predictions or decisions without being explicitly programmed. ML has been used in various fields to mimic human behavior and way of making decisions. Business, financial market analysis, recommendation systems, information retrieval, computer vision, robotics, medical diagnose, bioinformatics, and autonomous systems are all fields where ML has been applied successfully in order to process the available data effectively so that the machine (computer) can understand the situation and respond correctly to it.

There are many approaches to build an ML model depending on the type of learning. The most common approaches are as follows:

- **Supervised learning:** Labeled examples are used to learn the mathematical model. Classification and regression models are usually learned using this approach.
- **Unsupervised learning:** Unlabeled examples are used to learn the mathematical model. Most clustering algorithms use this approach.
- **Reinforcement learning:** Here, an agent learns to make decisions according to rewards assigned to the different available actions.

Additionally, we can divide learning methods into **online** methods and **offline** methods. Online methods keep updating the learned model as soon as new examples are available. On the contrary, offline methods do not update the learned model so often.

There are many shapes of mathematical models that can be built to address some learning tasks. The most common one is called **"artificial neural network (ANN)."** When these networks get deeper and deeper, they are called **deep neural networks** (DNNs) and studied under a subfield of ML called **deep learning** as shown in Fig. 10.3.

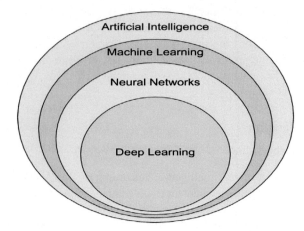

FIGURE 10.3 Deep learning is a subfield of artificial neural networks which is in turn a subfield of machine learning.

3.2 Artificial neural networks

An ANN is a type of ML model that is inspired by biological neural networks. In the brains of animals and humans, highly complicated neural networks take input signals from the surrounding environment and accordingly, learn some valuable information from these signals. These complicated biological structures consist of a large number of neurons. Each neuron takes its input signals through many dendrites attached to it. For each time, these dendrites give the neuron some message, and the corresponding neuron responds by producing an output signal which is carried on the attached axon that has some terminals to notify the neighboring neurons by the response [12].

Similarly, in ANN architectures, each network consists of many neurons that are organized in a number of consecutive layers. Each neuron receives the input signals from the neurons in the very previous layer and then responds by performing some mathematical operation and sending the corresponding result to the neurons in the next layer. The analogy between biological neurons and artificial ones is shown in Fig. 10.4.

More precisely, an artificial neuron takes the outputs of the neurons of the previous layer as its inputs, and multiplies each one of these inputs by some weight value that was learned previously. Then, it applies some mathematical function that is called "**activation function**" to produce the output signal. The output signal of the last layer is supposed to accomplish the task assigned to the neural network correctly. So, we can say that each neuron applies some predefined activation function on the weighted sum of inputs. Sometimes, it is

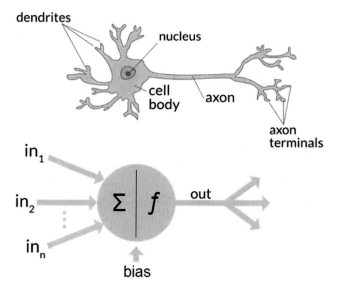

FIGURE 10.4 The analogy between biological and artificial neurons [13]. *Image is taken from P. Elavarthi, Semantic Segmentation of RGB Images for Feature Extraction in Real Time, M.Sc. thesis, University of Cincinnati, 2019.*

better to add some bias to the weighted sum. A simple mathematical form of the artificial neuron is given by the following:

$$h(x) = g(z(x)) = g(W^T x + b) \tag{10.1}$$

x represents the input vector, h represents the output of the neuron, g is the activation function, z is the weighted sum of the inputs of the neuron, W is the weights vector (that is, for each input element, it is multiplied by a weight value), and b is the bias value. An explanatory example of the described artificial neuron is shown in Fig. 10.5.

Typically, an ANN is organized into a number of layers. Each layer consists of some number of neurons. The first layer is called the "**input layer.**" The last layer is called the "**output layer.**" The layers in between are referred to as the "**hidden layers.**" The neurons of each layer send their output to at least one of the neurons of the next layer. Hence, the output of each layer is considered the input of the next layer except for the last layer whose output is considered the task accomplishment of the neural network. A simplified version of the ANNs is illustrated in Fig. 10.6. A fully connected neural network is shown where each neuron in each layer (except for the last layer) is connected to each neuron in the next one. This simple version contains only one hidden layer, but usually, we have more than one hidden layer.

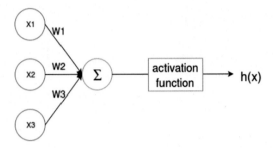

FIGURE 10.5 An artificial neuron applies an activation function on the weighted sum of the inputs in order to produce a response [14].

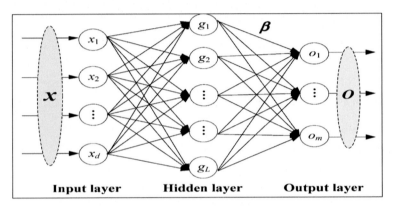

FIGURE 10.6 Illustration of a simple neural network [15].

3.3 Deep learning

Because of the rapid advancements of the hardware industry and the increasing capability of running complex and numerous mathematical calculations, which are required for ANNs to learn from the data, the research on ANNs has flourished recently, with wider and deeper architectures that have been proposed.

When ANNs get deeper and deeper to form what is referred to as DNNs, a new field of study emerges. This field is called "**deep learning.**" DNNs have been applied successfully in numerous areas including computer vision, autonomous driving, natural language processing, etc. The key feature of DNNs that makes them successful as an intelligent solution is their ability to capture the complex relationships between inputs and extract higher-level features so that they can be used for some difficult tasks such as representation learning. This characteristic limits the need for extensive feature engineering which is a significant advantage compared to old ML methods that required a huge effort to optimize the input features so that the model can learn perfectly [16].

A lot of DL models have been developed to solve various problems. The most common ones are convolutional neural networks (CNNs), recurrent neural networks, and autoencoders (AEs). In modern applications of DL, the input is directly mapped to the output in a single model without using many models. So, instead of having many models to process different types of data independently and then integrating the results in some master model, only one model is designed to receive data from all types and process them all to get the target output. This approach of learning and processing of data in a single model is called "**End-to-end Learning.**" This approach is increasingly used in DL applications as more and more data can be obtained due to the recent improvements in hardware and computing capabilities.

3.4 Learning process of deep neural networks

Deeper architectures are usually harder to train because of having a large number of trainable parameters (weights) so that the resulting mathematical model succeeds in mapping input values to output ones. The training process of DNNs is usually done in an iterative manner. Each iteration comprises two distinguished phases, namely forward propagation and back propagation. For those two phases to be done correctly, an appropriate collection of activation functions, loss functions, and optimization methods has to be decided.

Next, we illustrate some simple principles of the learning process of DNNs.

3.4.1 Forward propagation and activation functions

In forward propagation, the activation values are calculated consecutively starting from the first layer and ending by the last one. As mentioned earlier, the activation functions are applied to the weighted sum of inputs for each neuron.

There are many shapes of activation functions that are commonly used:

- **Sigmoid:** It is used widely especially for binary classification. It maps the weighted sum of inputs to a range [0,1] (Figs. 10.7 and 10.8). Sigmoid function is explained as follows:

$$\text{Sigmoid}(x) = \frac{1}{1 + e^{-x}} \qquad (10.2)$$

Tanh: It is less common than sigmoid. It maps the weighted sum of inputs to a range [−1,1] (Fig. 3.6). Tanh function is explained as follows:

$$\text{Tanh}(x) = \frac{2}{1 + e^{-2x}} - 1 \qquad (10.3)$$

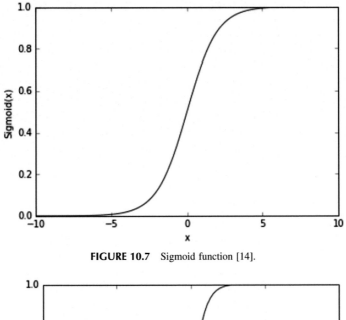

FIGURE 10.7 Sigmoid function [14].

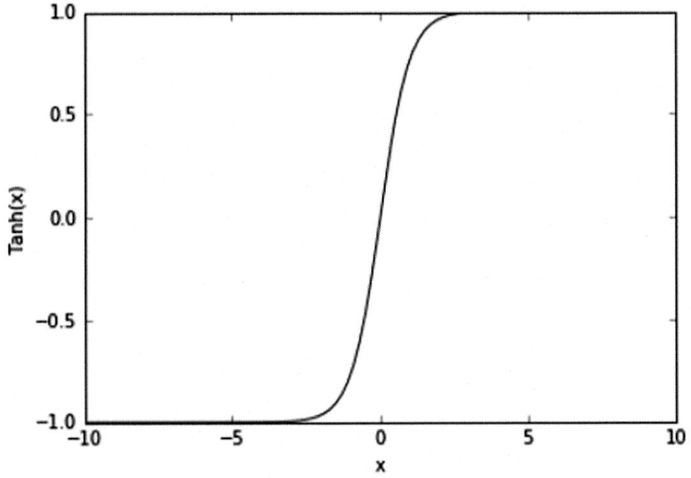

FIGURE 10.8 Tanh function [14].

- **ReLU (Rectified Linear Unit):** It is the most common activation function for DNNs. It accelerates the convergence of the used algorithm and is less computationally complex than other activation functions (Fig. 10.9). ReLU function is explained as follows:

$$\text{ReLU}(x) = \max(x, 0) \qquad (10.4)$$

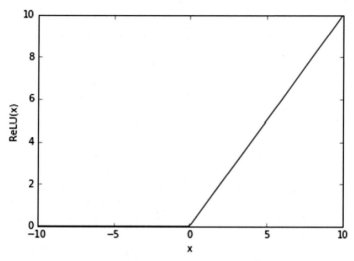

FIGURE 10.9   ReLU function [14].

- **Softmax:** It is commonly used for the output layer if it has more than one neuron. It has proven a high performance for classification tasks. Softmax function is explained as follows:

$$\text{softmax}\left(z^{i}\right) = \frac{e^{z^{i}}}{\sum\limits_{j=1}^{K} e^{z^{j}}} \tag{10.5}$$

3.4.2 Loss functions and optimization methods

Being able to calculate the error estimation is very crucial for training a neural network. This value represents the difference between the actual and predicted output of the network. The functions that are designed to estimate the error value are called loss functions. Loss functions are very important because they give a way to realize how far a solution is from the optimal one.

The most used loss functions in the field of DL are as follows (suppose p is the target output and $\widehat{p}$ is the predicted output):

- **Cross Entropy:** This loss measure is used for classification tasks where the output of each neuron is a probability between 0 and 1. It is defined as follows:

$$\text{CE} = -\left(p \log\left(\widehat{p}\right) + (1-p) \log\left(1-\widehat{p}\right)\right) \tag{10.6}$$

- **Focal Loss:** This type of loss function is used widely to increase the importance of hard examples compared to easy examples so that the learning algorithm can learn to distinguish the discriminant input features. It is defined as follows:

$$\text{FL} = -\left(\alpha\left(1-\hat{p}\right)^{\gamma} p \log\left(\hat{p}\right) + (1-\alpha)\hat{p}^{\gamma}(1-p) \log\left(1-\hat{p}\right)\right) \quad (10.7)$$

- **Dice Loss:** It is increasingly used in tasks that deal with images. It is defined in Eq. (3.8) where TP is the number of true positives, FP is the number of false positives, and FN is the number of false negatives. It is defined as follows:

$$\text{DL} = \frac{2\text{TP}}{2\text{TP} + \text{FP} + \text{FN}} = \frac{2|X \cap Y|}{|X| \cup |Y|} \quad (10.8)$$

Depending on the error estimation, an optimization method can be used to decide the amount of change of each trainable parameter so that it minimizes the value of the loss function. In other words, the main objective for every DL algorithm is to minimize the value of the used loss function using some designed optimization method.

A lot of optimization methods have been proposed for DNNs. The most common approach is called **"gradient descent"** (GD). This approach tries to minimize the loss function value by updating parameters by making steps to the negative direction of the gradient. Supposing that W represents the trainable parameters, $L(W)$ represents the loss function for the trainable parameters, $W\nabla L(W)$ is the gradient of the loss function, τ is the iteration number, and α is the updation step or learning rat, we generally define the updation process of weights based on GD as follows:

$$W^{(\tau+1)} = W^{(\tau)} - \alpha\nabla L(W) \quad (10.9)$$

The most used variation of GD is called "**stochastic gradient descent,**" where instead of calculation loss function for all examples of the dataset at once, only one or few examples are used for each iteration. Sometimes, we refer to the GD algorithm that uses a few examples each iteration by "**minibatch gradient descent**" as compared to the general one that uses all examples each iteration that is called "**batch gradient descent.**"

There are many extensions to the GD approach. The most common ones are as follows:

- **Adaptive Gradient Algorithm (AdaGrad):** [17] This algorithm keeps tracking of gradient history and uses it to update the parameters in each iteration. So, it stores a learning rate for each parameter so that it updates the parameters related to the least frequent features faster than parameters related to the most common ones. This algorithm is used for sparse gradients basically (e.g., natural language processing).

- **Root Mean Square Propagation (RMSProp):** RMSprop is an unpublished, adaptive learning rate method proposed by Geoff Hinton in a lecture on Coursera.org. This method also takes into account the frequency of features so that the higher the frequency, the lower its significance in parameter updation. It updates the parameters based on their recent values by introducing a parameter β so that the higher β value is, the higher the contribution of previous updation magnitudes in the learning process.
- **Adam Optimizer:** It combines the benefits gained by using AdaGrad and RMSProp optimizers. It is used mainly to train DL models for computer vision tasks [18].

3.4.3 Back propagation

Depending on the used loss function and optimization method, DNNs learn in a backward way from the last layer to the first one. While passing through different layers, the weight values of each neuron are updated according to the calculated errors. This process is referred to as "**back propagation.**"

Suppose $\delta_j^{(l)}$ is the error calculated for the neuron j is the layer number, and l and $a_j^{(l)}$ are the activation values of the same neuron. Providing that we have L layers, and y is the desired output of the network, we define the error of the last layer as follows:

$$\delta^{(L)} = y - a^{(L)} \tag{10.10}$$

The error for the layers before the last layer is computed by the following equation:

$$\delta^{(l)} = \left(\theta^{(l)}\right)^T \odot g'\left(z^{(l)}\right) \tag{10.11}$$

where $\theta^{(l)}$ is the weight of the links between the layer l and the layer $l+1$, g', while the derivative of the used activation function g and $\odot$ represents element-wise multiplication.

Giving that $J(\theta)$ is the loss function, the partial derivative of a single weight parameter $\theta_{i,j}^{(l)}$ linking between the neuron j in the l layer and i in the $l+1$ layer, with respect to the loss function, can be written as in the following equation:

$$\frac{\partial J(\theta)}{\partial \theta_{i,j}^{(l)}} = a_j^{(l)} \delta_i^{(l+1)} \tag{10.12}$$

In back propagation, we simultaneously update the weights in each layer from the last one to the first one. Suppose that α is the learning rate, we update each weigh parameter $\theta_{i,j}^{(l)}$ by the following equation:

$$\left(\theta_{i,j}^{(l)}\right)_{\tau+1} = \left(\theta_{i,j}^{(l)}\right)_{\tau} - \alpha a_j^{(l)} \delta_i^{(l+1)} \tag{10.13}$$

Fig. 10.10 represents the back propagation process.

Eventually, after some number of alternating forward and backward passes (each pass through the entire training examples is called an epoch), the model weight parameters will be tuned correctly so they make the model give the desired output if it is tested on input examples.

3.5 Challenges

Training of DNNs is a very hard process because the resulting network has to capture the training data complexity correctly and at the same time be able to generalize for new data. We illustrate the main points in the following.

3.5.1 Learning rate

Choosing a good learning rate is very important in the learning process of the neural network. A too small learning rate may result in a slow learning process, while a big learning rate could mean that loss value does not converge, leading to a failure in the learning process.

To get the maximum performance, it is recommended to use "**learning rate decay,**" by which we mean decreasing the learning rate as we iterate during the training process so that the learning rate value is a function of the

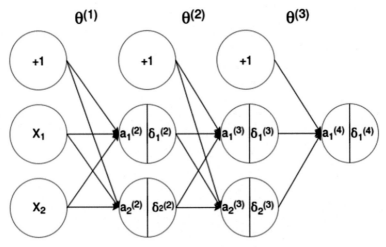

FIGURE 10.10 Back propagation process [14].

current number of epochs. In this way, we get a faster learning algorithm without the risk of our algorithm not converging to a minimum loss value.

3.5.2 Underfitting and overfitting

When the model fails to capture the complexity of the training data, the situation is called "**underfitting**" ("**high bias**"). Usually, the problem of underfitting can be solved by increasing the model complexity and training it for more number of iterations. Also, the used data have to be checked to see if it has noise that prevents the model from capturing the information.

The problem of "**overfitting**" ("**high variance**") occurs when the model fits the training data very well but fails to generalize for new data. This problem can be solved by either obtaining more data for the purpose of training so that the model can capture more useful information about the possible input data or applying some type of "**regularization.**" When obtaining new data is not a practical solution, or the dataset is already rich enough, regularization is the best choice.

Regularization does not have a unified method to be applied. Instead, there are many ways through which we can achieve a regularization effect that prevents the model from overfitting the training examples. The most used regularization methods are as follows:

- *L*1 and *L*2 **regularization:** these types of regularization are achieved by adding some regularization term to the cost function. This regularization term does not allow the weight values to be too large thereby reducing the captured complexity.
- **Dropout Regularization:** In this approach, each training iteration, random weights are chosen randomly to be ignored.
- **Data Augmentation:** If the training examples are not enough and it is hard to obtain new data, training the model on augmented training examples would be a useful approach. There are many ways to do so depending on the type of input data.
- **Early Stopping:** If the number of training iterations is too high, it can be better to consider stopping the training process at some point. To do so, the value of the loss function has to be monitored to stop the training whenever it converges so that the model does not become too complex.
- **Batch Normalization:** This technique may be needed to add some regularization effect in addition to speeding up the learning process. Batch normalization is achieved by performing normalization steps in each iteration so that the learning process considers the means and variances of each layer's inputs. Batch normalization limits the amount to which updating the parameters in the earlier layers can affect the distribution of values the current layer sees. This is due to the fact that the algorithm takes the mean and variance instead of the original values [19].

3.5.3 Dataset splitting

The most common practice regarding the use of available datasets is to split each dataset into three smaller datasets. The ratio of dataset splitting depends on the amount of available data and the type of application. The higher the amount of data, the less ratio of dataset is needed for validating and testing purposes. The main dataset is usually split into the following:

- **Training dataset:** This is the dataset used for updating the weight parameters of the model.
- **Validation dataset:** This dataset is used to ensure that the training process is done correctly. For example, using a validation dataset, it is possible to discover that some model is overfitting the training data and then some modifications can be applied to overcome the problem.
- **Testing dataset:** This dataset is used for actual evaluation of the final trained model to discover how much it generalizes to new data.

3.5.4 Gradient vanishing and gradient exploding

When gradient-based learning methods are used in training, the gradients on which the weight updation process depends may be too small so that the learning process stops or too big so that the learning process becomes incorrect. These problems became more frequent as deeper and deeper neural architectures were designed.

To overcome the problem of gradient vanishing, many approaches were proposed. The most used one in the DL design depends on the use of "**skip connections.**" In this approach, the model is given the choice to skip some layers if they are not participating actively in the learning process. Practically, some links are made between layers that are not consecutive, so some layers may be skipped if their response is not benefitting the learning. This process can be achieved in two main ways: skip connections by addition and skip connections by concatenation.

The problem of gradient exploding can be solved by clipping the exploded gradients or adding some modifications to the designed model.

3.6 Convolutional neural networks

A CNN is a class of deep, feed-forward ANNs, most commonly applied to analyzing visual imagery [20]. This type of DL model has been very popular recently due to the vast improvements in algorithms and computing capabilities.

A CNN is a DNN that contains some layers within which convolutional operations are performed. The normal design of CNNs uses three basic types of structure as shown in Figs. 10.11 and 10.12.

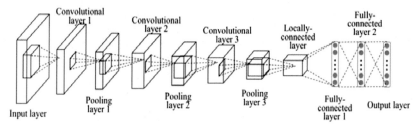

FIGURE 10.11 General structure of CNNs. *Image is taken from url: https://mc.ai/notes-on-deep-learning%E2%80%8A-%E2%80%8Aadvanced-cnn/.*

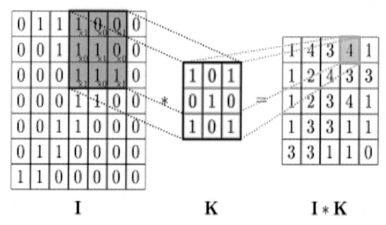

$$I \qquad K \qquad I * K$$

FIGURE 10.12 Example of convolutional operation. *Image is taken from url: https://medium.com/@cdabakoglu/what-is-convolutional-neural-network-cnn-with-keras-cab447ad204c.*

The first structure is called a "**convolutional layer**" where convolutional operations are applied on the input data and then the outputs are sent to the next layer. An example of a convolutional operation is shown in Fig. 10.11.

Each neuron of the convolutional layer receives only a small portion of the outputs of the previous layer after convolving them with some "**kernel.**" The group of output values a neuron can see is called the "**receptive field**" of that neuron.

The second main structure is the "**pooling layer.**" It combines each group of the outputs of the previous layer into a single neuron. There are two common variations of pooling operations: **average pooling** and **max pooling** (Fig. 10.13). An average pooling layer averages its input values by taking the mean of them. On the other hand, max pooling takes the biggest value.

The third type of layer is similar to that used in traditional ANNs where every neuron in every layer is connected to all neurons in the next layer. This type of layer is called "**fully connected**" layers (Fig. 10.14).

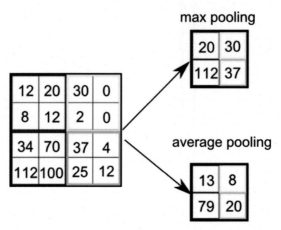

FIGURE 10.13   Types of pooling layers. *Image is taken from url: https://towardsdatascience. com/a-comprehensive-guide-to-convolutional-neural-networks-the-eli5-way-3bd2b1164a53.*

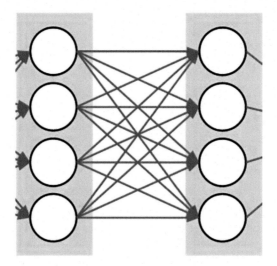

FIGURE 10.14   Fully connected layer. *Image is taken from url: https://numahub.com/articles/ why-do-you-need-fully-connected-layer.*

A CNN normally comprises the three previous types of layers. As shown in Fig. 3.9, the first part of CNNs is formed by a sequence of convolutional layers and pooling layers so that convolutional layers are organized into groups and a pooling layer is put after each group of convolutional layers. The second part begins by flattening the last layer of the first part and ends with a series of fully connected layers.

The main benefit of CNNs is that they are able to capture the complexity of the input data using a relatively small number of parameters. In a well-trained

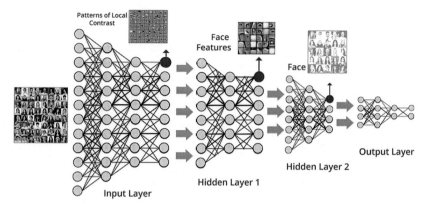

FIGURE 10.15 Feature hierarchy of CNNs. *Image is taken from url: https://livebook.manning. com/book/deep-learning-for-natural-language-processing/chapter-1/v-5/38.*

CNN, more abstract representations of data are learned as we go deeper in the CNN. This can be understood if there is some hierarchy of layers so that each part of this hierarchy is responsible for capturing a specific type of information. More abstract information is captured in the deeper parts of the hierarchy (Fig. 10.15).

3.7 Autoencoders

An AE is a type of feed-forward ANN used to learn efficient data coding in an unsupervised manner [21]. The main goal of using an AE is to learn a representation (encoding) for some type of data.

Two parts are necessary to build an AE (Fig. 10.16). The first part is called **"encoder."** It is responsible for deriving a correct encoding from the input

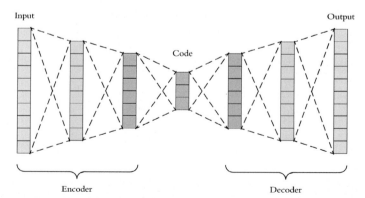

FIGURE 10.16 General architecture of the autoencoder. *Image is taken from url: https:// towardsdatascience.com/applied-deep-learning-part-3-autoencoders-1c083af4d798.*

data. This encoding is a compressed type of information which is a smaller version of the input data. The encoding can be used to reproduce these data. Actually, reproducing the input data is what the second part of the AE learns. This part is called "**decoder.**" The decoder uses the encoding to generate an output of the AE similar to the input of the same AE.

A special shape of AE is called "**convolutional autoencoder**" (CAE) that is an AE architecture where the encoding and decoding structures are mainly convolutional and deconvolutional structures, respectively (Figs. 10.17 and 10.18). This architecture is very efficient to reconstruct image data. The encoder of a CAE is similar to the normal CNN. The output of this encoder is the encoding that usually represents a dense form of visual input data. The decoder part of a CAE has a general structure of a reversed CNN. Instead of convolutional layers, there are deconvolutional layers. And we have upsampling (unpooling) layers instead of pooling layers.

4. Related work

Thanks to the rapid improvements in DL research last decade, great results have been achieved in the field of computer vision. Developing CNNs [23] had the biggest impact on this success as tasks such as object recognition and detection witnessed a huge jump in accuracy and speed. After the success of the early CNN models such as LeNet [24] and AlexNet [25] (AlexNet was proposed in 2012 but published in 2017), the number of proposed CNN works exploded. VGG [26], with its large number of parameters, performed well on the ImageNet dataset [27]. It increased the used number of hidden layers to 16 or 19 weight layers. At the same time, Inception [28] used the principle of network-in-network [29] to increase the depth of the CNN to 22 trainable layers. As the depth of the neural network increased, serious problems such as gradient vanishing and gradient exploding surfaced. Later proposals tried to overcome these problems by developing new techniques such as skip

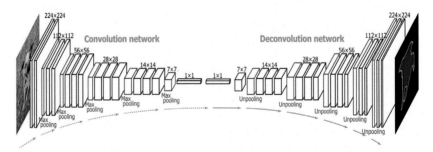

FIGURE 10.17 General architecture of CAE. *Image is taken from url: https://www.lri.fr/ ~gcharpia/deeppractice/2020/chap_3.html.*

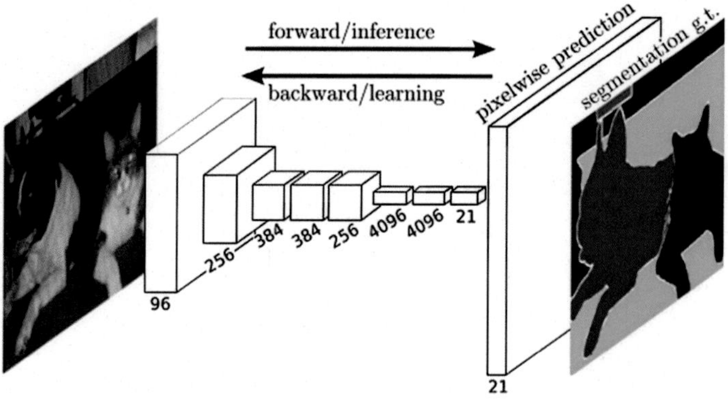

FIGURE 10.18   FCN model [22].

connections that were designed in the shape addition connections like in ResNets [30] or the shape of concatenation connections like in DenseNets [31].

However, in addition to the gradient problems, increasing the number of layers and trainable parameters made the use of these models limited, and any idea of implementing them within constrained environments or real-time systems is impractical. Xception [32], ShuffleNet [33], MobileNetsV1 [34], and MobileNetsV2 provided a convenient way of designing real-time CNNs by focusing on the use of depth-wise separable convolutions. This allowed researchers to design mobile vision applications that are both accurate and real time. Other solutions such as EfficientNets [35] made it possible to compromise between the performance of the designed model and its complexity. Similar to other computer vision topics, semantic segmentation research has experienced a huge improvement in the era of DL. In addition to CNNs, AEs were used to design semantic segmentation models that are much more efficient than old models. Recent semantic segmentation research focused on CAEs which are AEs whose encoder and decoder parts are convolutional and deconvolutional layers, respectively. CNN models that were developed initially for object recognition and detection have been used as the backbone architectures of CAEs developed for semantic segmentation.

FCN [36] used fully convolutional architecture with a large number of parameters to perform semantic segmentation. It was one of the first attempts toward getting rid of fully connected layers (Fig. 10.17).

SegNet [37] (Figs. 10.19 and 10.20) and SegNet-Basic [39] used VGG architecture as a backbone for the encoder and the decoder. It used the pooling indices of the encoder for the upsampling operation in the decoder.

Some other architectures such as UNet used some kind of skip connections between the encoder and the decoder and some other techniques such as data augmentation to increase segmentation accuracy (Fig. 4.3).

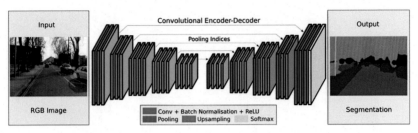

FIGURE 10.19 SegNet model [38].

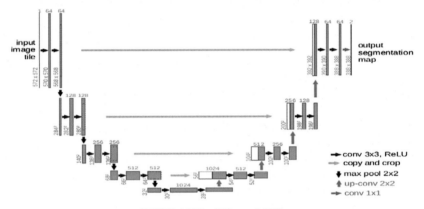

FIGURE 10.20 UNet model [7].

Although accuracy of semantic segmentation models improved, thanks to the above-mentioned models and some other architectures such as PSPNet [22], Dilated [38], and DeepLab [40], real-time semantic segmentation is still a hot research area, especially that some fields such as autonomous driving and robotics require very accurate semantic segmentation with a minimum amount of processing time. Because images are rich in semantic information, a significant number of trainable parameters are required to capture the complexity of possible images and it is very hard to develop lite segmentation models without sacrificing accuracy.

Some models were designed with a smaller number of parameters. FPN [4] and LinkNet [41] and other superlite models such as ApesNet [42], ENet [43], ESPNet [44], ESCNet [45], and EDANet [46] tried to minimize the number of parameters so that the semantic segmentation can be done in real time or embedded systems. Despite the fact that these models provided practical solutions to satisfy the real-time condition, crucial applications such as road scene understanding in autonomous vehicles need much more segmentation accuracy.

5. Experimental results

To do the comparative analysis among the existing models, a standard dataset is used using the pretrained models. The comparison work is implemented using Python frameworks that were designed for ML and computer vision tasks. The main frameworks we use are the following: TensorFlow, Keras, and Albumentations. The code was run on NVIDIA Tesla P100-PCIE-16GB. Fig. 10.21 shows more details.

The model is trained using one of the standard open source datasets named as CamVid. Random image crops of 320×320 are used to train the model. It is trained for 150 epochs with an initial learning rate of $= 5$ e $- 4$, a batch-size of 10, and using RMSProp optimizer.

The values of loss function over epochs are shown in Fig. 10.22. It shows that the value of the training loss function is decreasing as the model is trained for more epochs until it converges. Validation loss value may take more time until it eventually converges.

The evaluation metrics chosen for this work are mean of class accuracy (mCA), which is the ratio of correctly classified pixels to the total considered pixels. Suppose TP are the true positives, TN is the number of true negatives, FP is the number of false positives, and FN is the number of false negatives, we draw the confusion matrix shown in Fig. 10.23.

Then, class accuracy is defined as shown in the following equation:

$$CA = \frac{TP + TN}{TP + TN + FP + FN} \tag{10.14}$$

Because of the class count imbalance we have in image frames, the dominant classes will make us obtain misleading results if we take a global class accuracy, as even if we get good global class accuracy, the less dominant classes may be classified inaccurately, but their small count makes them less contributing to the calculated accuracy.

To ensure that class imbalance does not lead to misleading accuracy values, we follow the common practice of taking the average accuracy between all calculated accuracy of the defined classes. The resulting value is called mCA.

Mean Intersection over Union (mIoU) is one of the parameters which has been considered. It is defined as the number of pixel labels that are found in both the prediction frame and the ground truth frame over the pixel labels that

```
+---------------------------------------------------------------------+
| NVIDIA-SMI 440.82       Driver Version: 418.67       CUDA Version: 10.1    |
|-------------------------------+----------------------+----------------------+
| GPU  Name           Persistence-M| Bus-Id        Disp.A | Volatile Uncorr. ECC |
| Fan  Temp  Perf  Pwr:Usage/Cap|          Memory-Usage | GPU-Util  Compute M. |
|===============================+======================+======================|
|   0  Tesla P100-PCIE...   Off | 00000000:00:04.0 Off |                    0 |
| N/A   46C    P0    34W / 250W |  12343MiB / 16280MiB |      0%      Default |
+-------------------------------+----------------------+----------------------+
```

FIGURE 10.21 Details of hardware specifications.

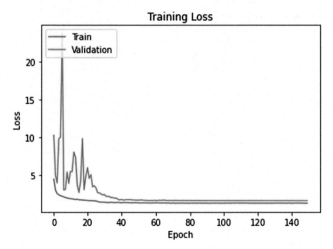

FIGURE 10.22 Training loss is decreasing over epochs until it converges.

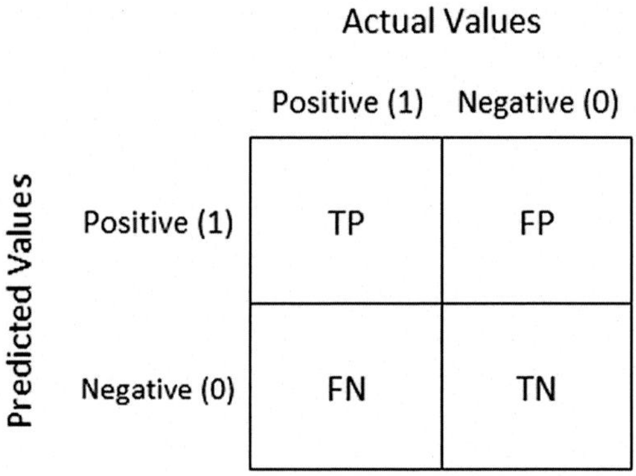

FIGURE 10.23 Confusion matrix.

are found in either the prediction frame or the ground truth frame. IoU is defined by the following equation:

$$IoU = \frac{|I|}{|U|} = \frac{|X \cap Y|}{|X \cup Y|} \qquad (10.15)$$

IoU takes values from a range $[0, 1]$; the closer the value to 1, the closer the predicted labels to the ground truth ones. Therefore, we aim at maximizing IoU value.

IoU is calculated for each segment class separately and then the average between all classes is taken to be the mean mIoU.

Ground truth
pixels in class

Predicted
pixels in class

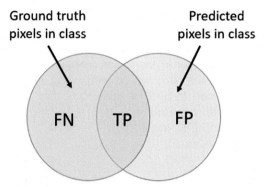

FIGURE 10.24 IoU is the area of intersection over the area of union. *Image is taken from url:*
https://in.mathworks.com/help/vision/ref/evaluatesemanticsegmentation.html.

To define IoU (or sometimes it is referred to as Jaccard index) in another
way, we use the confusion matrix shown in Fig. 10.24. IoU is defined as shown
in the following equation.

$$\text{IoU} = \frac{\text{TP}}{\text{TP} + \text{FP} + \text{FN}} \qquad (10.16)$$

Number of Parameters (#params): The measure of complexity of DL
models could be known by considering the number of parameters used in the
model.

We executed and evaluated the performance of the existing baseline
models and compared their complexity. The comparison results are shown in
Table 10.1.

TABLE 10.1 Comparison between different baseline models.

Model	mCA (%)	mIoU (%)	#Params (m)
SegNet [37]	65.2	55.6	29.5
FCN-8s [36]	–	57	134.5
ApesNet [42]	69.3	48	–
ENet [43]	68.3	51.3	0.36
ESPNet [44]	68.3	55.6	0.36
ESCNet [45]	70.9	56.1	0.185
DeepLab-LFOV [40]	–	61.6	37.3
Dilated-8 [38]	–	65.3	140.8
EDANet [46]	76.7	66.4	0.68

It can be observed that the trade-off between the number of parameters and both mIoU and mCA is inevitable; thus, some models like DeepLab-LFOV and Dilated-8 would achieve a higher mIoU or mCA but are less applicable in real time due to the higher number of parameters. ENet and ESPNet have a lower number of parameters than ours, but perform worse in terms of mIoU as models with a very small number of parameters may fail to capture the required complexity. Other models such as EDANet seem to give a higher mIoU, with less number of parameters.

6. Conclusion

Semantic segmentation is a very important process for the perception of autonomous vehicles. It plays a major role in the road scene understanding of the vehicle. Therefore, a lot of research is going on to develop the most accurate semantic segmentation system so that it contributes to making self-driving cars a dream come true. However, researchers on this topic are struggling to make their designed models satisfy the real-time operation requirement for any proposed system in order to be a part of a real driverless car so that it understands the surrounding environment and responds to it correctly all in real time. As DL methods have been improved during the last decade, more and more research is focusing on benefitting from DL so that better results can be obtained in all aspects of autonomous processes including perception and decision-making.

In this chapter, we presented the basic concepts behind the current advancements in semantic segmentation for self-driving cars and illustrated the state-of-the-art models used for this mission. For doing the comparison among the models, the pertained DL model architectures are tested on a single dataset. The model was trained and tested on the CamVid dataset for which a high accuracy was obtained with a relatively small number of parameters.

References

[1] C. Hoel, K. Driggs-Campbell, K. Wolff, L. Laine, M. Kochenderfer, Combining planning and deep reinforcement learning in tactical decision making for autonomous driving, IEEE Trans. Intell. Veh. 5 (2) (2019) 294–305.

[2] S. Lefèvre, A. Carvalho, F. Borrelli, A learning-based framework for velocity control in autonomous driving, IEEE Trans. Autom. Sci. Eng. 13 (1) (2016) 32–42.

[3] W. Zhou, S. Lv, Q. Jiang, L. Yu, Deep road scene understanding, IEEE Signal Process. Lett. 26 (4) (2019) 587–591.

[4] L. Jena, S. Mishra, S. Nayak, P. Ranjan, M.K. Mishra, Variable optimization in cervical cancer data using particle swarm optimization, in: Advances in Electronics, Communication and Computing, Springer, Singapore, 2021, pp. 147–153.

[5] D. Light, "A Scenario: The End of Auto Insurance" (Technical Report), Celent, 2012.

[6] E. Ackerman, Study: Intelligent Cars Could Boost Highway Capacity by 273%, Institute of Electrical and Electronics Engineers (IEEE), IEEE Spectrum, 2012.

[7] S.N. Roy, S. Mishra, S.M. Yusof, Emergence of drug discovery in machine learning, Tech. Adv. Mach. Learn. Healthc. 119 (2021).

[8] M. Taiebat, A.L. Brown, H.R. Sa, S. Qu, M. Xu, A review on energy, environmental, and sustainability implications of connected and automated vehicles, Environ. Sci. Technol. 52 (20) (2018) 11449−11465.

[9] P.K. Mallick, S. Mishra, G.S. Chae, Digital media news categorization using Bernoulli document model for web content convergence, Personal Ubiquitous Comput. 1 (2020) 1−16, https://doi.org/10.1007/s00779-020-01461-9.

[10] W. Wang, Y. Fu, Z. Pan, X.I. Li, Y. Zhuang, Real-Time Driving Scene Semantic Segmentation, vol. 8, 2020.

[11] S. Mishra, P.K. Mallick, L. Jena, G.S. Chae, Optimization of skewed data using sampling-based preprocessing approach, Front. Pub. Health 8 (2020) 274, https://doi.org/10.3389/fpubh.2020.00274.

[12] Y. Chen, Y. Lin, C. Kung, M. Chung, I. Yen, Design and implementation of cloud analytics-assisted smart power meters considering advanced artificial intelligence as edge analytics in demand-side management for smart homes, Sensors 19 (9) (2019) 2047.

[13] P. Elavarthi, Semantic Segmentation of RGB Images for Feature Extraction in Real Time, M.Sc. thesis, University of Cincinnati, 2019.

[14] S. Sahoo, M. Das, S. Mishra, S. Suman, A hybrid DTNB model for heart disorders prediction, in: Advances in Electronics, Communication and Computing, Springer, Singapore, 2021, pp. 155−163.

[15] W. Niu, Z. Feng, B. Feng, Y. Min, C. Cheng, Comparison of multiple lienar regression, artificial neural network, extreme learning machine, and support vector machine in deriving operation rule of hydropower reservoir, Water 11 (1) (2019) 1−17.

[16] Y. Lecun, Y. Bengio, G. Hinton, Deep learning, Nature 521 (2015) 436−444.

[17] J. Duchi, E. Hazan, Y. Singer, Adaptive subgradient methods for online learning and stochastic optimization, J. Mach. Learn. Res. 12 (7) (2011) 2121−2159.

[18] D.P. Kingma, J.L. Ba, Adam: a method for stochastic optimization, in: International Conference on Learning Representations, 2015.

[19] S.R. Chowdhury, S. Mishra, A.O. Miranda, P.K. Mallick, Energy consumption prediction using light gradient boosting machine model, in: International Conference on Emerging Trends and Advances in Electrical Engineering and Renewable Energy, Springer, Singapore, March 2020, pp. 413−422.

[20] M.V. Valueva, N.N. Nagornov, P.A. Lyakhov, G.V. Valuev, N.I. Chervyakov, Application of the residue number system to reduce hardware costs of the convolutional neural network implementation, Math. Comput. Simulat. 177 (2020) 232−243. Elsevier BV.

[21] M.A. Kramer, Nonlinear principal component analysis using auto associative neural networks, AIChE 37 (2) (1991) 233−243.

[22] H. Zhao, J. Shi, X. Qi, X. Wang, J. Jia, Pyramid scene parsing network, in: 2017 IEEE Conference on Computer Vision and Pattern Recognition (CVPR), Honolulu, HI, 2017, pp. 6230−6239.

[23] I. Goodfellow, Y. Bengio, A. Courville, Deep Learning, MIT Press, 2016, p. 326.

[24] Y. Lecun, L. Bottou, Y. Bengio, P. Haffner, Gradient-based learning applied to document recognition, Proc. IEEE 86 (11) (1998) 2278−2324.

[25] A. Krizhevsky, I. Sutskever, G.E. Hinton, ImageNet classification with deep convolutional neural networks, Commun. ACM 60 (6) (2017) 84−90.

[26] K. Simonyan, A. Zisserman, Very Deep Convolutional Networks for Large-Scale Image Recognition, 2014 arXiv:1409.1556.

[27] O. Russakovsky, J. Deng, H. Su, J. Krause, S. Satheesh, S. Ma, Z. Huang, A. Karpathy, A. Khosla, M. Bernstein, A.C. Berg, L. Fei-Fei, Imagenet large scale visual recognition challenge, Int. J. Comput. Vis. 115 (3) (2015) 211–252.

[28] C. Szegedy, S. Reed, P. Sermanet, V. Vanhoucke, A. Rabinovich, Going deeper with convolutions, in: IEEE Conference on Computer Vision and Pattern Recognition (CVPR), 2015.

[29] M. Lin, Q. Chen, S. Yan, Network in Network, 2013.

[30] K. He, X. Zhang, S. Ren, J. Sun, Deep residual learning for image recognition, in: CVPR, 2016.

[31] G. Huang, Z. Liu, L. Van Der Maaten, K.Q. Weinberger, Densely connected convolutional networks, in: 2017 IEEE Conference on Computer Vision and Pattern Recognition (CVPR), Honolulu, HI, 2017, pp. 2261–2269.

[32] F. Chollet, Xception: deep learning with depthwise separable convolutions, in: 2017 IEEE Conference on Computer Vision and Pattern Recognition (CVPR), Honolulu, HI, 2017, pp. 1800–1807.

[33] X. Zhang, X. Zhou, M. Lin, J. Sun, ShuffleNet: an extremely efficient convolutional neural network for mobile devices, in: 2018 IEEE/CVF Conference on Computer Vision and Pattern Recognition, Salt Lake City, UT, 2018, pp. 6848–6856.

[34] A. Howard, M. Zhu, Menglong, B. Chen, D. Kalenichenko, W. Wang, T. Weyand, M. Andreetto, H. Adam, MobileNets: Efficient Convolutional Neural Networks for Mobile Vision Applications, Google Inc, 2017.

[35] M. Tan, Q.V. Le, EfficientNet: Rethinking Model Scaling for Convolutional Neural Networks, 2019.

[36] J. Long, E. Shelhamer, T. Darrell, Fully convolutional networks for semantic segmentation, in: Proc. CVPR, June 2015, pp. 3431–3440.

[37] V. Badrinarayanan, A. Kendall, R. Cipolla, SegNet: A Deep Convolutional Encoder-Decoder Architecture for Image Segmentation, 2015 arXiv:1511.00561.

[38] F. Yu, V. Koltun, Multi-scale Context Aggregation by Dilated Convolutions, 2015 arXiv:1511.07122.

[39] V. Badrinarayanan, A. Handa, R. Cipolla, SegNet: A Deep Convolutional Encoder-Decoder Architecture for Robust Semantic Pixel-wise Labeling, 2015 arXiv:1505.07293.

[40] L.-C. Chen, G. Papandreou, I. Kokkinos, K. Murphy, A.L. Yuille, Semantic Image Segmentation with Deep Convolutional Nets and Fully Connected CRFs, 2014 arXiv:1412.7062.

[41] A. Chaurasia, E. Culurciello, LinkNet: exploiting encoder representations for efficient semantic segmentation, in: 2017 IEEE Visual Communications and Image Processing (VCIP), St. Petersburg, FL, 2017, pp. 1–4.

[42] C. Wu, H. Cheng, S. Li, H. Li, Y. Chen, ApesNet: a pixel-wise efficient segmentation network for embedded devices, in: IET Cyber-Physical Systems: Theory & Applications, vol. 1, 12 2016, pp. 78–85 (1).

[43] A. Paszke, A. Chaurasia, S. Kim, E. Culurciello, ENet: A Deep Neural Network Architecture for Real-Time Semantic Segmentation, 2016 arXiv:1606.02147.

[44] S. Mehta, M. Rastegari, A. Caspi, L.G. Shapiro, H. Hajishirzi, ESPNet: efficient spatial pyramid of dilated convolutions for semantic segmentation, in: Proc. ECCV, 2018, pp. 561–580.

[45] J. Kim, Y.S. Heo, Efficient semantic segmentation using spatio-channel dilated convolutions, in: IEEE Access, vol. 7, 2019, pp. 154239–154252.

[46] S. Lo, H. Hang, S. Chan, L. Jing Jhih, Efficient Dense Modules of Asymmetric Convolution for Real-Time Semantic Segmentation, 2018.

Chapter 11

Cognitive big data analysis for E-health and telemedicine using metaheuristic algorithms

Deepak Rai[1], Hiren Kumar Thakkar[2]

[1]*Department of Computer Science and Engineering, National Institute of Technology, Patna, Bihar, India;* [2]*Department of Computer Science and Engineering, School of Engineering and Sciences, SRM University, Mangalagiri, Andhra Pradesh, India*

1. Introduction

Nowadays, healthcare industries are experiencing the perfect storm with an exponential increase in volume and variety of data from various sources. Different sources of healthcare data are shown in Fig. 11.1.

Globally, the future of the healthcare industry is transforming. The technology is changing at a speed that most healthcare industries are unprepared and are in the mid of generational change [1]. With ever-increasing health data, today, the amount of health information is doubling every 73 days. Fig. 11.2 shows a small snap of today's healthcare data volume. The variety and amount of healthcare data required are multiplying, which needs to be managed regularly, analyzed daily, and shared with other organizations and professionals for securing from unethical use [2].

It is unreasonable to expect that today there are too much health data but very little insight into it. Industries aspire to deliver better quality care and outcomes at the most affordable cost but are generally limited by traditional computational approaches. The increasing amount of data requires enormous computational power that cannot be tackled with traditional approaches [3]. Therefore, machine learning—assisted and Artificial Intelligence—enabled approaches and adaptive [4] approaches are designed to tackle the problems in diversified areas such as healthcare [5,6], cloud computing [7], etc. However, the amalgamation of different sophisticated modeling approaches and optimization of skewed data [8] with cognitive computing can solve big data challenges and make the healthcare system smart. Cognitive technology enables real-time processing of massive healthcare data, understands, and learns while interacting with humans. That is one of the reasons that healthcare

Cognitive Big Data Intelligence with a Metaheuristic Approach
https://doi.org/10.1016/B978-0-323-85117-6.00003-0
239

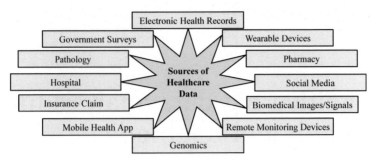

FIGURE 11.1   Sources of healthcare data.

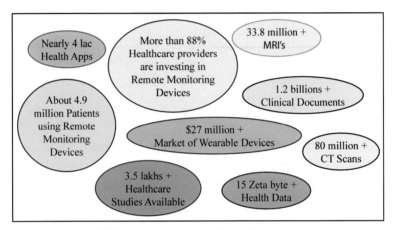

FIGURE 11.2   Volume of healthcare data generated.

industries are the earliest adopters of cognitive big data technologies. The 3 Vs of big data healthcare are shown in Fig. 11.3.

This chapter focuses on building cognitive big data applications that can help health experts to solve healthcare problems in new ways. At first, we try to look for the answer regarding the question, why E-health care system?

1.1 Why E-health care?

Nowadays, the development of information and communication technology has transformed our daily life. The quality of healthcare is enhancing comprehensively. The traditional healthcare system is becoming smarter with the amalgamation of modern technologies such as big data, cloud computing [34], artificial intelligence, machine learning [3], deep learning, reinforcement learning [7], and, especially, internet of things. Fig. 11.4 shows how this amalgamation changes traditional healthcare to E-health or smart healthcare.

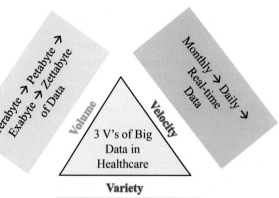

FIGURE 11.3 Three Vs of big data in healthcare.

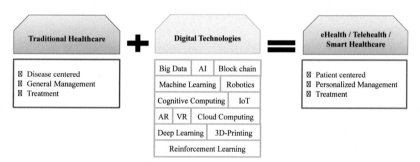

FIGURE 11.4 Traditional healthcare to Smart healthcare.

Today, the entire healthcare industry is in a remarkable position to benefit from these digital technologies' evolution. The significant cause of the shift from traditional to smart healthcare is the requirement to monitor health outside the boundary of hospitals, meaning healthcare is now free of the hospital's physical location. The patient can get access to the healthcare systems anytime and from anywhere. Further, the use of advanced digital technologies makes it possible to deeply analyze vast amounts of healthcare particulars, enhancing the quality of healthcare manifold. E-health care is benefiting the whole community through E-health and mobile health. E-health provides anytime, anywhere access to healthcare facilities such as telemedicine, online data sharing between patients and health professionals, online doctor consultation, and many other hospital services. Mobile health tries to provide some essential healthcare services through wearable devices, digital assistants, and other mobile devices [9]. One primary sector where smart healthcare is playing a vital role is the monitoring of old age patients. It makes use of intelligent devices placed in the environment to monitor the health of elderly persons round the clock and try to make their living independent [10]. The extent of E-health care is vast, it boosts the personal experience of the patients by taking care of their individual needs. It also gives a direction to the growth of modern medicines. In this chapter, we introduce cognitive big data technologies and how they are facilitating E-health care [11].

1.2 Advantages of E-health care

E-health care system has several advantages and they are listed below [12,35]:

- It significantly reduces the cost as well as the risk associated with manual healthcare processes.
- It automates the entire process of healthcare data recording, analyzing, and presenting with very little human intervention.
- It helps in lowering the need for direct supervision.
- It helps in getting continuous data points from our body, which facilitates continuous monitoring.
- It improves the utilization efficiency of medical resources.
- It promotes self-health care and facilitates the use of telemedicine.
- The overall medication process becomes more intelligent.
- It enhances the treatment of some particular diseases with an expert decision support system [13,14].
- It makes automatic pathology and imaging system have better accuracies than a manual system.
- It helps healthcare professionals personalize the course of treatment through the precise and real-time status of the individual.
- It makes the disease treatment process more precise.
- It assists in the easy formation and implementation of the surgery plans.
- It makes it possible for healthcare professionals to intervene timely in any diagnostic process through real-time feedback of the health data.
- It helps patients in self-managing their condition through health information platform.
- It eases the use of online advice and medication.
- It helps medical personnel in getting assistance from peer experts and researchers.
- It minimizes the chance of error during any diagnostic process.
- It makes healthcare services economical.
- It assists patients in getting timely healthcare services.
- It encourages the targeted prevention of diseases through self-monitoring.
- It helps in efficiently storing the patient records and seamlessly shares health information with patients and health professionals.

- It provides virtual assistants to patients, doctors, and healthcare organizations.
- It has the capability of language translation that helps the intercommunication of patients, doctors, and healthcare organizations.
- It has the facility of automatic interconversion of patients' common language into medical terminologies and vice versa.
- It helps in significantly reducing the requirements of healthcare organizations in terms of workforce and resources.

2. Cognitive computing technologies for E-health care

There are several technologies available that support cognitive computing. Here, we are considering only those technologies which facilitate cognitive computing application to E-health. There are several approaches including Machine Learning that analyzes the cardiac signals to generate the insights such as combined analysis of cardiac signals [15], comparative analysis of ML algorithms for heart disease prediction [16], and annotation of the cardiac signals [17,18]. One possible spectrum of these technologies is presented in Fig. 11.5. There may be many more technologies, but these are the primary ones that majorly support E-health care.

3. Cognitive big data analytics for E-health care

Over the last few decades, computing technologies' evolution has transformed machines into thinking devices, referred to as cognitive systems. The term *cognition* comes from the Latin word *cognito* which implies *to think*. Cognitive systems are fundamentally different in comparison to other forms of computing available. The cognitive system comprises of data, information, and expertise. It can learn from the interaction of individuals with data and

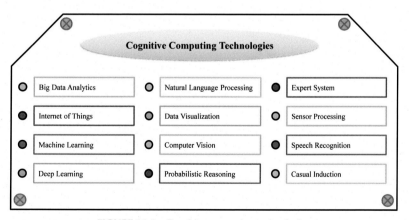

FIGURE 11.5 Cognitive computing technologies.

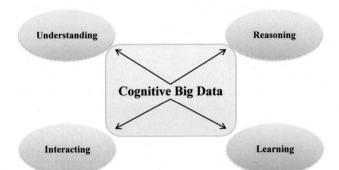

FIGURE 11.6 Capabilities of cognitive computing system.

situations without any interruption. Fig. 11.6 shows the capabilities of a cognitive system. The cognitive system has an auto-learning feature that learns over time through the experience and interaction with other systems. There are various standard properties of the cognitive system shown in Table 11.1.

TABLE 11.1 Properties of cognitive computing system.

S.No.	Properties	Description
1	Self-learning	The learning is unsupervised; it learns on its own without the need of explicit programming.
2	Stateful	It has memory which remembers the state of each transaction.
3	Adaptive and flexible	It is flexible in the handling of input data, if any unwanted data come up. It also adapts to both physical and logical conditions.
4	Dynamic	It is capable of handling the real-time data.
5	Probabilistic	It is not deterministic, it interprets the input probabilistically.
6	Interactive	It is interactive with machines and peoples.
7	Iterative	As it is self-learning, it is always iterative. It makes, learns, and updates.
8	Friendly with unstructured data	It is capable of handling several forms of healthcare data in the world.
9	Scalable	Its working ranges are from a small room to a whole city.
10	Context aware	It is aware of time, location, process, and goal.
11	Self-managed	It is fault tolerant and has the capability of diagnosis, troubleshooting, and maintenance.

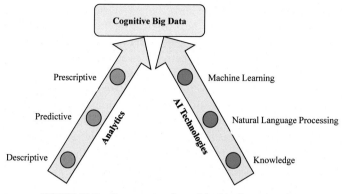

FIGURE 11.7   Convergence of cognitive big data computing.

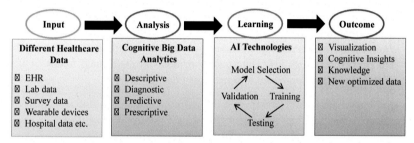

FIGURE 11.8   Process of cognitive big data in healthcare.

Fig. 11.7 shows how different forms of analytics, together with artificial intelligence technologies, converge to cognitive big data computing. In healthcare, the cognitive big data system understands massive data, reasons, and learns to strengthen the diagnostic process through interactions with different healthcare professionals. A healthcare cognitive big data system takes input in the form of several healthcare data, analyzes it, applies techniques to learn from it, and finally produces knowledge and different cognitive insights. Fig. 11.8 shows how cognitive big data performs healthcare.

3.1 Role of Hadoop and Apache Spark in E-health care analytics

Hadoop and Apache Spark are the two most common big data platforms used in healthcare analytics. The brief introduction of both the platform is presented here.

3.1.1 Hadoop

Apache Hadoop effectively deals with the challenges in healthcare organizations due to vast and complex data. In big data analytics, merely feeding the large volume of data even to the most potent clusters will not produce the desired results. Therefore, the best logical approach to deal with this complicated and huge data volume is to wisely distribute it on multiple nodes and process it in parallel. The nodes here represent the computing units present in the big data cluster. However, healthcare data are so massive that they require several computing nodes for their processing in considerable time. Additionally, parallel dealing with such a large number of computing nodes creates many challenges like distributing the data, parallelizing the computation, and handling failures. Hadoop is one such big data platform that is capable of dealing with these challenges. Hadoop uses the following methods for processing of data:

- *MapReduce:* It comprises of two primitives *map* and *reduce.* The former makes intermediate key/value pairs and suitably maps them to different logical records, and the latter combines the values with a similar key. It facilitates efficient parallelization of computations, schedules intermachine communication, and handles failures.
- *Hadoop Distributed File System:* It is the file handling system used by Hadoop. It provides efficient storage of data on distributed nodes. It is a scalable and replica-based storage.

Implementation of Hadoop system with big data will not set back the healthcare analytics. Few benefits offered by Hadoop are as follows:

- It makes data storage less expensive.
- It allows data to be always available.
- It allows storage and management of huge amount of data.
- It facilitates researchers in establishing the interdependence of data with different variables which is tough to perform for humans.

3.1.2 Apache Spark

It is another open-source faster alternative to Hadoop. It supports distributed data processing using the following higher level libraries:

- *Spark SQL:* It supports SQL queries.
- *Spark Streaming:* It supports real-time streaming of data.
- *MLib:* It supports different machine learning libraries.
- *GraphX:* It supports several graph processing.

These libraries help in increasing the productivity of healthcare organizations because they require lesser coding efforts. Spark supports in-memory processing of data by implementing Resilient distributed Datasets, making it 100 times faster than Hadoop for smaller datasets.

TABLE 11.2 Healthcare stakeholders.

Stakeholders	Healthcare input	Outcome
Doctors	Health tracking data	Better regulations and efficient healthcare.
Insurance companies	Claim and insurance cover report	Customized health insurance packages and user-specific rates.
Enterprise	Clinical trial data	Faster discovery and reporting.
Individuals	Sensor and wellness reports	Preventive and personalized care.
Government	Population data and public awareness	Efficient infrastructures and better policies.

4. Need for cognitive big data analytics in E-health care

Today, healthcare data are the most voluminous and complex data out of all other forms of data available in the world. According to VP of HP Software Marketing, the healthcare data in the world in the year 2012 were approximately 500 Petabytes, and the same is expected to grow 50 times, i.e., 25,000 petabytes by the end of 2020. There are various useful and essential healthcare information lying inside this massive pile of data. The big question is what can be done with this vast data to make it useful. More than 80% of all the healthcare data are unstructured, requiring specialized tools and methods to derive insights and manage the data for better healthcare outcomes. We lacked in analyzing these data a few decades ago, but in the last decade, the advancements in big data and cognitive technologies have made colossal healthcare data analysis a reality today.

Traditionally, healthcare providers used their clinical judgment to provide treatment, and therefore, they were very reluctant to use big data and associated technologies. However, the healthcare industries are inclined toward the technologies for better medical practice. The technologies are benefiting healthcare professionals in terms of enhanced productivity and efficiency of their work. Table 11.2 shows how different healthcare stakeholders are using healthcare data for getting better outcomes with the help of cognitive big data technologies.

5. Advantages of cognitive big data analytics in E-health care

Cognitive big data systems offer a wide range of benefits [19]. Some significant ones are presented here:

- Cognitive big data is materializing the healthcare sector with the triple aim, as shown in Fig. 11.9.

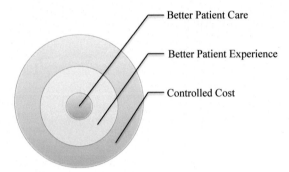

FIGURE 11.9 Aim of cognitive big data analytics in E-Health Care.

- It helps healthcare professionals to focus on more strategic initiatives and significantly minimizes the overall operational time.
- In case of emergencies, it provides a more superior user experience.
- It facilitates hospitals to use historical data analytics for optimization of the resource allocation process.
- It encourages online consultation.
- It suggests better support for the resolution of any healthcare problem.
- It maintains the proper proportion of cost and quality of care.
- It enhances the patients' and doctors' experience through better personal treatment.
- It upgrades the intercommunication of patients and healthcare professionals.
- It helps in the extraction of healthcare information from heterogeneous sources.
- It facilitates the exploration of more specific drugs and makes its development process convenient.
- It facilitates real-time collection of healthcare information from various sources.
- It helps in advance discovery of epidemics.
- It enhances the success rate of diseases detection and cure.
- It helps is preventing the frauds of insurance and mediclaim.
- It helps in enhancing the profitability of healthcare organizations.
- It allows to compare the treatment process of various healthcare organizations and helps in providing effective diagnostic process.
- It helps in associating various side effects of treatments.
- It assists diagnosis by grouping common symptoms and determining effective drug combinations to suit different sets of population.

- It helps in better healthcare management by allowing comparison across different healthcare groups.
- It makes the healthcare providers better understand the need of the individuals.
- It helps pharmacies by making them aware about the prescriptions of the doctors.
- It helps in tracking unusual practices of laboratories.
- It helps in expanding the reach of evidence-based medicine into domains not accessible with randomized clinical trials.
- It facilitates in conversion of the existing health records in the digital form accessible by every individual as and when they require.

6. Challenges of cognitive big data analytics in E-health care

It is well known for delivering correct healthcare inference automatically. Though there are number of advantages, it also has some specific challenges that cannot be overlooked [20,21]. Some of its challenges are as follows:

- To capture data: Capturing healthcare data is an ongoing battle as it does not always come from an impeccable source.
- To handle a large volume of data.
- To clean data: Most data cleansing processes are still manual.
- To implement high-end computing tools and protocols in the clinical setting.
- To report data.
- To visualize data: Clean and clear visualization of data at the point of care helps clinicians absorb information quickly.
- To share data: Sharing of healthcare data with external partners is essential to provide value-based care.
- Heterogeneity of data.
- To represent data in a format that helps in adding knowledge to the system.
- Ongoing supervision of the cognitive system to monitor the performance.
- Language understanding: It assists in understanding the specific symbolical healthcare knowledge.
- To train a cognitive big data system: It is very tedious to generate sufficient question—answer pairs to train the system.
- To update information: Healthcare data are not static; they require frequent updates to remain current and relevant.
- There is a scarcity of appropriate assets in the market.

- There is a lack of a reliable environment for the integration of new healthcare data produced.
- Interoperability of data.
- Transparency of data.
- Healthcare data have a long shelf life, which makes stewardship and curation a concern over time.

7. Metaheuristic approach for optimization of cognitive big data healthcare

The metaheuristic approach is used to enhance the performance of cognitive big data healthcare analytics. Nowadays, for the optimization of most problems, the research in metaheuristic-based approaches is trending. The term metaheuristic is the combination of two Greek words, "meta" and "heuristic." The former implies "higher level," and the latter implies "to find or discover." In summary, metaheuristics are groups of intelligent strategies that could find optimal or near-optimal solutions at sensible computational cost [22].

In cognitive big data analytics, the computing machines are expected to learn independently without the need for human intervention [23]. Consequently, machines require continuous improvement to provide predictive and prescriptive analytics [24]. Metaheuristic algorithms take other algorithms as input and help them find better solutions, run faster, return more accurate predictions, and enhance their performance. They help achieve the vision of autonomous cognitive computing and improve cognitive big data healthcare analytics's final results.

7.1 Benefits of metaheuristic approach over classical optimization methods

There have been debates on the selection of existing optimization techniques for optimizing cognitive technologies in the past. It was argued that metaheuristic algorithms could be a better choice in comparison to classical optimization methods [25]. Some benefits of metaheuristic algorithms over classical optimization methods are as follows:

- It avoids falling stuck at local minima.
- It is better at providing the optimum training weight in neural network–based cognitive healthcare analytics.
- Training cognitive technologies with the metaheuristics approach is faster than traditional gradient descent algorithm.
- It obtains an approximate solution fast in comparison to exhaustive search algorithms.
- In comparison to rule-based and deterministic algorithms, it provides a better result.

7.2 Applications of metaheuristics in cognitive big data—based healthcare

Some applications of metaheuristic algorithms with cognitive technologies for healthcare systems are as follows:

- In Ref. [26], Fruitfly Optimization, a metaheuristic algorithm, was used with a support vector machine (SVM) algorithm for the analysis of Wisconsin breast cancer dataset, Pima Indians diabetes dataset, and Parkinson's dataset for Parkinson disease.
- In Ref. [27], the Genetic Algorithm (GA), a metaheuristic approach, was used with the SVM algorithm to diagnose diabetes. GA was used for feature selection, and SVM was used as a classifier. The diagnosis was also conducted using the K-means clustering algorithm without any optimization approach. It was found that metaheuristic-based SVM classification has 2.08% more accuracy than the K-means algorithm.
- In Ref. [28], Firefly Algorithm, a metaheuristic optimization approach, was used with SVM for predicting malaria transmission. The prediction was also made using SVM only without any optimization approach. It was found that the SVM with a metaheuristic approach performed better than the only SVM.
- In Ref. [29], Chaos Firefly Algorithm was used for optimizing the computational burden of the Interval Type-2 Fuzzy Logic System for the diagnosis of heart disease.

In summary, it can be quickly concluded that these metaheuristics-based optimization approaches will become an essential part of data extraction, data preprocessing, and large-scale data analytics in the cognitive big data analytics—based healthcare system.

8. Cognitive big data analytics use cases in E-health care

It is so robust that we have created a revolution in the field of healthcare. Here, we present some of the use cases to show the revolution of cognitive big data technologies in healthcare. One important thing to mention here is that interactive diagnosis support systems (IDSSs) are meant to help us live better; they are not meant to get us worried.

- *Case 1: IBM Watson for Oncology:* It is one of the most well-known powerful cognitive big data computing platform healthcare analytics [30]. It has the capability of natural language processing and evidence-based learning to support healthcare professionals. It assists diagnosis in three steps as shown in Fig. 11.10. The most well-known application of IBM Watson is in the field of Oncology. IBM partnered with New York's Memorial Sloan Kettering Cancer Center to use Watson for elite cancer care from any corner of the world [31]. A hypothetical case of a patient

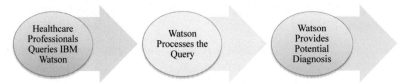

FIGURE 11.10   Steps followed by IBM Watson.

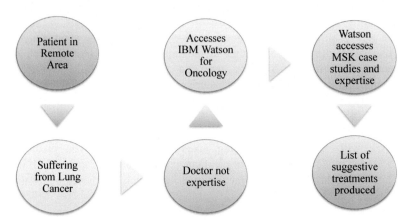

FIGURE 11.11   IBM Watson–based disease treatment process.

who is suffering from a rare form of lung cancer, getting suggestive treatment with the help of Watson for oncology, is shown in Fig. 11.11.

- *Case 2: IBM Watson - study reported from Japan in 2015:* A patient diagnosed with blood cancer showed prolonged recovery after chemotherapy. The concerned professionals used IBM Watson to cross-check the woman's genetic data with its database. Watson was able to find the cause of her illness in just 10 min, while professionals would have taken approximately 14 days to identify the same. Based on Watson's finding, the condition of the patient improved.

- *Case 3: IBM technology for Diabetic Retinopathy:* IBM uses IoT, big data technologies, deep learning, and visual analytics to solve the diabetic retinopathy problem in medically backward regions. The system analyzed around 35,000 images taken from EyePACs. A report tells that system was able to classify the severity of diabetic retinopathy with 86% accuracy.

- *Case 4: JVION Cognitive Clinical Success Machine:* It is the cognitive big data–based tool that consistently offers the complete healthcare solution for better patient care, experience, and successful outcomes. It has a self-learning component called Eigen Spheres that takes and interprets the data for each patient. In addition to different clinical factors, it also incorporates external and socioeconomic variables for better health outcomes.

- *Case 5: Apollo Hospital:* Apollo Hospitals, India's leading private hospitals, is one of the early adopters of digital technologies in healthcare. The CIO of Apollo Hospitals Group says that they are trying to use the best of computing technologies, including AI, cognitive computing, ML, DL, big data, and predictive analytics, to predict the disease risk in each area. Apollo hospital has already implemented big data analytics to control infection by predicting its risk.
- *Case 6: ImagineCare:* It reads blood pressure, blood sugar, oxygen saturation, weight, etc., in real time and sends them to the monitoring center where designated professionals monitor them round the clock. Whenever any parameter crosses the threshold value, professionals immediately contact the patient for necessary action. It also helps in reducing the unnecessary visit of patients to the hospital.
- *Case 7: UC Santa Cruz Initiative:* It is the world's largest cancer genomes repository, which facilitates the characterization of cancer at the molecular level.
- *Case 8: Sick Weather LLC:* It is the platform to track outbreaks of diseases through social media scanning. It offers forecasts to individuals regarding possible outbreaks similar to weather forecasts.
- *Case 9: Viz.ai:* It is an IDSS formed in November 2018, meant for highlighting stroke cases through analysis of CT results.
- *Case 10: IDx-DR:* It is an AI system formed in April 2018, which detects diabetic retinopathy in diabetic adults through analysis of Topcon NW400 retinal camera images. It provides a speedy diagnosis.
- *Case 11: DreaMed Advisor Pro:* It is an IDSS formed in June 2018, which computes and tells the insulin delivery level through analysis of self-monitoring glucose monitor data and insulin pumps data.
- *Case 12: EchoMD AutoEF:* It is an IDSS formed in June 2018, which measures cardiac function by analyzing cardiovascular images using deep learning algorithms.
- *Case 13: Arterys Oncology AI:* It is a web-based IDSS formed in November 2018 that assists healthcare professionals in analyzing MRIs and CT scans for liver and lung cancer.
- *Case 14: EXPLORER:* It is a whole-body scanner, the first of its kind. It scans the complete human body in just 20−30 s with compound CT and PET scans. It is 40 times faster than a PET scan.

9. Future of cognitive big data analytics in E-health care

It has enormous capabilities to modify the whole healthcare system. It is exciting to understand how cognitive big data analytics can be further

254 Cognitive Big Data Intelligence with a Metaheuristic Approach

improved and facilitate different healthcare stakeholders [32]. Some of the possible future directions are as follows:

- Use of Personalized Medicine on the basis of genetical variations for minimizing the side effects.
- Use of evidence-based care for better disease management.
- Explore the healthcare data in deep for the prevention of the spread of different infectious diseases.
- Explore ways of enhancing drugs and services transparency.
- Explore modern techniques for visualizing healthcare data.
- Investigate Fraud detection in real time.
- Studying and modeling the demands in future and the estimation of costs for predicting the trend of a particular disease.
- Explore ways to deal with the security and privacy of healthcare data.
- Trustworthiness of healthcare data.
- Enhancing the features of healthcare data in terms of its cleanliness.

10. Market analysis of cognitive big data analytics in E-health care

The advancement in cognitive computing technologies is rapidly transforming the healthcare industries throughout the globe. The integration of AI, ML, DL, and Big Data in cognitive computing has raised the market of healthcare [33].

- According to Data.gov, the market of these integrated technologies was USD 37.5 billion in 2019, and it is estimated that by 2022 the same will reach around USD 77.6 billion.
- Recently, the COVID-19 pandemic has caused economic troubles; several businesses have collapsed. However, the demand for cognitive technologies is increasing. The government is likely to invest more in cognitive technologies—based healthcare sector.
- Nowadays, cognitive big data analytics have become one of the significant market drivers; as per the Data Science Association report in 2018, the global revenue of cognitive big data analytics is around USD 189.1 billion.
- Investment in clinical analytics is estimated to reach USD 36.6 billion by 2025.

The detailed segmentation of cognitive computing market based on six different factors is shown in Fig. 11.12.

11. Cognitive big data players in E-health care

There are several cognitive big data health techs giants available in the market. Some top players assisting E-health care are presented in Table 11.3.

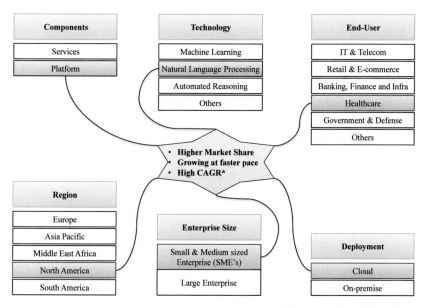

* CAGR: Compound Annual Growth Rate

FIGURE 11.12   Cognitive big data market analysis based on different factors.

TABLE 11.3 Cognitive big data healthcare players in market (data as on July 2020).

Name	Base country	Turnover (million)	Aim
Flatiron health	USA	USD 313	Fight against cancer.
Sema4	USA	USD 241	Personalized insights for patients.
iCarbonX	China	USD 199.5	To build an ecosystem of digital life.
Concerto HealthAI	USA	USD 150	Real-world evidence services for precision oncology.
Verana health	USA	USD 137.8	Platform for life science innovation.
Innovaccer	USA	USD 124.1	Data-driven value-based care world.
Evidation health	USA	USD 106	Connects individuals and the healthcare industry.
Exscientia	UK	USD 103.7	Accelerate drug discovery and development.

Continued

TABLE 11.3 Cognitive big data healthcare players in market (data as on July 2020).—cont'd

Name	Base country	Turnover (million)	Aim
Aetion	USA	USD 93.6	Real-world evidence for life sciences companies.
GNS healthcare	USA	USD 77.3	Empower health plan providers.
Nference	USA	USD 74	Knowledge synthesis from unstructured text.
Medopad	UK	USD 54	Connect patients and providers in real time.
Insilico medicine	Russia	USD 51	Extend human productive longevity.
Komodo health	USA	USD 50	Predictive analytics platform.
Abacus insights	USA	USD 47.7	Harness the power of the healthcare data.
SigTuple	India	USD 45	Detection of anomalies and trends in medical testing.
Perfint healthcare	India	USD 40	Developing diagnostic equipment for oncology space.
MDClone	Israel	USD 41	Enabling fast and direct access to healthcare data.
Holmusk	Singapore	USD 31.3	Reverse chronic disease and behavioral health issues.
Huimei healthcare	China	USD 30	Improving clinical quality.
Mfine	India	USD 24	Facilitates online consultation with doctors.
Qure.ai	India	USD 18	Analyzing diagnostic images.
Genoox	Israel	USD 12	Storing and managing genomic data in the cloud.
Somatix	USA	USD 10	Real-time gesture detection platform.
Human API	Canada	Dollar 6.6	Secure health data network.
Wysa	India	USD 4	Chatbot for managing mental health.
Prospection	Australia	10 CE	Deliver world class consulting.
Ybrain	S.Korea	Dollar 4.1	Measure and modulate brain signals.

References

[1] G. Aceto, V. Persico, A. Pescapé, Industry 4.0 and health: internet of things, big data, and cloud computing for healthcare 4.0, J. Ind. Inf. Integ. 18 (2020) 100129.

[2] P.-T. Chen, C.-L. Lin, W.-N. Wu, Big data management in healthcare: adoption challenges and implications, Int. J. Inf. Manag. (2020) 102078.

[3] H.K. Thakkar, P.K. Sahoo, Towards automatic and fast annotation of seismocardiogram signals using machine learning, IEEE Sensor. J. 20 (5) (2019) 2578−2589.

[4] S. Mishra, H.K. Tripathy, P.K. Mallick, A.K. Bhoi, P. Barsocchi, EAGA-MLP-an enhanced and adaptive hybrid classification model for diabetes diagnosis, Sensors 20 (14) (2020) 4036.

[5] S. Mishra, P.K. Mallick, H.K. Tripathy, A.K. Bhoi, A. González-Briones, Performance evaluation of a proposed machine learning model for chronic disease datasets using an integrated attribute evaluator and an improved decision tree classifier, Appl. Sci. 10 (22) (2020) 8137.

[6] H.K. Thakkar, W.-W. Liao, C.-Y. Wu, Y.-W. Hsieh, T.-H. Lee, Predicting clinically significant motor function improvement after contemporary task-oriented interventions using machine learning approaches, J. NeuroEng. Rehabil. 17 (1) (2020) 1−10.

[7] H.K. Thakkar, C.K. Dehury, P.K. Sahoo, Muvine: multi-stage virtual network embedding in cloud data centers using reinforcement learning-based predictions, IEEE J. Sel. Area. Commun. 38 (6) (2020) 1058−1074.

[8] S. Mishra, P.K. Mallick, L. Jena, G.S. Chae, Optimization of skewed data using sampling-based preprocessing approach, Front. Pub. Health 8 (n.d).

[9] P.K. Sahoo, H.K. Thakkar, M.-Y. Lee, A cardiac early warning system with multi channel SCG and ECG monitoring for mobile health, Sensors 17 (4) (2017) 711.

[10] N.V. Chawla, D.A. Davis, Bringing big data to personalized healthcare: a patient-centered framework, J. Gen. Intern. Med. 28 (3) (2013) 660−665.

[11] M.D. Lytras, P. Papadopoulou, A. Sarirete, Smart healthcare: emerging technologies, best practices, and sustainable policies, in: Innovation in Health Informatics, Elsevier, 2020, pp. 3−38.

[12] S.W.Y. Yee, C. Gutierrez, C.N. Park, D. Lee, S. Lee, Big data: its implications on healthcare and future steps, in: Impacts of Information Technology on Patient Care and Empowerment, IGI Global, 2020, pp. 82−99.

[13] J. Dhar, A. Ranganathan, Machine learning capabilities in medical diagnosis applications: computational results for hepatitis disease, Int. J. Biomed. Eng. Technol. 17 (4) (2015) 330−340.

[14] K. Polat, S. Güneş, Principles component analysis, fuzzy weighting pre-processing and artificial immune recognition system based diagnostic system for diagnosis of lung cancer, Expert Syst. Appl. 34 (1) (2008) 214−221.

[15] P.K. Sahoo, H.K. Thakkar, W.-Y. Lin, P.-C. Chang, M.-Y. Lee, On the design of an efficient cardiac health monitoring system through combined analysis of ecg and scg signals, Sensors 18 (2) (2018) 379.

[16] H.K. Thakkar, H. Shukla, S. Patil, A comparative analysis of machine learning classifiers for robust heart disease prediction, in: 2020 IEEE 17th India Council International Conference (INDICON), IEEE, 2020, pp. 1−6.

[17] D. Rai, H.K. Thakkar, D. Singh, H.V. Bathala, Machine learning assisted automatic annotation of isovolumic movement and aortic valve closure using seismocardiogram signals, in: 2020 IEEE 17th India Council International Conference (INDICON), IEEE, 2020, pp. 1−6.

[18] D. Rai, H.K. Thakkar, S.S. Rajput, Performance characterization of binary classifiers for automatic annotation of aortic valve opening in seismocardiogram signals, in: 2020 9th International Conference on Bioinformatics and Biomedical Science, 2020, pp. 77–82.

[19] S. Dash, S.K. Shakyawar, M. Sharma, S. Kaushik, Big data in healthcare: management, analysis and future prospects, J. Big Data 6 (1) (2019) 54.

[20] J. Hurwitz, M. Kaufman, A. Bowles, A. Nugent, J.G. Kobielus, M.D. Kowolenko, Cognitive Computing and Big Data Analytics, Wiley Online Library, 2015.

[21] M. Tarafdar, C. Beath, J. Ross, Enterprise Cognitive Computing Applications: Opportunities and Challenges, IT professional, n.d.

[22] Z. Beheshti, S.M.H. Shamsuddin, A review of population-based meta-heuristic algorithms, Int. J. Adv. Soft Comput. Appl 5 (1) (2013) 1–35.

[23] M. Sellmann, Meta-algorithms in cognitive computing, IEEE Intell. Syst. 4 (2017) 35–39.

[24] S. Fong, S. Deb, X.-S. Yang, How meta-heuristic algorithms contribute to deep learning in the hype of big data analytics, in: Progress in Intelligent Computing Techniques: Theory, Practice, and Applications, Springer, 2018, pp. 3–25.

[25] C.-W. Tsai, M.-C. Chiang, A. Ksentini, M. Chen, Metaheuristic algorithms for healthcare: open issues and challenges, Comput. Electr. Eng. 53 (2016) 421–434.

[26] L. Shen, H. Chen, Z. Yu, W. Kang, B. Zhang, H. Li, B. Yang, D. Liu, Evolving support vector machines using fruit fly optimization for medical data classification, Knowl. Base Syst. 96 (2016) 61–75.

[27] T. Santhanam, M. Padmavathi, Application of k-means and genetic algorithms for dimension reduction by integrating svm for diabetes diagnosis, Procedia Comput. Sci. 47 (2015) 76–83.

[28] X.-S. Yang, Firefly algorithms for multimodal optimization, in: International Symposium on Stochastic Algorithms, Springer, 2009, pp. 169–178.

[29] N.C. Long, P. Meesad, H. Unger, A highly accurate firefly based algorithm for heart disease prediction, Expert Syst. Appl. 42 (21) (2015) 8221–8231.

[30] Y. Chen, J.E. Argentinis, G. Weber, IBM watson: how cognitive computing can be applied to big data challenges in life sciences research, Clin. Therapeut. 38 (4) (2016) 688–701.

[31] S.S. Murtaza, P. Lak, A. Bener, A. Pischdotchian, How to effectively train IBM watson: classroom experience, in: 2016 49th Hawaii International Conference on System Sciences (HICSS), IEEE, 2016, pp. 1663–1670.

[32] P. Galetsi, K. Katsaliaki, S. Kumar, Values, challenges and future directions of big data analytics in healthcare: a systematic review, Soc. Sci. Med. 241 (2019) 112533.

[33] F. B. Insights, Cognitive Computing Market, n.d. https://www.fortunebusinessinsights.com/cognitive-computing-market-103377. (Accessed 9 September 2020).

[34] H.K. Thakkar, P.K. Sahoo, B. Veeravalli, RENDA: Resource and Network Aware Data Placement Algorithm for Periodic Workloads in Cloud, IEEE Trans. Parallel Distrib. Syst. 32 (12) (2021) 2906–2920.

[35] S. Mishra, H. Thakkar, P.K. Mallick, P. Tiwari, A. Alamri, A Sustainable IoHT based Computationally Intelligent Healthcare Monitoring System for Lung Cancer Risk Detection. *Sustain. Cities Soc.*, Elsevier, 2021, p. 103079.

Chapter 12

Multicriteria recommender system using different approaches

Chandramouli Das, Abhaya Kumar Sahoo, Chittaranjan Pradhan
School of Computer Engineering, KIIT Deemed to be University, Bhubaneswar, Odisha, India

1. Introduction

Currently, correct decision making is one of the most important factors in life—if we make a single wrong decision then we have to face its consequences. To make proper decisions we need some relevant data or recommendations. If we have proper recommendations, then only we can make the correct decision. Therefore, recommender systems can be seen to play an important role in decision-making.Recommender systems have been successfully applied to alleviate the problem of information overload and assist the user's decision-making. A multicriteria recommender system (MCRS) uses the client's multicriteria rating on dissimilar aspects of a set of items. MCRSs help in client's decision-making by generating personalized item recommendations, taking the information from the user preferences in different criteria to generate quality recommendations. MCRSs generate a list of recommendations for the user based on the user preferences.

The importance of recommender systems has been increasing rapidly, especially for business applications, with the use of recommender systems proving to be very successful in the ecommerce sector, (e.g., Amazon). Many businesses have started incorporating MCRS in a variety of other areas, including movie and music recommendation, books and e-books, tourism, hotels, restaurants, news outlets, etc. These systems assist the users in deciding the most relevant information based on their needs, instead of showing an indistinguishable amount of data that are irrelevant to the user. Hence it is crucial for recommender systems to have high predictive accuracy and for them to allocate the desired items at the top of the recommendation list based on the specific user's requirements [15].

Cognitive Big Data Intelligence with a Metaheuristic Approach
https://doi.org/10.1016/B978-0-323-85117-6.00011-X
259

The popularity of mobile devices among users has increased the dependency on mobile servers. A great deal of information, including business, product, and recommendation information is now widely available. One of the most popular applications is movie recommender systems. A movie recommendation system is an effective tool in movies to users, which helps viewers to cope with multiple movie options available to them and assists them in finding appropriate movies conveniently. However, recommendations are difficult to make, as they include different user preferences, different genres of movies, etc. Hence many techniques have been used to enhance the performance of recommendation systems [17].

The massive use of platforms for sharing opinions and reviews is one of the interesting trends that we have recently witnesses. As there is so much data flowing over the Internet, it is relevant to derive new strategies to gather and process this information. RS is an important component of every business. It mostly depends on the preference history of the users in order to provide them with suitable recommendations, whereas a traditional recommender system can provide only one rating value to an item [5].

Here we started with an introduction to multicriteria recommender systems, and next we describe some trending related works. After that we explain about the different phases and filtering techniques of recommender systems, before describing in depth our proposed three approaches. Then we discuss the dataset on which implementation of methods is done, and finally we show a comparison table of different approaches and an accuracy graph. This research activity ends with conclusion and future work section.

2. Related work

Multicriteria recommender systems are widely used in almost every sector of life, developed over time. Now-a-days there are many advanced recommender systems. Recommender system models can be made by various methods such as clustering technique, machine learning technique, deep learning techniques, neural networks, big data sentiment analysis, etc. There are many open-source projects being developed in the field of MCRSs. Researchers from all over world are creating recommender systems that will give the best recommendations. Some research work related to MCRSs is now outlined.

Wasid and Ali [2] came up with an MCRS using the clustering approach. The primary objective of their method was to enhance recommendation performance by identifying the most similar neighbors within the cluster of a specific user. To implement this method, they carried out two major operation. First, they extracted the user's preferences for the given items based on multicriteria ratings. Second, on the basis of the preferences of the user the cluster centers were defined.

Zheng [3] proposed a utility-based MCRS which was dependent on the utility function of every item for a client. He built the utility function by applying the multicriteria ratings to measure the similarity between the vector of user evaluations and the vector of user expectations. To calculate the utility score three similarity measures were incorporated. In addition, three optimization learning-to-rank methods were used to learn the user expectations.

Tallapally et al. [4] adopted a deep neural network technique known as stacked autoencoders to ease the recommendations problems. The functionality of the traditional stacked autoencoders was enhanced to include the multicriteria ratings by adding an extra layer that acted like an input layer to the autoencoders. The multiple criteria ratings input was connected to the intermediate layer. This intermediate layer was comprised of the items or criteria. This intermediate layer was further linked to N consecutive encoding layers.

Musto, Gemmis, Semeraro, and Lops [5] used an MCRS using aspect-based sentiment analysis. They utilized a structure for sentiment analysis and opinion mining. This automatically extracted sentiment scores and relevant aspects from users' reviews. They estimated the efficiency of the proposed method with other state-of-the-art baselines. The experimental product showed the commitment behind this work, as their method was able to beat both single-criterion recommendation algorithms as well as more sophisticated techniques based on matrix factorization.

García-Cumbreras et al. 's [6] method utilizes the pessimistic and optimistic behaviors among users for recommender systems. The objective was to categorize the users into two distinct classes, namely the pessimist class and optimist class, based on their cognition or behavior. The classes are defined according to the average polarity of users' reviews. Then the derived user's class is added as a new attribute for the collaborative filtering algorithm.

Zhang et al. [7] proposed an algorithm that considers virtual ratings or overall ratings from the user's reviews by analyzing the sentiments of the user's opinions by using the emoticons that were also included in the reviews to mitigate the sparsity problem which is still present in the recommender systems.

Bauman et al. [8] presented a recommendation system that suggested the items comprised of the most significant aspects to improve the user's overall experience. These aspects were identified using the Sentiment Utility approach.

Akhtar et al. [9] presented a technique for analyzing hotel reviews and extracted some valuable information and/or knowledge from them to assist the service providers as well as to help customers identify the loopholes and strengths in the service sector to improve their business performance.

Yang et al. [10] presented a technique consisting of three main components, namely aspect weight, opinion mining, and overall rating inference. The opinion mining component was responsible for extracting only the key aspects and opinions from the user's reviews based on which it computed a rating for each extracted aspect.

Wang et al. [11] proposed an approach on solving a problem when a user is particularly new to an environment. This problem is known as a cold start problem. We discuss about the cold start problem later in this chapter. Most recommender systems collect the preferences of users on some attributes of the items.

Musat et al. [12] explained a method called topic profile collaborative filtering (TPCF) that solved the problems occurring due to the data sparsity problems and nonpersonalized ranking methods that led to difficulty in finding sufficient reliable data for making recommendations.

Jamroonsilp and Prompoon [13] presented an approach for ranking items based on user's reviews. They considered five predefined aspects for the software items. The ranking of software was computed by comparing the sentences analyzing the different clients' ratings for every software aspect. This was performed in three phases including gathering user reviews, analyzing the gathered reviews, and carrying out the subsequent software ranking.

Zhang et al. [14] proposed a method that utilized the aspect-level sentiment of users' reviews with the support of helpfulness reviews.

Zheng, Shekhar, Jose, and Rai [16] proposed a multicriteria decision-making approach in the discipline of educational learning. First they integrated the context-awareness and multicriteria decision-making in the recommender systems considering the educational data as a case study.

These are some of the work carried out by various scientists around the globe. There are thousands of projects completed or on-going in the field of MCRSs with the aim of making the system fully efficient. Leading companies are now using recommender systems, such as Amazon which uses recommender systems to give accurate recommendations to its customers. Netflix also uses an MCRS to provide a list of movies and web series to users on the basis of user details and previous choices. These new techniques are being applied increasingly in recommender systems to achieve maximum accuracy.

3. Working principle

The most basic question that comes in mind is "what is a recommender system?" A recommender system is a subclass of information-filtering system that seeks to predict the "rating" or "preference" a user would give to an item. The basic working of a recommender system is to predict accurate recommendations for a particular user. The recommender system or single criterion recommender system explores only one criterion and gives the recommended result. This is the first recommender system concept. However, for real-world problems we cannot predict recommendation lists by exploring only one criterion at a time. This would give a false prediction. Therefore the MCRS concept comes into play. This kind of recommender system can explore multiple criteria simultaneously, giving excellent accuracy [17] (Fig. 12.1).

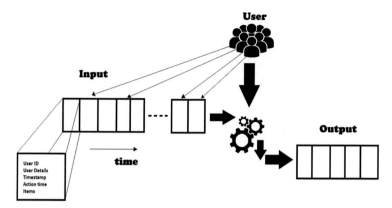

FIGURE 12.1   Working principle of MCRS.

Recommender systems are widely used in e-commerce systems, movie industries, and each many other sectors. For example, suppose we used amazon.com to buy a product then before checking out it shows a similar kind of product as an add-on. This list of items is predicted by Amazon's very own recommender system. Similarly, if we use Netflix then we can see that it regularly recommends new movies and web series to us. This prediction is based generally on two categories, on the basis of our previous choice and on the basis of out Netflix account details. That is how the recommender system generates a list which is most suitable to the user.

Every recommender system goes through three phases: the modeling phase, prediction phase, and recommendation phase.

The different phases of a recommender system are illustrated in Fig. 12.2. Now we discuss each of the phases and their significance.

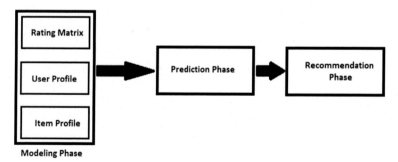

FIGURE 12.2   Phases of a recommender system.

3.1 Modeling phase

In the **modeling phase** the focus is on preparing the data that will be used in the next two phase. As can be seen in Fig. 12.2 it is divided into three cases. The first step is to build a ratio matrix. The rows of the matrix contain the names of the users, columns contains the items, and each cell contains a rating, which is by the user for a particular item. It then generates a user profile. This profile explains the preferences of a user. It is mostly a vector and each user has its own private profile of preferences. In the third step, it generates a profile for the items which contains the features of the items.

3.2 Prediction phase

This is the second phase of the recommender system. The main objective here is to estimate the rating or score of unrevealed or unspecified items for every client. This process is done by a utility function based on the extracted data which are provided by the modeling phase.

3.3 Recommendation phase

This is the third phase of the recommender system and is also an extension prediction phase. In this step various methods are used to select the client's choice by predicting the most acceptable items. As per the user's interest, new items are recommended in this step.

These are the three most important phases of an MCRS. We use different kinds of approaches in an MCRS to predict accurately. The most important and widely used approaches are content-based filtering, collaborative filtering approach, and knowledge-based approach; there is also a hybrid approach. We will take an in-depth look at these MCRS approaches (Fig. 12.3).

3.4 Content-based approach

A content-based (CB) approach generates suitable recommendations for a client depending on his previous behaviors. It analyzes the user's previous such as what they previously liked, bought, or watched, and accordingly make

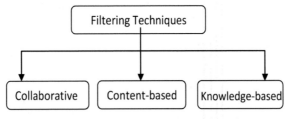

FIGURE 12.3 Filtering techniques of the recommender system.

predictions. It generates a user profile for every user based on their previously selected items and recommends items based on items with similar features. It does not compare his preferences to those of other users. The content-based filtering approach is divided into three steps, which are item representation, learning the user profile, and recommendations generator. In the **item representation** step, the information or the description of the item is extracted to create the item's characteristics. It produces the structured item's representation. In the next step, a user profile is generated. This user profile is based on the previous behavior such as liking or disliking, the rating, or by analyzing some text comment given by the user for a particular item. This step is known as the **learning the user profile** step. The final, but not least important, step is the recommendation generator. In this step a list of recommended items is generated and compared with the item's features on the user's profile. The item that is most likely to be suitable is added to the prediction list [1].

This method has been executed in various domains including textual details such as websites, news, and articles and also for recommending activities such as tourism, travel, TV, and e-commerce industries. This method works very efficiently if the item size is moderate. This approach relies on the content or characteristics of each item so that it gives several advantages such as offering a high level of personalization in recommendations, and it can increase its scale when the number of users increases, meaning that it is scalable. It also can make recommendations with a particular interest of a user and provides very good security. These are some of the advantages of the content-based filtering approach [1].

3.5 Collaborative filtering approach

This technique is the most popular technique among all the MCRSs. It interacts with multiple users and generates a recommendation list. If user 1 has similarities in their preference with user 2 then the item which is recommended to user 2 will also be recommended to user 1. The hypothesis behind this approach is that clients who agreed with other clients in the past will also agree in the future. For a new item the relationship with a user is determined by other users' reviews. We can represent this as a user terms matrix where each cell of the matrix represents the ratings given by clients for a particular item [1].

Collaborative filtering can be divided into two classes, model-based and memory-based. The memory-based approach is a kind of heuristic algorithm. It estimates the item's rating which depends on another client's ratings. It can also be classified into two methods: item-based and user-based. The other one, the memory-based approach, recommends items based on the similar interests of other users. It analyzes the behavior of other clients such as that they purchased, liked, or viewed before and then recommend the product to this client [1].

Collaborative filtering approaches have many advantages compared to all other filtering approaches, such as sometimes novel and unfamiliar items are recommended, it is very suitable and flexible in various domains, and it does not need to analyze the contents of a particular item [1].

These are some of the advantages of collaborative filtering in MCRSs.

3.6 Knowledge-based filtering approach

This is a comparatively new approach compared with the other two approaches. This method is used in those cases where both collaborative and content-based approaches failed or cannot work properly. This situation arises when there are insufficient ratings or reviews available for a particular item for the recommendation process. It generally happens for items that are rarely purchased, such as houses, cars, or financial services. The way this approach works is that it extracts the client's knowledge of the item domain for recommending the items that will satisfy his requirements the best. The core strength or advantage is that it does not need any previous rating of that particular problem, and so, by using this approach, it can overcome the cold start problem. However, it has a disadvantage also in that it requires experienced engineering with all of its attendant difficulties to understand the item domain satisfactorily [1].

There is another approach in the recommender system known as the hybrid **approach**. This approach is aimed at overcoming the weaknesses of both collaborative and content-based filtering approaches. It combines the strengths of the collaborative and content-based approaches by integrating two or more recommendation components or algorithm implementations into a single recommendation system to improve the accuracy of the recommendation system, which in turn allows better performance. The hybrid approach is generated by combining two or more algorithms. There are two major points that need to be addressed in this respect. First, keeping an account of the recommendation models that declare the required inputs and the determination of the hybrid recommender system. The second is determining the strategy that will be used within the hybrid recommender. However, there are also certain disadvantages to this hybrid approach, such as it not cost-effective as it is very expensive to implement because it is an amalgamation of other filtering methods. Moreover, it increases the complexity of the process and sometimes needs external information which is unavailable most of the time [1].

4. Proposed approaches

Now we discuss our approach using this activity. We chose K-nearest neighbor (KNN), support vector machine (SVM), and artificial neural network (ANN) approaches and compared the results, obtaining precision score, f1 score, and recall value. To measure the accuracy, we implemented a confusion matrix also. Now we take a deeper look into all three methods and also the accuracies of the measurement methods.

4.1 K-nearest neighbor (KNN)

The KNN algorithm is a very simple and easy to implement algorithm. It is used mainly for classification purposes and comes under supervised machine learning types (i.e., data sets are labeled). For example, we have two categories present as can be seen in Fig. 12.4.

The red one is category_1 and the green one is a different category; category_2. Now if we entered a new data point then the question would be into which category would this data point fall. To solve this kind of problem we used the KNN algorithm. At the end of the KNN algorithm we can see that the new data point is successfully placed in a suitable category. There are certain steps needed to implement this algorithm, these are:

Step 1: Choose the number K of neighbors—In this step we need to consider the K value. We can take a K value such as 2, 3, 5, or any other number. The default K value that is used most commonly is 5. Also, if we take a K value as an odd number, we get a better result.

Step 2: Take the K-nearest neighbor of the new data point, according to the particular distance formula—In this step, when a new data point is assigned, it measures the distance between all the categories present around

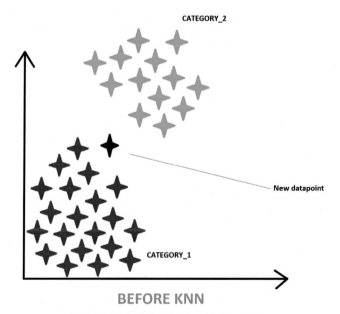

FIGURE 12.4 Labeled data set before KNN.

the data point. This distance measurement formula could be Euclidian distance, Manhattan distance, Minkowski distance, etc. Here we have used Minkowski distance.

Step 3: Among the K neighbors, count the number of data points in each category—Here it simply counts all the data points present in each category.

Step 4: Assign the new data point to the category where the most neighbors were counted —In this step we need to put the new data point in the category that has the greatest number of data points.

The KNN model is now ready. By following this step we can easily build a K-nearest neighbor algorithm (Fig. 12.5).

As can be seen, after applying this algorithm here it has successfully placed the new data point into category_1. For our research activity we have chosen 5 as the K value and Minkowski distance as the distance measurement formula.

4.2 Support vector machine (SVM)

Like KNN, the support vector machine is also a simple and easy-to-use algorithm. It is also a kind of supervised learning and is mainly used for classification and sometimes for regression also. SVM was founded in 1960s but was refined in the 1990s and now it is a very popular machine learning algorithm. It is little different from other machine learning algorithms. We now discuss how it works (Fig. 12.6).

Here let us take an example of two labeled data points, named category_1 and category_2. Now our main objective is to separate these in such a way that in future when we insert a new data point we can decide in which category it belongs. If we now try to differentiate those categories by a single line we can

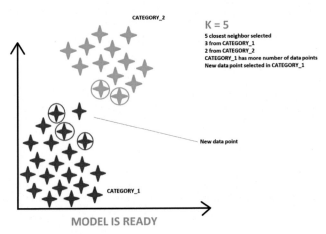

FIGURE 12.5 Classified after KNN model.

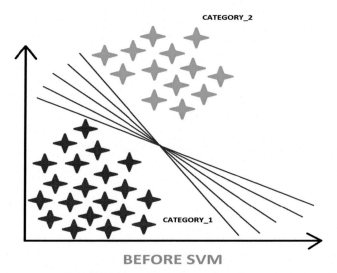

FIGURE 12.6   Labeled data before SVM.

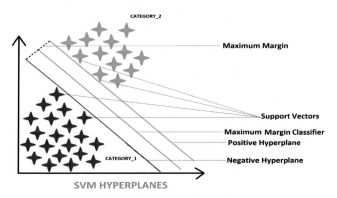

FIGURE 12.7   SVM details.

illustrate this in many ways, as shown in Fig. 12.7. However, we need to ensure that the divider is perfect, and so we need the help of a support vector machine.

SVM uses hyperplanes to separate different labeled data points, instead of dividing them using a single line. A hyperplane is drawn using the maximum width or margin that is allowed by the support vectors. These support vectors are the closest data points of two or more categories. In multidimensional space these data points act like vectors and with the support of these vectors we are able to draw the hyperplanes for the machine. That is why they are known as support vectors. The center line is known has the maximum margin classifier and each hyperplane is known as a positive or negative hyperplane.

Let us imagine that category_1 is apples and category_2 is oranges. The job of the SVM to distinguish between apples and oranges. By inserting the maximum margin classifier, it has successfully differentiated between oranges and apples. Now an apple appears which looks somewhat more like orange, however by other characteristics it is an apple. In these cases it will be placed somewhere in the negative hyperplane. Therefore, although its look like an orange it is still categorized as an apple by allowing for some error through the hyperplane. This is the main advantage of a hyperplane. In Fig. 12.8 this is illustrated, showing how a support vector machine works.

4.3 Artificial neural networks (ANNs)

Previously we used machine learning algorithms, now we implement a deep learning algorithm which is an artificial neural network algorithm. It is a supervised deep learning and very effective algorithm. To proceed with ANN, first we need to know what an artificial neuron is. An artificial neuron is similar to the neurons present in our brain, the dendrite part of the neuron is the input layer and the axon is the output value. Just like in neurons, artificial neurons are also connected to each other and act as input to another neuron. Fig. 12.9 represents a diagram of a neuron and an artificial neuron.

As we can see in Fig. 12.9, the artificial neuron is divided into three steps, input value, neuron, and output value. The input values are all independent variables. Those input values are connected by weights (w1, w2, ...) with the neuron. When an input enters a neuron, it is multiplied by its weight (X1.W1, X2.W2 ....) and, in the neuron, the value is calculated by summation of all inputted values. In the third step, the neuron value goes through an activation function. After that, the value goes to other nodes. This is the entire process of an artificial neuron. Since it is a deep learning approach, we illustrate how these neurons learn in Fig. 12.10.

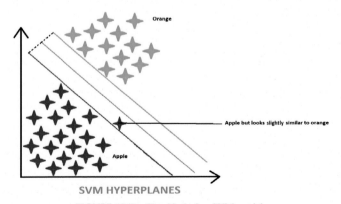

FIGURE 12.8 Classified after SVM model.

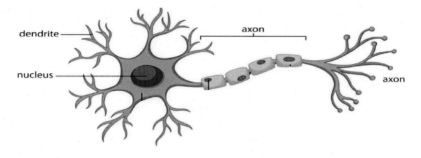

Neuron

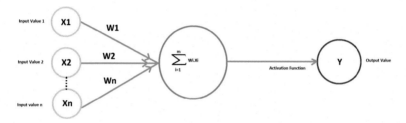

Artificial Neuron

FIGURE 12.9 A neuron and an artificial neuron.

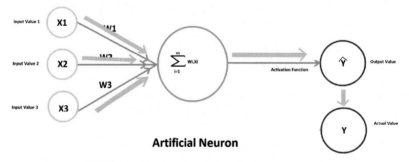

Artificial Neuron

FIGURE 12.10 Feed forwarding of an artificial neuron.

We have one neuron with three input values with three different weights. Initially the weights are taken randomly. Then the input value and weights are entered into the neuron section. Here all the inputs and weights are summed as shown in Fig. 12.11 and passed on to the next step. In the third step it goes through an activation function and gives a predicted output. Since this is a learning or training situation, we have the actual output. Then it is compared with an actual output via cost function to discover the difference. At the first

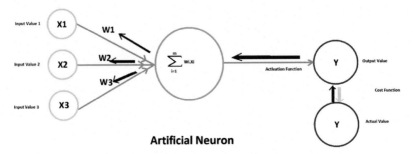

Artificial Neuron

FIGURE 12.11   Backpropagation of an artificial neuron

iteration it will predict inaccurately. Here, our job is to lower the cost function to obtain the correct output. Therefore it will feed back the value and will go backwards to the input layer and update the weights. This process will iterate more and more until the cost function value is at its minimum. This feeding backward is known as backpropagation. We also can choose good weights by the gradient descent method, which is how an entire artificial neural network works.

The model we have designed for our MCRS is as illustrated in Fig. 12.12. We have an input layer and two hidden layers. The activation function that we have used here is the Rectified Linear Unit Activation Function (Relu). This gives the output as 0 or 1.

These are the approaches used to implement our MCRS.

5. Experimental data analysis

In this research activity we used the IBDM move data set. Then we carried out a huge amount of preprocessing and made our own version of the data set. Then we manually added a column for the data set for calculating accuracy. We created a confusion matrix for each approach and calculated the precision, recall value, and f1 score. We will discuss each of these in detail.

5.1 Data set

We used the IMDB data set which consists of movies, TV shows, short movies, and other different types of movies. From IMDB data sets we chose four different types of data sets that are named as: name_basic, title_basic, title_-crew, and title_rating data sets. Due to these data sets being raw data sets, there are many blank columns present and many other columns present which are of no use for our model. We carried out a huge amount of preprocessing with these four data sets and merged the data into one data set which emerged as the perfect data set for our model. We discuss all the preprocessing steps in details. These data sets are in tab-separated Values format or TSV format. TSV files

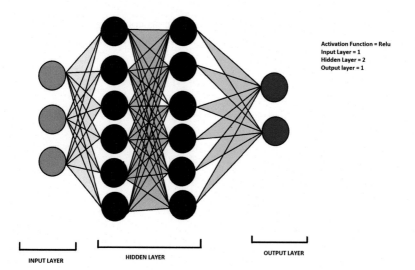

Activation Function = Relu
Input Layer = 1
Hidden Layer = 2
Output layer = 1

INPUT LAYER   HIDDEN LAYER   OUTPUT LAYER

Artificial Neural Network Model

FIGURE 12.12   Artificial neural network used in our model.

are used for raw data and can be imported into and exported from the spreadsheet software. TSV files are essentially text files, and the raw data can be viewed by text editors, although they are often used when moving raw data between spreadsheets.

At first we made four different data frames; name_basic, title_basic, title_crew, and title_rating to read the four data sets. The name_basic data set has six columns and 9,949,097 rows, title_basic has nine columns and 6,629,737 rows, title_rating has three columns and 1,037,488 rows, and title_crew has three columns and 6,629,737 rows. As can be seen, it has a huge amount of data. We noticed that each data set has many null values. Therefore, the using replace() function we put "NaN" in all the blank spaces for all the data sets. Then, title_basic has a column named "isadult" consisting of 0 and 1(0—not adult and 1—adult). We sorted the nonadult films from that data set using a pandas library. After that we merged title_basic and title_rating data sets into a new data frame called "title." This "title" now consists of 11 columns and 1,019,086 rows. There are some useless columns such as "originalTitle," "isAdult," "endYear," and "runtimeMinutes". Therefore we deleted these four columns from the title data frame. Then, from the name_basic we also dropped two columns: "birthYear" and "deathYear." Then we have merged title_crew with "title" data frame. Now the title data frame has nine column and 998,626 rows. This data frame has two columns named "averageRating" and "numVotes" that consist of integer data. After dropping all the unnecessary columns we saved the data frame in CSV format, named frame.csv. Then we manually inputted a threshold column in the data set and put a threshold value for each and every column. Our data set was then ready to use.

5.2 Confusion matrix

The confusion matrix, also known as the error matrix, is mainly use for statistical classification. It is a specific table layout that allows visualization of the performance of an algorithm. Each row of the matrix represents an instance in a predicted value while the column represents the actual value, or vice versa. The output matrix has four cells, true positive (TP), true negative (TN), false positive (FP), and false negative (FN). TP means the actual value and the predicted value are both positive, TN means the actual value is positive but the model predicted value is negative, FP means the actual value is negative but the model predicted value is positive, and, finally, FN means both the actual and predicted values are negative (Fig. 12.13).

5.3 Recall value

From the confusion matrix we can calculate the recall value. The recall value is also known as the sensitivity or hit rate, or true positive rate. The formula is:
 Recall value = (TP)/(TP + FN).

5.4 Precision value

From the confusion matrix we can calculate the precision value, also known as the positive predicted value. The formula is:
 Precision Value = (TP)/(TP + FP).

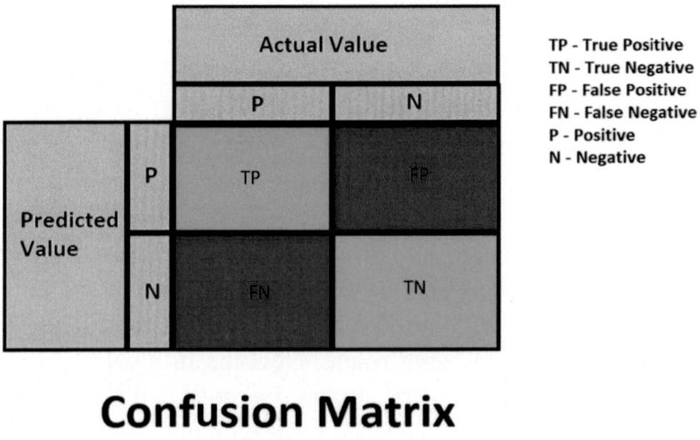

Confusion Matrix

FIGURE 12.13 Confusion matrix.

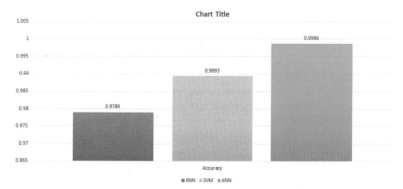

FIGURE 12.14   Accuracy comparison.

5.5 F1 score

The F1 score can also be determining from the confusion matrix. The formula is:
F1 Score = (2 TP)/(2 TP + FP + FN).

5.6 Accuracy

This is the main parameter for a confusion matrix. From this we are able to differentiate the performances of different models. The accuracy comparison graph is shown in Fig. 12.14:
Accuracy = (TP + TN)/(TP + TN + FP + FN).

6. Result

We have calculated the confusion matrix for each model and calculated the accuracy, precision, recall value, and F1 score separately. In Table 12.1 we show the comparison between these aspects.

TABLE 12.1 Comparison between accuracy, precision, recall, and F1 score.

Name	Accuracy	Precision	Recall	F1 score
K-nearest neighbors	0.9789	0.9862	0.9853	0.9866
Support vector machine	0.9893	0.9891	0.9882	0.9879
Artificial neural network (ANN)	0.9986	0.9983	0.9976	0.9989

7. Conclusion

Multicriteria recommender systems are becoming an essential part of modern life, which is why researchers are creating new algorithms and applying them in multicriteria recommender systems. There are several machine learning algorithms which are implemented or are yet to be implemented in recommender systems. In this chapter we have analyzed in depth the different filtering techniques of recommender systems, and the three most popular filtering techniques: collaborative, content-based, and knowledge-based filtering techniques. We also discussed hybrid filtering technique. Then we applied KNN, SVM, and ANN approaches in the recommender system to obtain a good accuracy score. In the future we plan to use many different MCRS approaches and compare them. We are also aiming to make our own multicriteria recommender approach which will give better results than the current traditional approaches.

References

[1] S.M. Al-Ghuribi, S.A.M. Noah, Multi-Criteria Review-Based Recommender System - the State of the Art, n.d.

[2] M. Wasid, R. Ali, An improved recommender system based on multi-criteria clustering approach, Procedia Comput. Sci. 131 (Jan. 2018) 99−101.

[3] Y. Zheng, Utility-based multi-criteria recommender systems, in: Proc. 34th ACM/SIGAPP Symp. Appl. Comput., 2019, pp. 2529−2531.

[4] D. Tallapally, R.S. Sreepada, B.K. Patra, K.S. Babu, User preference learning in multi-criteria recommendations using stacked auto encoders, in: Presented at the Proc. 12th ACM Conf. Recommender Syst., Vancouver, BC, Canada, 2018, pp. 475−479.

[5] C. Musto, M. de Gemmis, G. Semeraro, P. Lops, A multi-criteria recommender system exploiting aspect-based sentiment analysis of users' reviews, in: Presented at the Proc. 11th ACM Conf. Recommender Syst., Como, Italy, 2017.

[6] M.Á. García-Cumbreras, A. Montejo-Râez, M.C. Díaz-Galiano, Pessimists and optimists: improving collaborative filtering through sentiment analysis, Expert Syst. Appl. 40 (17) (2013) 6758−6765.

[7] W. Zhang, G. Ding, L. Chen, C. Li, C. Zhang, Generating virtual ratings from Chinese reviews to augment online recommendations, ACM Trans. Intell. Syst. Technol. 4 (1) (2013). Art. no. 9.

[8] K. Bauman, B. Liu, A. Tuzhilin, Aspect based recommendations: recommending items with the most valuable aspects based on user reviews, in: Proc. 23rd ACM SIGKDD Int. Conf. Knowl. Discovery Data Mining, 2017, pp. 717−725.

[9] N. Akhtar, N. Zubair, A. Kumar, T. Ahmad, Aspect based sentiment oriented summarization of hotel reviews, Procedia Comput. Sci. 115 (Jan. 2017) 563−571.

[10] R. Dong, M.P. O'Mahony, M. Schaal, K. McCarthy, B. Smyth, Sentimental product recommendation, in: Proc. 7th ACM Conf. Recommender Syst, 2013, pp. 411−414.

[11] F. Wang, W. Pan, L. Chen, Recommendation for new users with partial preferences by integrating product reviews with static specifications, in: Proc. Int. Conf. Modeling, Adaptation, Pers, 2013, pp. 281−288.

[12] C.C. Musat, Y. Liang, B. Faltings, Recommendation using textual opinions, in: Proc. Int. Joint Conf. Artif. Intell, 2013, pp. 2684–2690.

[13] S. Jamroonsilp, N. Prompoon, Analyzing software reviews for software quality-based ranking, in: Proc. 10th Int. Conf. Elect. Eng./Electron., Comput., Telecommun. Inf. Technol, ECTI-CON, May 2013, pp. 1–6.

[14] Y. Zhang, R. Liu, A. Li, A novel approach to recommender system based on aspect-level sentiment analysis, in: Proc. 4th Nat. Conf. Electr., Electron. Comput. Eng, NCEECE, 2015, pp. 1453–1458.

[15] N.R. Kermani, S.H. Alizadeh, A Hybrid Multicriteria Recommender System Using Ontology and Neuro-Fuzzy Technique, n.d.

[16] S. Zheng, R. Jose, A Sentiment-Enhanced Hybrid Recommender System for Movie Recommendation: A Big Data Analytics Framework, n.d.

[17] S. Raj, A.K. Sahoo, C. Pradhan, Privacy preserving in collaborative filtering based recommender system: a systematic literature review, Progr. Comput. Anal. & Netw. (2020) 513–522.

Chapter 13

Optimization-based energy-efficient routing scheme for wireless body area network

Aradhana Behura, Manas Ranjan Kabat

Department of Computer Science & Engineering, Veer Surendra Sai University of Technology, Burla, Odisha, India

1. Introduction

A wireless body area network (WBAN) is an interconnection of small biosensor nodes that are deployed onto different parts of the human body. It is an important research area and is used in different applications such as the medical, sports, entertainment, and social welfare fields. The sensor can measure certain parameters of the human body, either externally or internally. Sensor nodes (SN) normally have very limited resources due to their small size. Therefore, an essential design requirement of WBAN schemes is the minimum consumption of energy. Biosensor nodes (BSNs) or simply SNs are the main backbone of WBANs. They are used to sense health-related data such as heart beat rate, blood pressure, blood glucose level, electrocardiogram (ECG), electromyography (EMG), etc. and pass these readings to real-time health monitoring systems. Examples can include measuring the heartbeat, body temperature, or recording a prolonged electrocardiogram (ECG). Several other sensors are placed in clothes, directly on the body, or under the skin of a person, and measure the temperature, blood pressure, heart rate, ECG, EEG, respiration rate, etc. It can keep a check of changes in the above-mentioned parameters and many such applications in other fields. WBANs record and monitor biosignals. Increasing health monitoring needs and self-awareness of the population have created the need for the development of a low-energy and maximum-lifetime network-based routing protocol. The medical application of WBANs provides an efficient method for continuous human body monitoring. These WBANs are designed to operate autonomously, to interconnect the miniaturized nodes with sensor or actuator capabilities located in or around the human body. For example, if the sensor monitors a sudden drop in glucose, then a signal can be sent to the actuator in order to start the injection of insulin. This is a good example of a medical WBAN used for patient monitoring. WBAN can also be used to offer assistance to the disabled. A paraplegic can be equipped with sensors determining the position of the legs or sensors attached to the nerves. In addition, actuators positioned on the legs can stimulate the muscles. The interaction between the data from the sensors and the actuators makes it possible to restore the ability to move. Another example is an aid for the visually impaired. An artificial retina, consisting of a matrix of microsensors, can be implanted into the eye beneath the surface of the retina. The artificial retina translates the electrical impulses into neurological signals. WBAN can be found in the domain of public safety where the data are used by firefighters, police, or the military. The WBAN monitors, for example, the levels of toxic agents in the air and warns soldiers if a life-threatening level is detected. The introduction of a WBAN further enables the training schedules of professional athletes to be tuned more effectively. All these fields are able to maneuver WBAN effectively as it requires a low power consumption because of the limited capacity of the battery of each node, also it requires low latency and high communication reliability.

1.1 Three-tier wireless body area network (WBAN) architecture

The WBAN architecture is basically a three-tier system. It is composed of several biosensors which are deployed on the body. The first tier consists of body sensor nodes, the wireless communication system (devices) is the second tier, and the medical center or the application-specific center is the third tier. Tier 1 consists of an intelligent node which is capable of sensing, processing, and communicating. Some sensors used include an ECG (electrocardiogram) sensor for monitoring heart activity, and an EMB (electromyography) sensor for monitoring muscle activity, a blood pressure sensor, a tilt sensor for monitoring, and many others. Once the data of required parameters are collected from the biosensors, they are transmitted to a personal digital assistant (PDA). Usually the PDAs are within the transmission range of the biosensors. The PDA then transmits the data to tier 2 which can be IEEE 802.15.6 (for implantable nodes), IEEE 802.15.4 (ZigBee), IEEE 802.11 (WiFi), or IEEE 802.15.1 (Bluetooth), etc. In Tier 2, there is an interface in the WBAN sensor nodes through Bluetooth, ZigBee, IEEE 802, or, for example, ultra-wideband (UWB) technology, Zarlink technology, or ANT protocol (adaptive network topology). Wi-Fi cannot provide timing guarantees on packet delivery, while beacon-enabled ZigBee can provide real-time communication by supporting GTS. Zigbee's slow rate can be considered as a shortcoming. It is connected to the medical server through a cell telephone network (2G, GPRS, 3G) or WLAN—Internet. Its functions are as described next.

- Register type and number sensor node, manages the network channel sharing, time synchronization, and processing data, and sends data to MS;

    Next, tier 3 is a set of end points (PDAs) which are linked to a mega database system where the application-specific data are analyzed by the specialists in the area. The communication in WBAN takes place via the sensor nodes. The energy consumed by these nodes tends to be exhausted over a certain period of time, and it then becomes of prime importance to restore or replace the batteries of these sensor nodes. In tier 3 the major functions include:

- Authenticate users, save patient data into medical records, and analyze the data;
- Recognize serious health cases in order to contact emergency caregivers and forward new instructions to the user.

Therefore, we need a system which provides us with low energy consumption and maximum network lifetime. Clustering of the nodes is one such solution where the number of direct transmissions from the source to the sink is higher. Usually, the clustering approach is good for monitoring applications which require a continuous sensor data stream. To make an efficient clustering algorithm, various types of optimization algorithm can be used, such as PSO (particle swam optimization), ACO (ant colony optimization), and CS (cuckoo search). By using these nature-inspired algorithms, we can optimize the performance or enhance the quality of service. WBANs are emerging as a technology of great importance in the fields of health care, sports, military, and position tracking. They have a broader area of application because of their characteristics such as portability, real-time monitoring, low cost, and real-time feedback. Efficient data communication and limited energy resources are some of the major issues of WBANs. Despite the recent developments in communication technologies for WBANs, the reliability of packet transmission, especially for emergency and critical data transfer, remains a significant challenge. This may be because most of the existing techniques in WBAN use a single channel for data transmission, with no intelligence. The cognitive bonded channel provides a high data rate for emergency and demanding situations. WBAN consists of low-power sensor nodes where nodes are deployed on or inside the human body for the monitoring of various physiological parameters. It provides the daily activity of the patient and their health condition. In medical online monitoring environment, WBAN provides low cost and flexibility to monitoring for patients and medical professionals. Both healthcare and surveillance have been increasingly modified with recent technological advances. Advances in electronics, especially in communications technology and microelectronics, are leading to more and more personal health monitoring and advanced healthcare products with a wide range of products that already are widely available. Various sensor applications and systems have been developed with a wide range of features for heartbeat or temperature, insulin level, electrocardiogram (ECG), and for even wireless pacemakers. The introduction of advanced telecommunications technologies into the healthcare environment and the use of wireless communication solutions for healthcare products have led to increased user-friendliness and accessibility for users and health service providers. In the medical field, WBAN plays an important role in monitoring patient health situations for early diagnoses. These sensors sense human body activity and send the details to the cluster head or coordinator node. The cluster head is a high-power node that collects information from neighboring nodes and sends it to the base station or doctor. A number of sensor nodes can be implanted in the human body, with each sensor performing its own functions such as fear detection, heartbeat, blood pressure, etc. In WBAN, some events need high data rate transmission, such as in an emergency situation where a high data rate is required to send patient health information to a monitoring unit. In wireless communication, cognitive radio (CR) is a transceiver which senses a frequency spectrum and is capable of concatenating a free adjacent channel for a high data rate. In CR, the primary user (PU) transmits data and has the highest priority to use the channel. If the PU is not using the channel and the channel is free then it is allocated to the secondary user (SU). Many WBANs coexist, in which multiple WBANs communicate with medical staff for regular health monitoring. These WBANs consist of low-power sensor nodes which have a low data rate. These always rely on a single channel. Due to multiple adjacent WBANs and nearby IoT devices, their coexistence interference affects the reliability and overall performance of the system. However, numerous challenges are present in WBANs and their reliability is affected by wireless sensor nodes with limited resources. Also, because of the advent and advancement in sensor technology, low-power electronics, and low-power radio frequency (RF) design have enabled the development of small, relatively inexpensive and low-power sensors, called microsensors, which can be connected via a wireless network. These wireless microsensor networks represent a new paradigm for extracting data from the environment and enable the reliable monitoring of a variety of environments for applications that include surveillance, machine failure diagnosis, and chemical/biological detection. There are two main challenges to designing these kinds of networks, namely communication bandwidth and energy, which are significantly more limited in these kinds of WBAN networks as compared to any tethered network environment of the same above-described constraint. These constraints require innovative design techniques to use the available bandwidth and energy efficiently. In order to design good protocols for wireless microsensor networks, it is important to understand the parameters that are relevant to the sensor applications. While there are many ways in which the properties of a sensor network protocol can be evaluated, the following metrics are used by the authors.

1.1.1 Ease of deployment

Sensor networks may contain hundreds or thousands of nodes, and they may need to be deployed in remote or dangerous environments, allowing users to extract information in ways that would not have been possible otherwise. This requires that nodes be able to communicate with each other even in the absence of an established network infrastructure and predefined node locations.

1.1.2 System lifetime

These networks should function for as long as possible. It may be inconvenient or impossible to recharge node batteries. Therefore, all aspects of the node, from the hardware to the protocols, must be designed to be extremely energy efficient.

1.1.3 Latency

Data from sensor networks are typically time sensitive, so it is important to receive the data in a timely manner.

1.1.4 Quality

The notion of "quality" in a microsensor network is very different to that in traditional wireless data networks. For sensor networks, the end user does not require all the data in the network because (1) the data from neighboring nodes are highly correlated, making the data redundant and (2) the end user cares about a higher level description of events occurring in the environment being monitored. The quality of the network is, therefore, based on the quality of the aggregate data set, so protocols should be designed to optimize for the unique, application-specific quality of a sensor network.

1.2 Motivation and application scenario

The application of WBAN can be categorized depending on the domain of the application. In the following, major WBAN domain applications are presented.

(1) WBAN application for medical treatment and diagnosis:
   There are many possibilities where WBANs are useful for diagnosis or treatment of diseases. Many researchers have conducted research in this regard.
   - Remote patient monitoring
      Telemedicine and remote patient monitoring are the main applications of WBAN. Telemedicine means the diagnosis and treatment of patients located at a remote location using information technology. WBAN has made it possible for the delivery of certain healthcare services for patients at distant locations. Using telemedicine increased numbers of patients can be served. Body sensors collect signals from the body and transfer the data to distant physicians and doctors for processing. Doctors can use this information for health estimation,

medical diagnosis, and prescription. This will create a smart health-care system. Daily activities of patients can be monitored to collect vital parameters from the human body.

- Rehabilitation

  Through rehabilitative treatment methods, patients can restore their normal functional capabilities. Proper rehabilitation measures and therapy can enable a person who has experienced a stroke to function independently. These patients are constantly monitored to maintain a correct motion pattern. The main application of WBAN in this area includes sensor diversification, data fusion, real-time feed-back, and home-based rehabilitation through devices that constantly monitor bodily activities. This will create awareness regarding certain physiological activities.

- Biofeedback

  Through WBAN, remote monitoring of the human body can be done. The data collected by sensors can be accessed to gather valuable parameters from the body. Patients can look after and maintain their health through the mechanism of biofeedback including temperature analysis, blood pressure detection, ECG, etc. Biofeedback means maintaining and improving health through devices that constantly monitor bodily activities. This will create awareness regarding certain physiological activities.

- Assisted living

  This helps in improving the quality of life. Assisted living technologies enable elderly and disabled people to be monitored at their homes. This will lower healthcare costs. Through these devices and technologies, the health of these people can be estimated appropriately.

(2) WBAN application for training schedules of professional athletes

  WBAN further enables more effective tuning of the training schedules of professional athletes.

(3) WBAN application for public safety and preventing medical accidents

  Approximately 98,000 people die every year due to medical accidents caused by human error. A sensor network can maintain a log of previous medical accidents, and can notify the occurrence of the same accident and thus can reduce many medical accidents.

(4) WBAN application for safeguarding of uniformed personnel

  WBAN can be used by firefighters, police, or the military. The WBAN monitors the level of toxic agents in the air and warns firefighters or soldiers if a life-threatening level is detected.

(5) Application of WBAN in consumer electronics

  In addition to purely medical applications, a WBAN can include appliances such as an MP3-player, head-mounted (computer) displays, microphone, camera, advanced human−computer interfaces such as a neural interface, and gaming and virtual reality devices.

2. Related work

Data transmission in WBAN takes place either by the multihop transmission method or by a direct transmission method. Therefore there is a very limited number of energy-efficient routing protocols. Protocols like Probabilistic Routing with postural link Cost (PRPLC) [1], Distance Vector Routing with Postural Link Cost (DVRPLC) [2] and Energy Efficient Thermal Aware Routing in Body Area networks (ETPA) [3] use multihop transmission methods. ETPA has been proved to be the most efficient among the three, but the energy efficiency is not sufficiently achieved as it uses an individual link-based energy method, instead of an overall WBAN energy consumption method. Energy Aware Peering Routing Protocol (EPR) [4] performs better than the other protocols. It works by taking the residual energy and geographic information of the neighbor nodes. Adaptive Threshold based Thermal unaware Energy-efficient Multi-hop Protocol (ATTEMPT) [5] is a temperature-aware routing protocol which is designed for heterogeneous and homogeneous WBANs. The data rate of the nodes play a key role. The nodes are placed in descending order according to their data rates around the sink node of body. Nodes with lower data rates cannot participate or transmit the data further. Reliability Enhanced-Adaptive Threshold based Thermal unaware Energy-efficient Multi-hop Protocol (RE-ATTEMPT) [6] is another temperature-aware routing protocol developed to solve the issues that occurred using ATTEMPT [7]. In this a minimum hop count path is selected. The distribution of data takes place evenly, so that energy consumption in every round is equal, thus increasing the network lifetime. Based on cost function, a temperature-aware routing protocol called Stable Increased Multi-hop Protocol Link Efficiency (SIMPLE) [8] was proposed. Here, a forwarder node is selected based on the minimum cost function in every round. Cluster-based routing protocols are observed to be more energy-efficient routing protocols in WBANs. Even consumption of energy takes place throughout the network. The sensor nodes form a group in which some criteria cluster heads (CHs) are selected which directly transmit the data to the base station (BS), ultimately resulting in minimum energy consumption and maximum network lifetime. Reference [1] presents a routing protocol which tolerates changes in the network. A store and forward mechanism is used to increase the likelihood of a data packet reaching the sink node successfully. Each sensor is facilitated with buffers to store a data packet. In the source to destination route, each node stores a data packet and transmits it to the next node. Storing a data packet and then retransmitting causes more energy to be consumed and hence longer end-to-end delay. We can deploy some nonsensing, dedicated nodes with an additional energy source, while this technique enhances the network lifetime, however, additional hardware is required which increases the cost of the network. A clustering-based protocol was introduced. The feature of this protocol is to restrict the sensor nodes to transmit directly to the sink. This improves the efficiency of the network by changing the selection criteria of the cluster heads. Since both device and battery technology have only recently matured to the point where microsensor nodes are feasible, this is a fairly new research area. Researchers have begun discussing not only the uses and challenges facing sensor networks, but have also been developing preliminary ideas as to how these networks should function as well as the appropriate low-energy architecture for the sensor nodes themselves. There have been some application-specific protocols developed for microsensor networks. Clare et al. developed a time-divison multiple-access (TDMA) MAC protocol [2,3] for low-energy operation. Using a TDMA approach saves energy by allowing the nodes to remain in the sleep state, with radios powered-down, for a long time. Behura et al. [16] developed directed diffusion, a protocol that employs a data-driven model to achieve low-energy routing. Recently, there has been much work on "power-aware" routing protocols for wireless networks like LEACH. In these protocols, optimal routes are chosen based on the energy at each node along the route. Routes that are longer, but which use nodes with more energy than the nodes along the shorter routes, are favored, helping avoid "hot spots" in the network. In LEACH, randomized rotation of the cluster head positions is used to achieve the same goal. One method of choosing routes is to use "minimum transmission energy" (MTE) routing [4,5], where intermediate nodes are chosen such that the sum of squared distances (and, hence, the total transmit energy, assuming a power loss) is minimized. Another method of wireless communication is to use clustering. In this case, nodes send their data to a central cluster head that forwards the data to get it closer to the desired recipient. Clustering enables bandwidth reuse and can, thus, increase system capacity. Using clustering enables better resource allocation and helps improve power control. While conventional cluster-based networks rely on a fixed infrastructure, new research is focusing on ways to deploy clustering architectures in an ad hoc fashion. Another early work developed a linked cluster architecture, where nodes are assigned to be either ordinary nodes, cluster head nodes, or gateways between different clusters. The cluster heads act as local control centers, whereas the gateways act as the backbone network, transporting data between clusters. This enables robust networking with point-to-point connectivity. Another ad hoc clustering protocol, the Near Term Digital Radio (NTDR), uses a clustering approach with a two-tier hierarchical routing algorithm. Nodes form local clusters, and intracluster data are sent directly from one node to the next, whereas intercluster data are routed through the cluster head nodes. This protocol enables point-to-point connectivity and does not use low-energy routing or MAC, therefore it is not suited for microsensor networks. LEACH builds on this work by creating a new ad hoc cluster formation algorithm that better suits microsensor network applications. There are various protocols and techniques developed for traditional sensor networks or other wireless networks, but due to different working environments and their need to have a lot of physical wires, these protocols cannot be directly used in WBAN applications. WBANs are formed in or around the human body, which has a different network structure/environment as compared to other wireless networks. As WBANs are mainly used in medical/ health-related applications which can sense critical data from the human body, timely forwarding to the medical server for further analysis is of utmost importance. Data gathering and forwarding are typically done using technologies of different layers such as application, hardware/devices, security, network layer, MAC layer technologies, etc. Among all these mentioned technologies, routing is one of the main technologies, because the sensed data by the SN needs to be forwarded to the medical server quickly and efficiently. Furthermore, the clustering mechanism is considered as an optimum approach for routing schemes, which has many advantages such as network load balancing, etc. Therefore, researchers nowadays are more focused on developing efficient CH selection and routing mechanism for WBANs. The aim of developing an efficient CH selection and routing mechanism is to enhance the network lifetime, network stability, throughput, and end-to-end delay IRMB protocol, which is proposed to improve the performance of the CICADA protocol [5]. CICADA is a cross-layered protocol which works on MAC and routing layer, which support a multihop communication scenario. It supports high energy efficiency and offers low end-to-end delay by setting up a data gathering tree. It is based on the model of multihop probabilistic network connectivity. The main aim of this work is to enhance the reliability of data transmission in WBANs. It uses a path-loss model to cover the whole human body instead of covering only the circular area, as is normally done in most schemes. In this protocol, a time slot-based mechanism is used which assigns short but equal interval time slots to each SN in the network. Furthermore, this proposed work analyzes the CICADA protocol and some modification is done, such as to achieve high reliability. Many researchers have presented an energy-efficient routing mechanism called the low-overhead tree-based energy-efficient routing scheme (EERS) [6] for multihop WBANs. The proposed scheme mainly focuses on efficient utilization of energy and transmission power. In order to support their proposition, the authors have done some experimentation to describe the problem, that is, energy loss due to low reliability in transmission. The low reliability in transmission occurs due to body shadowing and fixed transmission power in WBANs by not considering the wireless link quality. To solve these problems, the proposed routing scheme establishes a tree-based and energy-efficient end-to-end wireless communication path by choosing the appropriate transmission power for each SN. The proposed protocol was implemented using real-time test bed of MicaZ WBAN test bed and extensive experimentation was done. The performance of the proposed scheme was compared with collection tree protocol (CTP) in terms of end-to-end delay, packet delivery ratio (PDR), and energy consumption/balancing. The results illustrated that the proposed scheme works better than the compared scheme in the mentioned parameters. Many researchers proposes IM-SIMPLE [7], which is an improved version of their previously proposed protocol, called SIMPLE. It is claimed to be a reliable and energy-efficient routing scheme which offers high network throughput. In order to select the forwarder node, the cost function is used which is based on the distance of the SN from the sink and the residual energy of the SN. An SN having least distance from the sink and maximum residual energy gets minimum cost function and is therefore selected as the forwarder node. The residual energy parameter used in the cost function is said to balance the energy consumption among the SNs. Meanwhile, the least distance parameter improves the packet delivery ratio to the sink, and also reduces the path-loss effects in data transmission. The performance results after experimentation show that the IMSIMPLE routing protocol in comparison with SIMPLE and M-ATTEMPT performs well in terms of network stability period, network throughput, and network life-time. Researchers proposed the Dual Sink approach using Clustering in Body area network (DSCB) [8,9]. The aim of the proposed protocol is to cover the path-loss issue using a clustering approach with the use of dual sinks. Two sink nodes are deployed on the human body at the front and back. In order to select the best forwarder node, a cost function is used which is based on the residual energy of the SNs, distance between the SNs, and required transmission power. An SN with minimum cost function is selected as the forwarder node. DSCB has been compared with DARE and SIMPLE routing protocols in order to check its performance. Researchers also proposed a novel energy-efficient and harvested-aware protocol called Energy Harvested-aware Routing protocol with Clustering approach in Body area networks (EH-RCB) [10,11]. This protocol aims to improve the energy efficiency of the routing process. It uses a clustering approach in WBAN, by forming two clusters with sink nodes as their predefined cluster heads to overcome the path-loss issue. To further enhance the energy efficiency, EH-RCB uses an energy-harvesting mechanism which generates energy from human surroundings. In order to select the best forwarder node for data transmission, the proposed protocol calculates the cost function for each SN in the network. The parameters used in the calculation of cost function are total energy (sum of harvested energy and residual energy), distance of the SN from the sink, and required transmission power. The performance of EH-ECB has been compared with DSCB, EERP, RE-ATTEMPT, and EECBSR. The results showed that EH-RCB outperforms the compared protocols in terms of network life-time, stability, throughput, end-to-end delay, and packet delivery ratio. Reference [12] proposed efficient routing protocols in terms of energy-aware links. It is mainly focused on developing a framework for green communication. In the first phase of the two-phased scheme, it presents a network model for efficient link selection. Meanwhile, in the second phase a model for path-cost calculation is presented. Using these two models, the proposed protocol focuses on selection of an efficient and energy-aware communication link. The proposed protocol is compared with some state-of-the-art techniques and achieves better results in the defined parameters. Ha et al. proposed the Even Energy Consumption and Back Side Routing (EECBSR) [1,13] protocol which mainly focuses on balancing energy consumption and routing among the nodes that are deployed on the back of the human body. This protocol is mainly proposed for efficient data transmission in WBANs in order to cover the path-loss issue (for the nodes that are attached to theback of the human body) and enhance network life-time. M-ATTEMPT is used as a base protocol and the improved version is presented. Based on the experimentation conducted using a simulation tool, the authors have claimed that EECBSR achieves better results as compared to its counterpart in terms of network stability and throughput. Low-Energy Adaptive Clustering Hierarchy (LEACH) [14−19], a protocol architecture for sensor nodes, has a cluster-based routing algorithm which reduces the energy consumption but increases the number of dead nodes, thus affecting the network lifetime. Researchers proposed a clustering protocol named LEACH. It is one of the pioneer protocols in WSN which uses the concept of clustering and CH selection. It uses a multiple-attributes probability-based weight function for selection of CH. TCH is randomly selected and used as the coordinator for its defined cluster. It receives the sensed data from cluster members and, after aggregation, forward them to the sink node. The main aim of proposing the concept of random selection of CH is to distribute the load evenly among all the SNs in the network.

M-ATTEMPT [20] is another routing protocol which is claimed to be an energy-efficient and thermal-aware routing protocol that supports nodes mobility in heterogeneous WBANs. In this protocol SNs with high data-rate capability and with more battery energy are placed on less mobile parts of the human body. SNs transmit the data to the sink node either using a single-hop or multihop communication scenario. The critical or on-demand data are always sent directly to the sink using single-hop communication, whereas normal data follow multihop communication. The proposed protocol estimates the hot-spot and wireless link and avoids those links for data communication. Battery energy is properly managed in order to enhance the network life-time. The results achieved after simulation show that the proposed protocol works better in regards to energy consumption, packet delivery, and reliability ratio. Routing protocols plays an important role in managing the energy consumption of the WBAN, where they define the path of transferring data packets from BANs to the destinations, either MDCs or NSCs. These routing protocols have to be designed in such a way that they save energy by establishing the route discovery by using the minimum number of hops for efficient data transmission. Hence, only one technique can be incorporated for the reduction of energy consumption using data aggregation. Data aggregation helps the network to reduce the load on the nodes before transmission. We used cluster-based routing protocols for data aggregation. This cluster-based routing protocol is very prominent for its scalability. It organizes the sensor nodes into clusters where each cluster has a cluster head which is responsible for receiving and aggregating data from all other members in that cluster group. In order to have better operation, the cluster-based routing protocol has to deal with the optimization in cluster formation and cluster head selection in order to achieve efficient data transmission to obtain high data throughput, reduce energy consumption, and increase the network life time. Many cluster-based protocols have been proposed, which are unable to achieve optimal network organization during formation and selection. One prominent well-known one is LEACH that is an energy-efficient protocol when compared with other conventional protocols. The clusters formed by LEACH are not uniform because of the uneven distribution of sensor nodes in each cluster which results in high traffic load and fast energy depletion at the cluster heads. Improvement of these protocols is needed with the support of novel optimization techniques for WBAN. In most BANs, when the communication range is limited, for a tree-based routing protocol, it may require more than two intermediate nodes to transfer data from the source to the destination. A tree-based routing protocol is used for multihop communication and also for data aggregation within the network which is the best way for energy conservation. Hence, the tree-based routing protocol construction where selection of the aggregation of nodes needs to be optimized and ordered to achieve the high energy efficiency of data transferring. Energy consumption in the node is the main concern when designing the routing protocols of the WBANs to increase the network lifetime. Efficient reduced-energy consumption routing protocols are needed to assist the operation effectively and in a better way. Clustering enables bandwidth reuse and can, thus, increase system capacity. Using clustering enables better resource allocation and helps improve power control. While conventional cluster-based networks rely on a fixed infrastructure, new research is focusing on ways to deploy clustering architectures in an ad hoc fashion.

3. Case study on an energy-efficient hybrid C-means donkey-smuggler optimization-based routing technique for a wireless sensor network

In this section, various optimization algorithms to get better results in terms of throughput, shortest path, and quick packet delivery ratio are discussed. In this case study section, a convolution neural network (CNN) is used for data training and testing purposes. By integrating a neuro-fuzzy inference system and rule-based system, a fuzzy-based routing scheme can be formulated. To find the shortest path among the network or from one node to another node is very important. The donkey-smuggler optimization algorithm is used to predict the shortest path among the sensor nodes.

4. Analysis of the previous approach

4.1 Network configuration

In the proposed algorithm, WBAN is assumed to be a network of sensor nodes which are deployed or implanted on the human body and have the ability to measure physiological values. The sensor nodes have limited communication and storage capacities. It is assumed that all the sensor nodes are constrained in energy and have different storage and communication capabilities. In the proposed work, Energy-efficient Harvested-Aware clustering and cooperative Routing Protocol for WBAN (E-HARP) are presented. The presented protocol mainly proposes a novel multiattribute-based technique for dynamic cluster head (CH) selection and cooperative routing. In the first phase of this two-phased technique, optimum CH is selected among the cluster members, based on the calculated cost factor (CF). The parameters used for calculation of CF are: residual energy of SN, required transmission power, communication link signal-to-noise-ratio (SNR), and total network energy loss. In order to distribute load on one CH, E-HARP selects a new CH in each data transmission round. In the second phase of E-HARP, data are routed with a cooperative effort of the SN, which saves the node energy by prohibiting the transmission of redundant data packets.

The greatest design challenge faced by WBANs is to achieve reliable data delivery and enhance the network lifetime under the imposed limited power supply constraint. A proper and well-designed routing scheme offers prolonged network life-time with high quality of services using efficient resource management strategies. As WBAN operating conditions and architecture are different to other traditional sensor networks, the routing schemes designed for those networks are not suitable to be implemented in WBAN applications. A typical WBAN contains a limited number of SNs with no provision for redundancy. These nodes have limited computational, storage, and power capacity. Therefore, routing protocols for WBANs need to be designed in a way that considers these limitations of SNs. The routing protocols which are based on a clustering mechanism are appropriate in applications related to WBANs. In a clustering approach, the network is partitioned into different logical subnetworks called clusters. Each cluster contains one header node called a cluster head (CH) and other cluster member nodes. The cluster member nodes transmit their sensed data to the CH in a single-hop manner. The CH of each cluster gathers the received data into a single packet called a datum. The CH then forwards this compressed datum to the BS/sink. In this manner the clustering approach ensures minimum utilization of energy and offers maximum data delivery with appropriate end-to-end delay. As the CH performs aggregation and forwarding of data toward the sink, it consumes more energy than member nodes. Therefore, in order to create a balance in the energy consumption, new CHs are selected dynamically for each transmission round. The dynamic selection of CHs distributes the load among different nodes throughout the life-time of the network and hence uniform energy consumption is achieved. The dynamic selection of CHs is a challenging job in which multiple aspects should be taken into account. The selection of a suitable node for the CH role is greatly dependent on multiattribute decision-making techniques. Such techniques determine high-ranked nodes as CH candidates based on the required attributes of nodes. These attributes include residual energy, proximity to sink, etc. The node with a high rank value according to the requirements of the network is selected as the CH. The background and motivation section presents some of the existing schemes which incorporate multiple attributes of nodes for CH selection decision. Here, the presented technique is an Energy efficient Harvested-Aware clustering and cooperative Routing Protocol for WBAN (E-HARP), which includes:

(1) Dynamic CH selection using CF which is based on multiple parameters. For CH selection, the proposed scheme considers four parameters of SN, that is, current/residual energy of SN, link statistics (SNR), required transmission power, and estimated total network energy loss.
(2) Cooperative efforts-based communication in which redundant sensed data by SNs in consecutive transmission rounds is omitted and not sent to the CH or sink. In the proposed scheme, each SN checks the sensed data for possible similarities. The sensed data are transmitted only if they are critical in nature or different from the data that are sensed in the previous transmission rounds, otherwise it is considered redundant and therefore is discarded. Hence, SN energy is saved from unnecessary consumption by not sending the redundant data repeatedly.

4.2 Protocol approach

The proposed WBAN system consists of 14 homogeneous SNs with limited hardware resources due to its small size. These SNs are deployed in/on the front side of the human body along with two sink nodes. Sink nodes are placed on the right and left hips. These sink node locations help in providing direct connectivity to all deployed SNs. Both of these sinks are advanced nodes with high-performance hardware as compared to SNs. The SNs sense the physiological data of the human body and transmit it to the sink either directly or through selected CH after minimal local processing. The sink node after receiving the data from the SN, aggregates it and forwards it to the personal server for further analysis. The communication scenario used in this scheme is both single-hop and multihop communication. Direct/single-hop communication is done in the following cases:

(1) If the sensed data are critical (different from the predefined upper and lower threshold limit);
(2) If the sensing node is closer to the sink node;

(3) If the sensor node is a selected CH.

If it is not one of the above-mentioned cases, then the SN transmits its data to the sink using a multihop scenario, by forwarding it to the CH first. The CH after receiving the data from SNs, aggregates them and then forwards them to the sink node. The sink is responsible for selection of the CH, based on the calculated cost factor (CF). The parameters for CF computation are estimated/calculated by SNs and sent to the sink node. After its selection, the new CN assigns time slots to each SN in the cluster at the beginning of each sensing/transmission round using the Time Division Multiple Access (TDMA) protocol.

There are some assumptions in the proposed work, as follows:

(1) Due to high mobility of the human body, the positions of the SNs may change frequently.
(2) The power consumption of SNs during processing data is ignored as it is very limited as compared to power consumption during the transmission/reception of data.
(3) In order to address the limited energy issue in WBANs, and to provide continuous energy supply, each SN is equipped with an energy harvesting (EH) functionality which generates energy from human surroundings based on solar energy and supply it to the SN. To predict the expected harvested energy $E_{Harvest_t}(t, iP_{setup})$ of each SN, a common model called the exponentially weighted moving-average (EWMA) is used (expressed in Eq. 13.1).

$$E_{Harvest_t}(t, P_{setup}) = \int_{t}^{t+P_{setup}} \lambda_i(\tau)d\tau \qquad (13.1)$$

where $E_{Harvest_t}$ is the estimated harvested energy by a SN_i in a defined time τ period, while the charging rate of node i in time τ is represented by $\lambda_i(\tau)$.
(4) A total of 14 SNs are deployed on the human body, therefore, two clusters are formed in the cluster formation phase, each having its own dynamically selected CH in each sensing/transmission round. The CH after reception of data from its cluster members, aggregates it and forwards it to the nearest available sink node.
(5) The on-body path-loss propagation model used in the proposed scheme is the same as that which is used in the IEEE 802.15.6 BAN channel modeling project. It is expressed in Eq. (13.2).

$$P_{Loss}(dB) = \propto \times \log 10(D) + \beta \times \log_{10}(f) + N_{df} \qquad (13.2)$$

where $P_{Loss}i$ is the path-loss or path-attenuation (in dB), D represents the distance between the SNs and the sink, f is the operating frequency, $N_{df}i$

is the distributed variable (158 dB), and $\propto$ and β are the linear coefficient whose values are -27.6 and -46.5, respectively.

(6) The distance between the SNs and the sink is calculated by the Euclidean distance, which is expressed in Eq. (13.3). As the distance has effects on path-loss, the path-loss factor is also included in the calculation of the distance.

$$D(i,j) = 10 \left(\frac{P_{Loss-j,i}(dB) - \beta \times \log_{10}(f) + N_{df}}{\propto} \right) \qquad (13.3)$$

(7) The estimation/prediction of energy consumption during data transmission, reception, and processing is done using a first-order radio model. Eq. (13.4) expresses the energy consumption during transmission of K bit of data to destination SN at distance D. Meanwhile, energy consumption while receiving K bits of data is expressed using Eq. (13.5). Eq. (13.6) represents the energy consumption during the data aggregation process done by CH.

$$E_{Tx}(K,D) = E_{Tx-Electronics} \times K + E_{Amplifier} \times n \times K \times D^{i} \qquad (13.4)$$

$$E_{Rx}(K) = E_{Rx-Electronics} \times K \qquad (13.5)$$

$$E_{D-Aggregation}(K) = E_{D-Aggregation} \times K \qquad (13.6)$$

$E_{Tx-Electronics}$, $E_{Rx-Electronics}$, and $E_{Amplifier}$ are the required amount of energy (Joule/bit) or can be called energy consumption, respectively, by the SN transmission unit, reception unit, and amplifier circuitry. Meanwhile, $E_{D-Aggregation}$ is the required energy for data aggregation (Joule/bit), and n represents the path loss coefficient of a human body.

4.2.1 Analysed scheme

In the proposed protocol, each sensing/transmission round works in the following phases.

4.2.1.1 Initialization phase

The initialization phase starts after the deployment of all SNs along with both sink nodes. The SNs and both sinks estimate/calculate their locations and calculate the distance from their neighbor nodes and sinks using the received signal strength indicator (RSSI) technique. After the calculation of the distance, all SNs including both sinks broadcast the BEACON message in the network. As first the time-slot is assigned to the sink node by TDMA protocol, therefore this process is initiated by the sink node. The BEACON message contains the sender node ID, distance from the neighbor nodes, destination node ID, current/residual energy (sum of harvested energy and residual energy) of the source node, node location, and transmitted signal power. Upon reception of the BEACON message, each SN identifies the sender node from its address and calculates the path-loss between itself and the SN. The computed path-loss between the receiving SN and transmitting node is expressed in Eq. (13.7). The receiving SN j also calculates the distance from sender SN i using the path-loss model, as expressed in Eq. (13.3).

$$P_{Loss-j;i}(dB) = P_t(dBm) - P_{rj,i}(dBm) \qquad (13.7)$$

where $P_{(rj,i)}$ is the power of the received BEACON signal at SN j.

With this whole process, SNs and both sinks in the network get information about their neighbor nodes, their position and distance from other nodes, and all possible routes leading to the sink node. Each node, including the sink, saves this information in its local memory for future use.

4.2.1.2 Cluster head selection and cluster formation phase

After the initialization phase is carried out, the proposed protocol selects CHs for both clusters. Clusters are the partitioned regions of the whole network each having its own coordinator/CH as shown in Fig. 13.3. The purpose of creating the cluster is to ease the network convergence and data transmission process, as only the defined cluster members communicate inside a cluster. Based on the collected information in the initialization phase, the process of CH selection and cluster formation is carried out. Two clusters are formed (one on the upper and the other on lower part of the human body) with a dedicated sink node as shown in Fig. 13.1. In each transmission round an SN, which fulfills the defined selection criteria, is selected as the CH dynamically in its respective cluster. The rationale of efficient CH selection is that it should be in a location where the communication link does not face high interferences. Furthermore, it should have maximum available total energy (i.e., sum of residual/current and harvested energy), and it should perform a data-routing process at very low network energy consumption. The dynamic CH selection process is discussed in the following subsections.

4.2.1.2.1 Cost factor computation for CH selection Based on the information obtained in the initialization phase, each SN predicts the estimated total energy consumption/loss of the network and total residual energy of the candidate SN in order to select the optimum CH for both clusters. The energy consumption/loss occurs due to the transmission, reception, and processing (aggregation) of data in the network. Total network energy loss is the sum of two energy losses, that is, energy loss of all cluster members and the loss of energy in the SN itself.

4.2.1.2.1.1 Estimation of energy loss of cluster members. In this step, each SN in the network imagines itself as the CH of the respective cluster and then predicts the total estimated energy loss of all the cluster members in the cluster, which can be expressed using Eq. (13.8). the energy of cluster members is consumed during different operations, such as sensing, local aggregation/processing, transmission, and reception of data.

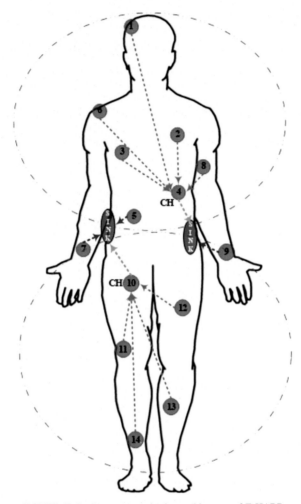

FIGURE 13.1 Data communication architecture of E-HARP.

$$E_{C-member}(i) = \sum_{j=1}^{N} \left\{ E_{Amplifier} \times n \times K \times D(i;j)^i + E_{Tx} \times K \right\} \qquad (13.8)$$

where $E_{C-member}(i)$ is the estimated total energy loss of cluster member i, and the total number of SNs in the network is represented by N. E_{Tx} and $E_{Amplifier}$ are the required amounts of energy (Joule/bit) required by an SN i for transmission, and amplification of a K bit size of data at a distance $D(i;j)$ from node i to node j.

The lower/minimum value of $E_{C-member}$ represents better connectivity with neighbor SNs.

4.2.1.2.1.2 Estimation of energy loss for SN. After the estimation of energy loss of all cluster members, the SN calculates its energy loss from its current energy which occurs due to sensing, reception, aggregation, and forwarding the data. The SN considers itself as a CH of the respective cluster and then calculates the energy loss if it receives the data from all of its cluster members, aggregates it, and forwards it to the sink node. The estimated energy loss from the current energy of the SN is expressed using Eq. (13.9).

$$E_{Loss-SN}(i) = \left(E_{Tx} + E_{D-Aggregation}\right) - K + E_{Amplifier} \times n \times K \times D(i, sink)$$
$$+ (N-1) \times E_{Rx} \times K$$

$$(13.9)$$

where $E_{Loss-SN}(i)$ represents the total estimated energy loss of the considered SN (CH candidate), E_{Rx}, $E_{D-Aggregation}$, $E_{Amplifier}$, and E_{Tx} are the energy consumption/loss in data reception, aggregation, amplification, and transmission, respectively, and $D(i, isink)$ is the total distance from node i to sink. The lower value of $E_{Loss-SN}(i)$ represents the better/closer proximity of SNs to the sink node.

The sum of both energy losses (expressed in Eq. 13.10) represents the predicted total network energy loss/consumption $E_{Loss-SN}(i)$ for the SN i.

$$E_{Total-loss}(i) = iE_{C-member}(i) + iE_{Loss-SN}(i) \qquad (13.10)$$

4.2.1.2.1.3 Calculation of sensor node energy. One of the other parameters used for the selection of CH is total residual/current energy of the SN. The total residual energy (expressed in Eq. 13.11) is the sum of harvested energy (generated from the external environment by SN) and residual/remaining energy of the SN.

$$E_{Total-curr}(i) = E_{Res}(i) + E_{Harvest}(i) \qquad (13.11)$$

where $E_{Total-curr}(i)$ represents the total current energy of the node i, $E_{Res}(i)$ is the residual/remaining energy (difference between initial energy and consumed energy) of the SN and $E_{Harvest}(i)$ is the total harvested energy from the energy harvester embedded inside the SN. The residual energy $E_{Res_i^j}$ of the SN at time t can be expressed using Eq. (13.12).

$$E_{Res_i^j}\left(t + P_{setup}\right) = E_{Initial_i^j}(t) - E_{T-round_i^j}(t) + E_{Harvest_i^j}\left(t, P_{setup}\right)$$

$$0 < E_{Harvest_i^j}(x) < E_{max_i} \qquad (13.12)$$

The initial energy $E_{Initial_i^j}(i)$ of the SN i is provided at the start of the deployment phase. $E_{T-round_i^j}(t)$ is the total energy consumed during the setup period P_{setup}.

E_{max_i} is the total capacity of the battery in the SN.

4.2.1.2.1.4 Estimation of required transmission power. In order to estimate the total required transmission power, which is expressed in Eq. (13.13), the SNR of the communication link needs to be calculated first.

$$TP = \frac{SNR}{\propto} \tag{13.13}$$

where "$\propto$" means path-loss exponent.

SNR is the ratio of the power of meaningful/useful signal P_{signal}, to the power of unwanted (noise) signals P_{noise}, which can be expressed using Eq. (13.14).

$$SNR = \frac{P_{signal}}{P_{noise}} \tag{13.14}$$

4.2.1.2.2 Reply to sink node After the necessary estimation and calculation, each SN sends the complete information in the REPLY message to the sink node. This message contains the SN ID, total current energy of the SN $E_{Total-curr}(i)$, predicted total network energy loss $E_{Total-loss}(i)$, required transmission power $T.P$, and other related information. These bits of information are useful for the sink node to take decision about CH selection.

4.2.1.2.3 Cost factor computation The sink node after receiving the REPLY messages from all SNs, computes the number of alive/dead nodes in the network, total current energy $E_{total-curr}(i)$ of all alive SNs, and required transmission power (TP) by SNs for transmitting data to the sink node. Using these calculated parameters, the sink node computes the cost factor (CF) for all the SNs in the network as expressed in Eq. (13.15).

$$CF(i) = \frac{E_{Total-loss}(i)}{E_{total-curr}(i)} \times TP \tag{13.15}$$

The SN with minimum CF is selected as the CH for the next sensing/transmission round. Thus, the CH is selected with minimum total network energy loss $E_{Total-loss}(i)$ and maximum total current energy $E_{total-curr}(i)$. The selected CH having these qualities is predicted to perform the data transmission, reception, and aggregation in the cluster with minimum energy loss from its residual energy.

4.2.1.2.4 Cluster formation and scheduling After the selection of the CH, the sink node broadcasts an ANNOUNCMENT message to all nodes in the network. All SNs upon reception of this broadcast message, decide to which CH will they register themselves. The SNs register with that CH, whose RSSI parameter is high. After this decision, each SN in the network sends JOIN-REQUEST to the newly selected CH. Based on this request message, the

CH registers the SNs in its cluster. This process results in cluster formation. Once the cluster formation is done, the respective CH assigns time-slots to each cluster member SN for communication on the shared wireless medium using the TDMA protocol.

4.2.1.3 Data sensing phase

Based on the allocated time-slot by the respective CH, each SN senses the physiological data of the human body such as blood pressure, blood glucose level, ECG, EEG, EMG, heartbeat, etc. After sensing the data, the analog-to-digital convertor (ADC) on-board unit in SN converts it to digital form for further processing. These data are also stored in its on-board memory unit for further use.

4.2.1.4 Cooperative decision-based data transmission

Once the SN senses some data, it needs to send them to the respective CH. Before transmitting the sensed data, each SN checks its total current energy $E_{total-curr}(i)$ against the defined energy threshold. If the total current energy is found to be lower than the defined threshold, then the SN has to wait for the next data sensing/transmission round, so that its on-board energy harvester unit can harvest enough energy for operation. If the total current energy $E_{total-curr}(i)$ is lower than the threshold energy, this means it has very limited energy and there are very high chances of its death if this SN starts transmission. SNs in WBAN may sense similar data in the repetitive/successive data sensing/transmission rounds. By sending the redundant data multiple times will result in more energy consumption. A significant amount of battery energy can be saved during transmission by avoiding the transmission of redundant/duplicate data. In the E-HARP protocol, redundant sensed data in consecutive rounds are restricted and not transmitted to the sink node. This is done by using the cooperative decision-based data transmission technique. In this technique, sensed data are first checked for any possible redundancy/similarity and then the transmission phase is followed. Each SN stores the data in its on-board local memory for each data sensing/transmission round. Therefore, in each new data sensing/transmission round, the SN compares these new sensed data with the stored data from the previous round for any possible redundancy. This minimal local processing is done before deciding whether to transmit the data to CH or not. The data are transmitted if either of the following conditions is true, otherwise the data are considered to be redundant and therefore discarded.

(1) Data are transmitted to CH if it is different from the data stored in the previous data sensing/transmission round.
(2) Data are considered critical and transmitted to the sink directly if they are beyond the upper/lower limits of the defined threshold.

FIGURE 13.2 Cluster head data packet format.

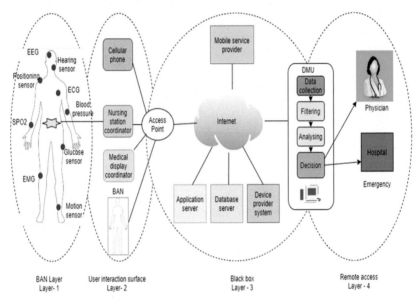

FIGURE 13.3 Remote data access through BAN.

Furthermore, the distance from the SN to the CH and sink is checked if condition 1 becomes valid. If the distance between the SN and CH is less than the distance between the SNs and sink $(D(i, CH)i < iD(i, isink))$, data are forwarded to CH, otherwise they are transmitted directly to the sink node using single-hop communication. As shown in Fig. 13.4, SN 5, 7, and 9 are deployed closer to the sink node, therefore the distance between these nodes and the sink is less than the distance between these nodes and their respective CHs. Therefore, in this case SN 5, 7, and 9 will send the data directly to the sink node. This cooperative decision-based data transmission minimizes the burden on the respective CH node. With this process the overall network performance also improves. Furthermore, the critical sensed data are also sent quickly without any delay by utilizing the communication channel bandwidth in an efficient way.

4.2.1.5 Process at the cluster head

After the reception of data forwarded from all the cluster members in a transmission round, the CH aggregates the whole data into a single packet/

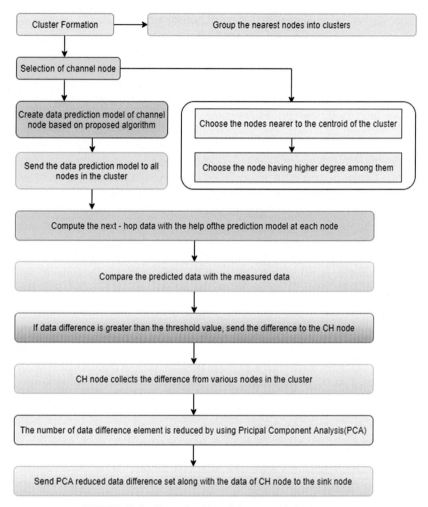

FIGURE 13.4   Cluster head based data transmission process.

message. This packet contains the cluster member IDs and their forwarded data. The CH adds cyclic redundancy check (CRC) bits at the end of this packet, as shown in Fig. 13.2. CRC bits are added for detection and correction of errors in the packet at the sink. The addition of the CRC bits ensures that the data packets that are forwarded to the sink node are error free and the same data sent by the CH.

5. Conclusion

In this chapter, various types of protocols mainly propose two mechanisms to improve the performance of WBANs, that is, the selection of a dynamic CH among the cluster members and the mechanism which omits the transfer of redundant data sensed by SNs in successive transmission rounds. The main goal of this research work is to enhance the network life-time, stability, throughput, and end-to-end delay. In order to enhance the network life-time and stability in WBAN, a technique called energy harvesting is used, which continuously provides energy to the SNs that is generated from the human surroundings (solar energy). Furthermore, dual sinks are used which help to cover the path-loss issue and also balance the network load. In order to distribute the network load evenly, E-HARP uses the concept of CH inside the cluster. The CH is selected on the basis of the cost factor, which uses multiple attributes such as link SNR, total current energy of the SN, total network energy loss, and required transmission power. To further enhance the network performance, the routing protocol uses a cooperative effort mechanism in SN, in which the redundant/similar data from the consecutive transmission rounds are ignored and not forwarded to the CH or sink and will also follow the concept of optimization or nature-inspired algorithms. The main goal of this research work is to enhance the network life-time, stability, throughput, and end-to-end delay. This saves the bandwidth of the overall network and also reduces the load on the CH and sink and ultimately improves the performance of the overall network.

References

[1] S. Hang, Z. Xi, Design and analysis of a multi-channel cognitive MAC protocol for dynamic access spectrum networks, in: Proceedings of the IEEE Military Communications Conference (MILCOM 2008), 16—19 November 2008, pp. 1—7. San Diego, CA, USA.

[2] N. Javaid, Z. Abbas, M.S. Fareed, Z.A. Khan, N. Alrajeh, M-ATTEMPT: a new energy-efficient routing protocol for wireless body area sensor networks, Proc. Comput. Sci. 19 (2013) 224—231.

[3] Q. Nadeem, N. Javaid, S.N. Mohammad, M.Y. Khan, S. Sarfraz, M. Gull, SIMPLE: stable increased throughput multi-hop protocol for link efficiency in wireless body area networks, in: 2013 Eighth International Conference on Broadband and Wireless Computing, Communication and Applications BWCCA, 2013, pp. 221—226.

[4] A. Ahmad, N. Javaid, U. Qasim, M. Ishfaq, Z.A. Khan, T.A. Alghamdi, RE-ATTEMPT: a new energy efficient routing protocol for wireless body area sensor networks, Int. J. Distributed Sens. Netw. 10 (4) (2014) 464010.

[5] S. Ahmed, N. Javaid, M. Akbar, A. Iqbal, Z.A. Khan, U. Qasim, LAEEBA: link aware and energy efficient scheme for body area networks, in: 2014 IEEE 28th International Conference on Advanced Information Networking and Applications AINA, 2014, pp. 435—440.

[6] Q. Tang, N. Tummala, S.K.S. Gupta, TARA: thermal-aware routing algorithm for implanted sensor networks, in: Proceedings of 1st IEEE International Conference on Distributed Computing in Sensor Systems, 2005, pp. 206—217.

[7] S. Ahmed, N. Javaid, S. Yousaf, A. Ahmad, M.M. Sandhu, M. Imran, Z.A. Khan, N. Alrajeh, Co-LAEEBA: cooperative link aware and energy efficient protocol for wireless body area networks, Comput. Hum. Behav. 51 (2015) 1205—1215.

[8]   X. Cai, J. Li, J. Yuan, W. Zhu, Q. Wu, Energy-aware adaptive topology adjustment in wireless body area networks, Telecommun. Syst. 58 (2014) 139−152.

[9]   D. Kim, W.Y. Kim, J. Cho, B. Lee, EAR: an environment-adaptive routing algorithm for WBANs, in: Fourth International Symposium on Medical Information and Communication Technology, 2010, pp. 1−4.

[10]   J. Wang, J. Cho, S. Lee, K.-C. Chen, Y.-K. Lee, Hop-based energy aware routing algorithm for wireless sensor networks, IEICE Trans. Commun. 93 (2) (2010) 305−316.

[11]   J. Kim, I. Song, S. Choi, Priority-based adaptive transmission algorithm for medical devices in wireless body area networks (WBANs), J. Cent. South Univ. 22 (2015) 1762−1768.

[12]   N. Kaur, S. Singh, Optimized cost effective and energy efficient routing protocol for wireless body area networks, Ad Hoc Netw. 61 (2017) 65−84.

[13]   C. Vimalarani, R. Subramanian, S.N. Sivanandam, An enhanced PSO-based clustering energy optimization algorithm for wireless sensor network, Sci. World J. (2016), https://doi.org/10.1155/2016/8658760.

[14]   A. Behura, Optimized data transmission scheme based on proper channel coordination used in vehicular ad hoc networks, Int. J. Inf. Technol. (2021) 1−10.

[15]   A. Behura, S.B.B. Priyadarshini, Assessment of load in cloud computing environment using C-means clustering algorithm, in: Intelligent and Cloud Computing, Springer, Singapore, 2021, pp. 207−215.

[16]   A. Behura, M.R. Kabat, Energy-efficient optimization-based routing technique for wireless sensor network using machine learning, in: Progress in Computing, Analytics and Networking, Springer, Singapore, 2020, pp. 555−565.

[17]   M. Buvana, K. Loheswaran, K. Madhavi, S. Ponnusamy, A. Behura, R. Jayavadivel, Improved Resource Management and Utilization based on a Fog-cloud Computing System with IOT Incorporated With Classifier Systems, Microprocessors and Microsystems, 2021, p. 103815.

[18]   V. Bhoopathy, A. Behura, V.L. Reddy, S. Abidin, D.V. Babu, A.J. Albert, IOT-HARPSECA: A Secure Design and Development System of Roadmap for Devices and Technologies in IOT Space, Microprocessors and Microsystems, 2021, p. 104044.

[19]   L. Das, S.B.B. Priyadarshini, B.K. Mishra, M. Sahu, A. Behura, Starring role of Internet of Things (IoT) in the field of biomedical peregrination for modern society, in: Handbook of IoT and Blockchain, CRC Press, 2020, pp. 175−185.

[20]   A. Behura, Congruence of Deep Learning in Medical Image Processing: Future Prospects and Challenges, Technical Advancements of Machine Learning in Healthcare, 197.

Chapter 14

Livestock health monitoring using a smart IoT-enabled neural network recognition system

Ricky Mohanty[1], Subhendu Kumar Pani[2]

[1]*Department of Electronics & Telecommunication, Orissa Engineering College, Bhubaneswar, Odisha, India;* [2]*Krupajal Computer Academy, Bhubaneswar, Odisha, India*

1. Introduction

Poultry farm health management is a significant aspect of poultry production. Many diseases in livestock are mainly due to infection-causing agents, and can extend throughout a bird flock rapidly resulting in reduced production and subsequent death of birds. Deficiencies of essential nutrients in feed such as vitamins and minerals also lead to reduced production. The key factors in poultry farm health management are: (1) early detection of disease; (2) if not detected, then prevention of disease; (3) if detected with disease, advanced treatment of disease; and (4) biosecurity management should be maintained regularly. A fundamental important concept is detection of disease which is seen as a way to prevent disease from spreading rapidly in a flock, and if the bird is identified as diseased it can be treated accordingly. The primary step in biosecurity management should be taken care of regularly: this principal theme includes a flock health-monitoring system, farm biosecurity practices, and a vaccination schedule to monitor diseased poultry in farms with the help of the Internet of Things (IoT) and wearable sensing devices. For recognition of disease in livestock, an intelligent system should be designed to identify diseased birds. Earlier research work carried out in the recognition of disease in animals was performed in Ref. [1]. In this work, the basis of classification was done using the coughing sounds of pigs by discriminating this from other noises, such as environmental sounds. The algorithm was conceptualized on a probabilistic neural network with 91.9% accuracy. The analysis of sounds has been used for evaluation of the emotional state of animals, as suggested in

Cognitive Big Data Intelligence with a Metaheuristic Approach
https://doi.org/10.1016/B978-0-323-85117-6.00007-8
305

many research works. For an intelligent system to be designed, different intelligent classifiers have been used by many researchers, some of which have included neural networks [2], decision trees [3], linear discriminant analyses [4], and support vector machines [5]. The work proposed here is based on neural network disease pattern recognition (NNDPR), that is, a spiking neural network to distinguish between healthy and unhealthy birds in a farm with subsequent treatment with the requisite medical help present in the local monitoring unit. If the local monitoring unit intervention is not sufficient to control the disease, then a consultant in the central monitoring unit will monitor the farm unit bird and advise on any medical measures to be taken by the local monitoring unit.

In view of the identification of diseased livestock, a wearable device for birds is proposed in this work. The rapid advancement of wearable devices has contributed to a growth in technology using sensors. Free scale uses micro-electromechanical systems (MEMS), which is applicable to examine and evaluate behavior patterns of humans with sensor devices such as accelerometers, gyroscopes, sensory units, and flexible computing units. This can be established by integrating sensor technology with an analog device. Recently, sensor technology has become increasingly popular due to its miniature size with low-power consumption features enabling its use in wearable devices which can measure human body parameters such as temperature, humidity, and blood pressure [6,7]. Wearable sensing has wide applications in many areas, such as sensing motion, physiological status, and pressure measurement [8]. They have more use in the health care of the elderly, therapy to address stress in the young or for mental health check ups, and therapy for those with behavior disorders [9]. Olguin et al. [10] conceptualized a wearable device to assess a particular individual's behavior by collecting their voice and unvoiced data. In the reference given in [11], wearable devices were used for measuring casual social interactions efficiently and effectively among different groups, areas, and subareas in an organization for research purposes by using wearable devices. In Ref. [11], rhythm is introduced as a platform that adds an online application with wearable electronic badges to gain group-level and network-level patterns of interactions in firms. Studies conducted by many researchers in the past have used collections of short-term information and analysis more than long-term examinations of social mental health. In connection with this, the privacy protection of wearable devices also has been included in various research studies. The data transmission protocol takes care of this, as discussed in many previous works. Das et al. [12] mentioned a modern robust authentication method which was apt for deployment of wearables. In Ref. [13], a set of lightweight authentication protocol with its privacy concerns regarding wearables usage were defined and compared. Ref. [14] proposed a new scheme of cloud storage-oriented user security for the security of clinical information authentication. Therefore, features extraction is the next important step to perform in the device mode to prevent dissemination of private data before information exchange [15,16]. The IoT is a concept that represents an interconnected series of things anytime and anywhere, providing a service through a network, with many opportunities in health care.

With this hypothesis, in this chapter, a wearable sensing band device is designed that continuously extricates the series of sensing data with conservative acquisition of signals, including audio and environmental information. The simulation is conducted while data are gathered for a 1-month period under the influence of the IoT. This chapter consists of the following sections. Section 2 introduces the system architecture, and also provides a well-defined introduction to the approach, including the design and development of the experiments. Section 3 presents the evaluation and analysis of the experiment, and discussion of the results and a summary of future research is given in Section 4.

2. System architecture

The system architecture is mainly constituted of two parts: (1) monitoring and controlling system; and (2) bird disease recognition.

2.1 Monitoring and controlling system

The livestock monitoring system, which is the poultry farm monitoring system discussed here, consists of a local monitoring system to monitor the basic needs while fulfilling the farm management of the utility, and the central monitoring unit which observes the function of the local monitoring system, and collect the bird data and information, which can help in decision-making with the help of a specialized consultant as required. The system architecture is defined in Fig. 14.1.

2.2 Central monitoring unit

The central monitoring unit tracks the local monitoring unit. This central monitoring unit consists of a monitoring system and also consultants/doctors. In central monitoring unit, it is the decision of the consultant whether medication will be provided after the detection of troubled bird using its bird id, sector id and farm id.

2.3 Functions of the central monitoring unit

The functions of the central monitoring unit include the following:

1. Monitor the basic function of each local unit (the poultry farm);
2. Collect the bird data and information from the farm, that is, temperature and humidity at the farm;
3. Assess and monitor the basic functionality at farm level;

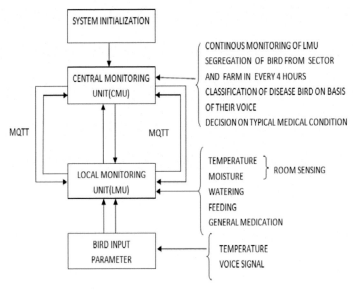

FIGURE 14.1   System architecture of the monitoring unit.

4. Using a classification technique for classification of birds as healthy, un healthy, or sick;
5. Give the appropriate instructions to the corresponding farm with the help of the consultant and monitor the unhealthy/sick birds periodically;
6. The above steps are repeated periodically and the decision on unhealthy/ sick birds has to take by the consultant and actions executed at the farm level.

2.4 Local monitoring unit

The local monitoring unit is installed in the farm, and consists of a local data acquisition system, local server, and farm operator (automatic or human-based operation). This farm operator helps in taking local decisions related to watering and feeding of livestock. The local server keeps a track of data acquired as voice frames, temperatures of respective birds, as well as the temperature and moisture of the sectors they are in. The local monitoring unit contains 20,000 birds divided into five sectors with 4000 birds in each. These sectors have a temperature recorder along with a moisture sensor (customized) to read the temperature and moisture conditions. This sensor helps in measuring the local requirements such as watering in regular intervals if the temperature is high and feeding of livestock. Every bird is provided with a flexible plastic band which consists of a temperature sensor using IR technology, a transceiver, a voice recorder, as well as a multicolored LED. The color of the LED indicates whether the bird is healthy or unhealthy. The voice recorder acquires the voice frame and the temperature sensor obtains the temperature of the individual bird. After acquisition of both the temperature and voice frames of the bird, the transceiver sends this information in regular intervals of an hour to the local monitoring unit for analysis and assistance if required. On the basis of the temperature conditions and the voice frame received, the consultant in the local monitoring unit has to take regular decisions. Any decision depends on the whether the bird voice is classified as a healthy or unhealthy voice by using a classifier algorithm (implemented on Raspberry Pi) installed in the local monitoring unit. If an acute situation is measured by the consultant in the LMU this is forwarded for further a decision to be taken by the central monitoring unit doctors/consultant. This central monitoring unit is connected to the local monitoring unit through long range (LORA) standard using message queuing telemetry transport (MQTT) protocols. The information related to the affected bird is sent to the central monitoring unit with the bird ID, sector ID, and finally the farm ID, which is related to the local monitoring unit. The bird multicolor LED indicates the healthy or unhealthy status of the bird, and in the worst case scenario removal of the bird from the farm.

2.5 Functions of the local monitoring unit

The functions of the local monitoring unit include:

1. Monitor the basic function of the local unit (the poultry farm), including watering, cleaning, feeding, and regular medical treatment;
2. Collect the bird data and information from the farm, that is, temperature and humidity, and send them to the central monitoring unit;
3. Monitor the basic functionality at the farm level;
4. Receive instructions from the central monitoring unit and execute these at the farm;
5. The above steps have to be repeated periodically and the decision on unhealthy/sick birds is taken by the consultant and executed at the farm level.

2.6 Basic hardware requirements

The basic hardware requirements include:

1. Features and specifications of the devices used in the collar bands of birds to detect the bird's health condition;
2. The multicolored LED for status if required;
3. The voice recorder for recording the bird's voice;
4. A transceiver to communicate between the local unit and the central unit, collecting the bird's information at the farm;

5. A temperature sensor using IR technology;

6. Features and specifications of the sector by the local server and central sever, a LORA-specified gateway has to used.

2.7 Wearable device platform

The design of a multisensory integrated wearable device (collar band) has been developed to combine audio and environment-based data irrespective of the living conditions of the bird, as described in Ref. [17]. As there is an assumption of no computational calculations being taken in the device, no high-end microcontroller has been adapted that is an integrated DSP module which would increase the costs of the project. For observations based on real time, we applies multicolored LEDs to indicate the current state of the bird information. In addition, to accomplish application testing, storage of data, and communication, a Bluetooth module was designed. The most suitable module includes integration of an HC05 wireless module RF transceiver module serial/TTL/RS in the band with IR temperature sensor. The power supply to the entire module is through a lithium battery (3.7 V, 2200 mAh), where each module is powered by a voltage powering unit circuit. Fig. 14.2 illustrates the system model that is based on a real-time thread operating system utilizing a multithreaded stage to enable maximum CPU utilization. While gathering audiovisual data, an analog-to-digital converter was used for sampling and filtering of the digital signal of the audio code unit APR chip APR2060 with an operating voltage of 3V. This APR 2060 is a powerful 16-bit digital audio processor and has a recording length of 40–80 s.

The sector in the farm or local monitoring system is equipped with an analog temperature sensor and analog humidity sensor to measure the room temperature and humidity as illustrated in Fig. 14.2. The temperature and humidity of the room affect poultry throughout all seasons, and avian diseases also vary with the room temperature and humidity.

FIGURE 14.2 A temperature and humidity device used for room sensing.

The connectivity protocol used in this work on the server of the central monitoring unit is MQTT, which stands for Message Queuing Telemetry Transport. This is an ISO standard (ISO/IEC PRF 20922) messaging protocol for publishing/subscribing. The connections between machines are established using the IOT connectivity protocol MQTT. The main purpose of this design was as a lightweight publishing/subscribing messaging transport. The connections in remote locations are easy due to MQTT, with a requirement for a small code footprint as the network bandwidth is at a high value. MQTT establishes communication related to the sensor from one individual passing data, for example for stock exchange through a satellite link, healthcare provider via dial up connections, and home automation. In mobile applications, MQTT is efficient due to the mobile having small size, lower power consumption, minimized data packets, and reliable circulation of data to one or many receivers. This connectivity is established with the help of the LORA gateway, which is situated in the nodes (farms). The nodes using the LORA WAN are not get affected by the MQTT OR server. The sending and receiving of data take place to and from the gateway. The gateway is at the intersection of the area covered by the LORA and MQTT. The task of the MQTT is to forward the collected data from the LORA WAN nodes to the server by publishing the appropriate node data to a specific MQTT point. The purpose of the LORA gateway device is to support the sniffer, soft AP, and WI-FI direct modes. The data rate is 150 Mbps and it transmits power at 19.5 dBm. The receiver sensitivity is up to -98 dBm with UDP proceeding with the amount by 135 Mbps, as shown in Fig. 14.3.

From Fig. 14.4, it can be seen that the audio data collected from the device used on the bird are acquired in an audio thread. Later in the server side, the raw data are preprocessed along with extracting the attributes of audio-related data, which are performed in the Pi device. These audio features are related to energy, waveform length [10], variance, and entropy [18]. The File-Thread includes the raw audio data collected with the help of an MEM microphone with a sampling frequency of 44.1 kHz. In addition, in the Activity-Thread, the information related to bird data is collected by sensors. In the Environment-Thread, the room parameters, that is temperature and humidity, are stored. The SD card in the File-Thread is used for temporary storage of sensor data. In the LORA gateway Thread, data from the SD card can be transmitted and data can be received from the server. The use of the Key-Thread is for human—computer interaction. The OLED-Thread is used for display of collected data and battery power supply.

2.8 Algorithm

In this research work, the local health monitoring unit sends values to the central monitoring unit.

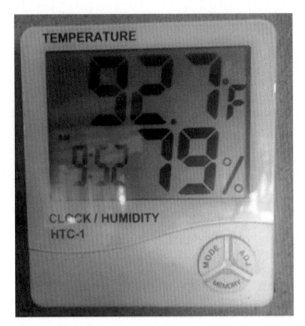

FIGURE 14.3   LORA unit at a farm node used for transmitting data collected by a sensor transmitted by using a Bluetooth module.

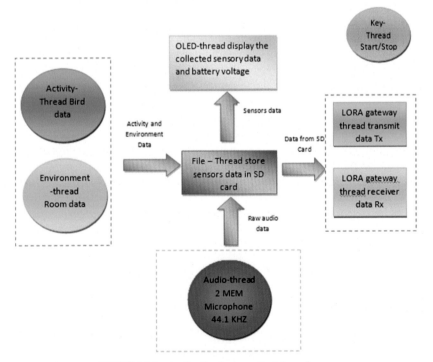

FIGURE 14.4   Application framework of the software.

Step 1: The system is first initialized.

Step 2: The central monitoring unit monitors the basic functionality at the farm/local monitoring unit level.

Step 3: The local monitoring unit also monitors the basic function of the local unit (the poultry farm), that is, watering, cleaning, feeding, and regular medical treatment.

Step 4: It collects the bird data and information from the Farm, that is, temperature and humidity at the farm, and sends these to the central monitoring unit.

Step 5: Segregation of bird information from the sector and farm is done every 4 h.

Step 6: Of the bird information, it uses the classification technique for classification of birds as healthy, unhealthy, or sick every 4 h.

Step 7: If the bird is unhealthy/sick, then the appropriate instruction is sent to the corresponding farm with the help of the consultant and the unhealthy/sick bird is monitored periodically.

Step 8: The local monitoring unit/farm receives instructions from the central monitoring unit and executes them at the farm.

Step 9: The above steps are repeated periodically and the decision on assigning birds as unhealthy/sick is made by the consultant and the resulting instructions executed at the farm level.

2.9 Data collection and transmission

In this chapter, wireless sensing technology is used to establish a connection with wearable devices, mobile phones, and server, databases, as illustrated in Fig. 14.5. Also, in this chapter, there is no requirement for real-time data transfer as evaluation of the long-term monitor data is conducted offline. The proposed platform in this chapter provides the facility of collecting data effectively and enabling the consultants to use the application to keep track of data collection related to bird's medical condition so that their privacy is reserved.

3. Recognition of a diseased bird by the central monitoring unit using Raspberry Pi

These birds are affected by four types of diseases: (1) metabolic and nutritional diseases; (2) infectious diseases; (3) parasitic diseases; and (4) behavioral diseases. The metabolic diseases and nutritional diseases can be controlled by regular feeding and watering of livestock, which requires proper monitoring. The monitoring part is discussed in an earlier section and takes place both at local and central locations. A farm can become rapidly affected by infectious diseases of poultry which result in a loss of production. Contact with an intermediate vector or direct exposure to infections can result in parasitic diseases. Abnormal bird behavior can cause injury and may lead to cannibalism

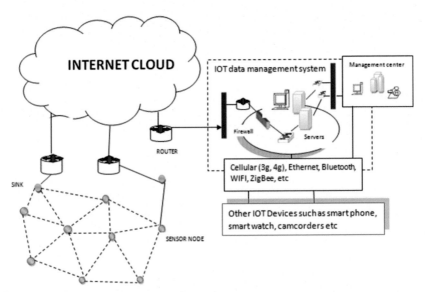

FIGURE 14.5   IoT-enabled monitoring and control unit.

(aggressive pecking). Therefore, for recognizing bird diseases, the following steps should be taken, as described in Fig. 14.6, of the proposed system using a Raspberry Pi. An experiment with bronchitis infection in Japanese quail is analyzed. The symptoms of respiratory distress include sneezing and coughing, which can be easily analyzed through their vocalization. Timely subsequent medical help can be done by adding an antibiotic (i.e., Tylosin) to the feed for 10 days, or by adding erythromycin to the drinking water for the same period of time. If not diagnosed in a timely fashion, it can lead to eradication of livestock from the farm. Data aggregation of field-recorded bird samples is followed by preprocessing, where the data samples are segmented into frames, as discussed in Ref. [19]. This is performed in the following steps.

❖ End-point detection: A vital feature of the recognition model is identifying the locus of the start and end of the frame. It distinguishes signals such as voice and silence categories present before and after the bird's call and consumes less time in analysis, where the sample duration is automatically minimized. Using the maximum amplitude model, the decrease in unvoiced part of an audio signal can be done easily or conveniently, as detailed in Ref. [20].
❖ Pre-emphasis: Among bird call signals, roll-off of a first-order low-pass filter at 6 dB/octave (20 dB/decade) exists symbolically. For eradication of this phenomenon, the signal has to undergo filtering by a zero first-order FIR filter with a 6dB/octave gain and is illustrated by:

$$y_1(m) = X_1(m) - \alpha X_1(m-1) \qquad (14.1)$$

where $x_1(m)$ represents the original signal, $y_1(m)$ represents the preemphasized signal, and the filter coefficient is α. The work here involves $\alpha = 0.9$.

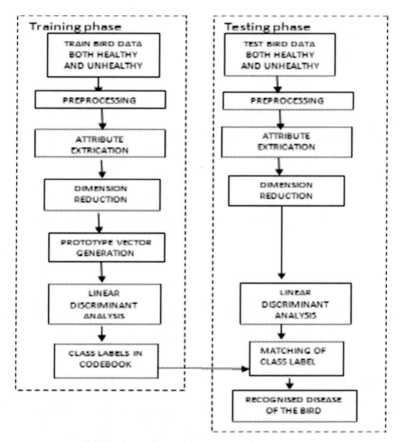

FIGURE 14.6   Steps of the disease recognition system.

❖ Windowing. The preemphasized signal is transformed into frames in a stationary form. The standard method is to use a fixed width window and overlapping features. To tackle this problem of a fixed window, the use of a variable window width of N_s samples is given by

$$N_S = \frac{f_s * s_l}{W_f} \qquad (14.2)$$

where f_s represents the sampling frequency, the length of the signal in time is represented as s_l, and W_f is the number of windows. The frame step S_f, which defines the overlap, is calculated as

$$S_f = \frac{N_S}{L} \qquad (14.3)$$

where L can be evolved to give the variable level of overlap. Here $L = 2$, in which there is a 50% overlap. Windows of variable size are used in Ref. [19]

and this is a good considerable conclusion that it is made more so than with fixed window sizes.

❖ Feature/attribute extrication. Attributes are extricated from each frame for bird call classification [21]. The attribute extrication method used in this work is discrete wavelet transform (DWT). The technique which is usually used for analyzing acoustic signals such as speech signal is wavelet transform. The Daubechies wavelet family (dbN) supports both scaling and wavelet functions also as they are orthogonal, therefore this wavelet is used in this work. On the basis of the experiment conducted, the best decomposition level (*N*) was six. The db10 was taken in this work for the wavelet function. Due to the results from the experiment performed, the best decomposition of the tested alternatives with the bird sounds was found.

❖ Principal component analysis. Dimension reduction is the subsequent phase of the proposed model and principal component analysis is used for the purpose [22]. It is so-called due to the orthogonal projection of data in a reduced dimension vector in such a way that the projected data's variance is greater without loss of data contained in it. The optimum classification accuracy is 91% with wavelet, whereas PCA's threshold value is constant at $\sigma = 0.97$.

❖ Prototype vectors generation. Frames produced from similar species of bird may differ to some degree [23]. A novel approach to solve this problem is to structure the audio samples of every species along with a summation of the corresponding vectors in a single class label. These vectors may be computed by classification of frames derived from similar bird hybrids into abstract sub-categories like frames with identical attribute vector kinds grouped together. It is achievable through the use of GMM for generating prototype vectors. Therefore, during implementation, this stage is embedded after feature extrication.

❖ Linear discriminant analysis (LDA) transformation. To generate a superior classification accuracy rate with fewer dimension attributes, LDA may be used to obtain better differentiation among several bird labels. LDA facilitates a reduction of the intraclass distancing, thereby increasing intraclass distancing. After attribute vector normalization is produced, PCA transformed matrix along with LDA transformation matrix performs the subsequent iteration to compute the final vector. The Fisher criterion is optimized for linear mapping of the transformation matrix, which is a popular method. It is observed that LDA strives to enhance the intraclass scatter and interclass scatter ratio by computing a transformation matrix. LDA transformation matrix is used to transform every PCA converted dimensional vector space into a lower dimensional vector where A $\geq$ 1.

❖ Classification: spiking neural networks. The final step includes conversion of the extricated DWT coefficients into linear spike trains and the work is completed by synaptic weight adjustment training [24]. The number of co-efficients extricated should be standardized, and the attributes are in the range −1 to 1. To transform these values into spike trains, the setting of all values by O_s by is by the following:

$$O_s = -1 - M_V \tag{14.4}$$

where M_v is the lowest value. These values are then multiplied by a factor of 10, resulting in a series of interspike intervals, which are then used to generate the spike trains.

❖ Hardware required for disease recognition in livestock. A Raspberry Pi adapter and API enable the Raspberry Pi to carry out offline disease recognition using the audio frames of the bird. This device helps in many applications including speech recognition. Using this device, the central monitoring unit can analyze diseased birds and take any necessary action. Figs. 14.7 and 14.8 illustrate the architecture of Raspberry Pi Zero used for the above proposed recognition method. This entire process of bird disease recognition is done on a Raspberry Pi Zero in the central monitoring unit where the programming code used is Python. Along with Pi, there is a keyboard, mouse, and 8-inch LED monitor. An open-source Python API for the Pi is used using an open-source Arduino IDE-based library. The Raspberry Pi Zero is designed for all types of audio processing with the features of Pi being fully compatible with the 40-pin GPIO. It has onboard WIFI and Bluetooth ports. It has a micro-USB for power, OTG host for data, and micro-CSI for the camera port. The input is provided by the collection of data from a sensor connected by the LORA gateway to the MQTT. This MQTT is on the server side of the central monitoring unit. Connectivity is also enabled to the consultant via an android phone in that unit for any medical emergencies.

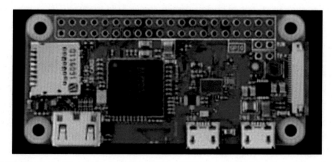

FIGURE 14.7 Raspberry Pi Zero wireless WH (presoldered header): front view.

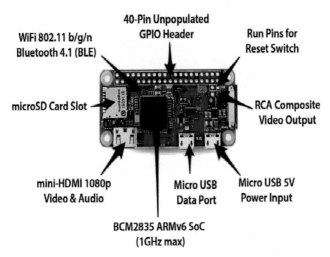

FIGURE 14.8 Raspberry Pi Zero wireless WH description.

4. Results and discussion

The experiment was carried out for 4 weeks. The data transmission in the particular farm unit was done through sensors in a wearable device on the bird using a collar device and also the room parameters. The collected data were analyzed in the central monitoring unit for recognition of disease birds so that the control unit could keep a check on livestock health. The samples used in this work were collected by the Central Poultry Development Organization (CPDO) Eastern Region, Bhubaneswar, Odisha, India, which retains four farms housing the same breed of adult Japanese quail (*Coturnix japonica*) affected with infectious bronchitis. The affected number of birds in the particular farm was 27. The collection of healthy bird audio frames along with unhealthy bird audio frames record varies from 100 audio frames in each farm in every 4 h, that is, 6 times a day. From these 100 frames, 70 frames of data were for training the classifier, 15 frames for validation of the classifier structure, and 10 frames for data used for testing classifier. Of the 70 bird audio frames, 40 were from healthy birds and 30 from unhealthy birds. The experiments are using the Python 3.7 version released in 2018, which is compatible with Raspberry Pi 3. In this work, attribute extrication results were given as an input to the GMM classifier and spiking neural network. The performance in the recognition of the spiking neural network was compared to the performance of an artificial neural network with one hidden layer [25,26].

Classification accuracy is universally used as a statistical criterion for evaluating bird species' calls. The classification rate is used in many works and is computed as follows:

TABLE 14.1 Classification accuracy for diseased Japanese quail using SNN along with wavelet.

Sl. no.	Evaluation day	Hidden neuron number	Classification accuracy	
			Testing data	Training data
1	15	2	67%	72%
2	20	2	69%	74%
3	25	2	79%	87%
4	30	2	88%	91%

$$C_r = \frac{N_c}{N_i} \times 100\% \qquad (14.5)$$

where C_r is the classification rate, N_c is the number of classified bird sounds; and N_i is the number of bird sounds. Table 14.1 shows the classification accuracy of both training and testing sets to be 91% and 88%, respectively, after evaluation of 30 days. Fig. 14.9 illustrates a comparison of the classification accuracy performance of SNN with wavelet and ANN with wavelet with test data.

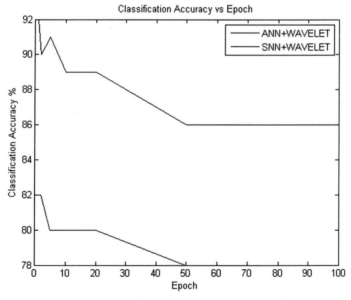

FIGURE 14.9 The classification accuracy performance of SNN along with wavelet and ANN along with wavelet on the test bird data.

5. Conclusion

In this work, the design of an IoT-based wearable device is carried out that integrates multiple sensors for measuring the audio and temperature parameters of livestock. Using this device, we monitored farms and livestock for 1 month. To collect and visualize data, an application has been developed based on a server and the use of android phones. Using a wearable device around the neck of a bird, the original voice is sent to the server side using a LORA gateway via MQTT to the server side in the central monitoring unit. After applying an algorithm for classification, it is discovered whether the bird is diseased and whether medical treatment is required. This was achieved using a spiking neural network model with an accuracy of 91%. With the research experiment conducted, it is observed that there are important correlations in the environmental conditions in which livestock reside and the physical parameters of the livestock health. The birds were subjected to wearable devices to prevent it from diseases along with their conditions that can be adjusted in time. In the near future, experiments will be conducted in livestock groups in farms to obtain consistent performance of the proposed method. For further work, various other diseases could be diagnosed using the proposed method on livestock to enable their better production.

References

[1] A. Chedad, D. Moshou, J.M. Aerts, A. Van Hirtum, H. Ramon, D. Berckmans, Production technology: recognition system for pig cough based on probabilistic neural networks, J. Agric. Eng. Res. 79 (4) (2001) 449−457.

[2] L. Boddy, C.W. Morris, M.F. Wilkins, G.A. Tarran, P.H. Burkill, Neural network analysis of flow cytometric data for 40 marine phytoplankton species, Cytometry 15 (1994) 283−293.

[3] S. Parsons, G. Jones, Acoustic identification of twelve species of echolocating bat by discriminant function analysis and artificial neural networks, J. Exp. Biol. 203 (17) (2000) 2641−2656.

[4] S. Mishra, H.K. Tripathy, P. Mallick, A.K. Bhoi, P. Barsocchi, EAGA-MLP—an enhanced and adaptive hybrid classification model for diabetes diagnosis, Sensors 20 (2020) 4036.

[5] F. Neri, Open research issues on advance control methods : theory and application, WSEAS Trans. Syst. 13 (2014) (in press).

[6] S. Patel, H. Park, P. Bonato, L. Chan, M. Rodgers, A review of wearable sensors and systems with application in rehabilitation, J. NeuroEng. Rehabil. 9 (1) (2012) 21.

[7] X.-F. Teng, Y.-T. Zhang, C.C.Y. Poon, P. Bonato, Wearable medical systems for p-health, IEEE Rev. Biomed. Eng. 1 (2008) 62−74.

[8] P. Bonato, Wearable sensors and systems. From enabling technology to clinical applications, IEEE Eng. Med. Biol. Mag. 29 (3) (May/June 2010) 25−36.

[9] R.R. Fletcher, M.Z. Poh, H. Eydgahi, Wearable sensors: opportunities and challenges for low-cost health care, in *2010 Annual International Conference of the IEEE Engineering in Medicine and Biology*, 31 Aug.−4 Sept. 2010; pp.1763−1766. https://doi.org/10.1109/IEMBS.2010.5626734.

[10] D.O. Olguin, et al., Sensible organizations: technology and methodology for automatically measuring organizational behavior, IEEE Trans. Syst. Man Cybern. B Cybern. 39 (1) (February 2009) 43−55. Conf. Eng. Med. Biol. Soc., 2010, pp. 1763−1766.

[11] O. Lederman, A. Mohan, D. Calacci, A.S. Pentland, Rhythm: a unified measurement platform for human organizations, IEEEMultiMedia 25 (1) (January/March 2018) 26−38.

[12] A.K. Das, et al., Design of secure and lightweight authentication protocol for wearable devices, IEEE J. Biomed. Health Inform. 22 (4) (July 2018) 1310−1322.

[13] A.K. Das, S. Zeadally, M. Wazid, Lightweight authentication protocols for wearable devices, Comput. Electr. Eng. 63 (October 2017) 196−208.

[14] J. Srinivas, A.K. Das, N. Kumar, J. Rodrigues, Cloud centric authentication for wearable healthcare monitoring system, IEEE Trans. Depend. Secure Comput. (n.d.). doi: 10.1109/TDSC.2018.2828306.

[15] L.R. Rabiner, M.R. Sambur, An algorithm for determining the endpoints of isolated utterances', J. Acoustic Society. American. Bell Syst. Tech. 54 (2) (1975) 297−315.

[16] A. Harma, P. Somervuo, Classification of the harmonic structure in bird vocalization, in: IEEE Int. Conf. Acoustics, Speech, Signal Processing (ICASSP 2004), Montreal, Canada, 2004, 2004.

[17] S. Yang, B. Gao, L. Jiang, J. Jin, Z. Gao, X. Ma, W.L. Woo, IoT structured long-term wearable social sensing for mental wellbeing", IEEE Int. Things J. 6 (No. 2) (April 2019) 3652−3661.

[18] J. Gu, et al., Wearable social sensing: content-based processing methodology and implementation, IEEE Sensor. J. 7 (1) (November 2017) 7167−7176.

[19] S. Mishra, P.K. Mallick, H.K. Tripathy, A.K. Bhoi, A. González-Briones, Performance evaluation of a proposed machine learning model for chronic disease datasets using an integrated attribute evaluator and an improved decision tree classifier, Appl. Sci. 10 (22) (2020) 8137.

[20] R. Mohanty, B.K. Mallik, S.S. Solanki, Automatic bird species recognition system using neural network based on spike, Appl. Acoust. 161 (2020) (April 2020) 1−8, https://doi.org/10.1016/j.apacoust.2019.107177.

[21] R. Mohanty, B.K. Mallik, S.S. Solanki, Normalized approximate descent used for spike based automatic bird species recognition system, Springer-Int. J. Speech Tech. (July 2020), https://doi.org/10.1007/s10772-020-09735-6.

[22] R. Mohanty, B.K. Mallik, S.S. Solanki, Automatic bird species recognition based on spiking neural network, Springer Book Chap. Lect. notes Electr. Eng. 652 (2020) 343−353, https://doi.org/10.1007/978-981-15-2854-5_30.

[23] R. Mohanty, S.S. Solanki, P.K. Mallick, S.K. Pani, A classification model based on an adaptive neuro-fuzzy inference system for disease prediction, Springer Book Chap. Bio-Insp. Neurocomput. 903 (2020) 131−149, https://doi.org/10.1007/978-981-15-5495-7_7.

[24] J.J. Wade, L.J. McDaid, J.A. Santos, H.M. Sayers, SWAT: a spiking neural network training algorithm for classification problems", IEEE Trans. Neural Network. 21 (11) (November 2010) 1817−1831.

[25] P.K. Mallick, S. Mishra, G.-S. Chae, Digital media news categorization using Bernoulli document model for web content convergence, Personal Ubiquitous Comput. (2020) 1−16.

[26] S. Mishra, P.K. Mallick, L. Jena, G.-S. Chae, Optimization of skewed data using sampling-based preprocessing approach, Front. Public Heal. 8 (2020) 274.

Chapter 15

Preserving healthcare data: from traditional encryption to cognitive deep learning perspective

Priyanka Ray, Sushruta Mishra
Kalinga Institute of Industrial Technology Deemed to be University, Bhubaneswar, Odisha, India

1. Introduction

Development of technology has helped the traditional medical practices to improve a lot. Earlier, people were treated through paper and prescriptions method and monitored in a hospital under full-time surveillance of medical professionals. With unprecedented improvement in mobile communications and high-speed internet over last decade saw the rise of e-health systems [1]. Nowadays, Electronic health record system (EHRS) and personal health record system have helped the patients to maintain their health record and helped the doctors in diagnosing and monitoring the patients. A patient may have many healthcare service providers including therapists and primary care physicians. In addition to this, a patient may be under multiple health insurances like for vision, dental, etc. Digitalization of healthcare data and maintenance of a database with all healthcare information helps doctors and medical insurance companies significantly. Therefore, e-health is already implemented in several countries, e.g., the United States of America, Canada, the United Kingdom, Korea, and several European countries [2−4]. It is understandable that a cloud-based system is suitable for storage and processing of this huge amount of data [5]. A schematic of the typical cloud-based e-health infrastructure is shown in Fig. 15.1.

But there are two inherent problems of storing these vital data in cloud, privacy, and security [6]. Firstly, due to the openness of the cloud, confidential data of a patient might be visible to unwanted persons with access to the cloud. Secondly, cloud-based system is prone to security attacks from hackers and third-party applications. This is the reason why the cloud requires strong

Cognitive Big Data Intelligence with a Metaheuristic Approach
https://doi.org/10.1016/B978-0-323-85117-6.00001-7

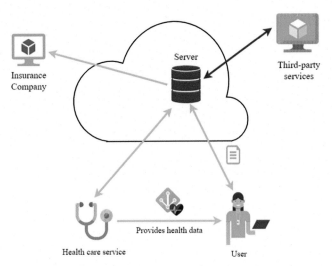

FIGURE 15.1   A schematic of cloud-based e-health system.

security and privacy to prevent easy access to the cloud. An intuitive solution to these challenges is encryption of data. Efficiency of a secure healthcare system revolves around the following five issues: (a) confidentiality (*Conf.*), (b) access control (*Acc.*), (c) privacy (*Priv.*), (d) data integrity (*Int.*), and (e) availability of data (*Aval.*). A summary of existing encryption-based healthcare system that addressed these five issues is provided in Table 15.1.

Encryption of data can be classified as (a) noncryptographic approach, (b) cryptographic approach. Noncryptographic approach is secure in the case of private clouds as their infrastructure is accessible to very few trusted members. But in the case of the public clouds, noncryptographic approach is inefficient due to the risk of information disclosure by insiders and other hackers. Therefore, in this chapter, our primary focus will be on cryptographic approaches. Cryptographic approach mainly focuses on converting a plaintext into a ciphertext with a help of a key and then decrypting it into normal text again. The typical data encryption and decryption model has been illustrated in Fig. 15.2. As shown in the figure, a plaintext also known as the original text (healthcare data in our case) is converted into the ciphertext using a secret key. Thereafter, the ciphertext is uploaded to cloud through the public channel. To access healthcare data, a user uses another secret key, using which the data are then decrypted into the plaintext.

Cryptographic approach is safer and secure in case of handling these sensitive healthcare data. However, when the data are encrypted, processing and sharing of data becomes difficult. Typically, information retrieval methods based on plaintext cannot be done on encrypted data. A simple solution for this problem can be that the user downloads the whole database locally, decrypts

TABLE 15.1 Summary of encryption-based healthcare systems.

Work	Author	Objective of the paper	Results				
			Conf.	Acc.	Priv.	Int.	Aval.
[7]	Mehraeen et al.	Review of the security challenges in healthcare cloud computing	☑	☑	☑	☒	☒
[8]	Waleed et al.	Study of privacy and security in cloud-based systems	☑	☒	☑	☒	☒
[9]	Christian esposito et al.	Study of cloud manufacturing from the aspects of security, privacy, and forensic concerns	☑	☒	☑	☒	☒
[10]	Sajid et al.	Review of cloud assisted IOT system the art and future	☑	☒	☑	☑	☑
[11]	Deshmukh	Cloud security designing in electronic health record system	☑	☒	☒	☒	☒
[12]	Premarathne et al.	A hybrid cryptographic approach on electronic health record system	☑	☑	☒	☒	☒
[13]	Marwan et al.	Challenges in cloud-based medical-image storage	☑	☑	☒	☒	☒
[14]	Kumarage et al.	Data analytics for cloud-based IOTs	☑	☒	☑	☒	☒
[15]	Barthelus et al.	Challenges of cloud-based healthcare system	☑	☒	☒	☒	☑
[16]	Chouhan et al.	Study of security attacks on cloud based system	☑	☒	☒	☒	☑
[17]	Alzoubaidi et al.	Possible architecture of nationwide cloud-based e-health services	☒	☒	☒	☒	☑
[18]	Rani et al.	Authentication protocol on cloud-based e-health care system	☑	☑	☑	☒	☑
[19]	Kaur et al.	Key exchange mechanism in healthcare system	☑	☑	☑	☑	☒
[20]	Noufal et al.	Monitoring and maintenance of e-health data using cloud	☑	☒	☒	☒	☒

Continued

TABLE 15.1 Summary of encryption-based healthcare systems.—cont'd

Work	Author	Objective of the paper	Results				
			Conf.	Acc.	Priv.	Int.	Aval.
[21]	Raval et al.	Protection of data in cloud-based system	☑	☑	☑	☒	☒
[22]	Tewari et al.	Review of security and privacy in body area network based health monitoring	☑	☒	☑	☒	☒
[23]	Desai et al.	Application of cloud computing in Indian healthcare system	☑	☒	☒	☒	☑
[24]	Zriqat et al.	Challenges of e-healthcare system	☒	☑	☑	☒	☒
[25]	Sangeetha et al.	Analysis of scalability and security of data sharing in cloud-based system	☑	☒	☑	☒	☒
[26]	Hanen et al.	Improved healthcare system using mobile cloud computing	☑	☒	☒	☑	☑
[27]	N.H. Hussein	Survey of challenges and solutions in cloud based system	☑	☒	☑	☑	☒
[28]	R. Kumar	Survey of security challenges faced in cloud-based system	☑	☑	☒	☑	☑
[29]	P. D. G. Vyawahare et al.	A survey of challenges and solutions in cloud system	☑	☒	☑	☑	☒
[30]	Rao et al.	Challenges and possible solution for storing data in cloud-based systems	☑	☒	☒	☒	☑
[31]	Griebel et al.	A review of cloud-based system in healthcare system	☑	☑	☒	☒	☒
[32]	Rezaeibagha et al.	A review of storing data in healthcare system	☑	☒	☑	☒	☒
[33]	Dubovitskaya et al.	A privacy aware architecture for cloud-based healthcare system	☒	☑	☑	☑	☒
[34]	Bhati et al.	Review of security in cloud-based system	☑	☑	☑	☒	☒

Continued

TABLE 15.1 Summary of encryption-based healthcare systems.—cont'd

Work	Author	Objective of the paper	Results Conf.	Acc.	Priv.	Int.	Aval.
[35]	Rathi et al.	Security of healthcare data in cloud systems	☑	☑	☒	☒	☒
[36]	Elmogazy et al.	Protection of data in healthcare systems	☑	☑	☑	☒	☒
[37]	Sengupta et al.	Hybrid RSA encryption algorithm for data security in cloud systems	☑	☒	☒	☒	☒
[38]	Sedem et al.	Architecture of cloud computing in electronic healthcare systems in Ghana	☒	☒	☒	☒	☑
[39]	Boyinbode et al.	Storage of e-Health record in cloud-based systems	☒	☒	☒	☒	☑
[40]	Plachkinova et al.	Architecture of data security in cloud	☒	☒	☒	☑	☑
[41]	Fabian et al.	Sharing of healthcare data securely in multiclouds	☑	☒	☑	☒	☒
[42]	Donald et al.	Comparison between the encryption algorithms in cloud based systems	☑	☒	☒	☒	☒
[43]	Ahmed E. Youssef	Architecture of healthcare system based on big data analytics in cloud computing	☑	☑	☒	☒	☑
[44]	Zafar 2014	Cloud based services in healthcare systems	☑	☒	☑	☒	☒
[45]	M. Tebaa and S. E. L. Hajji	Computation of privacy and fault tolerance from single to multicloud systems	☑	☒	☒	☑	☑
[46]	Sultana et al.	Development of cloud-based smart and connected data sharing in healthcare system	☒	☒	☒	☑	☒
[47]	Nagaty et al.	Mobile health care in hybrid cloud based systems	☑	☑	☑	☑	☒

Continued

TABLE 15.1 Summary of encryption-based healthcare systems.—cont'd

Work	Author	Objective of the paper	Results Conf.	Acc.	Priv.	Int.	Aval.
[48]	Y. B. Gurav et al.	Sharing of health records in cloud-based systems using attribute based encryption	☑	☑	☑	☒	☒
[49]	Thilakanathan et al.	Sharing of data securely in cloud based systems	☑	☒	☑	☒	☒
[50]	Raseena et al.	Sharing of health records securely in cloud-based systems using attribute-based encryption	☑	☑	☑	☒	☒
[51]	Jitendra Madarkar.et al.	Challenges of storing healthcare data securely in cloud-based systems	☑	☒	☑	☒	☒
[52]	Maya louket et al.	Storing of healthcare data in cloud-based system	☑	☑	☒	☒	☒
[53]	Ribeiro et al.	XDS-I outsourcing proxy: Ensuring confidentiality while preserving Interoperability	☑	☒	☑	☒	☒
[54]	Ikuomola et al.	Preserving of privacy in storing healthcare data using homomorphic encryption and access control	☑	☑	☒	☒	☒
[55]	Khan et al.	Architecture for storing healthcare data securely in cloud-based system using wireless body area networks	☑	☑	☑	☑	☑
[56]	Freire et al.	Survey of the challenges for storing data securely in cloud based system	☑	☑	☒	☑	☒

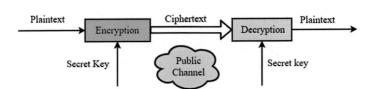

FIGURE 15.2 Typical model of data encryption and decryption.

the data, and then searches it locally. But this process requires a lot of space and is also not cost-efficient. It is also an impractical solution for users who require a very small portion of the database. Therefore, an ideal solution is employing searchable encryption. Searchable encryption is a cryptographic method which helps to search a keyword over the encrypted data. A searchable encryption mechanism uses four mechanisms: setup, encryption, token generation, and query. The setup algorithm is run by software to generate a private or a public key. The encryption algorithm is generated by data owner, who encrypts the data and uploads it to the cloud. The token generation algorithm is run by the data user to generate a keyword or token on the encrypted data. Afterward, the query algorithm is run by the cloud to give the matching results for the generated token. This complete process is illustrated in Fig. 15.3.

In recent times, cognitive-based deep learning algorithms evolved as a promising tool in diagnosis and prevention of disease. As deep learning algorithms exhibit cognitive abilities and acquire knowledge from previous observations or existing results (e.g., detection of brain tumor from magnetic resonance imaging), these algorithms are capable of works by accumulating knowledge from the experience of medical experts and thereby transforming it

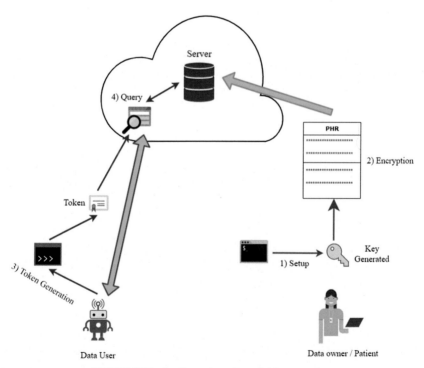

FIGURE 15.3   An illustration of searchable encryption.

into computer aided detection solutions. The challenging factor in applying deep learning algorithms over medical data is that it requires highest security and privacy, and therefore, sharing the medical reports to third-party deep learning servers to train them raises security concerns. Hence, it would be ideal if the medical data can be provided to deep learning servers in the form of encrypted data. As illustrated in Fig. 15.4, security in medical data is required in three levels: (i) when the cloud or processor directly processes the ciphertexts from uploaded health data, (ii) the cloud sends and receives the data from external deep learning servers in the form of ciphertexts, and these ciphertexts are only revealed to the client when decrypted, and (iii) the data must remain confidential in external third-party deep learning servers. This results in such a model from which the external party cannot get any information and the user is also unable to derive any information regarding this machine learning model.

As we can understand from the earlier discussion, efficient encryption algorithm and its applicability in cloud-based system is of primary concern. Recent cognitive-based deep learning models can also be used to secure healthcare-related data for encryption–decryption purpose. To the best of our knowledge, a robust performance comparison of different encryption algorithms with application to cloud-based e-health system is unavailable in literature. It motivates us to provide an analytical comparison between different e-health systems. Therefore, comparison of three state-of-the-art cryptography-based e-health systems has been done in this chapter. These algorithms have been compared on the basis of several performance metrics, e.g., efficiency, scalability, and load factor. Besides the performance comparison of these algorithms, this chapter also highlights the strengths and weaknesses of the presented algorithms.

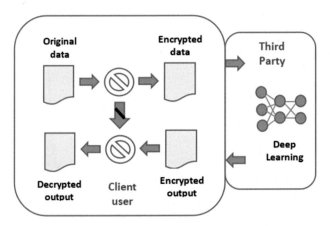

FIGURE 15.4 A sample encryption using cognitive deep learning.

The rest of this chapter is organized as follows: A brief literature survey, consisting of different available data encryption methods, and e-Health systems are presented in Section 2. Thereafter, a brief study of state-of-the-art encryption algorithms and discussion of their implementations is presented in Section 3. In the following part of the article, the experimental setup is defined to evaluate the performances of these encryption algorithms. Then, the algorithms are compared based on several performance metrics, such as efficiency and scalability factor in Section 4. Future challenges of digital healthcare systems are discussed in Section 5. Finally, this chapter has been concluded by discussing the advantages and disadvantages of these algorithms and direction of future research in Section 6.

2. Related works

To preserve the health data securely, relevant algorithms ranging from conventional encryption based to cognitive deep learning enabled models are presented in literature. Broadly, all these approaches can be classified into two groups: (1) cryptographic and (2) noncryptographic approaches. Cryptographic approaches can be defined as the approaches that encrypt the data using a randomly generated key. Conversely, noncryptographic approaches can be defined as policy-based authorization infrastructure that secures the health data based on some access control policies [57]. In this chapter, our main concern is the comparison of encryption algorithms. Therefore, the cryptographic approaches have been classified into (a) Private Key Encryption (PKE)—based approaches, (b) Symmetric Key Encryption (SKE)—based approaches, (c) Attribute-based Encryption (ABE)—based approaches, and (d) Cognitive Homomorphic Encryption (HE)—based approaches.

2.1 PKE-based systems

The PKE technique requires the use of two separate keys: a private key and a public key. The popular public key generation algorithms use the RSA and Elliptic Curve Cryptography. Some of the PKE-based approaches to protect the health data in the cloud are presented below.

Jafari et al. Ref. [58] proposed a system using Digital Rights Management (DRM) technology to maintain the privacy of patient's data stored in cloud based on a patient-centric approach. DRM is a popular system to securely manage the health record in cloud. In this approach, the data are stored in the encrypted form and the owner issues licenses which state that a user can perform some permitted operations on it only using a trusted terminal. In DRM systems, health data are encrypted in such a manner that only the users having a valid license can decrypt the data and use it accordingly. The heath record service provider provides the protected content to the authorized users, but they themselves do not have the content in clear text form. Doctors and patients can encrypt and decrypt data using the public and private key.

Mashima and Ahamad proposed a system that revolves around the concept of "accountable usage" to enable patient-centric monitoring while updating or adding of health records [59]. In this technique, the data which are to be shared are in the encrypted form and a special patient control monitoring system is introduced in this system which helps a patient to become aware if any requests for updating or accessing the data are made. Thus, this system will help a patient to know if any malicious entry tries to evade these data and the patient will remain accountable for allowing any such attacks. But the drawback of this system is that the recorder issuers have the knowledge about the patient's data while creating the records, and if it gets disclosed, it will become difficult for the system to manage the access control.

Pecarina et al. designed an architecture that provisions "selective anonymity" to remove privacy hurdles for information sharing through a user-centric approach [60]. This approach introduces anonymity boundaries between the cloud service providers (CSPs) and the users so that the users can upload health records in the cloud as an anonymous one. The patients encrypt the data using the public key of the CSP and upload it to the cloud. Thereafter, the CSP decrypts it and then stores the data and corresponding location information and then encrypts it using another key. The CSP pairing the patient's master key and the encrypted location preserves the data in the cloud storage.

2.2 SKE-based systems

The SKE approach uses a single key for encryption and decryption. The SKE due to better encryption of data procedures is more complex than the other forms of encryption. The SKE currently in use is Advanced Encryption Standard which is the most standard one as recommended by the National Institute of Standards and Technology. Under the AES system, the most common stream cipher system is RC4 and A5/1.

Li et al. Ref. [61] proposed a mechanism where the hospitals can apply for cloud storages without having their own setup to store electronic medical record information. The health records can be even shared among the hospitals through this platform. The medical personnel can log into the cloud platform and upload the patient's electronic health record in an encrypted manner through SKE. Every patient has a health card which contains an identity seed which is used to generate anonymity information and the key seed is the basic information used to encrypt the information. Therefore, the Electronic Medical Record Number, the identity seed, and serial number for treatment are necessary to access the patient's health records. The Medical Record Number is unique in two different parts to prevent malicious attacks over the patient's health records.

Chen et al. used SKE mechanism to encrypt health record of the patients in normal and emergency situations [62]. In this approach, there can be three types: New Electronic Medical Record Creation, Electronic Medical Record Access, and Emergency Electronic Medical Record Access. In the first type, a patient's health records are stored in an encrypted file format and uploaded into the cloud environment. In the Electronic Medical Record Access, there can be two situations: either the data will be available in the public and private cloud so that the data owner can access it any time and when necessary, the data will be accessible by the hospital only if the data owner gives such permission. In the Emergency Electronic Medical Record Access, the hospital will notify the data owner and immediately decrypt the patient's data at emergency center.

Zhang et al. introduced a functional-based and time-enabled access regulatory protocol that allows effective storing of encrypted EHRs [63]. Their mechanism is also applicable for the less trusted clouds which resolve key distribution—related concerns between users. Their proposed system works on the basis of an algorithmic integration of several access control protocols with hierarchical key control as such only an authorized entity of EHR system is permitted EHR data on basis of their role. Authors developed a dynamic key structure for role-based access and management of EHR data that addresses the privacy issues. Based on performance of access authorizations, the health records are encrypted using SKE. Still, this method is somewhat restricted because it needs an entity to operate in numerous functionalities. Subsequently, users need to acquire and regulate multiple keys, which is an additional burden to users, and thus, it is not a user-friendly system.

2.3 ABE-based systems

ABE is a cryptographic algorithm that works on top of an underlying PKE. In ABE, the messages are encrypted and decrypted based on user attributes. A user can decrypt a ciphertext only when it has both reliable attributes and the decryption keys. The ABE system enables the users to selectively share the encrypted data and provides a selective access. Some of the popular ABE-based systems are discussed below.

Sahai and Waters designed the primitive ABE system in Ref. [64], a Key policy ABE system where access policies are related to private key, while many attributes are utilized for labeling of ciphertext. A user can decrypt the ciphertext only if the data attributes satisfy the label of the ciphertext. In KP-ABE, ciphertexts are equipped with series of descriptive features, while keys of users are interlinked with norms. Therefore, encryptor in KP-ABE has no control over the users who can access the data, rather it needs to trust the key issuer in this regard.

To overcome the limitations of KP-ABE, a ciphertext policy attribute—based encryption (CP-ABE) was introduced in Ref. [65]. In this method, the private key of the user is formed with different attributes that is expressed in the form of strings. On the other hand, when a party encrypts a message in our system, they specify an associated access structure over attributes. In recent times, several extensions of KP-ABE and CP-ABE are presented in literature [66–68]. A complete ABE-based e-health system was developed in Ref. [69].

2.4 Cognitive HE-based systems

Cognitive HE is a special type of deep learning–based encryption algorithm that allows additional computations over encrypted data without the need of decrypting the data. For example, in a traditional cloud-based healthcare system, modification of an encrypted patient data may require a local workstation to download the encrypted data locally, then decrypt it, and only after that modify the data. For a trivial modification, it can cause unnecessary delay. To overcome this shortfall, an HE-based system is developed. There are two types of HE available in literature, partial homomorphic encryption (PHE) and fully homomorphic encryption (FHE). PHE supports only a single operation over the encrypted data, whereas FHE supports multiple operations. FHE was first proposed in Ref. [70]. The FHE system in Ref. [70] supports numerous addition and multiplication operations over encrypted data without decrypting the data. However, operations in FHE are limited to integers and cannot be applied to rational numbers [71]; also, HE-based systems are more time consuming than existing encryption-based systems. This limits the practical use of FHE, and therefore, a homomorphic encryption scheme that supports matrix-based operations is developed in Ref. [72].

3. Encryption algorithms

In this section, the four different encryption algorithms are defined, one for each approach (PKE, SKE, ABE, and Cognitive HE) and they have been compared based on couple of security parameters. For PKE-based approach, the system described in Ref. [60] is considered; for SKE-based approach, the system described in Ref. [62] is considered, and for ABE-based approach, the CP-ABE system [69] is considered.

The PKE-based approach, named SAPPHIRE, builds an anonymity boundary between the CSP and the user. Their approach toward the solution for anonymity is to allow recognition of health data to pass through a trusted agent. Then, user establishes a master key to manage their health data. Once the master key is established, the trusted agent allows delinking of the patient from his/her health data to provide greater privacy protection. The vital feature in this system is the establishment of a single master key that is shared between the CSP and the data owner. A simplified algorithm of SAPPHIRE system is given in Fig. 15.5.

As the primary concern is about the encryption of health data and its analysis, steps inside the cloud are not taken into account during performance comparison.

Step 1: User generates the master key (a 128-bit random integer).

Step 2: User encrypts the PHR using generated master key.

Step 3: User's master key is further encrypted using CSP's public key (RSA) and then both encrypted master key and PHR is forwarded to CSP.

Step 4: At the cloud, master key is decrypted using CSP's private key. Then the PHR is decrypted using the master key.

Step 5: Store PHR in a location and encrypt it using CSP's private key.

Step 6: Encrypt the location and pass this encrypted location to the user.

FIGURE 15.5   Algorithm of SAPPHIRE system (PKE-based approach).

The SKE-based e-health system in Ref. [62] modifies the privacy of health data to accommodate emergency situations. In this system, under normal circumstances, a user gives permission to access its PHR, but in emergency situations, user is just notified and the PHR is accessed by emergency centers. These two scenarios are incorporated in the system in Fig. 15.6.

PKE- and SKE-based systems suffer from the limitation of centralized key generation, as user has a secret key, and thus, it must be distributed from a single key distribution center. Therefore, it is prone to failures and denial of service in case of a failure in the key distribution center. To overcome this shortfall, Ruj et al. in Ref. [69] developed an ABE-based system that encompasses different attributes along with user ID in key generation for authentication. This supports a distributed access to cloud data where authorized users with valid attributes can access a data. The algorithm of the system is shown in Fig. 15.7.

A cognitive-enabled fully homomorphic system is a deep learning—based encryption model which can be used for securing medical data records. Vizitiu et al. developed a cognitive-enabled deep learning—based system that supports operations over encrypted data [71]. The overall algorithm of HE-based system is given in Fig. 15.8.

The cognitive deep learning that operates over encrypted data C uses six layers that support modifications over the encrypted data. The operations in these layers are convolution, pooling, convolution, pooling, and fully

Step 1: User creates the PHR and encrypt it using SKE (AES).

Step 2: Generate the license file which contains user ID, file identifier, and usage rights.

Step 3: License file is encrypted with patient's public key.

Step 4: License file is again encrypted (double encryption) by hospital's key.

FIGURE 15.6   Algorithm of SKE-based e-health system.

Step 1: Data owner receives a token from a trusted server after providing user ID.

Step 2: Data owner provides the token to a key distribution center to obtain the key to encrypt the data.

Step 3: Message in encrypted under access policy and obtained key.

Step 4: The access policy decides which users can access the uploaded data.

Step 5: Data owner signs the encrypted message and uploads it to cloud.

Step 6: If attributes of a user is matched with access policy then the user can edit or read the uploaded health data.

FIGURE 15.7   Algorithm of ABE-based e-health system.

Step 1: User creates the PHR (m).

Step 2: Develop an invertible matrix using m and a random variable r, $M = \begin{pmatrix} m & 0 \\ 0 & r \end{pmatrix}$.

Step 3: Generate the secret key S and develop the encrypted data $C = SMS^{-1}$

Step 4: Using a deep neural network, perform required operations over encrypted data C.

FIGURE 15.8   Algorithm of HE-based e-health system.

connected. The numbers of convolution filters in first and third layer are 8 and 16, respectively. Detailed operations in each of these layers are given in Ref. [71]. The basic idea of this approach is fetching information from an uploaded report (such as fetching coronary artery disease information from X-ray coronary angiography report) without downloading and decrypting the report separately.

Privacy of all these cognitive learning systems depends on some popular parameters, known as *Integrity, Confidentiality, Authenticity, Accountability, Audit, Nonrepudiation, Anonymity,* and *Unlinkability* [57]. These parameters can be defined as follows:

- *Integrity (IN):* makes sure that the health data recorded by the system do not get modified or altered in any way.
- *Confidentiality (CO):* makes sure that the information does not get accessible to unauthorized users.
- *Authenticity (AU):* the healthcare data should not be provided to anyone without knowing the identity. In this case, both the healthcare providers and the identities of the users asking permission to access them should be verified.

- *Accountability (AC):* refers to the responsibility or obligation to protect one's healthcare data. If an individual is accountable, then user remains responsible in case the healthcare data get misplaced or get misused by any third party.
- *Audit (AT):* refers to a kind of inspection to make sure that the healthcare data remain secured and also monitors the operations taking place in the cloud.
- *Nonrepudiation (NR):* it is a method of giving assurance if an individual denies after performing any activity in accessing the healthcare data.
- *Anonymity (AN):* it is an act of using an information without disclosing one's name or identity. This can be done if any user wants to remain anonymous to the CSPs while uploading any data into the cloud.
- *Unlinkabilty (UN):* refers to the multiple use of items by a user in such a manner so that other users cannot interlink the usage of these resources.

Privacy vulnerabilities on cognitive-based deep learning systems can be broadly identified in three dimensions, influencing threats, security violations, and threat specificity as shown in Fig. 15.9.

(i) **Influencing threats:** There are two types of influencing threats: (a) causative attack: these types of attacks attempt to gain control over the training data, and therefore, feeding wrong data to the deep learning model and (b) exploratory attack: these attacks utilize the misclassification or errors by deep learning models without intervening the training process of the model [73].

(ii) **Security violations:** it is mainly concerned with privacy and integrity of the data. This can be categorized into three types of attacks: (a) integrity attack: it tries to increase false-negative rate of classifier by giving wrong inputs to the deep learning models, (b) availability attack: it tries to increase the false-positive rate of the classifier in response to the inputs, and (c) privacy violation attacks: these attacks publicize the sensitive information used for training a model [74].

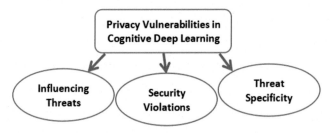

FIGURE 15.9 Possible privacy threats in a cognitive deep learning encryption model.

TABLE 15.2 Comparison between different e-health systems.

e-health system	Privacy parameters							
	IN	CO	AU	AC	AT	NR	AN	UN
PKE [60]	Yes	Yes	Yes	No	Yes	Yes	Yes	Yes
SKE [62]	Yes	Yes	No	Yes	Yes	Yes	No	No
ABE [69]	No	No	Yes	Yes	Yes	No	Yes	N/A
HE [71]	Yes	Yes	No	Yes	Yes	No	Yes	N/A

(iii) *Threat specificity:* These attacks can be classified into two types: (a) targeted attack: these attacks target specific input samples or a class of input samples, and therefore, reducing the accuracy of the deep learning model and (b) indiscriminate attack: this form of attack tampers every types of input data and results in a complete failure of the deep learning model [75].

A comparison between PKE, SKE, ABE, and cognitive-based HE-based systems based on these attributes is provided in Table 15.2.

4. Performance evaluation

In this section, the performance of three popular encryption algorithms is compared which has been discussed earlier in Section 3. Initially, the encryption efficiency of these three algorithms is compared. For efficiency evaluation, the time required for each algorithm to encrypt the data is calculated. For evaluation, the size of the healthcare data is taken as 1 KB. From the result in Fig. 15.10, it is observed that total encryption time for PKE-based approach is 740.9 ms, for SKE-based approach, it takes 853 ms, for ABE-based approach it takes 390 ms, and for HE-based approach, the encryption time is 345 ms. Therefore, based on encryption speed, Cognitive HE–based system is the fastest among these three. HE performs best because less number of encryptions are involved in storing the data in cloud. ABE-based system can secure the data even with a smaller number of encryption steps because access to data already depends on the attributes of a user. For SKE- and HE-based system, the key generation is faster because same key is used for encryption and decryption. Consequently, security issues are less severe for HE systems. Therefore, less computational heavy numerical operations are performed in encrypting (for example, matrix multiplications are performed in HE-based system) and uploading the data on the cloud server. Hence, HE-based system performs best among these systems.

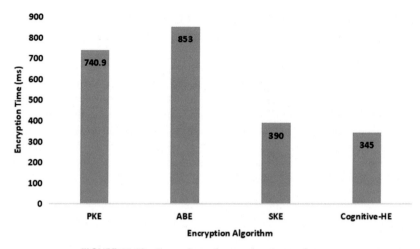

FIGURE 15.10 Comparison of encryption time performance.

In Fig. 15.11, the level of security that can be provided by these algorithms is compared. In this experiment, the maximum key size that can be used by these algorithms is compared, and this maximum value suggests the highest level of encryption that can be provided by the system. It is observed that PKE outperforms other systems by a large margin as PKE-based system in Ref. [60] can support a key size of 2048, whereas other systems like SKE and ABE can support maximum key size of 256. Cognitive-based HE model is also quite effective and supports up to 1024 key size. This key size analysis illustrates the scalability of the systems and results suggest that SKE- and ABE-based systems have a low scalability. Moreover, the key size of HE is flexible because operation of HE is not limited to any key size. However, bigger key size results

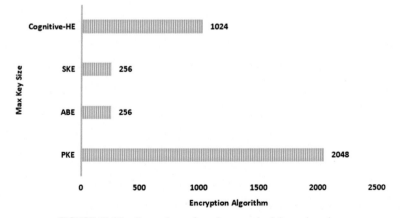

FIGURE 15.11 Comparison of maximum and minimum key size.

in a bigger matrix, and therefore, operations in the neural network sometimes become time consuming. In Ref. [71], keys of size 28 are used. We have observed that key sizes up to 1024 can be used practically, but sizes greater than that might be significantly time consuming.

To showcase functionality of the approach in learning from ciphertext records, the train and test accuracy rate, as the output from decryption, are highlighted in Fig. 15.12. Depicting accuracy of classification, the cognitive-based deep learning HE model trained on ciphertext data achieves a mean training accuracy of 93.2% of accurately classified data, and when validated with testing samples, the mean testing accuracy of correctly classifying the samples was observed to be 88.7%.

5. Future challenges of cognitive encryption models in healthcare

Although there is a significant advancement in encryption-based healthcare systems, still there are several challenges faced by a cognitive-based e-health system. Some of these challenges are listed below:

> **Increase in cyber attacks:** With the advancement of technology, the method of storing health records in the pen and paper form has become outdated. Countries like the United States and United Kingdom have been pushing to ensure that the health records are digitized as soon as possible. But with this E-health record system, the chances of cyber attacks have increased a lot. Therefore, development cyber security is falling behind the potency of cyber attacks.

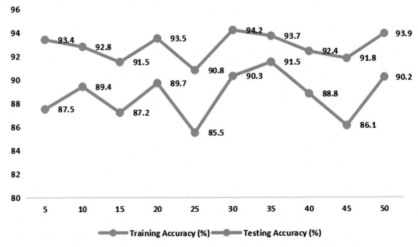

FIGURE 15.12 Testing and training accuracy of an HE-based system.

➢ **Outdated medical hardware and software:** as we all know, the medical equipment are not updated regularly due to high expenses. As a result, sometimes outdated software is used. These software applications are not supported by manufactures and do not receive necessary security updates. The WannaCry attack which affected NHS and many other institutions took place due to the usage of earlier versions of windows.

➢ **Less importance to cybersecurity attacks:** Most people till now are still ignorant to the cybersecurity attacks taking place frequently. Unfortunately, a serious breach of data is needed to wake organizations up to the importance of cyber security attacks.

➢ **Problems faced by the small organizations:** Nowadays, the small organizations are even using EHRS to store data. But due to lack of infrastructure, they are not able to prevent these cyber security attacks efficiently.

➢ **Healthcare systems are interconnected:** We always do not come to know about the attacks on smaller healthcare organizations. But as the healthcare systems are interconnected, these attacks on smaller organizations help the attackers to get access to the bigger healthcare organizations easily.

➢ **Importance of healthcare data:** By stealing the credit card information, one can typically use that information once before the card gets canceled. But it is not the same for medical record. Medical records can be used for almost 15−20 years or more. Medical records can be used for multiple times and for multiple purposes and there is nothing much to be done to stop this. Stringent IT auditing can help in increasing cyber security of the healthcare data.

➢ **Access of medical data to the patients:** Nowadays, patients are allowed to access the medical data as and when required. However, patients do not protect the healthcare data as they are concerned about the bank details. This leads to more attacks.

➢ **Limited resources for cyber security:** As the resources are limited, the healthcare data providers face problems in using the resources for IT security, staff, training, or in improving the technologies and supplies.

➢ **Lack of proper knowledge of cyber security:** One of the biggest problems faced by the healthcare data providers is that the doctors and the nurses do not know the security risks involved in storing these healthcare data thereby imposing more risks of cyber attacks. The most important thing to be kept in mind is that everybody including the patients plays an important role in handling the data.

6. Conclusion

In this chapter, a review of the current state of research in security of e-health systems and several cryptographic approaches is discussed. Evolution of conventional encryption to cognitive-based deep learning encryption on health records is highlighted. Some relevant cryptographic approaches are considered for secured digital healthcare system, and from the performance evaluation it is observed that cognitive-based HE system is most efficient as it takes the least amount of time to encrypt the data. The maximum key size suggests that the maximum level of encryption of health data can be provided by PKE-based system whereas the key generation complexity of the SKE model and HE-based system is minimum among the models discussed. Cognitive HE system also offers good performance in terms of maximum key size. Therefore, each system has its own merit and demerit. However, a general conclusion can be drawn that for cognitive enabled system HE-based deep learning method is preferable as it provides quick and reliable outcomes with a good key size in context to securing health records.

References

[1] D. Slamanig, C. Stingl, Privacy aspects of e-health, in: Proc. 3rd IEEE Int. Conf. Availability, Rel. Security, March 2008, pp. 1226−1233.

[2] L. Jena, S. Mishra, S. Nayak, P. Ranjan, M.K. Mishra, Variable optimization in cervical cancer data using particle swarm optimization, in: Advances in Electronics, Communication and Computing, Springer, Singapore, 2021, pp. 147−153.

[3] P.K. Mallick, S. Mishra, G.-S. Chae, Digital media news categorization using Bernoulli document model for web content convergence, Personal Ubiquitous Comput. (2020) 1−16.

[4] L. Tutica, K.S.K. Vineel, S. Mishra, M.K. Mishra, S. Suman, Invoice deduction classification using LGBM prediction model, in: Advances in Electronics, Communication and Computing, Springer, Singapore, 2021, pp. 127−137.

[5] S.P. Ahuja, S. Mani, J. Zambrano1, A survey of the state of cloud computing in healthcare, Netw. Commun. Technol. 1 (2) (September 2012) 12−19.

[6] N. Dong, J. Hugo, J. Pang, Challenges in e-health: from enabling to enforcing privacy, in: Foundations of Health Informatics Engineering and System, Springer, Berlin, Germany, 2012, pp. 195−206.

[7] E. Mehraeen, M. Ghazisaeedi, J. Farzi, S. Mirshekari, Security challenges in healthcare cloud computing: a systematic review, Global J. Health Sci. 9 (3) (2017) 511−517.

[8] A. Waleed, L. Chunlin, User Privacy and Security in Cloud Computing, vol. 10, 2016, pp. 341−352 (2).

[9] C. Esposito, A. Castiglione, B. Martini, K.K.R. Choo, Cloud manufacturing: security, privacy, and forensic concerns, IEEE Cloud Comput 3 (4) (2016) 16−22.

[10] A. Sajid, H. Abbas, K. Saleem, Cloud-Assisted IoT-Based SCADA Systems Security: A Review of the State of the Art and Future Challenges, vol. 4, 2016.

[11] P. Deshmukh, Design of cloud security in the EHR for Indian healthcare services, J. King Saud Univ. - Comput. Inf. Sci. (2016) 1−7.

[12] U. Premarathne, A. Abuadbba, A. Alabdulatif, Hybrid Cryptographic Access Control for Cloud- Based EHR Systems, 2016.

[13] M. Marwan, A. Kartit, H. Ouahmane, A. Jabran, K. Jabran, B.P. El, Cloud-Based Medical Image Issues, vol. 11, 2016, pp. 3713−3719 (5).

[14] H. Kumarage, I. Khalil, A. Alabdulatif, Secure Data Analytics for Cloud- Integrated Internet of Things Applications, 2016.

[15] L. Barthelus, Adopting cloud computing within the healthcare industry: opportunity or risk? Online J. Appl. Knowl. Manag. 4 (1) (2016) 1−16.

[16] P. Chouhan, R. Singh, Attacks on cloud computing with possible solution, Int. J. Adv. Res. Secur. 6 (1) (2016) 92−96.

[17] A.R. Alzoubaidi, Cloud computing national e-health services: data center solution architecture, Int. J. Comput. Sci. Netw. Secur. 16 (9) (2016) 1−6.

[18] A.A.V. Rani, E. Baburaj, An Efficient Secure Authentication on Cloud Based E-Health Care System in, 2016, pp. 53−59.

[19] E.R.A. Kaur, Data Privacy in Healthcare Networks with Secure Key Exchange Mechanism, 2016, pp. 2449−2451.

[20] M.M. Noufal, Smart e-Health Monitoring and Maintenance Using Cloud, 2016, pp. 61−65 (3).

[21] D. Raval, Cloud Based Information Security and Privacy in Healthcare vol. 150, 2016, pp. 11−15 (4).

[22] A. Tewari, Security and privacy in e-healthcare monitoring with wban: a critical review, Int. J. Comput. Appl. 136 (11) (2016) 37−42.

[23] V.L. Desai, Opportunity and Implementation of Cloud Computing in Indian Health Sector, July 2016, pp. 333−338.

[24] A. Zriqat, Security and Privacy Issues in E-Healthcare Systems: Towards Trusted Services, vol. 7, 2016, pp. 229−236 (9).

[25] Sangeetha, Analysis of an Effective, Scalable and Secured Data, 2016, pp. 135−141.

[26] J. Hanen, Z. Kechaou, M. Ben Ayed, An enhanced healthcare system in mobile cloud computing environment, Vietnam J. Comput. Sci. 3 (4) (2016) 267−277.

[27] N.H. Hussein, A Survey of Cloud Computing Security Challenges and Solutions II-Infrastructure as Services, vol. 14, 2016, pp. 52−56 (1).

[28] R. Kumar, A. Pandey, A Survey on Security Issues in Cloud Computing, vol. 3, 2016, pp. 506−517 (3).

[29] P.D.G. Vyawahare, R.B. Bende, D.N. Bhajipale, R.D. Bharsakle, A.G. Salve, A Survey on Security Challenges and Solutions in Cloud Computing, 2016, pp. 4069−4073.

[30] R.V. Rao, K. Selvamani, Data security challenges and its solutions in cloud computing, Procedia - Procedia Comput. Sci. 48 (Iccc) (2015) 204−209.

[31] L. Griebel, et al., A Scoping Review of Cloud Computing in Healthcare, 2015, pp. 1−16.

[32] F. Rezaeibagha, K.T. Win, W. Susilo, A Systematic Literature Review on Security and Privacy of Electronic Health Record Systems: Technical Perspectives, vol. 44, 2015 (3).

[33] A. Dubovitskaya, V. Urovi, M. Vasirani, K. Aberer, M.I. Schumacher, A Cloud-Based eHealth Architecture for Privacy Preserving Data Integration, vol. 2, 2015, pp. 585−598.

[34] M. Bhati, P. Rani, Review of Passive Security Measure on Trusted Cloud Computing, 2015 no. 3.

[35] G. Rathi, M. Abinaya, D.M.K. T, Healthcare Data Security in Cloud Computing, 2015, pp. 1807−1815.

[36] H. Elmogazy, O. Bamasak, Towards Healthcare Data Security inCloud Computing, 2009, pp. 356−361, no. 3.

[37] N. Sengupta, Designing of Hybrid RSA Encryption Algorithm for Cloud Security, 2015, pp. 4146−4152.

[38] A.A. Sedem, J.K. Panford, Cloud computing framework for E-health in Ghana: adoption issues and strategies: case study of Ghana health service, Int. J. Comput. Appl. 118 (17) (2015) 13−17.

[39] O. Boyinbode, G. Toriola, CloudeMR: a cloud based electronic medical record system, Int. J. Hybrid Inf. Technol. 8 (4) (2015) 201−212.

[40] M. Plachkinova, A. Alluhaidan, and S. Chatterjee, Health Records on the Cloud: A Security Framework, n.d. 152−158.

[41] B. Fabian, T. Ermakova, P. Junghanns, Collaborative and secure sharing of healthcare data in multi-clouds, Inf. Syst. 48 (2015) 132−150.

[42] A.C. Donald, M.P. Scholar, M.P. Scholar, A.C. Donald, A Comparative Analysis of Encryption Techniques and Data Security Issues in Cloud Computing, November 2014.

[43] A.E. Youssef, A Framework for Secure Healthcare Systems Based on Big Data Analytics in Mobile Cloud, vol. 2, 2014, pp. 1−11 (2).

[44] Z. Zafar, S. Islam, M.S. Aslam, M. Sohaib, Cloud Computing Services for the Healthcare Industry, 2014, pp. 25−29.

[45] M. Tebaa, S.E.L. Hajji, From single to multi-clouds computing privacy and fault tolerance, IERI Procedia 10 (2014) 112−118.

[46] S.N. Sultana, G. Ramu, P.B.E. Reddy, Cloud-based Development of Smart and Connected Data in Healthcare Application, vol. 5, 2014, pp. 1−11 (6).

[47] K.A. Nagaty, Mobile Health Care on a Secured Hybrid Cloud, vol. 4, 2014 (2).

[48] Y.B. Gurav, M. Deshmukh, Scalable and Secure Sharing of Personal Health Records in Cloud Computing Using Attribute Based Encryption, vol. 3, 2014, pp. 2012−2014 (7).

[49] D. Thilakanathan, S. Chen, R.A. Calvo, Secure Data Sharing in the Cloud, 2014, pp. 45−73.

[50] P.G. Scholar, Secure Sharing of Personal Health Records in Cloud Computing Using Attribute-Based Broadcast Encryption, vol. 102, 2014, pp. 13−19 (16).

[51] J. Madarkar, Security Issues of Patient Health Records in E-Hospital Management in Cloud, vol. 9359, 2014, pp. 46−51 (6).

[52] M. Louk, H. Lim, H.J. Lee, Security System for Healthcare Data in Cloud Computing, vol. 8, 2014, pp. 241−248 (3).

[53] S. Ribeiro, C. Viana-ferreira, C. Costa, XDS-I Outsourcing Proxy: Ensuring Confidentiality while Preserving Interoperability, vol. 18, 2014, pp. 1404−1412 (4).

[54] A.J. Ikuomola, O.O. Arowolo, Securing patient privacy in e-health cloud using homomorphic encryption and access control, Int. J. Comput. Networks Commun. Secur. 2 (1) (2014) 15−21.

[55] F.A. Khan, A. Ali, H. Abbas, N.A.H. Haldar, A cloud-based healthcare framework for security and patients' data privacy using wireless body area networks, Procedia Comput. Sci. 34 (2014) 511−517.

[56] M.M. Freire, P.R.M. Inácio, Security Issues in Cloud Environments: A Survey, 2014, pp. 113−170.

[57] A. Abbas, S.U. Khan, A review on the state-of-the-art privacy-preserving approaches in the e-health clouds, IEEE J. Biomed. & Health Inf. vol. 18 (4) (July 2014) 1431−1441.

[58] M. Jafari, R. S. Naini, N.P. Sheppard, A rights management approach to protection of privacy in a cloud of electronic health records in Proc. 11th Annu. ACM Workshop Digital Rights Manag., Oct. 2011, pp. 23−30.

[59] D. Mashima, M. Ahamad, Enhancing accountability of electronic health record usage via patient-centric monitoring, in: Proc. 2nd ACM SIGHIT Sympo. Int. Health Informat., January 2012, pp. 409−418.

[60] J. Pecarina, S. Pu, J.-C. Liu, SAPPHIRE: anonymity for enhanced control and private collaboration in healthcare clouds, in: Proc. IEEE 4th Int. Conf. Cloud Comput. Technol. Sci., 2012, pp. 99−106.

[61] Z.R. Li, E.C. Chang, K.H. Huang, F. Lai, A secure electronic medical record sharing mechanism in the cloud computing platform, in: Proc. 15th IEEE Int. Sympo. Consum. Electron., June 2011, pp. 98−103.

[62] Y.Y. Chen, J.C. Lu, J.K. Jan, A secure EHR system based on hybrid clouds, J. Med. Syst. 36 (5) (2012) 3375−3384.

[63] R. Zhang, L. Liu, R. Xue, Role-based and time-bound access and management of EHR data, Secur. Commun. Network. 7 (6) (2013) 994−1015.

[64] A. Sahai, B. Waters, Fuzzy identity based encryption, Adv. Cryptol. Eurocrypt 3494 (May 2005) 457−473.

[65] J. Bethencourt, A. Sahai, B. Waters, Ciphertext-policy attribute-based encryption, in: Proc. IEEE Sympo. Security Privacy, 2007, pp. 321−334.

[66] S. Yu, C. Wang, K. Ren, W. Lou, Achieving secure, scalable and fine-grained data access control in cloud computing, in: Proc. IEEE Infocom, March 2010, pp. 1−9.

[67] M. Chase, S.S. Chow, Improving privacy and security in multi-authority attribute-based encryption, in: Proc. 16th ACM Conf. Comput. Comm. Security, 2009, pp. 121−130.

[68] S. Agarwal, M. Chase, FAME: fast attribute-based message encryption, in: Proc. ACM Conf. Comput. Comm. Security, 2017, pp. 665−682.

[69] S. Ruj, M. Stojmenovic, A. Nayak, Privacy preserving access control with authentication for securing data in clouds, in: Proc. 12th IEEE/ACM Int. Sympo. Cluster, Cloud Grid Comput., 2012, pp. 556−563.

[70] C. Gentry, Fully homomorphic encryption using ideal lattices, in: Proc. ACM Sympo. Theory Comput., 2009, pp. 169−178.

[71] A. Vizitiu, C.I. Niță, A. Puiu, C. Suciu, L.M. Itu, Towards privacy-preserving deep learning based medical imaging applications, in: IEEE Int. Sympo. On Medical Measurements and Applications (MeMeA), 2019, pp. 1−6.

[72] A. El-Yahyaoui, M.D. Elkettani, Fully homomorphic encryption: state of art and comparison, Int. J. Comput. Sci. Inf. Secur. 14 (4) (2016).

[73] S.N. Roy, S. Mishra, S.M. Yusof, Emergence of drug discovery in machine learning, Tech. Adv. Mach. Learn. Healthc. 119 (2021).

[74] S. Mishra, P.K. Mallick, H.K. Tripathy, A.K. Bhoi, A. González-Briones, Performance evaluation of a proposed machine learning model for chronic disease datasets using an integrated attribute evaluator and an improved decision tree classifier, Appl. Sci. 10 (22) (2020) 8137.

[75] S. Mishra, P.K. Mallick, H.K. Tripathy, L. Jena, G.-S. Chae, Stacked KNN with hard voting predictive approach to assist hiring process in IT organizations, Int. J. Electr. Eng. Educ. (February 2021), https://doi.org/10.1177/0020720921989015.

Index

Note: 'Page numbers followed by "f" indicate figures and "t" indicate tables.'

Printed in the United States
by Baker & Taylor Publisher Services